THE LIMITS OF MILITARY INTERVENTION

SAGE SERIES ON ARMED FORCES AND SOCIETY

INTER-UNIVERSITY SEMINAR ON ARMED FORCES AND SOCIETY

Morris Janowitz, *University of Chicago*
Chairman and Series Editor

Charles C. Moskos, Jr., *Northwestern University*
Associate Chairman and Series Editor

THE LIMITS OF

MILITARY INTERVENTION

Edited by

Ellen P. Stern

 **SAGE PUBLICATIONS**   Beverly Hills / London

This volume was prepared in cooperation with the White Burkett Miller Center of Public Affairs, University of Virginia.

The United States Government has at least a royalty-free, nonexclusive and irrevocable license throughout the world for Government purposes to publish, translate, reproduce, deliver, perform, dispose of, and to authorize others to do so, all or any portion of this work.

This research was supported by the Advanced Research Projects Agency of the Department of Defense and was monitored by ONR under Contract No. N00014-76-C-0448.

The views and conclusions contained in this document are those of the authors and should not be interpreted as necessarily representing the official policies, either express or implied, of the Advance Research Projects Agency or the U.S. Government.

For information address:

SAGE PUBLICATIONS, INC.
275 South Beverly Drive
Beverly Hills, California 90212

SAGE PUBLICATIONS LTD.
28 Banner Street
London EC1Y 8QE

Printed in the United States of America

Library of Congress Cataloging in Publication Data

Main entry under title:

The Limits of military intervention.

    (Armed forces and society; 12)
    Includes index.
    1. Intervention (International law)   2. Military art and science.
3. United States—Military policy.   I. Stern, Ellen.   II. Inter-University Seminar on Armed Forces and Society.   III. Series.
U21.5.A74   vol. 12   [JX4481]   341.5'8   77-5588
ISBN 0-8039-0810-5
ISBN 0-8039-0811-3 pbk.

THE LIMITS OF MILITARY INTERVENTION

PREFACE

With the end of U.S. involvement in the war in Vietnam, it became clear that the changing role of force in international relations would come to be assessed from an academic and social science point of view. Power politics, national interests, and new technology would continue to determine the patterns of international military affairs. But it was important, further, to refine and clarify concepts and offer new hypotheses about the potentials and limits of military intervention.

In preparing this volume of analytic studies of military intervention, I have had the benefit of cooperation of a large group of colleagues whose assistance I wish to acknowledge. First, in order to sketch the outlines and issues to be investigated, a planning conference was held in Washington, D.C., in June 1975. James Arestad, Edward Beach, Davis Bobrow, John Faris, Morris Janowitz, Stephen Kaplan, Geoffrey Kemp, Richard Leighton, J. K. Milsted, Hugh Nott, John Schlight, Paul Schratz, and Anthony Wermuth participated and articulated the parameters of the undertaking.

Second, on June 17-19, 1976, a conference was held at the Center for Continuing Education, University of Chicago, at which twenty-two papers were presented. This volume was built on the basis of these papers. The participants engaged in pointed and critical debate, which made possible the identification of the areas of convergence and the areas of divergence in this study. I deeply appreciate the contribution of those in attendance: Bruce Bliven, Davis B. Bobrow, James Digby, Thomas A. Fabyanic, M. D. Feld, Paul H.B. Godwin, Lawrence Grinter, Roger Hamburg, Morris Janowitz, Morton Kaplan, Konrad Kellen, Geoffrey Kemp, Joseph J. Kruzel, Jack Ladinsky, Arthur D. Larson, James A. Linger, Charles Moskos, John E. Mueller, John Pickett, George Quester, Sam C. Sarkesian, Paul R. Schratz, Caesar D. Sereseres, Richard Smoke, Albert Williams, and Adam Yarmolinsky.

Third, it was deemed appropriate and important that the contributed papers be critically reviewed by a group of specialists concerned with the relations between social science research and policy. As a result, a seminar was held September 30-October 1, 1976, at the University of Virginia, under the sponsorship of the White Burkett Miller Center of Public Affairs, in order to further evaluate the prepared papers. As a result of this seminar, an alternative set of critiques ennerged, the results of which were incorporated in the final version of the papers presented in this volume. I am especially grateful for the efforts of those in attendance. They included James A. Barber, James Barco, Thomas A. Bartlett, Bruce Bliven, Thomas E. Cronin, Robert G. Gard, Jr., Robert Ginsburgh, Gwyn Harries-Jenkins, Samuel P. Huntington, Morris Janowitz, John B. Keeley, Jack Ladinsky, Franklin D. Margiotta, Frederick Nolting, Donald Nuechterlein, Donald Osborn, William Y. Smith, and William J. Taylor, Jr.

The conference "The Consequences and Limits of Military Intervention" was made possible by a research grant to Loyola University of Chicago from the Advanced Research Projects Agency, whose officers, Austin Kibler and Robert Young, were most helpful, and from the Norman Waite Harris Foundation of the University of Chicago. I am most appreciative to Sam C. Sarkesian of Loyola University, who coordinated all the administrative aspects of the project, and to Linda Roberts, Gloria Linger, JoAnne Leigh, Shelley Abelson, and Joy Neuman, whose varied efforts were much appreciated. The seminar held at the University of Virginia was arranged by James W. Barco and with the support of the White Burkett Miller Center of Public Affairs. I am pleased that this volume appears in the Sage Series on Armed Forces and Society and am grateful for the generosity and interest of Sara Miller McCune and Rhoda Blecker of Sage Publications, Inc.

Finally, I am particularly indebted to Morris Janowitz, without whose intellectual guidance and personal support this volume would not have come about. In the course of the preparation for this volume I have participated in sharp and highly pointed debate, all of which has served to clarify my thinking. I have been most impressed by the self-critical and intellectual bases of the presentations and ensuing critiques. It has been a rewarding experience, and I hope the result will serve to clarify the profound and awesome issues which the American leaders and critizenry face.

– E. P. S.

PROLOGUE

This book is an outgrowth of the need to identify the resolves and achievements, the misconceptions and mistakes of the recent past, to assess the direction of international relations, and to identify the changed potentials and consequences of military intervention from the point of view of the United States.

Intervention implies an active, calculated step, a forcible interference in another nation's external and internal affairs, to maintain or alter a condition or situation, presuming, further, that this coercion will in some manner benefit or protect the initiator. Such actions can be described by a wide spectrum of models. Military engagements can range from guerilla tactics to conventional battles between professionals with the most sophisticated equipment; from weaponry of the most minor, easily obtainable variety to the H-bomb.[1]

Further, intervention assumes, in most cases, a counter-intervention, whether it be steps taken to prevent initial intervention by an adversary or an answer in kind—more defensive, perhaps, than offensive. During a period of deterrence, there is great pressure to make counter-intervention capabilities readily available. But there exist powerful countervailing measures of politics and economics which limit or even displace military intervention activities. As a result, programs of military counter-intervention also require careful and continual reassessment.

This analysis focuses on the limitations of military intervention mainly as an analytical device. By a concern with limitations, it is possible to highlight changes which are taking place in the role of force and violence in international relations. Conventional, popular, and polemic thinking about military forces is fragmentary; therefore, our goal is to be more holistic and more systemic, and this requires an examination both of the consequences and of the limitations of military intervention.

The time reference is the immediate present and the years ahead. To accomplish our task, it is necessary to reach back at times, and the historical timeframe depends on the specific question at hand. Access to history requires reasoned judgment about relevant previous experiences. On the other hand, the goal of this analysis is not primarily to anticipate the future, but rather to clarify the present so that it can be better understood and thereby managed more effectively. Therefore, in organizing this endeavor, my collaborators and I took note of Harold D. Lasswell's notion of "developmental analysis." This is an outlook which is not limited to the analysis of that which has taken place, but is, rather, the analysis of that which is currently in process, on a basis of past experience and reasoned assessment of alternative paths into the future.[2]

Policy makers and academics, each for different reasons, see the need to consistently reevaluate the obvious but basic postulate that American capabilities for intervention have been limited in scope and pattern with the advent of nuclear weapons. The finale of the Vietnam epoch has provided an appropriate and much-needed moment in which to undertake such an evaluation. The tortured and unclear search for detente, volunteer force systems, precision-guided weapons, altered world economic relations, and shifting social structures are all factors which condition the resulting assessments.

The constituent elements of this study uniformly assume that a plateau in the nuclear arms race between East and West has been reached. A "limited adversary" relationship and the sense of nuclear "equality" have led American and Soviet leaders to search for alternative modes to express their cooperation and competition. It is an inescapable platitude to note that the East-West polarity has been augmented by a North-South imbalance. The growing participation of the nonindustrialized countries in the international arena cuts across cold war alliances. The cleavages are no longer solely designated as communist or non-communist.

The North-South schism does not center on ideologies, but on resources; the new materials and energy reserves needed by the East and the West are to be found in the nonindustrialized states. The growing tension between these nations and their former colonial masters has been expressed first economically and, in turn, in political-military dimensions. The United States and the Soviet Union continue to seek alliances and to support their client states among the developing nations; but the analyst of international relations is alert to emerging arenas of mutual interest between the two super-powers.

The transformations of the 1960s among youth have brought new patterns of social mobility and life style. In the West, one of the visible consequences has been the increased indifference to the basic symbolism of the nation-state where, as Anthony Mockler puts it, "patriotism is the only justification for taking up arms."[3] Conscription has been abandoned by the United States, Great Britain, and Canada, and constricted in various Western European nations. The generations born after World War II do not retain the perception of the "communist" or nuclear threat felt by their parents. The willingness of youth to serve in the combat arms is as limited as is its desire to see its government intervene in the conflicts of "others." The age gap not only includes life styles but also incorporates attitudes about national security and national defense.

The new social and political orders greatly influence the concepts of deterrence or, alternatively, stabilization. National consciousness and solidarity are strained. Writers as diverse as Joseph Schumpeter and Karl Manheim, as well as those concerned more specifically with the military profession, such as Morris Janowitz, have suggested that these complex cleavages result from the very success of democratic systems of government.[4] In a society where freedom of choice and expression is so heavily emphasized, it is inevitable that societal needs and considerations are often eclipsed by personal, almost hedonistic, satisfactions.

One repeatedly noted feature of the eighteenth- and nineteenth-century war machines was the centralization of the means of technology—of violence—by an increasingly professionalized force structure.[5] These trends have persisted in the twentieth century in most of the industrialized nations—with one notable exception. In the nineteenth century, the economics of war were also controlled by these force structures. But during the twentieth century, however, we have witnessed a reversal. Economics no longer directly respond to the requirements of military organizations. In the political democracies, resources available for military expenditures during a period of prolonged tension and deterrence are subject to powerful constraints. The demands for welfare expenditures become powerful competitors. Further, the unbalance of military institutions reflects the importance of and access to energy and raw material resources. The economics of these factors constrain (or may even control) the capability to wage war and to perpetuate existing political arrangements—that is, the dominance of the currently recognized superpowers.

Force and military intervention will not disappear. I would argue that this is not a banal simplification. However, their use is undergoing singular changes, and this volume seeks to clarify its changing dimensions. The contemporary compendia of articles and books dedicated to assisting nation-states in the search to abolish violence may prove more that violent expressions are endemic to men. As such, this study converges with those undertaken by pacifist philosophers and peace research groups. While the far-sighted goal may be a world without wars, our common sense directs us to focus on the mode of expression of violence, and how the inclination toward war-making will be directed, moderated, or restrained. We cannot ignore the oft-repeated observation that, from the point of view of Western nations, the role of violence in international relations has undergone "fundamental changes." Strategic planners need to accept the fact that the restrictions on the use of military power will expand in the future.[6]

The research design of this investigation of the limits of military interventions is based on a number of interconnected steps. These elements are designed to cover, in a holistic fashion, the various aspects of intervention. First, there is a discussion of the analytical dimensions of the study based on an American point of view, a perspective developed in terms of phases in decision-making theory. It is followed by an exploration of the Soviet perspective. The crux of the contemporary settings is dealt with in the second section which focuses on technology and systems of control.

The social science apparatus which has been offered is subsequently applied to concrete military settings. In the third and fourth sections, respectively, changing military operations—airlift, naval, and ground—are examined, followed by the main politico-military efforts—namely, military demonstrations, military assistance and military sales programs, and "stability operations," more properly designated as nation-building, and intelligence operations. The next two sections deal with a series of constraints and dilemmas—namely, the limitations on manpower under an all-volunteer force and the contradictory pressures of military professionalism, followed by domestic constraints, which include public opinion as well as political and administrative organization. In conclusion, the issues of conceptual reformulations are explicated.

As indicated, our endeavor is focused on organization or "institutionalization." We are concerned with military technology, but not at the expense of a consideration of societal trends and the accompanying organizational contexts. Our objective, which encompasses questions of theory and history, manpower and technology, politics and society, centered on the interplay of these factors in determining the role of force in future U.S. action.

Our approach must of necessity emphasize short-term trends, but we sought, further, to depart from oversimplifications which stress straight-line projections or which only appease some segment of the political body. We also recognized that the political context can be changed by events and by determined leaders. We considered how the issues of consequences and limits of military intervention are conceptualized both by social scientists and by policy makers who must develop operational strategies and the extent to which these perspectives converge or diverge.

In the first section, Richard Smoke's analytic discussion of military intervention deals with all the elements in our frame of reference. Food, energy, and mineral reserves are potentially just as valuable bargaining commodities as technology and weapons. The sophistication and diversity of military technology have engendered a self-perpetuating pressure for the accumulation of ever more advanced weapons, a pressure which is rapidly spreading to developing nations.

Smoke is a political scientist who is concerned with how military decisions are made. Identification of imperfections in the present working of the system make possible its modification by those actually involved. Smoke cautions against a tendency toward a "reductionistic cascade" in decision-making. By this, he means that the technical factors concerning weapons and strategies tend to overshadow the significance of various conceptual elements in the decision process. Smoke's major criticism of American military intervention capabilities lies in this deemphasis or general lack of policy analysis and planning in depth. However, the trend toward pre-programmed plans and options may be a step in the wrong direction, since this programming prevents easy transition to alternative crisis strategies. Another drawback to the deemphasis on conceptual factors is a tendency toward the premature "crystallization" of perceptions on the part of policy makers, which may deny or dismiss a meaningful hearing for possible solutions other than military intervention. In this context, it is predictable that escalation may result despite policy makers' original intentions to try to avoid it. An inability to be flexible due to overly rigid planning obviously can be as dangerous as a failure to plan at all.

Roger Hamburg's "Soviet Perspectives on Military Intervention" analyzes Soviet perceptions of U.S. foreign policy postures and the resulting mutual power calculus. He proceeds by means of drawing on an innovative approach—namely, an examination of the assumptions and content of the research generated by the Soviet specialists on the United States. Soviet strategy is always dictated by political objectives; this is a basic tenet of Marxism-Leninism, and the Soviets see no need to alter that key perception. The Soviets approach the intervention model differently than do the Americans: Outside of war, force is to be used potentially and symbolically, as a constraint against possible adversaries and to confound their diplomatic-strategic calculations. This is preferred to actual deployment (excluding naval demonstrations), where it loses its "bargaining chip" characteristics, except under the most highly favorable circumstances. Economic and political strategies, especially in the guise of a client state, are their most effective policy options. Nevertheless, the Soviets believe that there are great obstacles in their path. According to Hamburg, the Soviets obviously feel more secure in the American "businesslike" approach to "detente" than in the distortions of the cold war period. He asserts that they are well aware of their weaker economic base, both domestically and in the "third world," which does not permit them the variety of initiatives employed by the United States in the post-World War II world. However, it is necessary to keep in mind that the Soviets are prepared to allocate a much higher proportion of their limited resources to military programs.

Hamburg concludes that the initiative to prevent war and to increase stability remains a U.S. responsibility, and he is particularly concerned with the improvement of communicative networks. "Improvement of communicative networks" is critical in the sense that the Soviets must understand us in the way we intend to be understood, except where ambiguity is a deliberate strategy. An American military posture must act as a constraint on Soviet behavior without creating an exponential arms race or a series of escalating crises.

In the second section, the focus narrows to contemporary issues of technology and the control of military operations. To "New Weapons Technology and the Impact on Intervention," James Digby brings both a scientific and a managerial expertise to a highlight of new abilities to limit military intervention. He focuses on the progress and perfection of the American weapons arsenal and especially on precision weapons. The great concerns about the use of the most destructive weapons erodes the ability to resort "to all means" to gain victory. The result is a restraint which profoundly influences the course of political and military action and makes more urgent an understanding of the precise use of military power.[7]

If one assumes that the nuclear devices are so awesome in war that they are likely to remain relegated to their lockers or to underground or undersea testing for the immediate future, what weapons will the United States count in its arsenal for military intervention? In the decade of the 1970s, there has been a concern about the new generation of more technically advanced non-nuclear weapons, and concurrently in non-nuclear war.

The superpowers have two paths to follow in weapons acquisition and supply. The author indicated that one path stresses the modern (PGM's) and similar devices; the other leans on traditional weapons which would seem to have more varied uses. The PGM's are considered less expensive in the long run; they can be less vulnerable, and their precision makes them more suited to carrying out tasks precisely.

However, the widespread availability of the new generations of weapons can limit the capacity of a country to intervene militarily. While making the military power of the United States and the Soviety Union more usable, these weapons will reduce the "superpower monopoly on deterrence." Since the political and economic shifts of the last decades have increased the spread of equals, military technology can be readily bought on the open market; it is no longer the sole property of the industrialized and scientifically advanced. Some of the previously categorized lesser powers now have the ability to intervene, with either economic force or with the new conventional weapons, though the calculus of these new balances is quite difficult to estimate. Moreover, the attrition of those new weapons in battle is enormous, Digby argues, and their immediate destructive impact in the battlefield even greater, both of which may increase dependence on the supplier state. The results of the new technology seem to favor the defense, rather than the offense, at least for the near future. One clearly gets the impression that whether or not this is the case, the outcome of battle with these new weapons is more difficult to anticipate, and therefore they have added another dimension limiting military intervention.

There are several different steps along the military intervention continuum which are directly influenced by military technology and communications systems. Military alerts represent the initial steps of a posture of intervention. Joseph Kruzel critiques the existing signal system which, in his analysis, produces poor crisis-management and weakens the quality of decision making. It is difficult to successfully communicate a threat of intervention action, and it is equally difficult to distinguish, as the recipient, the negotiating implications of this threat of force. As situational stress mounts, this "gray area" between political overtures and war mobilization constricts, and decision makers view the action or response alternatives as diminishing, with the "enemy" appearing in an ever-improving position to manage the crisis.

Kruzel dissects the basic argument as an almost irreconcilable polemic between the civilian and military leaders responsible for the management of a possible intervention crisis. The military professionals are considered to demonstrate a lack of sympathy for diplomatic considerations, viewing them as constraints on necessary military preparations. In order to insure combat readiness, they tend to emphasize the necessity of military preparations. This is an elemental aspect of their responsibilities. However, in fact, frequently they recommend and suggest flexible or non-military responses. But in the management of a military alert, it would be an error to overlook the difference between military commanders and civilian political leaders. This difference limits the effects of military alerts. Moreover, the potential for diplomatic misunderstanding persists, as a real issue, when considering the basic differences between Soviet and American readiness levels. Not only is the eventual execution of a signal of paramount importance, but the understanding of "the enemy's" different perception of preparedness or posture level is key. As the costs of intervention rise, the importance of pre-intervention diplomacy rises correspondingly.

Davis B. Bobrow is a political scientist with expertise in the role of information in national security decisions and analysis of organizational behavior. The problematic issues of command, control, and communications (C^3) deal with the interface of technology and human behavior. Bobrow focuses on interactions which develop in large-scale defense organizations—both civilian and military. Once a diplomatic proposal has been tendered, the C^3 system must be at its peak performing capability to receive, relay, and interpret response signals to the initial alert. Bobrow emphasizes that an effective C^3 system should not be called upon to substitute for well-developed and meaningful policy and objectives. Nevertheless, it should be well advanced if prepared policies are determined to be weak or inaccurate. His analysis emphasizes realistically the importance of the system's place in the military intervention scenario.

The C^3 system of the 1970s has failed, in specific ways, to meet its challenges. For example, the 1975 Mayaguez crisis exposed serious flaws in the system: an inability to ascertain critical logistical information once the signals were received and, further, an inability to securely control the execution of the intervention through the chain of command. To what extent does such weakness inherently contribute to an ambiguous national security posture? As the author indicates, striking a vigorous political-military posture, either for domestic consumption or for international allies, may be a dangerous course unless an effective C^3 system exists to manage American initiatives or counter-initiatives and interpret the reactions of others.[8]

The trend toward reliance on advanced technology systems is certain; what then are the realities of actual use? The future roles of land, sea, or air forces, depend on an understanding of the technological advantages and limitations in military intervention. Despite the initiation of the "nuclear age of conflict," conventional conflict has continued to proliferate in the post-World War II period. Let us not forget that some theorists argued that future conflict would involve nuclear materials, by virtue of their existence. However, the weapons of the 1950s and 1960s were almost uniformly of World War II variety, with limited improvements; further, manpower procurement and training systems, supposedly a key factor in effective utilization of nuclear systems, were only marginally altered. The third section presents analyses of the impact of changed technological and organizational format on military operations.

Obviously, supply, support, and conveyance of military equipment and non-military goods are of crucial importance in the preparation for or in the conduct of military intervention. When one speaks of military intervention in the contemporary period, the role of air power encompasses airlift capabilities to assist allied states, as well as to support U.S. military operations.

John Pickett's discussion of airlift stresses the strained operational conditions affecting U.S. conduct of a conventional war. First, in the post-Vietnam period, there has been a reduction in manpower levels. Second, there has also been an extensive reduction in the base structure system which could seriously hamper the flexibility of an air force response.

The limitations on air lift capabilities are technical and organizational, as well as political. For example, the fuel supply question is crucial.[9] From a logistics point of view, fewer bases mean fewer refueling locales. With fewer places to refuel, alternatives are also reduced. The worst alternative is outright abandonment of support activity. In other cases, political allies may be approached for aid, or negotiations for refueling or base rights may be initiated with heretofore unaligned nations. This process would be time-consuming and might entirely checkmate interventionist actions. Further, as attested from NATO experiences, support for American military actions may be denied for fear of economic sanctions by oil producers. The political ramifications of these logistical problems must be seriously weighed in reviewing American capabilities for intervention.

In "Changing Naval Operations and Military Intervention," Michael MccGwire indicates that the new weapons systems increase the capability of rendering naval forces ineffective or obsolete. Again, the author's combination of a naval and academic career provides a perspective concerning the viability of naval activities. Consequently, the rights of maritime passage have succumbed to international tensions, and there now exists little unclaimed or uncontested marine space. Operationally, surveillance systems and technical weaponry can render a naval force immobile and helpless. Moreover, the acquisition by formerly minor powers, by purchase or "lend-lease," of advanced weapons systems further jeopardizes naval intervention, access to contested arenas, and, ultimately, self-preservation. While a vessel may be equipped with the most sophisticated and effective weaponry, the political and economic considerations may weigh heavily against unfettered naval intervention plans. Naval operations, especially those launched for specific intervention, must be conducted within narrow confines.

The case of conventional land warfare, with particular reference to the European theatre, is presented by Lewis Sorley, a former Army officer, in his analysis, "Changing Military Operations: Technology, Mobility, and Conventional Warfare." The assumption of the development of U.S.-Soviet nuclear parity underlies Sorely's analysis of changing military operations by ground forces, and Europe is the crucial theatre of operations. The crux of the role of the ground forces is the maintenance of a credible and effective conventional force, in order to reduce the threat of the outbreak of nuclear war. Military operations therefore involve the new personnel and organizational issues, when introduction of precision-guided missiles is considered. Given the destructive capacity of these weapons, the ground forces must become more and more of a force in being—in fact, a force in place. While the full impact of the new generation of conventional weapons has important problematic elements, Sorley's analysis converges with that of Digby. In this crucial dimension, the logic points to increased capacity of a defensive thrust response—that is, to an increase in the potential of counter-intervention, and thereby to an increase in the limits of military intervention.

Military operations have not, in the past, been limited to the actual application of firepower—there has been an intermediate area in which military systems —that is, weapons and military organization— have been intertwined with political negotiations and political presentations. The term politico-military operations is only a modern term for long standing practices—practices which have become more complex and more uncertain in their implication. Moreover, both the United States and the Soviet Union have found economic lines of intervention extremely effective, especially in situations where the employment of military force is ill-advised or not feasible. In section four, four different types of politico-military activities are assessed: military demonstrations, military sales and assistance programs, counterinsurgency (in which direct military action is undertaken), and finally, intelligence operations. The spectrum is broad and reflects the scope of U.S. actions in the world arena. By contrast, the Soviets have probably learned much from the American experiences in Vietnam, and may attempt to avoid the dilemmas of the political models devised for Vietnam by the United States.

Maury Feld approaches the analysis of military demonstrations from a sociological and political point of view; he is a sociologist with a strong interest in history, and his chapter seeks to compare nineteenth-century interventions with those of the twentieth century. He deals not only with the direct military impact, but with the symbolic and institutional results. "Military Demonstrations: The Flag and Intervention" reviews the concept and act of "showing the flag" as a centuries-old practice to reinforce political hegemony. Flag-showing, as intervention, was established when, as a "groundbreaker," an actor ventured into an area where the conventions of international behavior had yet to be established. The flag demonstrations of past centuries could be identified as the precursors of foreign aid. However, in the twentieth century, a more comprehensive and binding alliance system attached new meaning to the use of the flag; in Feld's words, it is displayed as "a token of mutual interest, rather than as an act of asymmetrical aggression." The Soviets retain a "state of seige" mentality from their 1917 experience and the aftermath of allied intervention. Whereas the "liberal" outlook inclines Western powers to accept most every nation-state as a de facto ally, the Soviets regard every non-Marxist society as a de jure opponent. Surrounded by enemies and adversaries, allies may be found in an assortment of geographical places and with an array of ideologies. The West, and most particularly the United States, has attained a cultural perspective which limits options in the establishment of a network of friends and allies; intervention originally was a gesture of parochial contempt—treating others as aberrations. Therefore, perhaps it may appear that the Soviets are more flexible, overall, in their approach to outright intervention, military assistance, or simply providing kindred support by the demonstration of the flag.

Caesar Sereseres combines the perspectives of an analyst for a professional research organization and the more introspective viewpoint of an academic in his analysis of military assistance programs. His study explores this more indirect form of military intervention, a form designed as a substitute for direct intervention. The support of a neutral or allied country by means of military assistance continues as a vital component of American foreign policy operations. Further, the author argues that for the domestic American public, the programs of military sales reinforce the notion of strength and dominance in the world arena. However, when carefully scrutinized, these programs—both military assistance and military sales—emerge as only marginally important to basic national security for the United States. There are, however, key elements in diplomatic interactions abroad, and for public relations between the American government and the American people.

Sereseres also maintains that the security assistance programs produce negative results which outweigh the outstanding benefits. Recipients are less eager to accept American arms and economic supplies in exchange for "blanket permission" to the United States to direct planning and operations, as was often the case in the past. The author's implication is that future decades will witness a decline in the use and effectiveness of this instrument of influence and diplomacy.

Stability operations, counterinsurgency, or effective nation building, have been at the core of U.S. politico-military intervention and counter-intervention plans. Lawrence Grinter draws on a wide background of familiarity with Southeast Asian political institutions and with the history of the American involvement in Vietnam. He quotes George Kennan that "it is important to recognize that not all places and regions are of equal importance to the major powers." During the 1950s, American leaders determined that Vietnam was a highly important region for U.S. security interests and that that locale would be an essential place to halt the "creep of communism" in Southeast Asia. Domestic political considerations and psychological warfare tenets meant that it was as important to propagandize effectively the giver, as well as the receivers, of aid. Indeed, throughout much of the twenty-five year U.S. involvement in Vietnam, the American people believed that Vietnam was a backward society greatly in need of American political, economic, and, finally, military support. The United States planted its "flag" on Vietnamese soil as a declaration that a stand was being made—an intervention which was designed to succeed.

Grinter asserts the widely held principle that the success or failure of past or future American "stability operations" depends on the character and capabilities of the regimes the United States elects to assist. While the principle was not totally ignored in Vietnam, it was eclipsed, which explains some of the determinants of the American failure. American pluralistic traditions were also a liability in our search for a Southeast Asian strategy. The assistance programs launched in Vietnam reveal the weakness of a variety of programs without a coherent single purpose. The multiplicity of American bureaucratic organizations contributed to a fragmented assistance and intervention effort.

Grinter describes the competing models which guided U.S. practices, some of which did not stand much of a chance of successful implementation because the United States did not appreciate the political climate and culture in which advice, money, and troops were being introduced. The Stability Operations/ Economic Development Approach model described by Grinter was conceptualized during the 1960-1963 Kennedy Administration. The goal was to bring a third world country through the modernization process, utilizing American economic, social, and technical resources. Also labeled "The Rostow Doctrine," this plan was the major tenet of a more general approach to problem solving by the United States in nonindustrialized areas. The major issue was seen as the communist proclivity to interfere by "subversion" of these transitional societies. The model was supplemented and finally supplanted by the Military Occupation Model relabeled "search and destroy." This approach had its roots in the French Indochina experience. The French colonial experiments of the late nineteenth and early twentieth centuries were only successful when there was a weak opposition or one without external support. The Americans found more success than the French in this pacification effort, but not enough to build a stable political climate.

The Administrative Approach—a tried and true colonial operation of the British— fared a bit better than most other models employed by the United States. Law and order and bureaucratic efficiency are emphasized and ideology is downplayed. The fact that the communists were utilizing elements of the same perspective was, however, a contributing factor to its low return value for the Americans. Nevertheless, the United States generally felt this model to be one of the more useful for Vietnam.

In general, the conventional response to problem solving has been to transplant Western values to a non-Western conflict setting. While this may appear to some to be a simplistic dilution of the cause of the American failure, I would suggest that this basic orientation must bear the burden, rather than more caustic indictments of individual strategic decisions. This is not to overlook a strong moralistic, even messianic impulse in the U.S. military intervention in Southeast Asia, which gave it the character of a "lost crusade."

Blackstock presents a history of past approaches to intelligence-gathering as they affected military intervention, and an analysis of the changes which the Congressional investigations of the mid-1970s seek to force on the intelligence bureaucracy. For one school of thought, the function of intelligence dictates the complete separation of intelligence procedures from the policy-making system. If, in this model, the policy maker must only be presented with new and objective facts of a crisis, there must be the ability to step back from already committed policy and to accept critical documentation indicating alternative policies.

The opposing view contends that a marriage between intelligence and policy is feasible. It would be hoped that individuals gathering intelligence would not permit their biases to permeate their reports. However, as has been pointed out by several observers, the results can be that the intelligence apparatus shoulders the blame for what works out to be wrong policy.

The core of Blackstock's analysis deals with the trend by which intelligence agencies seek to expand their function from information collection into covert operations. Covert operations include propaganda, bribery, deception, secret support for political groups, and, finally, covert military operations. Blackstock is engaged in the analysis of organizational behavior, for he sees this outcome as a widespread movement which both weakens the conventional intelligence functions and produces "adventurism," which is self-defeating, highly unproductive, and difficult to control. In this dimension, the limits of military intervention are profound, persist, and continue to enlarge.

In the post-Vietnam era, threat perception has changed and as a result the demand for extensive covert operations has substantially narrowed. But the pressure to launch a clandestine effort is always present. Proliferating Congressional intelligence control committees and continuous press exposure tend to limit intelligence operations. However, by emphasing sound data collection, the essential intelligence function can be maintained.

Many years of professional experience in U.S. military service plus social science expertise describe the backgrounds and perspectives from which Thomas Fabyanic and Sam Sarkesian explore the military manpower and professional variables limiting military intervention. In the era of volunteer force systems—with their lowered manpower levels—combat readiness and performance capabilities for a series of contingencies ranging from low-response, peacekeeping activities to conventional frontal battle engagements are of pointed importance in calculating emerging U.S. abilities for military intervention.

Thomas Fabyanic's combination of historical perspective and quantitative analysis shapes his presentation of recent trends in manpower levels of the U.S. military forces. Fabyanic focuses on the declining ability of the all-volunteer system to assure adequate forces-in-being of quality manpower and to provide a military force structure of adequate qualitative and quantitative dimensions to provide credibility for a strategy of deterrence.

A key question, then, is whether the United States can still represent itself as a "superior" nation militarily. In terms of its arsenal of weapons, there can be little doubt of U.S. strength and superiority. But what of that element of force, occasionally referred to as "brute force," that is men? There are two important issues that follow: To what extent has the all-volunteer formula reduced our numbers of men in uniform so severely as to affect combat performance, and to what extent has the new format altered the meaning of service in the combat arms?

Perhaps the major effort of manpower limitations with the all-volunteer force is the degree to which it will affect U.S. intervention capability. The era in which the United States could intervene militarily and escalate to extremes may have ended, and Fabyanic suggests that in the future, the United States may need to use de-escalation as a tool of reciprocity.

The issue of quality is not only a question of skill, but of the motivation and commitment once called patriotism. As Fabyanic points out, even the most highly skilled army may become overnight an anachronism in our "technetronic era." The creation of the all-volunteer force is only in part a response to technology; it is also a redefinition of civic responsibility and an expression of public disdain for the draft.

The external pressures on the all-volunteer force are matched by internal organizational pressures. The officer corps of the United States has come to think of itself as a professional group, with the concepts of "duty, honor, and country" as the hallmark elements. The question has been raised, especially by Charles Moskos, whether the introduction of the all-volunteer concept and the increased penetration of civilian values are shifting the officer corps from a profession, with a sense of calling, to more and more of an occupational model.[10] One of the attractions of the all-volunteer forces has been the higher salaries available than under the conscription formula. This leads the military to legitimize service in terms of the marketplace and thereby alter the basis of the military service.

Sam C. Sarkesian addresses the professional dilemmas that the officer corps faces in the limited war—that is, limited war of the Vietnam model, which is of protracted and unconventional nature. He argues that under such circumstances, ambiguity of purpose creates ethical gaps between society and the military which erode military legitimacy. Moreover, professional uneasiness has developed about the capability of volunteer forces which is compounded by the distinction between elite and conventional units with imputed negative impact of combat effectiveness. How can the professional carry out professional goals in an environment characterized by ambiguity and inherent conflict between societal and military goals? The implication of this analysis is to highlight the powerful factors which "militate" against a policy committing troops into an ambiguous, multidimensional environment associated with modern war. In this view, it is necessary for the military profession to assert itself on the basis of enlightened self-interest and accept these limitations and not merely rely on the traditional dogma of "duty, honor, country."

The issues of professionalism extend beyond those which have been explored here. However, professionals have traditionally been thought of as strengthening the capacity of the military to intervene; in the contemporary period, professionalism is a variable in the potential limits on intervention.

The tragic experiences of Vietnam may have indeed engendered the poten-tiality of a neo-isolationist national perspective. John Mueller, a political scientist trained in quantitative methods and at the same time deeply critical of the available public opinion data, has charted the change of attitudes toward American military intervention and the conduct of American policy in the international arena. His study, "Changes in American Public Attitudes Toward International Involvement," assesses American attitudes on defense expenditures, military involvements, isolationism, the campaign against communism, and the fear of war.

The first question which must be answered concerns the parameters of public opinion toward the military establishment itself. Mueller's study needs to be interpreted in light of the findings of David Segal and John Blair.[11] The U.S. military institution per se was held in significantly high esteem by the majority of the American public during the Vietnam period, and even immediately thereafter. It was the war itself, and the leaders of political and business institutions, not the military, which suffered a sharp decline in public confidence and esteem. It is civilians and non-military institutions which are perceived to have the greatest influence involving the military might of the United States in foreign conflict and military intervention.

The massive and continuing surveys of public opinion on which Mueller draws indicate that there has been some decline since the end of World War II in the level of support for defense spending. More recent data indicate that by 1975 this decline had ended. Of course, the responses in public opinion surveys are weak indicators of the political support that a president may well be able to mobilize in emerging conditions. For our purposes, the importance of Mueller's study rests in his analysis of the opinion concerning Korea and Vietnam—limited military engagements. Public support for these two limited military interventions declined with the passage of time. There is reason to believe that the same decline could operate, and even more rapidly, in potential cases of military intervention in the years ahead.

Current trends in public opinion influence U.S. political institutions and have repeatedly been described as sharply hampering the responsiveness of the military institution to pursue effective politico-military policies. Paul Schratz, a professional naval officer with extensive academic and civilian government experience, reviews the fragmentation of American political institutions as a factor controlling military intervention. His chapter, "National Decision Making and Military Intervention," offers an explanation for the seeming decline of military power during a period of intensified concern with military technology. His argument focuses on political and administrative organizations which have proliferated tasks, to their mutual detriment.

Nevertheless, Schratz concludes that under prevailing circumstances the military establishment suffers no lack of access and influence. In fact, the military input, which is periodically too oriented toward individual services, is too extensive. His interpretation of the effect of the War Powers Resolution on congressional-executive relations in future military interventions is prophetically intriguing. The weakness of the Congress in foreign policy—disclosed in a survey commissioned by Congress itself—is quite disturbing. It is impressive that Congress and the President authorized such an extensive analysis of the governmental role in policy formulation. The findings confirm the long-held view that a new relationship between the legislative and executive branches is essential if the military is to be made fully effective and responsive to national aspirations as well.

As an epilogue, the chapter "Beyond Deterrence: Alternative Conceptual Dimensions," by Morris Janowitz, serves in various ways to integrate the themes presented in this study. His approach is that of the military and political sociologist concerned with the linkages between domestic sociopolitical order of industrialized societies, especially the United States, and the changing international order. Internally, the United States is experiencing a dispersion of political power which is paralleled by a diffusion of power in the international community. Because these international changes take place at varying rates in different regions of the world, new elements of instability become operative.

As Janowitz says at the beginning of his remarks, "The classical categories for analyzing military organizations and strategy must be reconceptualized." And this is his goal and those of the authors of this volume. Policy makers and leaders concerned with the daily stream of events—crisis-oriented or otherwise—often do not present adequate concern with the "larger picture." Such a posture, obviously, is one of the hazards of responsible decision-making. "Beyond Deterrence" strives to present a larger framework which makes use of the concept of stabilization. His effort to make the vocabulary of stabilization more precise is a major innovation; it rests on an interdisciplinary perspective. The analysis of international relations and the changing role of the United States can no longer be limited to military or economic resources. The full gamut of sociopolitical and sociopsychological stimuli influence the conduct of U.S. foreign policy. In turn, these factors condition the reception—or perception—of these policies by adversaries and third parties. "Destabilization" thus results not only from military and economic factors, but from political definitions and lack of clarity about the intention of key actors. Thus, Janowitz is searching for conceptions and formulations which both analyze the reality of international politics and help political leaders control the flow of events by making their intentions clear. It is important to emphasize that stabilization is offered as such a concept, because it does not mean the maintenance of the status quo, but the basis of orderly and justified change.

There is always the possibility of unexpected developments—political and even technological. Moreover, the scope and intent of the adversaries' programs are subject to wide differences of assessment, as has been the case in the Soviet military buildup of the 1970s. But my assumption and that of my collaborators is that the main outlines of the international military balance emerge gradually and with reasonable clarity. The result is that the contending powers can adjust their responses in a deliberate and measured pace. Hence, it does appear sound to assume that the effective nuclear parity between the United States and the Soviet Union will be maintained, rather than greatly altered; the U.S. political leadership could not and would not tolerate a distinct imbalance. In other words, in a more basic sense, there is a worldwide system of strategic military forces with a reasonable degree of stability, which provides the framework within which issues of the limitations and consequences of military intervention can be analyzed. Given the analytic perspective of those involved in this study, there was little chance of utopian thinking.

One of the aims of this volume has been to avoid strategic cliches; likewise, mechanical extrapolations of trends also have been discouraged. The limits on emerging military intervention are real. The clearest and notably obvious conclusion of this study is that they are increasing. But the reality of the constraints does not negate the likelihood of particularized military intervention. Crisis situations will arise where a military answer is deemed proper; but the decision makers will have to operate within a narrow scope and delimited time frame. Moreover, the analysis of the limits of military intervention serves to clarify the strategy of counter-intervention as an essential mechanism of deterrence and of stability. But, in this regard, the limits on the United States and the Soviet Union need to be seen in their stark reality. Hopefully, the successes and failures of the cold war period and the agonizing lessons of the Vietnam period will caution those who advocate the use of military force to be more precise about the goals to be achieved and the price to be paid.

— Ellen P. Stern

NOTES

1. For an interesting diagramatic explanation, see Nordal Akerman, *On the Doctrine of Limited War,* trans. Keith Bradfield (Lund: Berlingska Boktryckeriet, 1972), p. 17.

2. For a more detailed presentation, consult Harold D. Lasswell, "World Politics and Personal Insecurity," in *A Study of Power* (Glencoe, Ill.: The Free Press, 1950), pp. 3-9.

3. Anthony Mockler, *The Mercenaries* (New York: Macmillan, 1969), p. 16.

4. Morris Janowitz, "Military Institutions and Citizenship in Western Societies," *Armed Forces and Society* 2 (Winter 1976): p. 200. See also, Morris Janowitz, *Social Control of the Welfare State* (New York: Elsevier Press, 1976).

5. Michael Howard, "Change in the Use of Force, 1919-1969," in Brian Porter, ed., *International Politics, 1919-1969* (London: Oxford University Press, 1972), p. 140.

6. For a converging summary, consult Klaus Knorr, *The Power of Nations: The Political Economy of International Relations* (New York: Basic Books, 1975).

7. For a more detailed presentation of this issue, see the classic pieces by Raymond Aron, *A Century of Total War* (Garden City, N.Y.: Doubleday, 1954) and *On War* (Garden City, N.Y.: Doubleday, 1959).

8. See Richard Burt, "New Weapons Technologies: Debate and Directions," *Adelphi Paper No. 126* (London: International Institute for Strategic Studies, 1976), p. 30.

9. Consult Geoffrey Kemp, "The New Strategic Map," paper presented for the conference, "The Consequences and Limits of Military Intervention," University of Chicago, June 1976.

10. Charles C. Moskos, Jr., discusses the issue of the emerging military model at length in a paper, "The Emergent Military: Calling, Profession, or Occupation?" presented at Symposium on Representation and Responsibility in Military Organization, University of Maryland, January 1977.

11. David R. Segal and John D. Blair, "Public Confidence in the U.S. Military, *Armed Forces and Society* 3 (Fall 1976): 3-11.

PART I. ANALYTIC DIMENSIONS

ANALYTIC DIMENSIONS OF INTERVENTION

DECISIONS

Richard Smoke

Whether to intervene militarily in a distant conflict and, if so, how and to what extent, have always been troublesome decisions. But there are several reasons for thinking that, in the world of the present and foreseeable future, such decisions are becoming harder than ever to make rationally and well. This paper attempts, first, to outline very succinctly why this seems to be the case. Against this background, then, it attempts to suggest some limitations in the analytical approaches and perspectives usually taken to this kind of decision, and some directions for improvement, to better meet the challenges of today's and tomorrow's world.

THE CONTEXT OF DECISION: PRESENT AND NEAR FUTURE

Morris Janowitz, in this volume, argues that we have been experiencing, and will probably go on experiencing, a diffusion of centers of power and decision. The emerging world cannot be adequately conceptualized in bipolar terms, or in "tripolar" or "pentapolar" terms. The system is no longer one in which the great majority of players orient themselves around some small number of poles and may be regarded as allied to, subordinate to, or de facto clients of, the polar powers. Rather the system is increasingly one of numerous independent and semi-independent players in varying degrees of conflict and cooperation among each other.

The complications this introduces for the decision maker represents one aspect of the problem. Another is the multiplication, now occurring, in the *kinds* of conflicts that may spring up—economic conflicts in particular. The economic gap is continuing to widen between the few developed, Northern, mostly white nations and the many underdeveloped, Southern, mostly nonwhite ones, as GNPs and per capita incomes go on rising among the former and largely stagnate among the latter. Among the Group of 77 nations—actually numbering over a hundred by now—the revolution of rising expectations is becoming what one observer has termed a "revolution in rising frustrations,"[1] More and more the preconditions are in place for international conflicts generated not principally by the traditional ideological competition, but directly or indirectly by economic demands, and simply by basic economic and material needs.

Economic issues provide a medium for international conflict as well as a source of it. Only four nations possess some 80% of the world's copper ore reserves; and another four, some 95% of the tin reserves.[2] (Both metals have been almost completely mined out of North America and Europe.) Though no cartels have yet formed among these countries to fix prices or exact other demands, fewer players are needed to form them than are needed to maintain OPEC, the existing oil-producers' cartel, which numbers about a dozen significant members. Reserves of other minerals essential to advanced industrial societies are owned by slightly larger, but still comparatively small, collections of Third World nations. On the other hand, North America has been the world's breadbasket for some time and may continue to be. There is at least a potential, widely noted in recent years, for this food reserve to be employed as a bargaining chip. In both directions along the North-South dimension of world politics, then, there is an economic "layer" of interactions that represents both a medium for conflict and an increasingly serious source of it.

Where competition becomes acute in this layer, furthermore, it is likely to set the stage for overt political-military conflict. We have already seen powerfully argued proposals by certain American political specialists, for instance, that the United States use its military power to seize Middle Eastern oil fields.[3]

At the same time, the traditional East-West ideological competition also remains, as does the competition between Moscow and Peking. And so do some standing territorial competitions, e.g., in the Middle East. These better-understood layers of potential conflict intersect with the newer layer of economic competition. In a world of many new centers of decision, the number of possible combinations and crosscurrents of national interests is some multiplication of the previous range of possibilities, not merely a simple addition to them. Decision making is correspondingly complicated.

But there is yet a third aspect to be considered. What is perhaps most disturbing about the emerging world constellation—apart from the profound human and moral dimension of the looming economic disaster—is that it is occurring at the same moment in mankind's history that increasingly diverse and destructive military technology is passing into more and more hands. When, during the autumn of 1974, Giscard d'Estaing said of the world economy that "all the curves are leading us to catastrophe,"[4] he did not add, at least in public, that "catastrophe" in the military-technological context of the late twentieth century could not be like "catastrophe" in earlier eras. The military possibilities are more numerous, more complicated, and much more destructive.

Indeed it is not much of an exaggeration to say that we are presently entering an era of "military plenty." The world's nations are now much better armed than they were during the cold war era, and the long-term trend seems to be toward ever growing armories. As recently as 1960, total world military expenditures, outside NATO and the Soviet bloc, were only about $8 billion per year, and the bulk of this sum was accounted for by just three nations: China, India, and Japan. By 1974, these expenditures had exceeded $20 billion a year and were continuing to accelerate. In the five years 1970-74 inclusive, the total came to almost $100 billion, and a growing number of nations spent significant sums. The sophistication and diversity of the military technology spreading outside the two traditional blocs is rising also, in tandem with its quantity. Today a number of countries possess much of the technology which was current in the American armory when the U.S. entered the Vietnam War. Meanwhile, the "exotic" technology of the seventies has already spread to the Middle East—e.g., advanced electronic countermeasures, F-16's, hand-held antiaircraft missiles, and precision-guided missiles. The most likely prospect for the 1980s is of this technology spreading to a number of middle-rank powers. Most serious of all is the very real possibility that nuclear weapons and their makings may proliferate in the years ahead to a growing number of countries, and perhaps to terrorist and criminal groups. The multiplication and dispersion of reactors, the sale of fuel-processing plants, the known development of inexpensive laser isotope-separation, and the risk of theft or covert distribution of finished weapons combine to make nuclear blackmail, and warfare employing a few nuclear weapons, disturbingly unremote.

Terrorist and criminal groups may also be riding a trend toward more destructive weaponry, quite apart from their possible possession of atomic explosives. Twice within the last three years, for example, terrorists have been captured with Soviet-made STRELLA missiles (hand-held antiaircraft missiles) in their possession. In the future such a group, armed with only a modest number of these weapons and using skillful bargaining and demonstrative tactics, might be able to bring civil aviation to a halt within a nation or region, or conceivably worldwide.[5]

In at least three major respects, then, the world of the late twentieth century seems likely to differ markedly from the world existing when most foreign policy and national security specialists took their training. The number of independent and semi-independent centers of decision is vastly greater than before, and some players are not organized governments. Conflict may occur on a greater number of layers of the world social system—economic, political, ideological, territorial, tribal, etc.—and these layers are interlinked in numerous intricate ways. In at least one layer, the economic, actual or potential conflict is becoming more serious, while in few if any other layers is it lessening. And more and more players are coming to possess a wide range of advanced, very destructive military capabilities, with both the number of such players and their capabilities likely to go on increasing. There may now be a real danger of the threat, or actual use, of one or more nuclear weapons within the near to medium future.

THE CONTEXT OF DECISION: IMPLICATIONS OF THE WORLD CONSTELLATION

If this is a fair, if extremely terse and oversimplified, summary image of the probable emerging world constellation, it represents an essential point of departure for a fresh analysis of the problems of military intervention. For this sort of world constellation is highly *intervention-prone*. It is more intervention-prone, almost certainly, than an essentially bipolar (or tripolar) world system, in which conflict runs mainly along one or two layers and most actions of global significance are taken by, or at the instigation of, the two polar powers. In a world of "military plenty" and a substantial number of independent or semi-independent actors, there is a considerably higher probability that a minor conflict may seem to threaten the interests of—or present opportunities to—regional powers who are prepared to intervene largely on their own and who have the capability to do so.

In addition, the number of players, and the multiple layers of diverse interests and involvements connecting players to local situations, will usually present a rich menu of possibilities for low-level, "subthreshold" interventions of various kinds, as well as more overt military intervention. Numerous options are likely to present themselves for economic pressure tactics, for political threats and promises, and for many sorts of covert or semicovert "political warfare" devices. In this kind of constellation, opportunities often abound for playing ends against middles, for agent-provacateur types of tactics, for "psywar" and "disinformation" operations, and for "destabilizing" political proceses, groupings, and governments (à la the CIA "destabilization" campaign against Allende's Chile). The likely flourishing of these and similar kinds of *relatively* nonviolent, occasionally not even entirely coercive, possibilities for "subthreshold" interventions may give a Byzantine or medieval-Florentine flavor to many political affairs of the near future.

Finally, this kind of world constellation is intervention-prone in another sense having to do with self-feeding processes. Increasing instabilities in local situations (perhaps partially a result of subthreshold interventions) often tend to create conditions inviting more and larger interventions. Consider, for example, the Lebanese civil war of the spring of 1976. We may note in passing that both the predominantly Christian rightists and the predominantly Moslem leftists were beneficiaries of subthreshold interventions from outside Lebanon, in the sense that both were evidently resupplied with ammunition—and, on the rightist side, apparently with light and heavy weapons as well—after the stocks that each side had captured when the regular Lebanese Army had dissolved were exhausted. The more significant point, however, concerns the self-feeding process at work. The continuation and periodic intensification of the fighting led, during one period of five days in May for example, to the offer (threat?) of French military intervention, and the standing threat of a major Israeli military intervention. Here is a case, then, like many others, where the consequences of an important local instability—and the consequences of subthreshold interventions—included the fact and threat of much greater interventions.

IMPLICATIONS FOR DECISION OF SELF-FEEDING PROCESSES

The possibilities raised by self-feeding processes of this sort have enormous implications for decision making—in particular for policy makers' perceptions of other players, motives and actions, and evaluation of their own options. This is a difficult subject to sketch briefly, but it is important enough that some attempt must be made.

Overt military interventions (as opposed to subthreshold interventions) have an interesting characteristic in an era of "military plenty." They generally succeed against opposition *currently* in existence at the time of the interventory act. Until the contemporary period, such had not been the typical case (except in interventions by the mother country in colonial affairs). Such was definitely not the case, for example, in the Soviet intervention in the Spanish Civil War of 1936-39. For several reasons the USSR was simply unable to intervene decisively in the Spanish theater, although a very significant effort was made. Soviet logistics were inadequate to sustain more than a relatively modest flow of equipment, supplies, technicians, and advisers to the Republican side in Spain; a blockade by the Nationalist side interrupted the logistical link with increasing effectiveness and the Soviets lacked the naval force to escort cargo vessels through the blockade; and the Soviets proved to have insufficient quantities of the most critical goods, especially tanks and aircraft, to be able to spare enough for Spain.[6]

But in many, probably most, situations in the contemporary period, an outside power intervening in an ongoing conflict will commit an intervention sufficient to turn the local tide decisively. Decision makers are likely to have a wide range of interventory options available, and generally will select one that is adequate, even ample, to deal with the existing opposition. In such situations, their decision concerning the size of their military commitment is often influenced heavily by the tradeoff between securing a rapid and sure victory on the one hand, and minimizing costs on the other. Both considerations argue for a decisive stroke, though the latter may suggest an upper limit on the size of the interventory force as well. The original American interventions in Korea (1950) and Vietnam (1965-66), the Anglo-French intervention in Egypt (1956), the Soviet-Cuban intervention in Angola (1975), and the American intervention in Lebanon (1957), to name five, all had these features.

Such calculations leave a margin for minor errors, and the consequences of such interventions are, indeed, quite predictable so long as the opposition is not reinforced by a counterintervention from a fourth (or Nth) party. The Angola and Lebanon (1957) cases provide examples. The analytically more interesting and pragmatically more important situation arises, however, when such a counterintervention does occur. In the cold war and immediately post-cold war periods we have witnessed a number of such situations, including the other three just named; and in the world of numerous players, military plenty, and multiple layers of actual and potential conflicts that may be coming, we seem likely to witness many more. The danger of escalation clearly ranks among the most important potential consequences of intervention.

By "escalation," I mean something moderately specific. I am not referring to the kind of escalation that is also sometimes called "eruption" or "explosion," where the fighting shifts very quickly to a high order of violence. Everyone knows that deploying Cuban and Soviet elements to Angola or American Marines to Lebanon will not be answered by a fusillade of the other superpower's ICBMs, or even by a flight of tactical aircraft with nuclear bombs in the theater. The "eruption" concept is relevant mainly to an outbreak of a NATO/Warsaw Pact or a Soviet/Chinese battle. By "escalation" I am also not referring to minor commitments of additional troops or other forces within a local theater, or even a substantial commitment by one side if it is clear that this represents the best that it can do.

Rather, by referring to the dangers of escalation in this context, I am pointing to the complicated hazards that can arise in conflicts involving several players, at least some of whom dispose of major usable capabilities applicable to the situation and as yet untapped. An initial intervention may receive a "moderate" counterintervention, reasonable on its own terms, which in turn inspires a counter by the original intervenor or another party, also reasonable on its own terms, which in turn inspires another move, and so on. A *sequence* of escalations back and forth may occur, in which each step makes sense in terms of its own context in the immediate situation, yet the cumulative effect is to drive the level of violence to a much higher level than anyone originally intended or perhaps even anticipated. The stakes to be won or lost grow as each of the two (or more) sides increase their military and political and psychological commitments, and the point may be reached where one or all sides find that there is so much at stake that they cannot deescalate.

To some extent this occurred in Vietnam, and in a different way it occurred in the weeks just preceding the outbreak of World War I. It almost occurred in the Spanish Civil War, which at the time was widely expected to become the launching pad for a second world war (but never quite did, substantially because it was so widely expected). If the characterization sketched earlier of the likely shape of the world to come proves accurate, such escalation sequences would well be a recurrent danger in the years ahead. A web of complicated, multilayered relationships among numerous independent players would provide a maximum of involvements and national interests through which nations could become involved in local and regional conflicts. And the widening range of military capabilities available to a growing number of players would present them with attractive and reasonable options—or the appearance of attractive and reasonable options—for intervening in these conflicts with real effectiveness at acceptable cost. The emerging world constellation may turn out to be not only intervention-prone but also, in the wake of interventions, *escalation-prone*.

The rise and spread of precision-guided missiles could prove particularly salient in this context, because PGMs may well create among national decision makers the belief that they can intervene in conflicts in precise, "surgical" ways, at a very reasonable cost. But, in fact, precise weapons do not necessarily make for precise consequences. The perception and evaluation of events by policy makers in other countries involved in the conflict are by no means entirely calculable. And while precise targeting may sometimes assist in communicating one's own political intentions to them, it certainly does not guarantee that this communication will be clear, or that those policy makers will evaluate the "message" in the way that is anticipated. Their decisions about possible counteractions depend, naturally, on how *they* perceive and evaluate the action.

It is primarily this inability of each national decision-making group to be highly confident about the perceptions and evaluations of their counterparts abroad, rather than sloppy targeting in tactical operations, that makes for such great uncertainties in trying to anticipate escalation sequences.

But there is another side to this decision problem. One of the paradoxes of the logic of military intervention is that early recognition by decision makers of the escalation-prone character of a local conflict can generate an antidote to it in the form of greater caution in policy making. Their comprehension of the hazards which the political complexity and military plenty of the coming world may create could lead them to accept the danger as a real limitation upon the feasibility of interventory strategies—even in specific situations where the exact route by which the hazards could materialize might not be clear.

Indeed to some extent they already accept this. One need only compare most policy making on military intervention in the contemporary era with, for instance, the blithe fashion in which British decision makers used to dispatch Royal Navy squadrons to local hot spots. The power and diversity of modern weapons systems, the number of states that have them, and the never entirely forgettable nightmare that nuclear weapons could somehow become involved have engendered a sense of caution all around. A feeling that dangerous possibilities are becoming more numerous and more hazardous, and a sense of restraint—born of caution—in contemplating intervention options, could become more pronounced as time passes. The emerging world might then turn out to be less escalation-prone, and even less intervention-prone, than the preceding discussion has suggested.

SOME ANALYTIC DIMENSIONS OF INTERVENTION DECISIONS

The problems of self-feeding processes are not the only difficulties policy makers face in dealing with intervention-prone and escalation-prone situations. There are others of related kinds. To explore them, it is useful to introduce two abstract dimensions of interventory decision making that are not only analytically useful and interesting in their own right, but also provide a framework for investigating some of the less obvious problems that arise in this process.

Although they overlap in practice, these two analytic dimensions must be conceptualized as "stages" or "phases" of the decision-making process. First, there is the phase in which policy makers faced with a crisis derive an understanding of what the local and regional situation is, and what the significance of it seems to be. Second, there is the phase in which they reach an action decision on what, if anything, to do about the situation—a decision that may include or exclude military intervention in some form. Let us call the first phase the *diagnosis* of a situation and its significance, and the second phase *option-handling*—the search for, creation of, evaluation of, choice among, and implementation of options for dealing with the situation.[7]

Most of the remainder of this discussion explores the utility of this distinction and some of its applications. But at the outset, the very great overlap of these two "phases" in practice must be emphasized. Military intervention is usually an ongoing process, in which interactions among a number of players require a stream of many decisions, not just one "for" or "against" intervention. Through the trajectory of this stream, policy makers constantly move back and forth between diagnosis and option-handling. Even in the making of a decision, the distinction may not be clear-cut practice. For instance, the exploration of available options, at a given moment, may suggest to policy makers some important aspect of the situation which they had previously overlooked or deemphasized in their diagnosis. There is also a tendency for their perceptions of the significance of events to be influenced by the options which seem most ready to hand or most probably useful. For example, policy makers who believe that numerous and effective options are readily available for counterinsurgency and low-level warfare are more likely to perceive a situation such as Vietnam in the mid-1960s in primarily military terms. Also, there is feedback between options executed and policy makers' perceptions of the problem. If the initial action decisions do not work out as expected, decision makers will usually try to reassess the nature of the situation as well as the limitations of the option(s) selected.

Despite these and other overlappings in practice, conceptually and analytically the distinction is a useful one. It also has *prescriptive* value; as is suggested in what follows, clarity among decision makers on which phase they are in at any particular time can improve the quality of their policy making. Let us explore these dimensions of decision making, then, in a little more depth.

DIAGNOSIS: ON THE ROLE OF INFORMATION

Policy makers faced with a sudden international crisis, or a more gradually developing problem situation, must come to an understanding of what that situation is, what its significance is and what policy issues (if any) it creates. They may do so carefully and explicitly, or they may feel that "what the problem is" is clear, and pass on quickly to the stage of considering intervention options. But one way or another—explicitly or implicitly, consciously or unconsciously—they form some kind of diagnosis of the situation. They *must* do so before they can begin to consider what to do about it, and their option-handling will depend on their diagnosis, whether this is fully recognized or not. This is so both in the obvious sense that the option-handling will depend on the content of the diagnosis; and in the slightly less obvious sense that the quality of the option-handling will be heavily dependent on the comprehensiveness, explicitness, accuracy, and perceptiveness of the diagnosis.

It is probable that both policy makers and the community of analysis within and without the government have tended to be less attentive to the requirements of this diagnosis stage than they might have been. Specifically, the nature of the internal "structure" of a diagnosis—its analytical elements and the logic of how these elements fit together—as well as the importance of this structure, may be less widely appreciated than they deserve. There are two aspects of the analytics of diagnosis which may merit more attention: the limited role of factual information, and the role of images of others. First we will consider the former.

Consider, at the outset, the limited value of intelligence information in assessing the intentions of other players in an emerging situation. It has become a truism in intelligence circles that even the short-term intentions of others, to say nothing of their overall objectives, are almost never indicated unambiguously by available information. For example, data about a new force deployment by one country, and its supporting logistical operations, may demonstrate pretty clearly that that country is positioning itself to be able to activate certain military options, but will not say much about which options are most likely to be chosen. Diagnosis of the real significance of even such relatively tangible developments depends on estimates—always somewhat uncertain—about the longer-term objectives, preferred strategies, and political-behavioral style of that nation's policy makers.

A single example will illustrate. Prior to the Nazi attack on the USSR in 1941, ample high-quality intelligence of Hitler's military dispositions and plans was available to Stalin. The Soviet leader, however, simply did not believe that Hitler would launch a surprise attack. Stalin's image of Hitler's style encouraged him to believe that Hitler would first present demands and attempt to bargain before resorting to force. The menacing Nazi buildup on the Soviet border, Stalin believed, was intended to set the stage for serious negotiations and bargaining. There are a number of explanations of why Stalin may have miscalculated Hitler's intentions in this way; but in any case it is clear that he did so not because hard intelligence was scanty or equivocal, but because for various reasons he did not believe in the contingency that, in the end, actually emerged.[8]

This is a case where the number of players involved and the number of possible patterns of development were both very small. In most conflict situations in the contemporary world where outside intervention is a possibility, the number of possible players and the number of potential patterns of development are much larger; and often the relevant hard intelligence is of lesser quality and/or quantity. The role of uncertain political estimates in diagnosing other players' intentions is concomitantly greater.

We may not be as analytical as we could be about all the ingredients that go into this kind of estimating. Certainly two ingredients seem to be important which have received comparatively little attention from analysts, at least in the open literature. One is the conceptual and doctrinal component in the political perspective of policy-making groups abroad. Military intelligence analysts give great weight to the military doctrines of foreign armed forces, but it is not clear that the doctrinal assumptions of political policy makers abroad have received equivalent attention from political specialists (beyond such relatively straightforward things as learning what Marxism-Leninism says).[9] The second ingredient concerns the personality structures of high-level policy makers abroad. There is much to suggest that the temperaments and cognitive styles of decision makers play a heavy role in their policy making, but only recently have such factors begun to catch the eye of political-military specialists. Lucian Pye's recent study of Chairman Mao from this point of view may turn out to be a harbinger of a new interest in this approach.[10]

If we turn from the comparatively specific problem of assessing other parties' fairly short-term intentions to the more general aspects of forming high-quality diagnoses of emerging problem situations that may require or invite intervention, we find that factual information probably plays a still less central role. A proportionately greater role seems to be played by what I shall term "conceptual presuppositions," which may be of several sorts.

One sort is the historical analogy. A generation of decision makers tended to shy away from policies that appeared to be "appeasement," on the analogy of Munich and the Franco-British policy of the late 1930's that had proved so disastrous with Hitler. President Truman, for instance, was quite explicit in saying that this analogy had weighed heavily in his decision to repel the North Korean attack on South Korea by the use of American forces. Ernest May offers a powerful argument in his book, *"Lessons" of the Past*, that a historical analogy, comparing a current situation with one from the past, can have a remarkably compelling impact on policy makers' perceptions of their problem. [11] Of course, a rich understanding of history usually offers multiple analogies suggesting diverse policies. But particular events of the fairly recent past which decision makers have lived through themselves apparently can have a vivid and dramatically persuasive effect. After World War II, for instance, decision makers in the United States coalesced fairly rapidly around a perception of Stalin as "another Hitler." As May points out, the evidence available at the time (as well as more recently) supports at least as well the analogy of Stalin as another Peter the Great or Catherine the Great—analogies which would have suggested quite different American policies from the ones pursued. But U.S. decision makers were not familiar with Peter or Catherine. They were very familiar with Hitler, however, and their diagnosis of Stalin may have been skewed as a result.

Similar to historical analogies are generalizations, or "laws," which policy makers may believe history "proves." Secretary of State John Foster Dulles, for example, was persuaded that most of the great wars of modern times had begun because the aggressors—Hitler, Kaiser Wilhelm, and others—had underestimated the strength of the military alliances that would ultimately be brought to bear against them. Had they not miscalculated in this way, he believed, they would never have opted for war. In short, war was generally the result of a miscalculation of forces. Dulles's effort to construct a system of formal U.S. alliances ringing the Communist world rested in part on the premise that this would make clear to Moscow and Peking the U.S. and allied defense commitment to the lands threatened by communism. This time the potential aggressors would not miscalculate the forces, because the military alliance that would be brought to bear had been constructed in advance.

Dulles did not consider a very different, and conflicting, historical "law"— that wars can also result from a cycle of provocative acts reciprocating back and forth between potential belligerents, and escalating. This "law" implies a rather different policy conclusion. Had both "laws" been recognized and mutually balanced, U.S. policy makers might not have applied containments so ambitiously and so rigidly on such a global scale—for instance, interfering in the Chinese civil war, even to the point of hazardously defending islands lying a couple of miles off the Chinese mainland.

A third sort of "conceptual presupposition" is the fundamental, often semi-conscious, assumption about long-term historical trends. We have heard much, for example, about Henry Kissinger's alleged belief that in the long run the tide of history is running against the West, and that therefore the best statesmanship is to delay the inevitable through a succession of compromises. Another example may be provided by the current North-South negotiations over economic issues. It seems likely that policy makers in the developed countries presuppose, at least to a considerable degree, that great economic disparities between their nations and the Third World will persist for a long time. Many policy makers among the Group of 77 nations, however, clearly presuppose that, within a couple of generations at the very most, the standard of living and per capita incomes of their peoples must roughly equal those of, say, Europe. Clearly the perceptions in various capitals of the significance of specific negotiations must differ greatly when such underlying assumptions are so widely opposed.

Historical analogies, purported historical "laws," and fundamental assumptions about long-term historical patterns clearly play a central role in decision makers' diagnoses of the significance of events. (There may be other important kinds of "conceptual presuppositions" as well.) Their exact roles in specific cases may be difficult to ascertain and to demonstrate unambiguously. But in this area we probably do not know as much as we could about the analytics of diagnoses. To the extent that we are concerned with improving the quality of policy makers' diagnoses, as well as understanding scientifically the bases of foreign policy behavior, more attention to these kinds of elements could prove quite useful.

DIAGNOSIS: ON THE ROLE OF IMAGES OF OTHERS

The second aspect of the analytics of diagnosis may merit more attention from policy makers than analysts. It concerns what may be a tendency to accept as sufficient a somewhat oversimple image of the decision calculus of policy makers abroad. More specifically, there may be a tendency for the apparent or imputed *objectives* of the policy makers of other nations to receive the lion's share of the analysts' attention, to the comparative exclusion of those policy makers' underlying perspectives, assumptions, and expectations relevant to the situation—their complete "frame of reference."

Consider an example. Let us take, in fact, the example of one of the worst military and foreign policy setbacks in American history—the decision, in the fall of 1950, to permit the U.S. forces in Korea, then advancing rapidly up the peninsula in the wake of the triumphant Inchon landing, to proceed all the way to the Yalu River, the border with China. The consequence of this decision and its execution was a massive military intervention by the Peoples'

Republic, for which the American forces were ill-prepared, and which sent them reeling back in one of the longest and bitterest military retreats in U.S. history. After great difficulties a stable defensive line was finally established, and there followed two and a half years of a painful and costly war of attrition, before a cease-fire was finally arranged in the summer of 1953.

How did this setback occur? At the outset of the Korean engagement, President Truman and Secretary of State Acheson had clearly defined the U.S. objective as limited to pushing the North Korean aggressors back behind the 38th parallel. Subsequently, the clarity of this limitation became eroded as General MacArthur, commander in Korea, and the Joint Chiefs of Staff asked permission for flexibility in operations to ensure tactical defeat of the North Koreans. And, during the fall, a series of directives from Washington progressively relaxed the geographical limitation on U.S. operations, finally abandoning it entirely so long as the forces remained within Korea. It is true that the "decision" to proceed to the Chinese border was made gradually and in stages, and never as the result of a well-defined debate in which the full weight of arguments pro and con were considered. What partly made this possible, though, and what was equally or more significant, was the comparative simplicity of the model which Washington decision makers were using of the probably Chinese decision calculus.

President Truman, Secretary Acheson, and other high-ranking policy makers were perfectly aware, of course, that the Peking regime would be highly sensitive about its border with Korea, and that protecting the security of that border and of nearby Chinese territory would be a major objective. This awareness was reflected in very strict orders to MacArthur not to cross the Yalu with either ground or air forces under any circumstances. It was also reflected in a declaratory campaign, during the summer and fall of 1950, aimed at reassuring Peking that the U.S. harbored no designs against China. Decision makers in Washington quite clearly believed that these and related policies should relieve Chinese security anxieties sufficiently that Peking would have no reason to accept the costs and risks of a military intervention in the Korean conflict.

However, this belief reflected an inadequate comprehension of the Chinese perspective. In Peking's eyes, U.S. policy in Asia had begun to harden and to assume an increasingly threatening posture with the outbreak of the Korean War. Chinese Communist leaders saw, in Truman's "neutralization" of Formosa early in the war, an ominous reversal of U.S. policy toward China. In 1949, the U.S. had acquiesced in the Communist victory in the civil war, and early in 1950 had publicly excluded Formosa, as well as South Korea, from its defense perimeter in the Far East. Now, in June 1950, the U.S. was suddenly intervening in what Peking saw as a Korean "civil war," and also immediately reversed its policy of tacitly allowing Nationalist Chinese-held Formosa to fall to the Communists.

Peking may also have seen, in the brilliant success of MacArthur's advance up the Korean peninsula in the summer and fall, something alarmingly like the Japanese invasion of Korea many years previously, which had culminated in an all-out attack on China. What might U.S. strategic intentions really be? In adopting the objective of reunifying Korea under a pro-West regime, the United States for the first time was using its enormous military power to eliminate a Communist government. Might this be the beginning of a general policy of "roll-back"? Such a policy was being advocated by the Republican opposition to the Democratic administration within the United States, and by many military officers, including General MacArthur. Why was he being allowed to remain in command if this were not secretly the administration policy as well?

All the "facts" just mentioned were known to American policy makers, but insufficient attention was given to what might be the Chinese perspective on them. They miscalculated the feasible limits of their military intervention in Korea, because they failed to comprehend adequately the frame of reference through which Chinese decision makers were assessing the significance of U.S. activities in Asia.[12]

Many other case histories could be cited where similar inadequate comprehension resulted in similar grave consequences. Roberta Wohlstetter, Ole Holsti, Robert Jervis, and others have all stressed the importance, in successful decision making, of a clear understanding of other parties' perspectives and assumptions.[13] The general importance of this factor is also appreciated by many officials experienced in foreign and national security policy making. Indeed, the general need to appreciate the other side's point of view is an idea that will almost always command assent among decision makers and their staffs.

Assenting to the idea, however, is not the same thing as policy makers' initiating analytic efforts, when faced with fresh crises, to bring to light as much as possible of their adversaries' perspectives. The attention which they usually pay to the other side's immediate objectives does not substitute for this wider conceptual understanding. And policy makers may not be aware of the real extent of their analytic deficiency. For many reasons of governmental organization and bureaucratic politics, working-level officials—who may be familiar with relevant factors in the frames of reference of foreign governments, as they operate in a particular situation—may not be adequately tapped in the policy process. In the absence of alertness to such factors on the part of high-level policy makers themselves, decisions may be made on the basis of inadequate assumptions about the sources of other players' behavior.

OPTION-HANDLING

As policy makers complete their diagnosis of an emerging situation, they may conclude that it involves important national interests, and that some form of intervention may be desirable. In most capitals, however, policy makers may be compelled to realize that they lack acceptable options, or perhaps any options, for a unilateral intervention, and must act in concert with others or not at all.

In the Soviet Union, however, and above all in the United States, decision makers possess a great range of options for many kinds of unilateral interventions almost anywhere on earth. The number and variety of military options physically available to the United States are completely unprecedented; they are significantly greater now than they were even ten years ago, and with the advent of plentiful cruise-missiles and other new technology, they are still increasing. It is a challenging task for U.S. decision makers to search out their options and review them in a new, specific context, and perhaps to create new options by combining, subdividing, or otherwise manipulating existing capabilities—to evaluate, then, the alternatives and to choose wisely among them.

Partly because of this range and diversity of military options open to the U.S., there may be some tendency for American decision makers to pass rather quickly from the stage of diagnosing a problem to the stage of option-handling—particularly when there is time pressure. Even when time is not a pressing factor, the exceedingly busy schedules of high-level policy makers make it difficult to bring the subtleties of a situational diagnosis to their attention until the issue has become so "hot" that the pressure is on to find something to do about it.

The tendency of decision makers to jump quickly to the option-handling stage may also be due to a bias toward action rather than contemplation in American culture. There tends to be a prevailing feeling that to draw out the diagnosis is negative and unconstructive because it makes problems seem larger and more difficult, whereas to turn to the search for "solutions" is positive and constructive. This bias for action, however, can easily lead to what psychologists and management specialists call "premature closure" of the diagnosis stage.

Yet the task of finding effective, high-quality "solutions" to foreign policy problems in fact depends very greatly on the diagnosis stage not being closed prematurely. This is perhaps particularly true where policy makers are faced with a choice between a set of *military* intervention options and *other ways* of exerting influence over the developing situation. There are a couple of reasons for this. First, military options, unlike most nonmilitary ones, run the risk of triggering escalation sequences; diagnosing the degree to which this danger may be present in particular situations requires the most careful possible analysis that time permits to reduce the inevitable uncertainties. Secondly, military options require more preconditions in place, for the options to have a reasonable chance of success at reasonable cost, than do most nonmilitary options. This is a point that is sometimes overlooked. Because military intervention is, in a sense, the most "unilateral" kind of policy to undertake (since, for the U.S. at least, it demands the least cooperation from others), it is not always recognized that in most circumstances there are *more* preconditions to be satisfied before this policy can promise a favorable ratio of expected benefits to expected costs.

The consideration of military intervention from the angle of ascertaining the number and kinds of preconditions for success is a productive analytic approach that is not always emphasized. Among U.S. policy makers, Secretary Acheson in particular is notable for having stressed it. When faced with situations where an American intervention seemed to be a possible policy, Acheson would regularly ask what were the "missing ingredients" in the situation which, if supplied by the United States, would lead to a decisively more favorable outcome. When he could not identify such "missing ingredients," or if they could not be provided by the U.S. at acceptable cost, he would recommend against intervention.

Among scholars and analysts, the most systematic attack on the intervention question, using this approach, was a study undertaken several years ago by Alexander George and two associates, David Hall and William Simons.[14] The researchers compared three crises where the U.S. intervened with "coercive diplomacy"—military force and/or diplomatic threats backed with military force. The three were the Cuban Missile Crisis, assessed as essentially a success, and the U.S. intervention in Laos in 1960-61, and the initial U.S. intervention in Vietnam in 1964-65, both assessed as predominantly failures.

Analysis led to the identification, among other things, of eight preconditions for a successful intervention, at least by the U.S. under that class of historical conditions. These are as follows:

(1) The strength of the U.S. motivation

(2) An asymmetry of motivation favoring the U.S.

(3) The clarity of U.S. objectives

(4) A sense of urgency to achieve the U.S. objective

(5) Adequate domestic political support

(6) Usable military options

(7) Opponents' fear of unacceptable escalation

(8) Clarity concerning the precise terms of settlement

(Note, incidentally, the extent to which the assessment of several of these, in any particular situation, depends on the assessment of the opponents' frame of reflection, as discussed above.)

The analysis which led to these conclusions is too complicated to be reviewed here. The study represents, however, one attempt to examine at least a certain set of intervention situations systematically, from the viewpoint of what preconditions need to be satisfied before an intervention strategy is likely to pay off. Other studies, approaching intervention from a similar viewpoint, might expand or modify the list. The preconditions suggested by this particular study, though, are neither few in number nor easy to achieve. The conclusion seems at least likely that military intervention, despite being the most "unilateral" of strategies, is one whose preconditions for success are numerous and substantial. Premature closure of the diagnosis phase in favor of rapidly turning to a search for "solutions" is likely to obscure this fact for policy makers.

If the tendency toward premature closure does indeed occur, it has additional implications. If one side of the coin represents an underemphasis on the analytical preconditions of intervention, its opposite side represents an over-emphasis on what might be termed the "technical" aspects of option-handling.

This overemphasis has certainly occurred, for instance, in theorization about deterrence and in the actual execution of deterrence strategies in U.S. foreign policy. (I refer to general foreign policy deterrence and not to the special mutual deterrence by the two superpowers' strategic armories.) Deterrence in this sense is a fair test of the argument being offered here. As Janowitz and others have pointed out, there is probably no concept that has received greater attention over the last several decades from scholars and analysts of foreign policy than this one.[15] And if we accept "containment" as the equivalent of a general strategy of deterrence, then there is nothing that has been more central in U.S. foreign policy.

Yet a recent review of theorization about deterrence in the U.S., in which the author was involved, remarked that this theorization has had "a somewhat narrow, mechanistic, and technical character. Deterrence theory to date has seemed to presume, de facto, that the scope, desirability, form and appropriateness of a deterrent relationship among the U.S., a potential aggressor, and a third nation were either not problematical or not germane issues, and has passed on to the technician's questions—by what tactics does one become committed once the decision has been made to do so, and how then can the commitment be effectively signalled?"[16] The same study attempted to show that this observation applies not only to theorization, but also rather systematically to the practice of U.S. deterrence strategies in the post-World War II period.

The empirical and theoretical arguments supporting this thesis cannot be reviewed here. Suffice it to say that there is at least suggestive evidence to indicate that the theory and practice of deterrence strategies have included a tendency to overemphasize technical aspects of option-handling at the expense of a relative underemphasis on the analytical preconditions for attempting such a strategy in the first place. The same tendency may very well apply, *mutatis mutandis,* to many other aspects of U.S. foreign policy making. For reasons of space, just one more example will be considered.

ON OPTION-HANDLING: THE EXTREME CASE
OF PREPROGRAMMED OPTIONS

A relatively new development in American military policy making seems to offer a particularly clear bit of evidence for this imbalance in the emphasis given the technical side of option-handling. This is the emergence of "preprogrammed options"—tactical plans, command/control/communications arrangements, and logistical arrangements set up in advance to make *a specific menu* of preselected options easy and quick to carry out in various hypothetical scenarios. I would argue that this development may turn out to be a very long step in a very wrong direction.[17] This is not to deny that value of major attention and planning in advance as to the range and flexibility of the military options available for intervening in various situations. But to design actual options in advance and in detail, and program them into the forces, seems likely to have the practical effect of reducing decision makers' flexibility in the name of increasing it.

There are two reasons for this. First, as a technical matter, preprogramming certain options usually has the effect of making other options more difficult to carry out in a crisis. Unless extremely careful attention is given to just this danger, the tangible steps taken at various intermediate levels of the military bureaucracy to set up certain patterns of action to be quick and easy tends to introduce rigidities that make other patterns of action more difficult. Yet it is impossible for contingency planners to anticipate in advance the full range of considerations that may apply in a future crisis, and to program the forces to cover all of them. High-level policy makers know this so well, *when it comes to a crisis,* that it is not unusual for their first step to be the immediate rejection of all contingency plans! Exactly this was done, for instance, by the Executive Committee at the beginning of the Cuban Missile Crisis.

Second, as a psychological matter, preprogramming certain options is likely to bring these options to prominence in the minds of high-ranking military officers and civilian officials familiar with them. The result could well be a kind of premature "crystalization" of their perceptions of what the possibilities are in a fresh crisis. Other options, other *kinds* of options, or even just creative variations on the programmed options (which might be technically feasible in some cases) would tend not to get thought of, or to be prematurely dismissed.

In short, preprogramming some options is likely to "deprogram" others—in fact, to make others at least somewhat "unprogrammable." And it should be fairly obvious that the whole idea of preprogrammed options (and their apparent desirability to the military bureaucracy) represents, among other things, the ultimate in the tendency toward emphasizing technical aspects of option-handling, at the relative expense of analytical and conceptual aspects.

CONCLUSION

It will have become clear in the course of the preceding discussion that the various issues raised can really be taken as variants on a single theme. In each successive context, I have attempted to point to a certain kind of simplification that probably occurs too often. And each time it has been of the same general kind—a simplification in the direction of policy makers' implicitly reducing the perceived significance of "analytical" or "conceptual" elements in their decision making in favor of the perceived significance of comparatively physical, material, or "technical" factors. To borrow a term from philosophers, there may be a tendency toward a kind of "reductionism."

In utilizing information to form diagnoses, this reductionism appears in the guise of an underestimation of the way policy makers' "conceptual presuppositions," not always articulated, shape their understanding of the significance of information. In utilizing their knowledge of the decision calculus of policy makers abroad, it appears in the guise of an underemphasis on the background "frames of reference" of these policy makers. In the somewhat narrower context of forming estimates of other players' short-term intentions, it appears in the guise of an underemphasis on doctrinal and personality attributes of decision makers abroad, in favor of "hard" intelligence-gathering. And in the context of option-handling, it appears in the guise of an underemphasis on the analytical preconditions for various strategies, in favor of emphasizing "technical" aspects of carrying them out.

To be sure, *how much* this sort of reductionism occurs, and how important its consequences are, will vary substantially from case to case. But it would seem suggestive that the tendency, in each of several contexts, is for the same general kind of reduction to occur. If this is true, then in both their diagnoses and their option-handling, American policy makers may find themselves unnecessarily handicappped in coping with the problems and hazards of an intervention-prone world.

NOTES

1. Geoffrey Barraclough, "The World Crisis" (pt. 1), *New York Review of Books* (January 23, 1975): 20-29.

2. *Ibid.*

3. See, for instance, Robert W. Tucker, "Oil: The Issue of American Intervention," *Commentary 59* (January 1975): 21-31

4. *New York Times* (October 25, 1974): 1.

5. *Aviation Week & Space Technology,* January 20, 1975, pp. 7, 29.

6. This effort in Spain was by far the largest military intervention attempted by the Soviet Union to date, outside areas contiguous to its own borders. For one analysis, see Richard Smoke, *Controlling Escalation* (Cambridge, Mass.: Harvard University Press, 1977), chap. 4.

7. The distinction between "diagnosis" and "option-handling" in the military and foreign policy context was introduced by Alexander L. George in the introduction to his book with David K. Hall and William E. Simons, *The Limits of Coercive Diplomacy* (Boston: Little, Brown, 1971). The distinction was further developed in subsequent work by Professor George and this writer, separately and together. It is discussed from a viewpoint somewhat different from that being developed here, in Richard Smoke, "Policy-applicable Theory," a chapter in Alexander L. George et al., "Towards a More Soundly Based Foreign Policy: Making Better Use of Information," Appendix D to the *Report of the Commission on the Organization of the Government for the Conduct of Foreign Policy, 1973-75* (Murphy Commission) (Washington, D.C.: Government Printing Office, 1975). The discussion immediately following draws in part from that paper.

The diagnosis/option-handling distinction is similar to the distinction between "conclusions" and "decisions" as these terms are used in the "methectic" theory of decision developed by T. T. Patterson in *Decision Dynamics* (forthcoming).

8. For an analysis of Stalin's miscalculation, see Barton Whaley, *Codeword Barbarossa* (Cambridge, Mass.: M.I.T. Press, 1973). The discussion surrounding this example is drawn from a somewhat more extended discussion of the same point in Alexander L. George and Richard Smoke, *Deterrence in American Foreign Policy: Theory and Practice* (New York: Columbia University Press, 1974), chap. 20.

9. Nathan Leites pioneered one approach to this problem, termed the "operational code" technique; see his *The Operational Code of the Politburo* (New York: Greenwood Press, 1972). The technique has since been pursued by Alexander George and others; see, for instance, George's "The 'Operational Code': A Neglected Approach to the Study of Political Leaders and Decision-Making," *International Studies Quarterly* 13 (1969):190-222.

10. Lucien Pye, *Mao Tse-tung, the Man in the Leader* (New York: Basic Books, 1976).

11. Ernest May, *"Lessons" of the Past* (New York: Oxford University Press, 1972).

12. This example is drawn from a longer discussion in George and Smoke, *Deterrence in American Foreign Policy,* chap. 7.

13. See, for example, Ole Holsti, *Crisis, Escalation, War* (Montreal: McGill-Queen's University Press, 1972); Robert Jervis, *Perception and Misperception in International Politics* (Princeton, N.J. Princeton University Press, 1976); and Roberta Wohlstetter, *Pearl Harbor: Warning and Decision* (Stanford: Stanford University Press, 1962).

14. George, Hall, and Simons, *The Limits of Coercive Diplomacy.*

15. Morris Janowitz, "Toward a Redefinition of Military Strategy," *World Politics* 26 (1974): 473-508.

16. George and Smoke, *Deterrence in American Foreign Policy,* p. 65.

17. The argument made here appears in slightly different form in the epilogue to Smoke, *Controlling Escalation.*

SOVIET PERSPECTIVES ON MILITARY

INTERVENTION

Roger Hamburg

Soviet military policy seeks to further the overall strategic-political objectives of the Soviet state. These include deterrence of external attack and recognition by other powers of the Soviet Union's dominant position on the Eurasian land mass as this is reflected on its western and eastern borders. A related, important subsidiary purpose is to extend the reach of Soviet military power in the Third World through selective, opportune use of air and naval forces and military personnel in these areas.

The Soviet economy is smaller than that of the United States and plagued by bottlenecks, shortages, and inefficiencies that are admitted even by Soviet authors. The buildup of armed forces remains a critical objective of the leadership, despite these strains, and the defense burden is accepted for what are deemed overriding diplomatic-strategic objectives. Aside from internal and bloc defense, large Soviet armed forces also provide a means of legitimation, both to the population when the Soviet economy fails to deliver up to enhanced consumer expectations and to possible conservative critics. It may also reduce the divisive effects of the nationalities issue.

Soviet diplomatic-military moves have reflected an awareness of the opportunities the external environment offers as well as the constraints, both external and internal, that confront the Soviet leadership. Highly significant, if not ultimately decisive, in the external realm will be the future international conduct of the United States. Soviet scholarly analysis is seeking increasingly to explain the motives and probable tendencies of American foreign policy. Soviet commentators approve of what they perceive as a new realism in American actions and policy analysis in the wake of the Vietnam experience; but this American mood may be evanescent. The United States is still a hostile force and cannot objectively withdraw into isolation, because its existing and future stake in any emerging international order will not allow it to do so. Future Sino-American relations are important in this regard.

Future American-Soviet relations will offer both opportunities and dangers for the United States, as American policy makers seek to avoid either overreacting to any particular Soviet diplomatic-strategic initiative or failing to make clear to the Soviet leadership what American purposes and objectives are.

SOVIET STRATEGIC THEORY: SOME BASIC CONSIDERATIONS

It is basic to Soviet views on intervention and military force that strategy is always dictated by political objectives; the intensely political nature of Soviet thinking on these matters is a traditional foundation of Marxism-Leninism.[1] Soviet thinking on military matters reflects the view that conflict and coercion, though not military force necessarily, are dominant in international affairs, although military force is available where appropriate. Marxists "do not deny the role of force in politics" but "emphasize that force comprises only part of the political process, not fulfilling it completely."[2] The "objective" factors of power include a state's population, its social structure, its level of science and technology, the availability of raw materials, and "space-geographic conditions" (size and location of productive forces). These, among others, constitute the moral, political, and military potential of the state. But the "subjective" factor is critical: a commander's ability to choose "unexpected means, places and times of military operations for the enemy" as well as his ability to "lead the enemy into error relative to his intentions and actions and successfully realize the decision adopted."[3]

Such statements reflect the nature of the Soviet regime, founded on hostility to all existing regimes and dedicated to transforming the international environment, yet prevented from doing so fully by the existence of powerful external adversaries and internal constraints.[4]

Bolshevik leaders initially emphasized consolidating internal control and building strength for future contingencies. Revolutionary rhetoric and Comintern manipulation of external political forces formed the only realistic option. The emphasis, even after World War II, was to be primarily on maintaining significant deterrent and defensive power. Resort to war with a nuclear power would be very dangerous, but the general rule remained that "the more military power the country has, the better, especially as instruments for foreign policy purposes.[5]

Military aid and advisers were used after 1923 in the Middle and Far East. The Soviet Union did make important gains as part of its pact with Nazi Germany in 1939 and during and shortly after World War II as a result of combat operations. But cold war "probes" in the Berlin blockade and the Korean War were largely unsuccessful; similar operations in Northern Iran were halted in the face of Western opposition. The Soviet Union's efforts to improve its position by direct military deployments after World War II were "minimal."[6]

Soviet leaders have used military power in circumstances within their capabilities and when the risk to the territorial base of Soviet power was inconsequential. This is a policy of "political offensiveness" and "military defensiveness," as in the "power play" against the Japanese in the summer of 1938.[7] In this instance, a combination of military force and political firmness inflicted a limited defeat on the Japanese.[8]

The Soviet Union has shown an ability to cut losses, withdraw from exposed and declared positions, and avoid wars or situations that would not be acceptable internally, but manipulate risks where suitable for Soviet objectives.[9]

The Soviets have been circumspect where a strong Western response might be expected but have supported revolutionary movements where prospective gains appeared to warrant doing so and the possibility of extensive direct Soviet military involvement was remote.[10] The Western powers have used force on more occasions than the Soviet Union has since 1945; and the Soviets have not relied on war to advance—as opposed to preserve—Soviet territory except in the context of an imminent war.[11]

V. M. Kulish, in a seminal monograph published in Moscow in 1973, under the auspices of the Institute of World Economics and International Relations of the Academy of Sciences of the USSR, stated what may be the closest approximation to Soviet doctrine on the use of force in international relations. It reflects Soviet experience with the use of force in conflicts and as a "presence" for Soviet diplomacy. His and his colleagues' views reflect the caution with which force has been employed, the circumstances where it might be used, and some indication of the constraints on Soviet planners.

Kulish reminds us that a state's military might is durable "only when its development is not in conflict with the national economy and when all aspects of the country's life, economic, political, social, cultural, and military . . . are being developed in a harmonious manner." States must find the proper form that will be congruent with the "foreign political goal of the state on one hand and with the international-political situation on the other." He cautions that war is an "extreme and dangerous political means" and military threats can also "summon forth a definite reaction on the part of either international or domestic forces, the consequences of which are difficult and even impossible to anticipate, particularly in the case of opposition between the two world systems."[12]

Even if a state has an advantage in a particular weapon or use of military force, it may be neutralized by the other side, which can utilize another weapon or create "a political situation somewhere in the world or region, or in the relations between the countries, that will prevent the enemy from realizing his military advantages." Political or military-strategic superiority is the result of a "complicated opposition of forces" which is impossible to express in terms of simple qualitative indices, even though it may prove "impossible to analyze the balance of forces in the absence of such indices."[13]

The United States is described as having great strategic mobility and manipulating a broad military presence, but *"no direct dependency exists between the level of strategic mobility and the actual potential for employing it to achieve political goals."* The military-strategic and international effectiveness of strategic mobility depends on objective factors like the armament, strength, and development of the armed forces but also upon "many intra-political and international-political conditions, in which military power and its mobility are realized in terms of political and military-strategic effectiveness."[14]

The words of the Institute of World Economics and International Relations (IMEMO) associates may be a warning against excessive zeal and posturing by Soviet military or political figures tempted to overplay the Soviet military card, take unwarranted risks, and paint an excessively optimistic picture of what can be derived by expenditures of money and/or manpower in various critical regions. This modern unrealistic syndrome could easily be nurtured at a time of rising Soviet military capabilities and what many perceive to be a corresponding relative decline of American and Western military capabilities and of motivation to resist Soviet probes and Soviet-assisted clients.

SOVIET INTERVENTION POLICY AND INCREASING MILITARY CAPABILITIES

The current debate in Western strategic, governmental, and academic quarters concerned with Soviet affairs deals with serious questions. Is traditional Soviet caution in deploying forces beyond the Soviet Union and Eastern Europe gradually being supplanted by a "forward" posture—the use of Soviet ground, air, and naval forces to support various allies and client states in various contingencies with eventual incalculable consequences for world peace? A Soviet Union operating in an ascending curve of Great Power dynamism may collide with a United States disillusioned with the results of its forward deployment policies yet determined to resist Soviet moves. There is also the fear that the United States may not resist gradual encroachments until some extremely dangerous Soviet move develops from miscalculation—and a nuclear war occurs.

It is clear that there has been a net increase in Soviet military capabilities in gross terms under the Brezhnev-Kosygin leadership, an apparent desire to "erase the image of a Soviet Union strategically inferior to its major adversary," and a parallel effort to improve the reach of Soviet general-purpose forces. Despite the priority on major investment reforms and attempts to stimulate economic growth, there have been successive annual increases in the military budget between 1965 and 1970 and thereafter.[15] Meanwhile, in 1974 the United States armed forces fell by 78,000, to 2,174,000, while those of the Soviet Union were

100,000 higher, at 3,525,000. American forces fell another 44,000 in 1975 and Soviet forces increased another 50,000 to 3,575,000.[16]

The 1968 incursion into Czechoslovakia resulted in the placement of five combat divisions in Central Europe. There were additional divisions in Europe, and no diminution of strength because of Soviet manpower deployments in the Far East, where separate but powerful mobile armed forces remain—Soviet manpower there is about a half-million, with more than 10,000 tanks plus impressive tactical air capability. Generally, there is greater emphasis on increased mobility, greater firepower, more use of air transport, and better logistical performance. Soviet armies in Eastern Europe have maintained existing manpower levels and improved the ratio of advanced equipment and weapons. The Soviet European commitment still consists of 75% of available ground-force strength and 70% of tactical air strength.[17]

The more dramatic, novel changes in naval strength reflected in part the belief of Khrushchev's successors that the Soviet Union needed a wider range of military capabilities, particularly as a reaction to U.S. policy in Vietnam and a perceived U.S. willingness to suppress "national liberation movements" in the Third World, accelerating Soviet efforts to project a presence into the Middle East, Africa, and the Indian Ocean. Strong imphasis was placed on improving the world's largest submarine fleet, whose missions included launching sea-based missiles and inter-dicting seaborne supplies, but there was also a renewal of the surface-ship construction begun under Khrushchev. The merchant marine grew and there were significant increases in trawler and oceanographic activities. Soviet submarines ranged farther into distant areas within missile range of the Atlantic and Pacific coasts of the United States. Two helicopter carriers, designed presumably to support shore-based ground forces, were built.[18] The Soviet naval presence increased in the Mediterranean. Naval units were used politically from 1968 in the Indian Ocean, from 1969 in the Caribbean and West Africa, and in 1970 in Southeast Asia, apparently in support of a decision by the 23d Party Congress of March 1966 that the Soviet Navy was to "Contest the West's unhindered use of the seas for the projection of military power and take on the guise of guardian against imperialist aggression."[19] The Soviet Navy also introduced new classes of support and landing vessels.[20]

The qualitative and quantitative growth of the Soviet Navy was called forth statements by senior Navy officials who emphasized that the Soviet Navy was now a "global, ocean-going, long-range submarine and aircraft navy" fully capable of "great independence of operations, navigational abilities," great striking power, and combat stability. Admiral Gorshkov, in a series of articles in *Morskoi Sbornik,* seemed to be making a case for a powerful surface unit, as opposed to a "submarine/aviation" naval mix, and for a strong naval-air arm under naval control.[21]

Airlift capabilities improved, and high-performance, all-weather interceptors were introduced. This was demonstrated in Prague in 1968, and perhaps more significantly, in the logistical sense, in the airlift supply operation to replenish

Nasser's forces after the June 1967 Arab-Israeli war. Soviet interventionary capabilities were highlighted by the appearance during that war of a tank-landing ship and a couple of troop-landing ships carrying black-bereted naval infantry forces. This seemed designed to convey the impression that the Soviet Union would intervene with local landing parties, although the crisis had passed before they appeared.[22]

These buildups reflect traditional world power concerns given a particular dimension by the historical experience of the Soviet Union and the close wedding of Soviet military power to specific strategic-diplomatic objectives during periods of economic scarcity and strain. The Brezhnev leadership sought to avoid nuclear war and maintain the Soviet Union's traditionally strong European military position plus a credible military presence against an increasingly troublesome Peking. In addition, it sought to develop naval and maritime capabilities to support Third World interests and compete successfully on a global basis with the United States.[23] The danger, of course, was that "instead of armed forces being the instrument of foreign policy," foreign policy might "become the hand-maiden of military requirements."[24]

Besides these general strategic purposes, other reasons—partly internal—for the buildup must be considered. Soviet commentators emphasize that the "balance of forces" is as much a political as a military concept, but "something more than a refined calculus of the utilities and disutilities of military power helps to shape the attitudes of the Soviet leadership toward its accumulation."[25]

Military power, in terms of what may be perceived at home and abroad as parity with the United States, is basic to the official Soviet world view. Possession of strategic might and conventional forces commands respect; on any major international issue the Soviet Union's voice must be heeded and its cooperation, or at least acquiescence, is imperative.

> The Soviet Union is a great power situated on two continents, Europe and Asia, but the range of our country's international interests is not determined by its geographic position alone. ... The Soviet people do not plead with anybody to be allowed to have their say in the solution of any question concerning the maintenance of international peace, concerning the freedom and independence of the peoples and our country's extensive interests. This is our right, due to the Soviet Union's position as a great power. During any acute situation, however far away it appears from our country, the Soviet Union's reaction is to be expected in all capitals of the world.[26]

Georgi Arbatov charges that Americans are guilty of a system of "double measures" and "double standards" when they express concern about the "mortal danger" supposedly hanging over the United States in the new strategic and conventional balance of forces in the world.

> If American navies are permanently stationed thousands of kilometers away from the United States, close to the Soviet borders, Americans once again regard this as a normal state of affairs. But if Soviet warships so much as move out into the Mediterranean, which adjoins Soviet borders and is a long way from the United States, this too is assessed as an unparalleled threat and is a violation of the legitimate order of things.[27]

Other comments by high Soviet officials link the buildup of military power with détente and the "onward rush of socialism" in the world. Gromyko, in an article in the authoritative *Kommunist,* declared:

Socialism is the most dynamic and influential force in the world arena. On three continents, from the Republic of Cuba to the Democratic Republic of Vietnam, the new society of the peoples of Socialist states thrives and is being successfully constructed. *The inexhaustible resources of these countries,* imposing in their economic achievements, *the power of their offensive might* is placed at the service of peace and only peace. . . .

. . . *The tasks of the further strengthening of unity and solidarity, of the defensive might of the socialist commonwealth will remain henceforth the foremost concern of the CPSU and its Central Committee.* [28]

Similarly, Brezhnev contended that:

The development of the socialist countries, their growing might, the increased beneficial impact of their international policy–that is what constitutes the main direction of mankind's social progress today. The attractive force of socialism has become still greater against the background of the crisis that has broken out in the capitalist countries.

Our Party's 24th Congress emphasized that "The attempts of capitalism to adapt itself to the new conditions do not mean its stabilization as a social system. The general crisis of capitalism continues to deepen." Events of the past few years are convincing confirmation of this. [29]

Soviet diplomacy has seen no inherent contradiction between forcing concessions from the United States by threats and pressures and seeking limited agreements. The United States' ability to use military means has been neutralized by growing Soviet military power; the U.S. has been forced to accept the logic of détente.

The change in the balance of power throughout the world in favor of socialist countries has resulted in the establishment of a dynamic equilibrium in military sphere or such a relationship in the strategic forces of the two world systems (primarily between the USSR and the U.S.A.), that the imperialist powers will be unable to use their military might with impunity in carrying out their foreign political plans.

. . . The Soviet Union, while displaying concern for the security of all countries in the Socialist Bloc and for creating favorable conditions for socialistic and communistic organizational development has at the same time been *forced* into building up its own defensive capabilities. As a result, it succeeded to a considerable degree in neutralizing American military might and, at the same time, it ensured the conditions required for peaceful co-existence between the two world systems. [30]

Soviet Military Capabilities: The Internal Dimension

The internal dimension of the military buildup is both critical and puzzling. The economic strain of achieving and maintaining global "parity" and mounting a global military effort in competition with an economy that has more than double the gross national product must be great and the overall performance of the Soviet economy in recent years has been inconsistent. While the military share of the national output has been small enough to be "accompanied by rapid economic growth and rising living standards," the rate of growth of factor productivity, the "effectiveness with which the inputs have been utilized," has declined; Soviet deficits to hard-currency nations continue to grow.[31]

The total Soviet economic picture does act as a constraint in that what the Soviet leadership considers necessary for a Soviet military effort will be provided, but not to the extent proposed in some military quarters. Military leaders know that, if they push demands too heavily, "they run the risk of starving the economic goose that lays golden military eggs," and this is a factor in Soviet force deployments and their possible utilization.[32]

Soviet military-strategic planners and economists have not succeeded in discovering a Marxist-Leninist philosophers' stone; but apparently competing internal considerations override whatever forgone opportunity defense spending represents. One consideration is clearly Brezhnev's own version of consensus politics, economically reassuring a Soviet military leadership naturally dubious about a détente that could lead to a dangerous relaxation of pressure abroad and a lessening of proper Soviet vigilance and discipline at home. Therefore, it was hardly surprising to hear Grechko, the late Soviet defense minister, insist that positive changes in international relations were largely the "outcome of the Party and the people's great work in boosting the country's economic potential and strengthening its defense capability, the direct result of the fact that the policy of the Soviet Union combines the firm will for peace with the constant readiness to deal any aggressor a decisive rebuff."[33]

Brezhnev and other political leaders share the military's concern about the dangers of Soviet military inferiority. Possibly Brezhnev, who cannot reform the command economy for fear of possible adverse political consequences, seeks to improve the capacity of the economy to produce military power. The economy raises the question, "How much butter must be produced in order to obtain the highest rate of military growth?" with military growth a desirable end, not a regrettable necessity.[34]

In addition, some elements of the military and political leaders share an interest in internal discipline, suppression of dissidence, and *large armed forces and deployments* (excluding unpopular wars) *as an instrument of internal legitimation,* a time-honored technique of political systems hardly unknown today in societies lacking the resources of the Soviet Union. Brezhnev, for example, described the military as a "good school of ideological and physical tempering, discipline and organization." *The army enables the Soviet male population to "graduate, so to speak, from a unique nationwide university."*[35]

Hedrick Smith, in his conversations with Soviet citizens, has found that patriotic indoctrination appeals had an audience. Russians, he notes, have a "primeval sense of community," of "Victorian pride in power and empire." Soviet soldiers envied the East German standard of living but felt superior to Germans, "as if their affiliation with the muscle of Moscow compensated for all else." A Russian writer, vacationing in Sochi when reports of Soviet intervention in Czechoslovakia were aired on Western radio frequencies, noted that "The people down there were really very happy with what happened. 'Finally—our troops have gone into Czechoslovakia. We should have done that a long time 'ago. Now we must go on and do the same in Romania.' These people were glad to see that Russia had used its force. They respect that force very much. They like to see Russian power exercised."[36]

Whether this visceral patriotism would survive a critical test of combat, especially if it were prolonged and indecisive (as perhaps in a war with the Peoples Republic of China, hereafter PRC), or whether patriotic rhetoric can perpetually neutralize internal strains and poor performance in the Soviet economy, is problematical. But the burden appears tolerable now, given the perceived advantages of military power internationally and its "bonus effect" internally.

However, calls for moral rather than material incentives and appeals to patriotic fervor cannot completely compensate for declines in agricultural production, the lowest growth rate of civilian industrial production since World War II, and the overall decline in the growth of per capita consumption observed recently.[37] Soviet force levels and deployments inevitably reflect these constraints but are designed to have maximum political and psychological influence in furthering the aims of Soviet foreign policy and in serving as instruments of "coercive diplomacy."

Soviet Intervention Policy and Ground Forces

There has been a great deal of speculation about the intentions of Soviet forces deployed along the Sino-Soviet border in recent years. After the hostilities at Chenpao Island on the Sino-Soviet border and Manchuria on March 2 and 15, 1969, and along the Sinkiang border in July and August of the same year, Colonel General Tolubko was appointed commander of the Far Eastern Military District. Commemorating the Sino-Soviet war of 1929, Tolubko had published an article in *Red Star* noting that after "all efforts to settle the conflict had failed," the Soviet forces struck a "sudden and decisive blow."[38] There were reports that, in August, Soviet diplomats had asked East European leaders how they would react if Chinese nuclear installations were attacked and more Soviet reinforcements were sent to Soviet Asia. These and other gestures appeared to be elements of political pressure designed to force the Chinese into the border talks arranged later in the year. Soviet force deployments since that time have been designed to put pressure on China as a means of fanning pervasive anti-Chinese feeling in the Soviet Union.[39] Soviet moves and statements are intended to deter a major Chinese attack (highly unlikely, given the great disparities in the military strengths of the two nations), and also to preserve the possibility of a partial rapprochement with the post-Mao leadership. The Soviet leaders may respond to Chinese "provocations" but not in a way that would alarm domestic or foreign opinion and thus foreclose the possibility of reconciliation.[40] Brezhnev, for example, after attacking "Peking's feverish attempts to wreck détente," indicated that the Soviet government was "prepared to normalize relations with China on the principles of peaceful coexistence" and, if Peking returned to a policy "truly based on Marxism-Leninism," this "would find an appropriate response from our side."[41]

Any Soviet *attack* on the PRC would be fraught with risks, including that of a long, inconclusive war with an opponent whose ideological zeal and motivation might match or exceed those of the Soviet soldiers. It would be difficult to envision a Chinese leadership that, having lost a Chinese province to a sudden Soviet armed assault, would be politically able to make a settlement with the Soviet Union. The imminent *possibility* of Soviet attack might drive the Chinese closer to the very alliance with the United States the Soviet Union professes to fear. (Goldhamer notes that far more attention is devoted to political indoctrination against the United States and the West than against China in the Soviet armed forces. This is in part because Soviet military personnel can acquire large amounts of anti-Chinese material in the civilian press and radio and in part because the "threat" of the imperialist power is needed to justify military expenditures,[42] particularly when there is the goal of "catching up with and overtaking" a technologically superior opponent.)

The capabilities and intentions of Soviet ground forces in Eastern Europe and the USSR have, of course, always been of concern to the defense planners and armed forces of the United States, despite Korea and Vietnam. Concern about a massive Soviet attack or other political-military contingency in Europe—the military focal point of the cold war as early as 1947 when Soviet forces outnumbered U.S. troops by about two to one,[43]—appears to be reemerging in public and official discussion.[44]

A Soviet commentator observed that the advantages of one ideology or social system "cannot be solved with the aid of nuclear arguments," but nevertheless "it is naïve to suppose that nuclear missile parity predetermines the preservation of the sociopolitical status quo."[45] This has usually been taken to apply to non-European contingencies, but there have been recent indications that it may also apply to Europe, which shows signs of being susceptible to "sociopolitical change" for the first time since the early cold war years.

Soviet military planning and deployments proceed from the assumption that deterrence may fail, or indeed that even successful deterrence is linked with a war-waging, i.e., war-winning, ability to wage a nuclear or nonnuclear war in Europe and win it.[46] Soviet forces in Europe outnumber NATO forces by about three to one in armor and two to one in combat aircraft; even though some of these forces are deployed for "policing" duties in Eastern Europe and the Soviet Union, they constitute a formidable striking force. This is part of a "rapid roll-over" technique, using Soviet and non-Soviet Warsaw Pact forces with a stress on their *preemptive* potential. The Soviet Union is also favored by geographic proximity, and her theater-force levels are larger than those of all the Western allies combined.[47]

Soviet forces are deployed for high-speed offensive operations, a "shock power" army which "tries to create the impression of great strength, often by reliance on mobility to augment its force by velocity (and deception) for the purpose of sapping the morale of its opponent and paralyzing his command and control."[48] Soviet writings depict an offensive coordinated at high rates designed to seize important areas and economic centers, of "smashing the enemy with nuclear weapons," of destroying the enemy defensive line "simultaneously throughout its entire depth," even without numerical superiority over the enemy at every point. High-speed offensive operations along the entire front will "deprive the enemy of the capability to close breaches." Enemy tactical means of nuclear attack (a major offsetting factor in NATO defense planning) are to be neutralized by *"immediate destruction of nuclear means as they are discovered, and preemption in the launching of nuclear strikes, that is, destruction of nuclear means before they can be put into action."*[49] High rates of military advance reduce the possibility of manpower destruction by enemy nuclear strikes. A rapid advance deep into the enemy's rear exposes his long-range nuclear force to capture and deprives him of the "time needed for occupying launch positions and for preparing for launch, since this time is rather lengthy."[50]

Experience in past wars shows that "surprise combat actions make it possible to achieve the greatest result with a minimum expenditure of forces, means, effort and time." The enemy must be hit at his most sensitive point; one must concentrate superior forces in the battlefield "unexpectedly (secretly and swiftly) for the enemy and place them before the battle in as favorable a position as possible."[51]

This major emphasis on initial combat power for short, intense war utilizes Soviet advantages to the fullest and is designed to downplay their vulnerabilities. Soviet ground armies are more labor-intensive forces, supported by fewer (and less complex) weapons, than is true of the West. Mass armies emphasizing numerical superiority have always been a Russian characteristic.[52] Only in a prolonged war would Soviet organizational advantages disappear because of the Soviet inability to supply and maintain forces. NATO is designed to fight a sustained, long-term war of the World War II variety. Soviet doctrine seeks to ensure that NATO will not survive organizationally to fight such a war.

Soviet steamroller tactics and organizational practices permit "a high teeth-to-tail ratio" and "higher visibility of military power" than their opponents. A

Warsaw Pact assault must concentrate attacks, because the pact is vulnerable in a longer war and must avoid the possibility that key NATO industrial nations will develop superior *(but latent)* military resources. Soviet emphasis on the total economic strength of a nation as a critical factor would not be so applicable to a short conventional war using peacetime forces in being and readily mobilizable forces, but it would be a "binding constraint" in a prolonged war.[53]

Soviet writers speak less of all-out nuclear war in Europe and more of swift, even sustained conventional war, for "without a political goal the most fierce battle, in the words of Lenin, will not be a war but simply a fight."[54] If nuclear missile parity does not guarantee the "preservation of the sociopolitical status quo," how would or could Soviet forces be deployed in Europe to affect that status quo? The "worst case" would involve a rapid advance across Europe with nuclear strikes before NATO could reinforce its units, or a massive conventional assault so sudden and so rapid that NATO could not bring its nuclear forces to bear. A sudden attack might commence at a time of ostensible cordial relations with the West, perhaps following an American withdrawal. Or European and Western capitalism might be perceived as so eroded that they would succumb quickly to a display of Soviet military prowess.[55] The vulnerability of Western economic structures to energy shortages and generally deteriorating economic conditions that would bring about a favorable "correlation of forces" within particular European countries would be pertinent here. Brezhnev's recent emphasis on the growing influence of Communist parties in the Western world and the need to deepen ties with "progressive non-Communist parties" in Finland, Great Britain, and France is instructive and an assessment of dètente as leading to "more favorable conditions for peaceful socialist and communist construction."[56]

Soviet forces might attempt a *fait accompli,* incorporating Hamburg or Bornholm Island into the Soviet bloc or probing in Berlin, testing U.S. resolution and political will. The Soviet Union has a great advantage on land and sea in the area of northern Norway, where it might be assumed that the West would accept Soviet expansion. Soviet military forces also constitute a possible threat to southern Europe, especially the Balkans, where Greek-Turkish difficulties have roiled NATO and where Tito's death could create a crisis that the Soviets might exploit by direct military action.[57]

Conceivably, a crisis in Eastern Europe on the Czech model of 1968 might lead Soviet troops to pursue refugees across borders to trace the "heresy" to its foreign source. Less apocalyptically and unpredictably, there is the utilization of the diplomatic "deployed threat," "psychological coercion" exercised by the "passive threat implications of Soviet forces in being." Western European nations would consider Soviet interests and adjust to them, there would be a neutrality "tilt" toward the East, and the result would be de facto acceptance by outside powers of Europe as a Soviet area of special interest. The Soviets would prevail in diplomatic negotiations, not by force of arguments, but by perception of strength.[58] At a minimum, the large Soviet military presence in Europe casts a shadow over its Western neighbors and is ubiquitous in negotiations on arms reduction and European boundaries.

Soviet Intervention Policy and Naval Forces

The Soviet naval deployment, involving a challenge in military and geographical areas where Western and especially American forces have long been predominant, is of relatively recent origin. In his celebrated series of articles in *Morskoi Sbornik* [Naval collection], Gorshkov enumerated the peacetime political tasks of the Navy. These include: (1) demonstrating Soviet power beyond Soviet borders, for prestige and influence; (2) increasing Soviet control over the oceans to obtain food, industrial raw materials, and energy resources; and (3) surprising, intimidating, and lowering the morale of and securing objectives on shore without fighting.[59]

Navies permit "the achievement of political goals without resorting to military operations by merely threatening to initiate them." The emergence of a modern Navy allows the Soviet Union to "deliver punishing retaliatory blows and to disrupt the plans of the imperialists," to defend the country "from attacks by aggression from the direction of the ocean." Official visits and business calls by the warships of the Navy are "making a significant contribution to improving mutual relations between states and peoples" and "strengthening the international influence of the Soviet Union."[60]

Soviet naval units have averted attacks on client states, e.g., after the June 1967 war in the Middle East, to deter Israel from attacking Alexandria and Port Said. They also served to avert the direct threat to the USSR posed by the presence of the sixth Fleet's aircraft carriers in the late 1950s and Polaris submarines in the 1960s. But they also played a more discreet, "show-the-flag" role in support of one side in a regional dispute; they backed the negotiating position of Iraq in its dispute with Kuwait, for example, without pressing Kuwait. This was designed to increase Soviet influence and deny the West any advantage detrimental to the Soviet Union's clients.[61]

The Soviet deployment in the Indian Ocean was designed in part to raise the specter of a naval race (but not create one) and deflect Third World hostility to the American-British presence. It sought to show the flag, support an anti-Polaris and anticarrier role, and serve the cause of denuclearization of the Indian Ocean. Soviet support of Third World clients in this fashion coaxes them into nonalignment. This is consistent with visits of, but not permanent bases for, Soviet warship.[62]

In the Indo-Pakistani crisis of December 1971, Soviet naval moves in the Indian Ocean were apparently intended to counterdemonstrate against "imperialist provocations" (U.S. Naval Task Force 74) and win favor with India. It was an attempt to maintain solidarity with and control the actions of a client. Each side sought to maintain the "right" to intervene and to avert intervention.

In the tacit rules of the game, a superpower can support a friend who is on the strategic defensive, avert defeat, and restore balance (Soviet moves in support of Nasser, and U.S. moves in mining Haiphong Harbor during the Vietnam War), but not assist the client to a conclusive victory. Soviet naval deployment policy seems to follow these rules. It has supported with force, or demonstrated on behalf of, governments having internal difficulties (Yemen, 1967; Somalia, 1970; Sierra Leone, 1971; and, of course, Egypt). Basically, Soviet initiatives have not sought to interfere directly with Western initiatives. Soviet moves in the Indo-Pakistani crisis, for example, seem to have been designed to restrict the "scope of U.S. intervention and confine it to defensive ends." Formal Soviet naval equality, however, does not in fact mask a still substantial U.S. advantage; the interests at stake and the will of the respective superpowers are ultimately conclusive.[63]

The "new" Soviet naval role is significantly different from the past, as it seeks to protect Soviet state interests and clients worldwide, but this has not yet evolved in a design to directly challenge vital Western interests, nor has it evidenced a serious intention to fight limited wars at sea with the United States or other Western navies, as some believe.[64] While there is a growing Soviet naval presence in the Mediterranean, even at the end of the October War in the Middle East the Soviets had more ships at sea than the United States, although they were inferior in firepower and military effectiveness.[65]

The Soviet Navy has logistic support weaknesses and has no transamphibious capability. It has some "sea denial" capability, but it is questionable whether this can be maintained without mobile seaborne air support. It still must depend on facilities in foreign countries, and these are potentially vulnerable to the vagaries of Third World internal politics, as the Soviet Union has discovered in Egypt. Soviet logistics ships are very vulnerable and their amphibious forces are designed for "short duration amphibious lift near the homeland."[66]

MccGwire has observed that the Soviet Navy has been given more ambitious goals than before but not the means to fulfill them. There are occasional hints that the Soviet Navy cannot obtain all it wants, especially where huge capital costs for large surface ships like aircraft carriers are involved.[67] The Soviet Navy does not seek classic command of the sea, in the Western sense. Resource limitations would make this difficult. It does seek control over sea areas where it is possible at reasonable cost. This is a form of command denial, in countering the West's strategic delivery capability. In operating close to its own shores, the Soviet Navy practices "command by exclusion," in more distant areas it adopts "command denial," and in specific areas it may seek temporary command with a local superiority of force. This is not "command of the sea," but, as in the Indian Ocean, it cannot be easily countered if it is used as a political instrument against another fleet and to increase its own authority and importance. If it does more than this, it risks becoming "a Potemkin village on a raft" in the sense that Indian Ocean-based units, once deployed in a critical confrontation, become hostages to fate. Should such a critical confrontation ensue in an area of minimum Soviet naval strength, it is doubtful that Soviet units could engage in serious gunboat diplomacy, to interrupt oil shipping, for example.[68]

The Soviet Union is not challenging the United States for command of the sea, but it is challenging the commands that Western navies formerly exercised. A Soviet source, for example, contends that a Soviet military "presence" with adequate strategic mobility helps to oppose the "aggressive aspirations of imperialism on a global scale." But "military presence" is *"first of all an economic and political problem and only thereafter does it become a military problem."* In this sense, *"we immediately note that the USSR is following a policy that is basically different from the American plan. It has its own historical, economic and geographic peculiarities which, distinct from those of the U.S.A., will not allow it to or require it to maintain a military presence in remote regions of the world."*[69]

Soviet armed forces on land and sea seek to create an impression of great military strength. In Europe they constitute a large military force able to fight a war at different levels, either nuclear or conventional. This formidable, constant military presence is recognized by other nations and casts a corresponding diplomatic shadow. It undoubtedly could have some sudden, "shock" military uses, but it is mainly intimidating, rooted in part in traditional Russian preferences and perceived needs for such a force; it is not likely to become military master of the continent, assuming a reasonable nuclear balance, a maintenance of political will, and the continuing economic and technological superiority of the Western countries. The Soviet naval forces are smaller and have less firepower in relation to their chief adversary than is the case with the traditionally dominant ground forces of a continental power like the Soviet Union. The Soviet naval units seek primarily to deny access, or at least complicate the deployment calculations of Western military and political leaders, but they manifest no readiness to risk any shoot-outs or limited naval engagements with American or other Western naval forces. While they extend their range and increasingly engage in audacious maneuvers, as in the Caribbean, the extent and duration of their reach are limited.

Yet there is the danger of miscalculation, especially of being drawn beyond the point that Soviet capabilities and more prudent interests might dictate if a client state or movement were doing poorly in a crisis, as occurred in the October War in the Middle East. There are precedents for large quantities of Soviet weapons and some personnel being used to "support those nations fighting for their freedom against the forces of internal reaction and imperialist intervention." The Soviet Navy, by its very presence in the Mediterranean, would "restrain the imperialists and local reaction, prevent them from dealing out violence to the local populace, and eliminate a threat to world peace and security." "Mobile and well trained and well equipped armed forces" are required for this role. The situation may require the Soviet Union to "carry out measures aimed at restraining the aggressive acts of imperialism." The Soviet Union has already "begun to resolve the task of furnishing military-technical support for its military presence in rather remote parts of the world," although "foreign political support" for a Soviet military presence may "become more complicated and difficult" than economic and military technical support.[70] In these instances Soviet policy has recently reflected a more forward-oriented stance. They reveal, more than possible Soviet moves in Europe or naval interdictions of Western oil tankers, the acutely political nature of Soviet deployment policy, whatever its domestic underpinnings.

CASE STUDIES IN SOVIET INTERVENTION POLICY

Vietnam, Middle East, Angola

Soviet moves during the second Vietnam War, the October War in the Middle East, and the recent events in Angola, resulted from a perceived threat to "fraternal" or client states or movements—a situation demanding and inviting some form of Soviet military presence without an immediate danger of confrontation with the United States, and requiring a correct assessment of the probable reaction of the latter.

Soviet policy in the second Vietnam War reflected the facts that only the Soviet Union could provide the North Vietnamese with the sophisticated weaponry they needed to continue the war after the introduction of American combat forces in the South and the bombing in the North, and that only Soviet assistance could deter the United States and keep it from taking advantage of its technological superiority.[71] As American combat troops were introduced into Vietnam in spring 1965, the Chinese had to give the Soviet Union land access to Vietnam. This enabled the Soviets to open up a secure land supply route to the North and gave them the power to raise and maintain the level of combat in Vietnam as their interests dictated.[72]

Late in 1964 Gromyko told the North Vietnamese that they could plan for a military push in the South. In this connection, Le Duan said to party cadres in 1965: "The attitude of the Soviet party today regarding strengthening the socialist camp as well as regarding the national liberation movement in general and Vietnam in particular is different from that of Khrushchev before." The Soviet comrades "agree completely with our path."[73]

Soviet policy was to aid the North Vietnamese, isolate and curtail China, and outmaneuver and ultimately outlast the United States without seriously risking confrontation with it. The Soviets sent the DRV advanced military equipment, especially defense weapons, convoys of Soviet freighters, and Soviet technicians.[74]

The 24th Party Congress in 1971 sought détente with the United States and simultaneously sought to strengthen the Soviet position around China, including

Vietnam. The Chinese had spurned a negotiated settlement in Vietnam, wanting the war protracted until final victory could be won. The Soviet Union probably wanted to create doubt about the Chinese formula in North Vietnamese calculations and sought a negotiated settlement, favoring a united front of all Communist forces relying on Soviet support and influence. The North Vietnamese wanted some diplomatic step from the Soviet Union that would make it clear that dètente was impossible while the United States intervention in South Vietnam and the bombing of the North continued. Evidence suggests that the Soviets and Chinese were unwilling to reduce arms supplies to push the DRV into concessions in their negotiations with the United States but intended to reduce aid after an agreement was reached, implying a veto over any subsequent North Vietnamese offensive in the South.[75]

Soviet military-diplomatic steps from that point seemed to reflect a desire to strengthen the North Vietnamese for negotiations, prolonged combat, and intermittent major offensives. The Soviet Union increased its supplies to North Vietnam in preparation for an assault in the South. It began shipping heavy weapons to the North Vietnamese, including T-54 medium tanks, 130mm artillery pieces, and SA-7 missiles, new nondefensive items not part of earlier Soviet aid efforts. These were key elements in the North Vietnamese offensive of the spring of 1972 that began after Nixon's return from Peking but before the Moscow summit meeting. The offensive would have strengthened the North Vietnamese in the negotiations and possibly led to a more pliable government in Saigon. There was heavy use of massive artillery barrages with 130mm weapons, and at least 100 NVA tanks were deployed against units unversed in antitank warfare. Prisoner interrogations revealed that at least 3,000 North Vietnamese tank crewmen in this offensive had graduated from the Russian armored school at Odessa four to five months earlier. The size and scope of the North Vietnamese offensive were made possible in part by a massive stockpiling of Soviet weapons, following Podgorny's trip to Hanoi in October 1971.[76]

Nixon's bombing of North Vietnam, the emergency shipment of weapons, and the blockade of Haiphong Harbor followed. The Soviet Union did not react in a military manner, perhaps because of the very massiveness of the assault [77] and because they wanted the Nixon summit visit with Brezhnev to take place for what appeared to be compelling reasons.[78]

The peace agreement of January 1973 needed the forbearance of all the major powers involved to be effective. Indeed, the Soviet Union and China "significantly decreased their supply of arms to North Vietnam" (in Graham Martin's words) in 1973 and were "not resupplying them with massive weapons of war" in 1974.[79] The North Vietnamese, for this and other reasons, practiced prudence, maintaining limited military pressure but avoiding steps that could lead to a resumption of the U.S. bombing of the North. Following the Paris agreements, the Communists strengthened their forces in the South by building an all-weather road and a pipeline across the 17th parallel. They sent in enough tanks, trucks, artillery, manpower, and missiles to sustain themselves for a year of heavy fighting or several years of low-level fighting. The force in being could exert political pressure or be used to launch an offensive against the South Vietnamese should the need arise.[80]

A Soviet observer, reviewing 1973 in North Vietnam, provides an insight into Soviet thinking at this time:

> The government of the DRV, in the course of the year, came out with a number of statements, in which it resolutely condemned the numerous attempts of the Saigon administration, supported by the United States, to wreck the fulfillment of the Paris agreements and called on the Vietnamese people to intensify the struggle for the peaceful reunification of Vietnam. In particular, in a statement published in the middle of November, it noted that in spite of the agreement, the USA continued to strengthen the Saigon administration in the capacity of an arm of neocolonialism in South Vietnam, kept thousands of its military advisers there, in the guise of civilian advisers, and brought in a large quantity of weapons and military materials.[81]

The restriction on U.S. air support, the growing military potential of the North Vietnamese forces, and the combined military-political efforts of the North Vietnamese and NLF forces eroded the ARVN military position and probably suggested that it was time for a renewed major military effort.[82] The North Vietnamese offense began—at first tentatively—in spring 1975, and the comprehensive scope, firepower, and equipment gave evidence of Soviet assistance. The liberal use of heavy artillery, especially tanks, against disintegrating South Vietnamese opposition also suggested Soviet tactics.[83]

The role of Soviet assistance and particularly the complex international background of the final North Vietnamese thrust are suggested by Gromyko's remarks: While the victories won by the peoples of Indochina were "primarily by their own efforts . . . all-around and effective" Soviet aid was a decisive factor.

> The successful development of the concluding phase of the liberation struggle on the Indochinese peninsula was facilitated by the circumstance that it took place in new conditions, in the situation that had come about in the world under the influence of the process of the easing of international tensions, at the beginning of which was placed the active foreign policy operations of the USSR, of the entire Socialist commonwealth.[84]

When the continuing Middle East conflict is assessed, Soviet political-military aid to "confrontation states" opposing Israel, chiefly Egypt and Syria, furnishes an example of Soviet military assistance to selected regimes or movements on a worldwide scale. Here the area involved is closer to the Soviet Union, the stakes are far greater, the Soviet client states far weaker, the regional adversary far stronger than in Vietnam, and American reactions more unpredictable.

The Soviet Union pursued multiple objectives with its buildup in the then UAR, especially after the defeat of Arab armies in the Six-Day War in June 1967. One goal was to strengthen the Soviet military and political position in the

Mediterranean, to limit Western actions there. Another was to strengthen the UAR side in a way that would be favorable to the Soviet Union and its position in the Arab world, to build up a "base" with stable boundaries, protected by an agreed territorial frontier between the UAR and Israel.[85] From the Egyptian perspective, "only the Soviets could be looked on to bolster Egypt's ability to wage war against Israel, offensively or defensively, while only the Americans could help them to make peace." As the October War broke out, Soviet aid and influence weighed heavily in the balance—assistance for a limited military operation that could set in motion American diplomatic pressure on Israel.[86]

Soviet combat personnel, especially pilots, became increasingly involved in Egyptian defense. It was imperative to shore up a client state demonstrably inferior to its regional antagonist but not to make it so strong that Egyptian moves might result in setting major American counterintervention in motion.[87]

The exact nature and extent of the Soviet role in the coordinated Egyptian-Syrian attack on the Israeli Suez position in the October War are difficult to establish. But the Soviet Union was aware of preparations for war in May-June 1973 because Soviet media referred to alleged Israeli troop concentrations and provocations.[88] The USSR would not back an effort to eliminate Israel as a state: "The USSR, because of its world responsibilities could not support us in this because such support would mean it would have to be prepared for war with the United States." But Soviet military support was available for "eliminating the consequences of the 1967 aggression," because in part the United States would not unconditionally guarantee Israel's post-1967 boundaries.[89]

The Soviets were cautious. Pressed to supply surface-to-surface missiles or MIG-25s to Cairo, they temporized and obfuscated. Sadat indicated, for example, that "They say, yes, yes, yes, to make things easy for us, but then we are caught in a whirlwind." Heykal (then Sadat's close adviser) contended that the Soviets could tolerate the state of neither war nor peace better than the Egyptians but that did not mean that the Russians wanted it to continue. They wanted it to end, a peaceful end if possible but one that did not involve them with the United States. *"As for the alternative, the Soviet Union does not prevent anyone from pursuing it nor does it push anyone towards it."*[90]

Soviet officers and troops were distributed among Syrian field forces as advisory teams, and preparations for the October 1973 offensive could not have been hidden from them. Both Egypt and Syria needed Soviet weapons and ammunition; Sadat either knew from prior consultation or assumed that the Soviet Union would supply him what he needed to avert defeat. These arms included antiaircraft and antitank missiles not previously supplied outside the Warsaw Pact countries. A limited number of "offensive" longer-range surface-to-surface missiles as well as light and medium bomber aircraft were also supplied. Soviet military authorities could assume that a limited offensive against Israel would succeed. Soviet media had previously endorsed "all forms of struggle" by the Arabs and agreed that, given Israel's unwillingness to reach a political settlement, the Arabs were justified in using other methods to regain their land.[91]

Sadat's troops crossing the Suez Canal were protested by a Soviet missile screen and had unlimited quantities of arms and equipment. In addition, the use of surprise and deception as a means of disorganizing the adversary seems to have been taken "from the Soviet Union's doctrinal book" by the Egyptian forces in the October War.[92]

The fact that Washington had never endorsed Israel's post-1967 boundaries may have encouraged the Soviet belief that a limited offensive would not invite an American response. The war would be an instrument of diplomacy and pressure on Israelis. It ended with neither losers nor winners; only after the war was over was Sadat able to achieve a partial Israeli withdrawal through Washington pressure.[93]

In one Soviet view, Israeli hawks, under Moshe Dayan, sought to permanently annex (assimilate) Arab lands seized during the Six-Day War in 1967. The Israelis in their military actions ("clinical strikes") sought to eliminate the capacity of the Arab countries and the Palestinians to oppose them. The Israelis would not settle the conflict in the Middle East but "sought to guarantee the preservation and stabilization of the results of the 1967 aggression" in spite of international public opinion and U.N. resolutions to the contrary. The Israelis believed that preservation of the "neither war nor peace" situation would cause a move to the right in the Arab world, and "weaken revolutionary democratic regimes" as well as "facilitate the possibility of maneuvering" by "openly reactionary and pro-Islamist Arab countries." The Israelis sustained great losses in the October War and, although Arab losses were greater, the Israelis were especially sensitive because of the disparity in their human resources and those of the Arab countries. Kissinger said that, in his opinion, Israel had to "avail itself" of the possibilities of negotiations for a settlement, for it could not withstand such losses indefinitely. The Israeli military-political positions aimed at "perpetuating the results of the 1967 aggression" failed and the road to a peace conference on a political settlement was opened.

> The combination of the resolute measures of the Soviet Union in support of the struggle of the Arab countries for the liquidation of the consequences of the Israeli aggression with the constructive course, directed at the development of the process of the easing of international tension, exerted a definite influence on Washington's position. Under the influence of Soviet policy and also considering those changes which appeared in the military situation in the Near East and the political situation in other areas of the world, the U.S. was forced to introduce a number of corrections in its policy.[94]

There was no question of "Washington's retreat from aid to Israel," and the United States demonstrated its support for the Israelis with a "continuous flow of American weapons and military equipment and the shifting of the 6th U.S. fleet, strengthened with aircraft carriers, to the eastern part of the Mediterranean." But, at the same time, "the United States was forced to change a number of emphases in its policy, that was established at the time of the contact of the Soviet Union with the United States on problems of settling the Near East conflict."[95] Gromyko warned that the "Israeli aggression" was doomed to failure as the "historical experience and recent events in Indochina" illustrated. As long as Israeli aggression and expansion continued "there will be no peace in the Middle East, just as there will be no security for Israel." Israeli government circles must understand that *"while they are guided by aggressive ambitions, the very existence of the state of Israel cannot be reliably guaranteed.''*[96]

In Angola, the last of the case studies of Soviet military assistance, the United States worried that the MPLA, the faction backed by the Soviet Union over a number of years, had gained a military advantage over its two rivals in a struggle for ultimate control while the Portuguese were departing. Fearful of a Vietnam type of involvement but concerned about Soviet influence in Africa, the United States apparently increased covert support for one of the two rival factions, the FNLA. The Soviet Union interpreted this as a Washington challenge and began smuggling in AK-47 rifles, machine guns, bazookas, and rockets; from March to July 1975, fighting and Soviet arms shipments increased. Part of this was a response to what was obviously perceived as a raising of the stakes by Washington, and part a desire to compete successfully with the Chinese, who were also active in supporting one of the factions. The United States responded with additional military assistance through neighboring black African states.[97]

American aid would challenge a Soviet-backed faction, but it would be too little and too late, because of the general fear of greater involvement felt by Congress and the public. As one black African leader said, "The declarations of Ford and Kissinger even do us harm. Whenever they bang their fists on the table against our enemies, the Russians take them seriously and increase military aid to the MPLA. The Americans don't match this by aid to us."[98] The Soviets were also helped when South Africa marched north into Angola near its border with Namibia (Southwest Africa) in October, complicating the tasks of American-African diplomacy.

The Soviets soon supplied twice as much aid in a single month as they had supplied to the MPLA in an entire year during its guerrilla war against the Portuguese. This included tanks, rocket launchers, MIG-21 fighters, small arms, and clothing for up to 30,000 troops. Along with the presence of up to 12,000 Cuban fighters, such equipment rapidly changed the balance; the conventional war ended with an MPLA victory.[99]

The size and rapidity of the Soviet arms buildup and the quickly augmented Cuban presence reinforced congressional and popular doubt (some State Department personnel had been skeptical from the very beginning) about the Angolan affair; Congress voted to cut off economic aid in December 1975. Some congressional quarters believed that a much greater U.S. effort, eventually involving military personnel and advisers, or closer cooperation with South Africa, would be required.[100]

Uniquely among the three cases examined, in Angola the Soviet Union intervened swiftly and decisively and outmaneuvered the United States militarily and diplomatically. The Soviets freely admitted giving "moral and material support to the patriotic forces of Angola and the Popular Movement for the Liberation of Angola [MPLA] in their struggle against colonialism." Such a course of action was "fully in accord with the well known decision on decolonization, adopted by the United Nations as well as by the Organization of African Unity."[101]

Subsequent Soviet commentary stressed that the MPLA was recognized "as the vanguard of the Angolan people." Kissinger's allegation that the Soviets had intervened was "not in harmony with the facts." "Real" intervention was practiced by the South African armed forces; Soviet assistance was given to the "legal government at its request in order to suppress foreign aggression against the new African state." It was the opposing Angolan factions, the Soviet commentary alleged, inspired from outside, that prevented a peaceful settlement and "opened the path for foreign armed intervention. The Soviet Union would continue to render moral, political, diplomatic and other aid." Given the overwhelming military preponderance of the MPLA, the Soviets could remonstrate that they were "far from seeing the possibility of settling the Angolan problem only by the military path and don't speak against a political solution of the Angolan problem."[102] This did not preclude a compromise and may have been intended to lessen concern in the United States.

The Angolan episode occurred during the beginnings of the quadrennial American presidential campaign, and that added weight to increasing American domestic suspicion about the Soviet Union's motives and modi operandi in applying its version of détente American foreign policy toward the USSR hardened in various ways; the manifestations, at first treated as so much campaign oratory by Soviet analysts, began to cause worry.[103]

All three examples of Soviet diplomatic-military moves manifest increasingly that détente does not bar extensive military aid to client states and factions that the Soviet Union favors according to its interests of the moment. But in all these cases, reactions by the United States, either political or military, were considered and weighed. Therefore the Soviet assessment of American foreign policy and the assumptions on which it is based, as well as the congressional and popular milieu in which it is constructed, is clearly vital in evaluating future Soviet actions.

SOVIET ELITE PERCEPTIONS OF AMERICAN FOREIGN POLICY

What connection do "assessments" or "perceptions" have with policy? This question inevitably arises when consideration is given to writings by Soviet specialists professionally concerned with areas of the world critical to Soviet foreign policy. Of course, it is difficult to trace the intellectual source of any decision or group of decisions for policy makers in any political system. But there are certain characteristics of Soviet foreign policy formulation that make the problem appear less insoluble than it might otherwise have been.

The burden of office and the fact that most Politburo members are more familiar with internal and administrative matters than with foreign policy matters often oblige them to turn to specialists in the Foreign Ministry and Academy of Sciences. But neither the Foreign Ministry nor departments of the Central Committee dealing with foreign affairs conduct foreign area studies in any systematic way; only limited research is done at country desks or in regional offices. When new problems arise or old ones require new information, officials search for people with scholarly expertise, an expertise provided by specialized research institutes under the Section of Social Sciences or Academy of Sciences.[104]

One of the sections is the Division of Economics, which supervises, among other agencies, the institutes of World Economics and International Relations (IMEMO) and United States Studies (now United States and Canada). Research programs of all institutes must be approved by appropriate divisions and sections and ultimately by the Presidium of the Academy of Sciences, which works with appropriate organs of the Secretariat of the Central Committee of the CPSU. This centralized administration makes it possible for research to be closely directed and coordinated, and facilitates more efficient use of talent. Further coordination is provided by the Editorial Publishing Council of the Academy of Sciences, which approves publication programs.[105]

Occasionally, Soviet scholars are admonished to avoid adopting Western concepts "uncritically," especially Western empirical techniques, and to avoid assuming the pose of the "disinterested researcher."[106] However, in research dealing with the external world, "disinterested research" is more of an imperative as an information base for Soviet foreign policy decisions. Brezhnev himself indicated the need for such information in his remarks to the 24th Party Congress.

> I have already spoken of our scientists' tasks in the field of scientific and technical progress and the introduction of the achievements of science in production. No less important tasks confront the social sciences. In the period under review, the CPSU Central Committee adopted a special comprehensive resolution of the problem. The tasks of the Institute of Marxism-Leninism and the Academy of Sciences under the CPSU Central Committee have been expanded and clarified. In the past few years, a number of new humanities institutes have been set up in the system of the Academy of Sciences, and this has made it possible to intensify the study of problems of the social and economic development of the USSR and foreign countries and of the world revolutionary process and to improve scientific information. What we need is an increasingly resolute turn by the social sciences toward the elaboration of problems that are urgent for the present and future.[107]

Added to the official linkage is the fact that administrators of policy-oriented institutes maintain close working relations with the appropriate offices of the

Ministry of Foreign Affairs and the International Department of the Central Committee. When the latter request it, "emergency studies," are launched in the institutes, and other programs are deferred; the priority needs of party and government are paramount. The link between institutes and ministries is further consolidated because prominent officials serve on the scientific councils of the institutes and often participate in their deliberations. In addition, scholars are appointed to high Central Committee and government positions. N. N. Inozemestev, director of IMEMO, is a member of the Central Committee; G. A. Arbatov, director of the renamed Institute for the Study of the U.S.A. and Canada, is a member of the Central Auditing Commission. Arbatov was also included in the official party which accompanied Brezhnev on his 1973 visit to the United States. Politburo members consult informally with academic experts in their fields of interest.

While the bureaucrats, as in other systems, have the final say, the social prestige, income, and job security of social scientists mean that they do have a growing role in the high councils of decision making in the Soviet foreign policy and government bureaucracies.[108]

Soviet evaluations of American presidential administrations are that the United States, as early as the Eisenhower administration, realized that it was not omnipotent. Only in the Kennedy administration, however, was it recognized that the "new correlation of forces in the world arena," the "process of changes in the correlation of economic, military, and political forces between the two systems," were developing unfavorably for the United States. But the Kennedy administration, although it understood the suicidal nature of nuclear weapons-rattling for the United States, *sought not to prevent conflicts but to work out rules for war in conflict itself.*[109] There was flexibility in creating a broad spectrum of U.S. military forces, but the military commitments assumed by the United States were inflexible

Soviet analysts no longer depicted a united bourgeoise elite in the Kennedy and Johnson administrations. There were, on the one hand, new "realists" who sought to normalize relations with the USSR and coexist peacefully, and, on the other hand, "wild men" who advanced a policy of militarism, blackmail, and intervention. Soviet analysts disagreed on the relative strengths of the two groups. However, the undisciplined character of the Kennedy foreign policy machinery, in the Soviet view, was paralleled by fluctuations in moods and policies. There was and is no powerful Left with a political leader who could counter the influence of the Right. The "center" in the political process could still be pushed to the Right in foreign and domestic policy and, while occasionally "realistically thinking American politicians" correct this tendency, the "rightward list" soon recurs.[110]

Only in the Nixon administration, according to the Soviet view, did policy decisions reflect the new "realism," a "pragmatic conservative reaction to changes occurring in the world" which would adjust U.S. capabilities to international realities. Rigid foreign policy commitments adopted in the past would be abandoned to avoid dissipating resources in secondary directions.[111] But the new policy of "selective" intervention was "inconsistent" and "contradictory," producing the "illusion" that relaxation would allow certain elements of the "policy of strength" to remain untouched.[112]

The intellectual bases and assumptions of American foreign policy planning are of great interest to Soviet analysts. One study traced the U.S. policy of creating a favorable equilibrium of forces to Wilson's vow that the United States must be the arbiter of a peace settlement after World War I. Later, foreign policy advisers recommended that the United States stay out of a Russo-Japanese war, settling it without victory so that the balance between the Soviet Union and the other powers "not be disturbed." American foreign analysts in the 1940s, such as Nicholas Spaikman, advocated a policy of creating equilibrium between the Soviet Union and "outlying states" where the United States could exert a decisive influence. Kennan and Kissinger sought to "split the states of the old world into hostile groups," the material base of the "balance of forces," and strengthen England, Japan, and Germany against the Soviet Union, "utilizing the contradictions" between them.[113]

Naturally, Soviet writers are concerned with the most current example of the policy of "equilibrium," the exploitation of Sino-Soviet antagonism. In their view, the United States would choose between strict neutrality and strengthening China, the weaker of the two Communist competitors. China policy would be part of an attempt to encircle the Soviet Union, a modified version of the old containment policy whose cost has become militarily and economically prohibitive. Soviet specialists alternately downgraded the significance of Chinese-American ties and Chinese diplomatic or economic capabilities and warned the United States that China would be a military threat in the future.[114]

The Chinese policy, like all American policies of balance of forces, bore an anti-Socialist, anti-Communist character and was aimed at world rule by the United States. All American military doctrines—like containment, limited war, graduated response, etc.—were also integral parts of the balance of power doctrine, but the diplomatic aspects of the latter became dominant. This was particularly true because the United States broke the rules of the balance of power by using its own forces in Vietnam and failing to prevail militarily.

The United States, confronting increasing military parity with the USSR, sought to change containment to "more convenient means" for achieving its objectives, chiefly economic and scientific. American doctrines of flexible response, limited war, and crisis diplomacy demonstrated their unreliability in Vietnam. U.S. "hegemonic aims" on Berlin, the Caribbean, Indochina, and elsewhere were not achieved. Recognition of these factors, growing domestic frustrations, and the increasing strength of the Socialist countries, headed by the Soviet Union, contributed to the realism of the 1970s. This realism, "in all its contradictory character, expresses positive changes in the minds of American ideologues, but these changes are engendered not by their good intentions and altruism, but are an acknowledgment of stern truths, the change of the relationship of forces in favor of socialism." Despite the fact that American foreign policy had not really changed, that there was no new foreign policy course but only a "more flexible policy more in agreement with the real possibilities," the "moderate realists" should be encouraged and their "liberalism" should not be underestimated.[115]

"Moderate realists" recognized that the Soviet Union had counterbalanced U.S. strategic forces with its own and had changed the role of the military factor in international relations. The Soviets would counterbalance U.S. conventional forces in the "not-too-distant future," especially naval forces, which would restrict political-military actions of the United States in different parts of the world. Faced with these and other realities, American foreign policy in the 1970s could take several forms. One would involve a mobilizing of resources and using them in the traditional plane of military force. Another would mark a gradual transition to neoisolationism, "a retreat from participation in international policies at least beyond the boundaries of the Western hemisphere." A third would involve a "flexible and long-term accommodation to changing conditions, oriented to a certain preservation of basic U.S. positions in the world." Domestic and foreign social and economic difficulties were such that "it can be said confidently that no American government could carry out at the beginning of the 1970s the mobilization of resources for foreign policy on such a scale and military-political character as at the beginning of the last decade."[116] But the "neoisolationist" option was "unacceptable" to U.S. "ruling circles." U.S. dependence on the outside world would not only fail to decrease but would grow in succeeding years, and the interests of the U.S. ruling class "objectively demanded" a U.S. presence in world politics. The third option, of accommodation, was the only viable one, and the new political strategy involved a realistic assessment of the relation of forces between the U.S. and USSR, especially parity in the military-political sphere.[117]

American political leaders recognized that they confronted "irreversible deep social-economic changes in Asia, Africa, and Latin America" and no longer declared that the Soviet Union was the "instigator" of a "global conspiracy" which the United States must oppose everywhere by military means. The United States must give less direct aid to developing countries, and use more economic levers in foreign policy. It would seek to replace its policies of military intervention against the Socialist countries with one of fostering their economic dependence through the forging of scientific-technical links. But the Soviet Union had been able to attract specialists and use the technical achievements of capitalist countries without changing the character of the country, and would do so again. The American policy of balancing, of using "power centers" possessing nuclear missiles, especially the PRC, would *not* be an alternative policy, despite Kissinger's statements. Instead, the U.S. would adhere to a "less risky direction" in international relations, such as those outlined above.[118]

Soviet assessments of U.S. foreign policy directions and philosophies reveal the same ambivalence that the subject itself affords. The United States has been chastened by the Vietnam experience; the traditional military and political doctrines that led it are discredited. But it cannot and will not withdraw from the world; it is unable to do so, and it has no new foreign doctrines or directions to utilize. "Moderate realist circles" in American foreign policy should be encouraged, but what is the best or proper way to do that—a Soviet forward posture to chasten American "wild men" still more and strengthen the moderates, with the risk of a sharp American turn to the Right? Or a less militant posture that might risk forgoing opportunities offered by the "change in the correlation of forces" that Soviet military strength and forward posture had purportedly helped to bring to fruition? The analyses suggest no definitive answers; these await other forums and other situations. The lingering concern with an American-Chinese link is evident, but there too no specific policy emerges. Too strong an emphasis on Soviet military power in a number of situations of common concern to the two countries would risk driving America and China closer together. Any lessening of military pressure and deployed strength, however, might erode Soviet bargaining power and reveal weakness and vacillation before foreigners—a trait traditionally despised by Soviet leaders—as well as carry unacceptable domestic costs and risks.

Soviet evaluations of the internal political climate in the United States, and especially the post-Watergate relationship between the President and Congress, give evidence of the same uncertainty and ambivalence. These may even be accentuated because of the great imponderables involved and the Soviet inability to understand a phenomenon that has no exact counterpart in the USSR. One Soviet work on U.S. policy making concluded that, in the domestic struggle surrounding the Watergate affair, even the most vocal critics of the government found no argument against its foreign policy. Indeed, the Nixon administration used its foreign policy actions in its defense. Nixon administration policies aimed at easing international tensions "found and find a positive response from the American people and other countries as well," and the attempts of the Ford administration to strengthen that foreign policy course, to institutionalize it, are "logical and natural."[119]

One Soviet Americanist, assessing the results of the 1974 congressional elections, approved the losses suffered by conservatives and the "presence in the United States of a stable opposition to militarism and anti-Sovietism, which became a constant factor in the fight for the détente policy."[120] Another noted that "eminent U.S. congressmen" had positively approved Ford's trip to the Soviet Far East (Vladivostock) and the continuation of improving relations between the United States and the Soviet Union.[121] Congress's role was now more independent and stable than before and, while still secondary in foreign policy matters, was increasingly important.

But the doubts and hesitations of Soviet Americanists persisted. There were always the Soviet bêtes noires—the Zionists, elements of the U.S. labor movement, and hostile political figures in Congress whose influence at any particular time was hard to assess. The views of many U.S. political figures, especially liberals, revealed a definite "ebb" or "flow," "depending upon which direction the political winds are blowing." Anti-Vietnam liberals especially, who were not opposed to détente talked about "human rights" and stressed the provisions in the Helsinki Declaration concerning the exchange of people and ideas, a form of intervention in Soviet internal affairs. There were still signs of anticommunism in U.S. domestic policy, and pro-Zionist and pro-Israeli organizations exerted influence, even though they were not supported by "the majority of Americans." In addition, Soviet commentators were concerned that "the most important problems of international relations, problems of war and peace, affecting the fate of people are all the more objects in the U.S. of shameful preelection speculation and politics."[122]

Congress was seen as especially unpredictable—especially if a populist backlash over foreign policy were to envelop it. While it could exert a notable influence on political circles formulating U.S. policy and was an important element of the state mechanism " on all important questions (especially foreign policy), Congress, as a rule, does not oppose the President." The significance of that for Soviet foreign policy would depend on the nature and policies of the Congress and the President. Nevertheless, Soviet specialists recalled that Congress, without prolonged debate and delay, confirmed legislation for additional funds for the Vietnam war. They also noted that until the election of 1968 only a very few members criticized the conduct of the war and demanded its end. The majority of the same Congress "approved every step of the U.S. government and American military figures in expanding the aggression in Vietnam." *After* the signing of the Vietnam cease-fire in January 1973, Congress "undertook a number of steps to reestablish its position, which forced the President to step back somewhat." [123]

A Soviet Americanist put an uncharacteristic emphasis on "subjective factors" in determining the direction of government policy. The choice of political line "depends greatly on persons found at a given instance in leading state posts, of their capability of realizing the true interests of the country and selecting the most realistic line."[124] While he cites Nixon's détente policy as a positive example of the personal factors, there is nothing in Soviet analysis which would suggest that a return to a hard anti-Soviet line in American foreign policy, either because of external-internal pressures or because of a deliberate presidential tactic, is precluded.

THE FUTURE COURSE OF AMERICAN
RELATIONS WITH THE SOVIET UNION

In assessing the future course of Soviet intervention, I was struck by Adam Ulam's view that "the main difficulty with American-Soviet relations has been that for the most part the policies of the two countries moved at different levels and reflected different understandings of the realities of international life." Inevitably, each country "betrayed the other's expectations of its prospective role in international affairs."[125]

Soviet specialists discerned anti-Soviet designs in American circles in the 1930s and, after World War II began, a duality—in particularly a lack of confidence in Soviet military prowess. Soviet military emphasis today may be designed partly to compensate for past weaknesses and to discourage such external disparagement. Another commentator, looking at post-World War II relations, saw a U.S. attempt to bludgeon the Soviet Union with atomic blackmail and economic blockade.[126]

Soviet specialists could understand a firm American diplomatic stance toward the Soviet Union with military power in the background. But they have attacked Washington's military emphases that have been either divorced from or supplanting diplomacy. One Soviet writer professed to be puzzled by the "extreme reaction" to the Yalta decisions. The United States, in his view, could not have prevented these events in Eastern Europe and was physically incapable of attacking the Soviets. Having been bested diplomatically and strategically, the United States sought to attack the original agreements. As Maxim Litvinov observed in June 1945, "Why did you Americans wait till right now to begin opposing us in the Balkans and Eastern Europe? . . . You should have done this three years ago. Now it's too late and your complaints only arouse suspicion here." Litvinov admitted that his country's seeking power and influence beyond its security requirements was the cause of conflict, but the West's failure to resist it early enough was an important secondary cause.[127]

Interestingly, one Soviet commentator lauded U.S. diplomacy of the 1970s, which was more "businesslike" in comparison with the "narrowly propagandistic approach" which had characterized many diplomatic "feats" of U.S. foreign policy in the past, especially in relation to the Socialist countries.[128] In this connection, Khrushchev gave Kennedy's conduct in the latter stages of the Cuban Missile Crisis the highest praise a Soviet political figure can offer.

> I'll always remember the late President with deep respect because, in the final analysis, he showed himself to be sober-minded and determined to avoid war. He didn't let himself become frightened, nor did he become reckless. He didn't overestimate America's might, and he left himself a way out of the crisis. He showed real wisdom and statesmanship when he turned his back on right-wing forces in the United States who were trying to goad him into taking military action against Cuba.[129]

The Soviet Union is in an assertive mood at present, roughly coterminous with the end of the American assertive period in 1968. The Soviet Union sees its mounting military power leading to an acceptance of Soviet positions and influence in areas where it was previously absent or not without challenge. But economically the Soviet Union still operates under significant constraints, and its military might lacks the global character of U.S. military forces. Soviet analysts express concern about the emerging, but still inchoate, American-Chinese-Soviet triangular relationship. In addition, Third World conditions would hardly allow the Soviet Union to exercise even the relatively strong influence the United States once exercised. The Soviet Union can deny the United States certain positions and advantages in Third World areas, but it has not found any significant way of converting this denial capability into assets of its own. The Middle East is a case in point; while Vietnam in one sense was a victory and vindication of Soviet arms, the circumstances of that example were very local in origin and the ultimate extent of Soviet influence in the area is highly problematical.

The United States still has great appeal because of its social and technological innovation and its enormous economic and moral residual strength.[130] Soviet diplomatic and military postures are designed in part to cover Soviet weaknesses, both those cited in this paper and those of morale and discipline, which are not always so high as the regime's deliberate attempts at "military legitimation" for domestic reasons would suggest.[131]

A U.S. posture will have to be found that does not seek or appear to seek to intimidate the Soviets. They will not passively accept intimidation and will react to it in exactly the opposite way to that desired. The U.S. posture should communicate to them firmly and confidently, through preventive diplomacy, what American purposes and intentions are. Military power will always be a necessary accompaniment to such dealings, for the United States must never be put in the position of negotiating from fear or fearing to negotiate.

NOTES

1. For a discussion of Soviet views on war and related matters, with appropriate citations from Marx, Engels, and Lenin, see P. H. Vigor, *The Soviet View of War, Peace and Neutrality* (Boston: Routledge & Kegan Paul, 1975), esp. p. 444.

2. A. Karenin, *Filosofia Politicheskovo Nasilia* [Philosophy of political force] (Moscow: International Relations Publishing House, 1971), p. 27.

3. I. A. Grudinin, *Dialektika i Sovremennoe Voennoe Delo* [Dialectic and contemporary military affairs] (Mowcow: Military Publishing House of the Ministry of Defense of the USSR, 1971), p. 25.

4. On the subject of risk taking, dictated by the image of the external adversary, along with caution, dictated by external constraints, see Hannes Adomeit, *Soviet Risk-Taking and Crisis Behavior: From Confrontation to Coexistence?* Adelphi Papers no. 101 (London: International Institute for Strategic Studies, Autumn 1973), pp. 34-35.

5. Quotation from Ken Booth, *The Military Instrument in Soviet Foreign Policy 1917-1972* (London: Royal United Services Institute for Defense Studies, 1973), pp. 10, 11, 13, 18, 20.

6. Ibid., pp. 35, 39, 40.

7. Ibid., pp. 41-42.

8. Martin Blumenson, "The Soviet Power Play at Changkufeng," *World Politics* 12 (January 1960): 249, 263.

9. Christopher D. Jones, "Just Wars and Limited Wars: Restraints on the Use of the Soviet Armed Forces," World Politics 28 (October 1975): 51, 59, 60-61, 68; and Booth, *Military Instrument*, p..45.

10. Booth, *Military Instrument*, p. 47. For a general discussion of Soviet sponsorship of revolutionary violence, see Brian Crozier, "The Soviet Involvement in Violence," Soviet Analyst 1 (July 6, 1972): 5-7; and "The Soviet Involvement in Violence, II," *Soviet Analyst* 2 (July 20, 1972): 3-5.

11. Booth, *Military Instrument*, p.60.

12. V. M. Kulish, *Military Force and International Relations,* JPRS 58947 (Arlington, VA: Joint Publications Research Service, May 8, 1973), p. 25. This is a multiauthor work; Kulish wrote the section quoted here.

13. Ibid., pp. 14, 15, 23, 24, 28.

14. A. M. Dudin and Yu. N. Listvinov, ibid., p. 98 (italics added).

15. Thomas W. Wolfe, *Soviet Power and Europe 1945-1970* (Baltimore: Johns Hopkins University Press, paperback, 1970), pp. 441, 428-429.

16. *The Military Balance, 1974-75* (London: International Institute for Strategic Studies), p. 4; and *The Military Balance, 1975-76,* p..4.

17. John Erickson, "The Soviet Military, Soviet Policy and Soviet Politics" (Lecture at the U.S. Army War College), Strategic Review 1 (Fall 1973): 27-28.

18. Wolfe, *Soviet Power,* pp. 428, 443, 444, 445.

19., Michael MccGwire, "Soviet Naval Programmes," *Survival* 15 (September-October 1973): 225.

20. *Military Balance, 1975-1976,* p..4.

21. John Erickson, *Soviet Military Power* (London: Royal United Services Institute for Defense Studies, 1971), p. 52; and Erickson, "Soviet Military," p. 27.

22. Wolfe, *Soviet Power,* pp. 444, 448.

23. Ibid., p. 428.

24. Booth, *Military Instrument*, p. 62.

25. Thomas W. Wolfe, *Military Power and Soviet Policy,* RAND-5388, March 1975 (Santa Monica, Ca.: The Rand Corp.), pp. 11-12.

26. Andrei Gromyko (speech before the Supreme Soviet, June 1968), quoted in Herbert Block, "Value and Burden of Soviet Defense," in Joint Economic Committee, *Soviet Economic Prospects for the Seventies* (Washington: Government Printing Office, 1973), p. 201.

27. G. A. Arbatov, "Soviet-American Relations in the 1970's," *U.S.A.: Economics, Politics, Ideology,* no. 5 (May 1974), translated in Joint Publications Research Service (JPRS) 62191 (June 6, 1974): 21.

28. A. Gromyko, "Programma Mira v Deistvii" [Program of peace in action], *Kommunist* 14 (September 1975): 7 (italics added).

29. Brezhnev's Report to the 25th Congress of the Communist Party of the Soviet Union on February 24, 1976 (*Pravda* and *Izvestia,* February 25), in *The Current Digest of the Soviet Press* (hereafter abbreviated *CDSP*) 28 (March 24, 1976): 12.

30. Dudin and Listvinov, in Kulish, *Military Force,* pp. 86, 97 (italics added). On Khruschev's policy of forcing concessions and seeking limited accommodations, see Robert M. Slusser, "America, China and the Hydra-Headed Opposition: The Dynamics of Soviet Foreign Policy," in *Soviet Policy Making: Studies of Communism in Transition,* ed. Peter H. Juviler and Henry W. Morton (New York: Praeger, paperback, 1967), esp. p. 196.

31. Adomeit, *Soviet Risk-Taking,* p. 33; see also Erickson, "Soviet Military," p. 31; Statement of Holland Hunter, U.S., Congress, Subcommittee on Economy in Government of the Joint Economic Committee, *The Military Budget and National Economic Priorities: Hearing,* 91st Cong., 1st sess., pt. 3, *The Economic Basis of the Russian Military Challenge to the United States,* June 23, 1969, pp. 917, 913. Keith Bush, "Soviet Economic Growth:

Past, Present and Projected," in "The Soviet Union in the Era of Negotiation and Compromise," U.S. Army Institute for Advanced Russian and East European Studies, 8th Annual Soviet Affairs Symposium 1973/1974 (Garmisch, Germany), pp. 15, 17.

32. William E. Odom, "Who Controls Whom in Moscow," *Foreign Policy* 19 (summer 1975): 13.

33. Marshall Grechko, "The Danger of War Remains a Grim Reality," *Krasnaya Zvezda* [Red star], June 5, 1974, quoted in Peter Kruzhin, "Grechko: The Danger of War Remains a Grim Reality," *Radio Liberty Dispatch* (Munich), RL-200/74 (July 8, 1974), p. 1. For a stimulating article describing Brezhnev's attempts to deal with assorted economic ills, pursue détente, and appease critics in the military and security branches, see Grey Hodnett, "Succession Contingencies in the Soviet Union," *Problems of Communism* 24 (March-April 1975): 9-11.

34. William E. Odom, "The Party Connection," *Problems of Communism* 22 (September-October 1973): 25; and Odom "Who Controls" pp. 113, 122. For an analysis of the "retardation" in the Soviet economy revealed by the Tenth Five-Year Plan (1976-80), the reduced rate of overall growth and curtailment of consumer production but continued emphasis on the industrial base and military might, see Gregory Grossman, "An Economy at Middle Age," *Problems of Communism* 25 (March-April 1976), esp. p. 33.

35. Brezhnev at the 24th Party Congress, *Pravda,* July 22, 1975, quoted in Herbert Goldhamer, *The Soviet Soldier: Soviet Military Management at the Troop Level* (New York: Crane, Russak, 1975), p. 235 (italics added). Goldhamer's study indicates the depth of military involvement in the Soviet civil sector: civil defense preparations, preinduction military training, and other activities.

36. Hedrick Smith, *The Russians* (New York: Quadrangle, 1976), pp. 313, 314. Whether all Soviet citizens regard deployed military power as a magic lingua franca that can forever overcome the divisive tendencies inherent in a multinational and multicultural state is another matter. For a discussion of this internal time bomb, see Edward L. Keenan, "A Majority of Suppressed Minorities: Soviet Time Bomb," *The New Republic,* (August 21 and 28, 1976): 20-21. An alternate possibility is that military power and pro-Stalinist sentiment may reflect deep uneasiness, a desire to avert the "political anarchy" that a nationality crisis and related developments could bring in their wake. William E. Odom, "A Dissenting View on the Group Approach to Soviet Politics," *World Politics* 28 (July 1976): 560.

37. Hodnett, "Succession," p. 10, and n. 38, p. 11. Connor believes that a regime that seems to be stable in meeting the "mass expectations of the Soviet people" might be in considerable straits if "circumstances" reduced its capacity to "deliver" (Walter D. Connor, "Generations and Politics in the USSR," *Problems of Communism* 24 [September-October, 1975] : 26).

38. Tolubko, in *Krasnaia Zvezda* [Red star], August 6, 1964, quoted in Jurgen Domes, "Chinese Communist Strategy in the Sino-Soviet Conflict," in "Agenda for the Politburo: Critical Issues of Soviet National Security Policy," U.S. Army Institute for Advanced Russian and East European Studies, 6th Annual Soviet Affairs Symposium 1971/1972 (Garmisch, Germany), p. 82.

39. Goldhamer, *Soviet Soldier,* pp. 229-34, discusses political indoctrination against the Chinese.

40. Ibid., p. 234. Domes indicates that Soviet China specialists he had talked to did not anticipate a major Chinese military attack on the Soviet Union for the "next one or two decades." Domes, "Chinese Communist Strategy," p. 83.

41. Brezhnev, quoted in *CDSP,* 28:7.

42. Goldhamer, *Soviet Soldier,* p. 233.

43. Wolfe gives the figures as a minimum estimate of 2.8 million in the Soviet armed forces in 1947 (Khrushchev's figure) as opposed to 1.4 million in U.S. forces in that year. He also indicates that the Soviet reserve system would have permitted rapid mobilization of

Soviet forces to World War II levels. This manpower disparity may have been, as Wolfe argues, a deliberate move which, aside from Soviet internal reasons, was designed to create the impression that Europe was a hostage to Soviet arms and not a harbinger of an intention to invade (Wolfe, *Soviet Power*, p. 26). The fear of invasion has remained, however, for many years.

44. See Drew Middleton, *Can America Win the Next War?* (New York: Scribner, 1975), esp. chaps. 5, 8, 9, and 10; and Secretary of Defense Rumsfeld's remarks about the capabilities of Soviet tactical aviation in support of ground troops: *"Of particular concern for the future is the nascent but increasing capability to execute effective conventional deep strike ground attacks against NATO tactical air and nuclear reserve resources, and to do so through sudden attacks without prior deployment"* (Donald H. Rumsfeld. *Annual Defense Department Report FY 1977 to the Congress*, January 17, 1976, p. 127 [italics added]).

45. A. Bovin, "Facets of Détente," *Izvestia*, February 5, 1975, trans. in *Soviet Press: Selected Translations*, no. 75-3 (March 1975) [Translated and distributed by the Directorate of Threat Applications, AF/IN, HQ USAF], p. 4.

46. John Erickson, "Soviet Military Policy: Priorities and Perspectives," *Commonwealth Journal of International Affairs* (October 1974): 373.

47. Ibid., p. 375; Erickson, "Soviet Military Capabilities in Europe," *RUSI Defense Journal* (March 1975): 67; and Thomas W. Wolfe, *Soviet Military Capabilities and Intentions in Europe*, RAND P-5188, March 1974 (Santa Monica, Ca.: The Rand Corp.), p. 7

48. Jeffrey Record, *Sizing Up the Soviet Army* (Washington: Brookings Institution, 1975), p. 14; and Steven L. Canby, *NATO Military Policy: Obtaining Conventional Comparability with the Warsaw Pact*, RAND 5-1088 ARPA, June 1973 (Santa Monica, Ca.: The Rand Corp.), p. 10.

49. A. A. Sidorenko, *The Offensive (A Soviet View)* (Moscow, 1970 [Translated and published under the auspices of the United States Air Force, 1970]), pp. 3, 57, 59, 134 (italics added).

50. V. Ye. Savkin, *The Basic Principles of Operational Art and Tactics—A Soviet View* (Moscow, 1971 [Translated and published under the auspices of the United States Air Force, 1972]), p. 173.

51. Ibid., pp. 232-31. On surprise, see Colonel A. Krasnov, "Faktor Vnezapnosti" [The factor of surprise], *Krasnaia Zvezda* [Red star] (February 3, 1974).

52. Record, *Sizing*, p. 24. Record concludes that Soviet airlift capability indicates less a desire to move Soviet forces abroad than the need to supply client states in the Middle East (p. 30).

53. Canby, *NATO*, pp. 23, 38, 82. Goldhamer *(Soviet Soldier)* contends that the Soviet emphasis on economy of resources in training and the great stress placed on psychological conditioning and motivation in training are in part attempts to substitute moral for material motivation and to overcome a technologically superior opponent by a high level of indoctrination as well as the shock use of firepower emphasized in Soviet military works. The Soviets keep the costs of their conscript army very low; while this provides extra resources for a modern military machine, its effects on morale are uncertain.

54. Savkin, *Basic Principles*, p. 75. Jacobsen notes that Moscow "no longer dismisses the possibility of more strictly limited conventional wars in Europe, especially given the "constricted conventional potential" of the allies, and depicts a growing Soviet doctrine of "flexible response." See G. Jacobsen, "The Emergence of a Soviet Doctrine of Flexible Response?" *Atlantic Quarterly* 12 (Summer 1974): 236; and Jacobsen, "Deterrence or War Fighting? The Soviet Case: Soviet Military Posture and its Relevance to Soviet Concepts of Strategy," *Canadian-American Slavic Studies* (Spring 1975), esp. p. 21.

55. R. J. Vincent, *Military Power and Political Influence: The Soviet Union and Western Europe*, Adelphi Papers no. 119 (London: International Institute for Strategic Studies, 1975), p. 13.

56. Richard E. Foster and John C. Scharfen, *Study of Possible Soviet Strategy of Controlled Conflict* 1 (Stanford: Stanford Research Institute, June 1975), p. 76; Brezhnev, quoted in *CDSP*, 28:13, 14. For a discussion of alleged Soviet organization of a subversive apparatus in some West European armed forces, "sleepers" who in a crisis could be activated by the KGB to paralyze Western military operations, see Arnaud de Borchgrave, "'Sleepers' in NATO," *Newsweek* (March 8, 1976): 42. Strong Soviet military forces might also remind "dissident" Communist parties like the Italians where their "true" interests would lie in peace or in war.

57. Vincent, *Military Power*, p. 13; see also Rowland Evans and Robert Novak, "Arms for Yugoslavia—A Message for Moscow," *Chicago Sun-Times,* (April 16, 1976).

58. Vincent, *Military Power*, pp. 16, 17; and Benjamin Lambeth, *Selective Nuclear Operations and Soviet Strategy*, RAND, P-5506 (September 1975), pp. 11-12.

59. Franklyn Griffiths, "The Tactical Uses of Naval Arms Control," in *Soviet Naval Policy Objectives and Constraints* ed. Michael MccGwire, Ken Booth, and John McDonnell (New York: Praeger, 1975), p. 643.

60. Sergei G. Gorshkov, "Navies as Instruments of Peacetime Imperialism," in *Red Star Rising at Sea*, trans. Theodore A. Neely, Jr. (Annapolis: U.S. Naval Institute, 1974), pp. 115, 119.

61. George S. Dragnich, "The Soviet Union's Quest for Access to Naval Facilities in Egypt Prior to the June War of 1967," in MccGwire, Booth, and McDonnell, *Soviet Naval Policy*, pp. 267, 268.

62. Geoffrey Jukes, *The Indian Ocean in Soviet Naval Policy*, Adelphi Papers no. 87 (London: International Institute for Strategic Studies, May 1972), pp. 11, 22, 20.

63. James M. McConnell and Anne M. Kelly, *Superpower Naval Diplomacy in the Indo-Pakistani Crisis*, Professional Paper no. 108 (Arlington, VA: Center for Naval Analyses, February 1973), pp. 7, 8, 10. McConnell and Kelly cite an exception to their depiction of the Soviet defensive stance, the West African patrol against Portuguese Guinea (Bissau) since 1970. It deterred sea raids on Guinea and prevented the overthrow of the Toure government, but resulted in Guinea's being able to mount an offensive against the Portuguese colonial regime (n. 47, p. 13). See also Anne M. Kelly and Charles Petersen, *Recent Changes in Soviet Naval Policy: Prospects for Arms Limitations in the Mediterranean and Indian Ocean*, Professional Paper no. 150 (Arlington, VA: Center for Naval Analyses, April 1976), esp. pp. 17-18, 19.

64. See Desmond P. Wilson and Nicholas Brown, *Warfare at Sea: Threat of the Seventies*, Professional Paper no. 79 (Arlington, VA: Center for Naval Analyses, November 1971).

65. Victor Zorza, "Soviets' Great Debate: Cost of Building Up Navy," *Christian Science Monitor,* (December 13, 1973).

66. Erickson, *Soviet Military Power*, p. 60; Michael MccGwire, "Current Soviet Warship Construction and Naval Weapons Development," in MccGwire, Booth, and McDonnell, *Soviet Naval Policy*, p. 444; and Rumsfeld, *Annual Report*, p. 129.

67. MccGwire, "Current Soviet Warship Construction," p. 44; see also "Russ, Too, Put Pinch on Navy," *South Bend Tribune,* (March 28, 1973).

68. MccGwire, "Command of the Sea in Soviet Naval Strategy," in MccGwire, Booth, and McDonnell, *Soviet Naval Policy*, p. 634; and J. Bowyer Bell, "Strategic Implications of the Soviet Presence in Somalia," *Orbis* 14 (Summer 1975): 408. Gorshkov, in *The Sea Power of the Soviet State*, published in February 1976, argued that gaining command of the sea is subsidiary, a supporting task linked to the main operation on land. The navy's geographical sway is limited to a portion of a theater or, occasionally, to a whole theater, and its time is also circumscribed. Command of the sea is "only a vehicle for creating the definite preconditions that will allow fleet forces and means to successfully accomplish particular tasks in definite regions of the world in a concrete time period" (Gorshkov,

quoted in James M. McConnell, *The Gorshkov Articles, the New Gorshkov Book and Their Relation to Policy,* Professional Paper no. 159 [Arlington, VA: Center for Naval Analyses, July 1976], pp. 59-60).

69. MccGwire, "Command of the Sea," p. 634 (italics added). Quote from Dudin and Listvinov, in Kulish, *Military Force,* p. 99. Before this passage is the interesting accusation that the United States was "trying to force the Socialist Bloc countries into further distributing their forces among many centers of resistance and thus weaken their direct resistance to the U.S.A."

70. Dudin and Listvinov, in Kulish, *Military Force,* Soviet sources often explain this as a policy of restraining and halting local wars, as the "probability of the outbreak of local wars and military conflicts caused by imperialist policy remains a real one." See I. Shavrov, "Local Wars and Their Place in the Global Strategy of Imperialism," *Military Historical Journal* (April 1, 1975), in *Soviet Press: Selected Translations,* no. 75-3 (September 1975): 15.

71. Paul F. Langer, "North Korea and North Vietnam," in ed. Adam Bromke and Teresa Rakowska-Harmstone *The Communist States in Disarray, 1965-1971,* (Minneapolis: University of Minnesota Press, paperback, 1972), pp. 273, 275.

72. Richard C. Thornton, "Soviet Strategy and the Vietnam War," *Asian Affairs, An American Review* 4 (March-April 1974): 217.

73. Le Duan, "We Will Certainly Win. The Enemy Will Certainly Be Defeated" (Nha Xuat Ban Tien Phong, 1966), p. 7, quoted in Gareth Porter, *A Peace Denied: The United States, Vietnam, and the Paris Agreement* (Bloomington: Indiana University Press, 1975), p. 24.

74. Langer, "North Korea," pp. 277-278, gives some figures on the magnitude and composition of the aid.

75. Porter, *Peace Denied,* pp. 113, 114, 188.

76. Thornton, "Soviet Strategy," p. 227; Ian Ward, "North Vietnam's Blitzkrieg: Why Giap Did It: Report from Saigon," and Brian Crozier, "Revolutionary War: Fact versus Theory," in *North Vietnam's Blitzkrieg—An Interim Assessment,* Conflict Studies, no. 27 (October 1972), pp. 3, 5, 14. Crozier reveals that captured documents of COSVN (Central Office for South Vietnam) mentioned Podgorny's visit in terms which support the assumption that Moscow knew of preparations for the offensive in advance (p. 16).

77. A Soviet analyst observed that the Nixon administration practiced "great severity in using military force, if the United States decides to apply it after all." G. A. Trofimenko, "Voenno-Strategicheskie Aspekty 'Doktrina Niksona'" [Military-strategic aspects of the Nixon Doctrine], in *Doktrina Niksona* [The Nixon Doctrine] (Moscow: Main Publishing House of Eastern Literature, 1972), p. 68.

78. John Osborne, "The Nixon Watch: The Pressure of Fear," *The New Republic,* June 3, 1972): 14. Osborne indicates that the Soviet leaders would be inviting "unmanageable domestic trouble for themselves" if they canceled the summit. One Soviet journalist said, "Do you believe that our leaders are totally divorced from public sentiment? If you do, you are foolish."

79. Porter, *Peace Denied,* p. 188.

80. Stanley Karnow, "Avoiding Bloodshed in Saigon: Hanoi's Design," *The New Republic,* April 26, 1975, pp. 11, 12.

81. E. Glazunov, "Demokraticheskaia Respublika Vietnam: Novy Étap Razvitia" [The Democratic Republic of Vietnam: New stage of development], *Mezhdunarodny Ezhegodnik 1974: Politika i Ekonomika* [International annual 1974: Politics and economics] (Moscow: Publishing House of Political Literature, 1974), p. 69. Earlier, Glazunov had indicated that the North had sought to reconstruct its economy, but systematic violations by the Saigon regime of the Paris agreement caused the DRV "constant concern for strengthening its defense capability" (p. 67).

82. Porter, *Peace Denied*, p. 272.

83. Guy Halverson. "Hanoi Military Impresses Pentagon: U.S. Analysts Surprised by Speed of Thrust and Power of Red Units," *The Christian Science Monitor*, (March 28, 1975).

84. Gromyko, "Programma," pp. 8, 9.

85. Malcolm Mackintosh, "The USSR and the Near East," in "The Present State of Soviet Global Expansion: Sources, Goals and Prospects," U.S. Army Institute for Advanced Russian and East European Studies, 5th Annual Soviet Affairs Symposium, April 20-22, 1971 (Garmisch, Germany), pp. 44-45.

86. Malcolm H. Kerr, "Soviet Influence in Egypt, 1967-1973" (unpublished paper), pp. 29, 6.

87. For a discussion of evidence in the Soviet press of a split between hawkish Soviet military leaders and a more cautious Soviet leadership about the extent of Soviet military and diplomatic engagement in the Middle East, see Ilana Dimant-Kass, "The Soviet Military and Soviet Policy in the Middle East 1970-73," *Soviet Studies* 26 (October 1974), esp. p. 508.

88. Galia Golan, *The Soviet Union and the Arab-Israeli War of October, 1973* (Jerusalem: Leonard Davis Institute of International Relations, The Hebrew University of Jerusalem, 1974), p. 11.

89. Heykal in *Al-Ahram*, December 3, 1970, quoted in Abraham S. Becker, *The Superpowers in the Arab Israeli Conflict, 1970-1973*, RAND P-5167 (December 1973), p. 37.

90. Sadat, in his report to the Central Committee of the Arab Socialist Union on the expulsion of the Soviets on July 24 *(New York Times*, July 25, 1972), quoted in Becker, *Superpowers*, p. 38; H. Heykal, "Soviet Arms and Egypt," *Al-Ahram* June 30, 1972, as broadcast by "Voice of the Arabs," June 30, 1972, *Survival* 14 (September-October 1972): 235 (italics added).

91. Elizabeth Monroe and A. H. Farrar-Hockley, *The Arab-Israeli War, October 1973: Background and Events*, Adelphi Papers No. 111 (London: International Institute for Strategic Studies, 1975), p. 32; and Foy D. Kohler, Leon Goure, and Mose L. Harvey, *The Soviet Union and the October 1973 Middle East War: The Implications for Détente* (Coral Gables: University of Miami Center for International Studies, 1974), pp. 39, 43.

92. John Kimche, "Fall, 1973: The Soviet-Arab Scenario," *Midstream* 19 (December 1973): 15; and Wolfe, *Soviet Capabilities*, p. 24.

93. Edward R. F. Sheehan, "How Kissinger Did It: Step by Step in the Middle East," *Foreign Policy*, no. 22 (Spring 1976): 13-15.

94. E. Primakov, "Blizhevostochny Krizis v 1973" [The Near East crisis in 1973], in *Mezhdunarodny Ezhegodnik 1974*, pp. 220, 223, 225, 226, 229.

95. Ibid., p. 230.

96. Gromyko, "Programma," p. 9 (italics added).

97. This account is taken from John A. Marcum, "Lessons of Angola," *Foreign Affairs* 54 (April 1976): 414, 416, 416, 418.

98. Henry Kamm, "Angolan Premier Sees U.S. Harming His Side's Efforts," *New York Times* (January 25, 1976).

99. Robin Wright, "Huge Soviet Aid Tips Angola balance," *The Christian Science Monitor* (January 23, 1976).

100. See, for example, "Abandon Angola to Russia? Soviets Are Not apt to Gain a Tremendous Amount," interview with Senator Dick Clark of Iowa, *U.S. News and World Reports* (February 23, 1976): 35.

101. Observer, "On the Events in Angola and Around It," *Pravda* (January 3, 1976), in *Soviet Press: Selected Translations*, no. 76-2 (February 1976): 11.

102. Observer, "K Polozheniiu v Angole" [On the situation in Angola], *Pravda* (February 11, 1976).

103. "Moscow Plays Down U.S. Tough Talk," *Soviet World Outlook* 1 (April 15, 1976): 1, 9, 10.

104. Morton Schwartz, *The Foreign Policy of the USSR Domestic Factors* (Encino, CA: Dickenson Publishing Co., 1975), p. 175; and Vladimir Petrov, *Soviet Foreign Policy Formulation: Formal and Informal Inputs*, XR/RESS-6 (Washington, D.C.: Department of State, March 30, 1973), pp. 20-21.

105. Petrov, *Soviet Foreign Policy*, p. 21

106. Terry McNeill, *Ideological Trends and Portents: A Review of Some Recent Developments*, Radio Liberty Dispatch (Munich) RL 332-74 (October 4, 1974), p. 3.

107. Brezhnev, *CDSP* 23 (May 14, 1971): 7.

108. Petrov, *Soviet Foreign Policy*, Schwartz, *The Foreign Policy*, pp. 171, 175.

109. G. A. Trofimenko, USSR–U.S.A.: Peaceful Coexistence Is the Norm," *U.S.A. Economics, Politics, Ideology*, no. 2 (February 1974), *JPRS* 61346 (February 28, 1974), p. 7 (italics added).

110. See various Soviet sources cited on pp. 32, 33 of Roger Hamburg, "Soviet Perceptions of Détente and Analysis of the American Political Process," *Naval War College Review* (May-June 1975); see also Robert Hansen, "Soviet Images of American Foreign Policy: 1960-1972" (Ph.D. diss., Princeton University, 1975), p. 211; and Anatoli Andreyevich Gromyko, *Through Russian Eyes: President Kennedy's 1036 Days*, trans. Philip A. Garar (Washington, D.C.: International Library, Inc., 1973), p. 225.

111. See Soviet sources cited in Hamburg, "Soviet Perceptions," p. 33, n. 44, p. 40.

112. V. Z. Zhurkin, "Foreign Policy Debates: From 'Globalism' to 'Selectiveness,'" *U.S.A.: Economics, Politics, Ideology*, no. 6 (June 1974), *JPRS* 62492, (July 17, 1974), p. 32.

113. Karenin, *Filosofia*, pp. 124, 128, 154-155.

114. Ibid., pp. 166, 169. On conflicting themes in U.S.–PRC relations from the Soviet viewpoint, see V. P. Lukin, "Sino-American Relations: Conceptions and Realities," *U.S.A.: Economics, Politics, Ideology*, no. 2 (February 1973), *JPRS* 58418 (March 8, 1973), esp. pp. 17-20; and B. N. Zanegin, "Some Aspects of American-Chinese Relations," *U.S.A.: Economics, Politics, Ideology*, no. 2 (February 1975), *JPRS* 64262 (March 6, 1975),esp. pp. 43-47.

115. V. F. Petrovsky, "Novye Tendentsii v Amerikanskikh Burzhuaznykh Kontsepsiakh Mezhdunarodnykh Otnoshenii" [New tendencies in American bourgeoise concepts of international relations], *Novaia i Noveishaia Istori* [Modern and contemporary history], 1 (January-February 1975): 80, 81; V. V. Zhurkin, "Evoliutsia 'Krizisnoi Politiki' i 'Krizisnoi Diplomatii' SShA" [The evolution of U.S. "crisis policy" and "crisis diplomacy"), *Voprosy Istorii* [Problems of history] 4 (April 1975): 83, 89; and Karenin, *Filosofia*, pp. 275, 286.

116. A. A. Kokoshin, *Prognoziroyanie i Politika. Metodologia, Organizatsia i Ispol'zovanie Prognozirovanie Mezhdunarodnykh Otnoshenii vo Vneshnei Politike SShA* [Forecasting and politics: Methodology, organization and utilization of forecasting international relations in U.S. foreign policy] (Moscow: International Relations Publishing House, 1975), pp. 139, 151, 152.

117. Ibid., p. 153.

118. Ibid., pp. 153, 155, 157, 161, 167.

119. S. B. Chetverikov, *Kto i Kak Delaet Politiku SShA* [Who makes U.S. policy and how it is made] (Moscow: International Relations Publishing House, 1974), p. 220.

120. Ye. I. Popova, "The Senate and Strategic Arms Limitation," *U.S.A.: Economics, Politics, Ideology*, no. 4 (April 1975), *JPRS* 64720 (May 8, 1975): 24.

121. A. D. Turkatenko, "An Important Stage in the Development of Soviet-American Relations," *U.S.A.: Economics, Politics, Ideology*, no. 1 (January 1975), *JPRS* 64129 (February 20, 1975): 14.

122. V. A. Shimanovsky, "Liberaly i Razriadka Napriazhennosti" [Liberals and the easing of tensions], *SShA: Ekonomika, Politika, Ideologia* 1 (January 1976): 42, 45, 48; and M. V. Valeriani, "SSSR-SShA: Itovi, Trudnosti, Perspektivy" [The USSR and U.S.A.: Results, difficulties, prospects], ibid., p. 6.

123. Boris Dmitriev, *SShA: Politiki, Generaly, Diplomaty* [U.S.A.: Politics, generals, diplomats] (Moscow: International Relations Publishing House, 1971), p. 237; and Chetverikov, *Kto*, p. 65 (italics added).

124. Chetverikov, *Kto*, p. 178.

125. Adam Ulam, *Expansion and Coexistence: Soviet Foreign Policy 1917-73*, 2d ed. (New York: Praeger, paperback, 1974), pp. 410-11.

126. Ernst Henry, "Against Historical Truth," *U.S.A.: Economics, Politics, Ideology*, no. 5 (May 1975), *JPRS* 64956 (June 10, 1975): p. 25; and V. M. Berezhkov, "The Potsdam Decisions and After," *U.S.A.: Economics, Politics, Ideology*, no. 5 (May 1975), *JPRS* 65458 (August 14, 1975): 60.

127. Ye. V. Ponomareva, "Yalta: 30 Years Later," *U.S.A.: Economics, Politics, Ideology*, no. 2 (February 1975), *JPRS* 64262 (March 6, 1975): p. 68; and Vojtech Mastny, "Reconsiderations: The Cassandra in the Foreign Commissariat: Maxim Litvinov and the Cold War," *Foreign Affairs* 54 (January 1976): 373.

128. Kokoshin, *Prognoziroyanie*, p. 155.

129. Edward Crankshaw, ed., *Khrushchev Remembers*, trans. Strove Talbott (New York: Bantam, 1971), p. 555.

130. Zbigniew Brzezinski, "The Competitive Relationship," in *Caging the Bear: Containment and the Cold War*, ed. Charles Gati (Indianapolis: Bobbs-Merrill, paperback, 1974), pp. 188, 191-92.

131. John Erickson, "Soviet Military Performance. Some Manpower and Managerial Constraints," in "The Soviet Union in 1972-1973," U.S. Army Institute for Advanced Russian and East European Studies, 7th Annual Soviet Affairs Symposium, 1973 (Garmisch, Germany), pp. 16, 22, 24.

PART II. TECHNOLOGY AND CONTROL

MILITARY ALERTS AND DIPLOMATIC SIGNALS

Joseph J. Kruzel

Military alerts and mobilizations are the continuation of diplomacy by other means. They fall into a gray area between war and politics. Because they are steps beyond the normal limits of diplomacy, yet short of actual military intervention, alerts are inherently difficult to manage. Soldiers and statesmen may find themselves equally ill-equipped to direct a military alert for maximum diplomatic effect. Civilian officials may not understand the complexities and implications of military alert procedures, and military men may be reluctant to accept artificial constraints on military forces imposed by the requirements of statecraft.

If war is too important to be left to generals, and diplomacy is too important to be left to diplomats, then surely actions between war and diplomacy are too important to be left to either group.

Military alerts have often been used without regard for their diplomatic impact. When alerts have been employed as a means of conveying diplomatic signals, they frequently haven't had unintended consequences. The process of alerting military forces and the use of alerts for diplomatic purposes deserve careful study and reflection *before* a crisis erupts.

DIPLOMATIC CRISES AND MILITARY ALERTS

Crises are not a new phenomenon in world politics. Unanticipated threats to critical national values have erupted throughout history. In many cases the time available for decision makers to act and react has been extremely limited.

Many crises have been resolved diplomatically, with no threatened use of force. Some have resulted in military intervention by one of the involved parties.

And every crisis, almost by definition, involves at least some threat of military action.

The existence of nuclear weapons magnifies the risks involved in poor crisis management. The amount of destruction which is possible in a nuclear war imposes a special obligation on the actors in a crisis to act with wisdom, restraint, and foresight.

The United States and the Soviet Union now possess nuclear missiles capable of reaching each other's shores within thirty minutes. Over the next two decades, many other nations may develop nuclear weapons and the means of delivering them. In any confrontation with even a faint hint of escalation to nuclear war, all parties must manage their diplomatic moves and countermoves with utmost caution. So long as nations continue to disagree over world goals and methods for achieving those goals, crises of varying intensity can be expected to erupt in the future. Each nation must design and execute its diplomatic signals with great care. Each must evaluate its adversary's moves with imagination and sensitivity.

Diplomatic crises frequently entail precautionary military measures by one or more of the involved parties. Such measures may include the mobilization of key reserve units, cancellation of leaves for military personnel, redeployment of forces, or the ordering of a military alert to enhance overall readiness for combat.

Mobilizations and alerts serve two functions. First, they bring military forces to an enhanced state of combat readiness. It is physically and economically impossible to maintain troops and equipment in a constant state of readiness for war, and every military establishment has developed a series of steps for bringing peacetime forces up to a wartime footing.

A military alert may also be used for political purposes, as a means of conveying a diplomatic signal. An improved military posture can often serve notice to other nations that military action is possible if a crisis cannot be resolved through peaceful means.[1]

The use of military alerts to convey diplomatic signals is a risky business. By its very nature an alert transmits an ambiguous signal. If a state wanted to reinforce its diplomacy with a military threat, it might consider putting its forces on alert. On the other hand, if a state decided to abandon diplomacy and take military action, it also would alert its military forces. Usually there is no way to tell whether an alert is a last step in an effort to bring about a peaceful settlement or a first step toward war.

This ambiguity poses a problem for decision makers in other countries attempting to evaluate the alert. Is an adversary's alert simply a prudent precaution in a crisis? Is it a military threat designed to induce a peaceful resolution of differences? Or is it a prelude to inevitable armed conflict?

Whatever its true purpose, a military alert may trigger similar precautionary actions by other states. Paradoxically, an escalation of alerts may lead to the sort of military conflict which the original mobilizations were designed to prevent.

The outbreak of World War I can be explained at least in part as the result of competitive mobilizations by the major European powers.[2]

DECISION MAKING IN CRISIS SITUATIONS

It is a cruel paradox of human behavior that people seem to function worst when it matters most. In situations of great stress decision makers are less likely to forge innovative responses to new problems, to perceive nuances and shades of meaning, and to examine problems from different frames of reference.[3]

Decision makers are more likely to react to a crisis by focusing on immediate rather than long-term consequences, by filtering out dissonant information, and by adopting comfortable routines and standard procedures which may be inappropriate to new circumstances. Ole Holsti has suggested an additional consideration about crisis decision making: as stress continues, decision makers tend to perceive their range of alternatives as narrowing, and that of their adversaries as expanding.

Little can be done to eliminate these psychological tendencies. Stress is, after all, a natural response to crisis. It would be useful for decision makers to be aware of these dangers and to be on guard against them, but we could hardly ask public officials to avoid situations of stress. Some stress may be a good thing. As much as we might want political leaders to keep cool in a crisis, we would probably prefer them to endure stress than to face their problems with an unconcerned serenity.

If little can be done to eliminate stress, something can be done to reduce the other impediments to proper crisis management. A number of procedural and organizational factors influence crisis decision making in ways that are inconsistent with rational policy making.

The first factor concerns the role of military advisers in crisis decision making. The advice of senior military officials invariably assumes a great importance during international crises. As a crisis intensifies, military advice tends to become increasingly significant. This is an understandable but lamentable phenomenon. As the threat of war increases, civilian leaders must necessarily give more thought to possible military alternatives. Unfortunately, military men may not appreciate the subtleties of diplomacy or the process of achieving diplomatic objectives. Even if they are aware of diplomatic considerations, they are likely to underestimate their importance.

The basic responsibility of a professional soldier is to be prepared if war should break out. When a crisis occurs, senior military officers will want above all else to maximize the combat readiness of their forces. They will be attracted to policy options which ensure that objective. But such precautionary measures may be counterproductive in a diplomatic sense. Military advisers will invariably prefer initiatives which improve military readiness, even if such improvement occurs at the expense of diplomatic flexibility.

A second problem may obtain once a military alert or other show of strength is chosen as a means of conveying a diplomatic signal. Every military establishment has devised procedures for alerting its forces. Such plans usually specify a limited number of steps between a peacetime and a wartime footing, as well as a limited range of contingency plans for meeting various types of threats. Plans for military alerts are designed with one basic objective in mind: to enhance the combat readiness of military forces. Few contingency plans consider the diplomatic impact of military mobilization. Thus political leaders may find themselves confronted with a limited array of options, none of which are designed with diplomatic objectives in mind. A military alert or show of force may easily convey an incomplete signal. The action may be a credible "stick," but unless it is accompanied by a diplomatic "carrot," the alert may be misinterpreted.

A third difficulty involves the psychological effect a military alert may exert on decision makers and the general public. An atmosphere in which the danger of war is perceived to be high may in itself raise the risk of conflict. Military forces may be put on alert initially in order to avoid war, but with forces on alert national leaders may be tempted to give more weight to military alternatives than they might otherwise have done. The inflated attractiveness of military solutions is an unpleasant but probably unavoidable aspect of crisis decision making.

A final problem concerns the implementation of an alert. As every student of bureaucratic politics knows, deciding on a policy option is only the first step in the policy-making process. Serious problems are apt to arise in the implementation of a policy. The executors of a policy, for example, may simply misunderstand their orders. Or they may understand the guidance perfectly but refuse to carry it out. Quite possibly the details of execution may be unclear to decision makers and operatives alike.

In a crisis, senior officials often fail to supervise the details of implementing a military alert. In most day-to-day government activities it is probably wise for senior officials to delegate considerable authority to their subordinates, but in an international crisis a failure to supervise the details of an alert may have disastrous consequences.

One example occurred during the most critical moments of the Cuban Missile Crisis. An American U-2 reconnaissance plane flew a routine flight over the North Pacific on a mission totally unrelated to the crisis. The aircraft took its bearings on the wrong star and strayed over the Soviet Union. The overflight occurred despite the fact that President Kennedy had specifically ordered such flights suspended for the duration of the missile crisis. Khrushchev pointed out to Kennedy the frightful implications of the U-2 incident:

> How should we regard this? What is this, a provocation? One of your planes violates our frontier during this anxious time we are both experiencing, when everything has been put into combat readiness. Is it not a fact that an intruding American plane could easily be taken for a nuclear bomber?[4]

Khrushchev's point was well taken. When informed of the U-2 overflight, Kennedy muttered to his advisers, "There is always some son of a bitch who doesn't get the word." Kennedy's complaint is a bureaucratic fact of life. It suggests that great caution should be used in employing military alerts or shows of force, and that during a crisis decision makers should supervise the details of implementation to the maximum extent possible.

U.S. AND SOVIET MILITARY READINESS

The proper use and evaluation of military alerts depend on a number of factors. First, civilian officials need to understand their own military forces. They must be familiar with the standard level of military readiness, the process by which forces are alerted, and the various types of alerts which can be implemented. It is equally important that decision makers have some knowledge of foreign military forces and alerting procedures. Without such an understanding, alerts by other nations cannot be properly interpreted.

For American and Soviet leaders an understanding of each other's military forces and alerts is particularly important. The normal risks involved in alerts are compounded by the fact that the two military superpowers take quite different attitudes toward military readiness. The most dramatic difference in U.S. and Soviet practices lies in the area of strategic forces.

The United States generally maintains all of its strategic forces in a high state of readiness. Intercontinental ballistic missiles (ICBMs) are in a constant ready-to-fire condition, and virtually the entire force can be launched within a few minutes of receiving an authenticated order to fire.

In the submarine force, more than half of the U.S. submarine-launched ballistic missiles (SLBMs) are at sea within range of their assigned targets at any given time. With the introduction of the longer-range Trident missile, submarine "on-station" time will increase considerably.

A substantial portion of the B-52 bomber force is also on alert, with crews standing by ready to go. B-52s on alert can be airborne within several minutes.

The strategic forces of the Soviet Union are generally at a far lower level of readiness than their American counterparts. Soviet ICBMs take much longer to prepare for launch; some American intelligence analysts believe that it may take over an hour to prepare Soviet ICBMs for firing.

Only a small fraction of the Soviet SLBM force is ever on station at any given time. Often no more than one or two submarines will be within range of American targets. The U.S. Navy goes to great effort to keep no more than a few SLBM submarines in port at any given time; the Soviet Navy keeps more of its missile-carrying submarines in port most of the time.

Russian long-range bomber aircraft are never kept on a standby alert status, as are the American B-52s. Aside from practice alerts and periodic Arctic staging exercises, Soviet Bear and Bison aircraft are maintained in a fairly relaxed status.

This basic difference in American and Soviet alert practices appears to be the result of various historical, strategic, and economic considerations. One possible explanation for the American practice stems from the longstanding U.S. preoccupation with the threat of surprise attack. A means of reducing the possibility of surprise attack is to maintain forces in a high state of readiness so they can be launched quickly and not be destroyed on the ground. One Pearl Harbor in a nation's history is enough.

A second explanation for the American practice stems from the dictates of deterrence theory. American nuclear strategists have long argued that stability in the nuclear age is enhanced by reducing the incentives for either side to strike first in a crisis. The smaller the advantage in preemption, the less the temptation, and the less dangerous a crisis will be. Forces at a high state of readiness therefore make for greater stability.

A nation would have little incentive to launch a preemptive attack against an opponent's submarine base if there were only one submarine in port; with twenty or thirty submarines in port the incentive would be much greater. Bombers which can be airborne in three or four minutes provide less temptation to an attacker than bombers which require half an hour or more of warning time and can be caught on the ground. The United States has long considered the improved strategic stability which results from a high state of readiness to be well worth the cost.

A third reason for the American practice may stem from the nature of Soviet society. A closed society inherently affords greater opportunities for secrecy than does an open society, and there is some concern within the U.S. government that the Soviet Union could disguise its preparations for war. If the Soviets did plan a preemptive attack, the critical deliberations in the Kremlin could involve a relatively small group of officials. There might be no press reporting or public debate to suggest the possibility of war. It is conceivable, although highly unlikely, that the United States could be denied any general warning of an impending nuclear war.

In contrast to the Soviet system, the nature of American society virtually guarantees the Soviet Union a good deal of warning time. This social asymmetry may be one reason the United States has chosen to keep its strategic forces at a higher state of readiness.

The more relaxed Soviet attitude may be linked to three different concerns. The first is cost. The Soviet method is a far less expensive way to maintain strategic forces. Keeping submarines in port, for example, is certainly cheaper than having them on station. To maintain most of its submarine missile force at sea and ready to fire, the United States is required to keep two fully manned crews for each sub. That alone doubles the manpower costs of the American SLBM fleet. In addition to manpower, the costs of maintenance, fuel, and supplies are substantially greater under the American system than the Soviet. Similar expenses are evident in the ICBM and heavy-bomber components of strategic forces. Maintaining strategic forces on the American model costs a great deal of money. It is a cost which the Soviet Union has thus far shown no interest in assuming.

The second explanation for the Soviet practice may be a greater concern on their part with the problems of command and control. Reliable means of maintaining command and control of strategic forces are necessary in order to minimize the risk of an accidental or unauthorized nuclear attack. As the readiness of strategic forces increases, the importance of command and control also increases. Something is far more likely to go wrong when forces are spring-loaded for action than when they are at rest. An unauthorized or accidental launching of nuclear weapons, à la *Dr. Strangelove,* is more likely in a force at high readiness than in one at low readiness.

To minimize the possibility of such a nightmare ever occurring, the United States has invested a great deal of money and ingenuity in the development of a sophisticated and reliable network of communications, command, and control. The Soviet system is not so technically advanced as the American, and that may be one reason for the relatively low state of Soviet strategic readiness.

In recent years the USSR has embarked on a major effort to improve command and control, but whether that will lead to a higher readiness level remains to be seen. Even with a command and control network as good as the American system, a case could be made for keeping forces in a more relaxed day-to-day posture in order to reduce still further the danger of an accidental or unauthorized attack.

Another explanation of the related Soviet defense condition may be that the Kremlin appears genuinely unconcerned about an unexpected nuclear attack. Soviet leaders anticipate that any nuclear exchange will be preceded by days and perhaps weeks of international tension. That period will provide them with more than enough time to generate a strategic alert. It goes without saying that neither the United States nor the Soviet Union considers a surprise attack very likely. The difference is that the United States is willing to take expensive precautionary steps to minimize the possibility, however slight; the Soviet Union is not. The Kremlin is literally betting most of its SLBM fleet, most of its bombers, and some of its ICBMs on the prospect of receiving at least several hours' advance warning of an impending nuclear attack.

These two models of readiness for strategic forces provide an interesting and significant contrast. Neither the American nor the Soviet system is inherently better. Each has its pros and cons. The American practice is more expensive, less susceptible to surprise attack, and strategically most stable; at the same time it is somewhat more prone to accident. The Soviet system is relatively inexpensive and a bit safer, but it also presents a more tempting array of targets for surprise attack. In addition to the contrasts, the two systems also provide quite different opportunities for conveying diplomatic signals through the use of alerts.

Before turning to the diplomatic implications of military alerts, a word must be said about the general readiness of conventional forces. In contrast to strategic forces, U.S. and Soviet readiness procedures for conventional military units are rather similar. Both sides maintain several divisions of troops at full strength, ostensibly in a permanent condition of combat readiness. An alert of these forces generally involves only final preparations for deployment. It may include a cancellation of military exercises, the recall of furloughed personnel, and even a forward deployment of troops to a position nearer the area of conflict.

TYPES OF ALERTS

Military alerts cover a wide variety of possible military activities, and there are two important ways in which alerts may differ. The first is the level of readiness which the alert entails. The second is the number and type of forces involved.

American military forces have for some time maintained five discrete conditions of defense readiness, covering the entire spectrum from tranquility to hostility. Defense condition 5 (DEFCON 5 in military parlance) is the lowest state of readiness. In this condition forces are not in any state of readiness; recruits lack any training. At the other end of the spectrum, DEFCON 1 means that troops are deployed for combat.

For the past several years most U.S. forces have remained at DEFCON 4 (normal peacetime condition), with the notable exception of a period during the 1973 Yom Kippur war when forces were moved to DEFCON 3. This condition places troops on standby to await further orders. Little is known publicly about the various stages of Soviet defense readiness, but it is reasonable to assume that Soviet forces operate under a similar type of system.

For purposes of signaling the breadth of an alert may be as important as the level of readiness. Most alerts are selective and affect only specifically identified military units. During the 1970 civil war in Jordan, for example, the United States alerted an airborne division in this country and two airborne battalions stationed in West Germany. Selective alerts are fairly common occurrences. Since 1960 the United States has used them on several occasions. The 1961 Berlin crisis, the seizure of the *Pueblo* in 1968 invasion of Czechoslovakia all prompted selective alerts of American military forces. Soviet armed forces have gone on selective alerts in response to most of the same crises; in addition, the Soviet Union called selective alerts during several border disputes with China and during the Indo-Pakistan war of 1971.

The alternative to a selective alert is a universal alert involving a nation's entire military establishment. A worldwide alert has been used by the United

States only rarely since World War II. Once was during the Cuban Missile Crisis of 1962; another was in October 1973, to counter the Soviet threat to send forces into the Middle East. In a universal alert, all of a nation's military forces—land, sea, and air; strategic and tactical; conventional and nuclear—are directed to stand by and await further orders.

It may be instructive to examine one crisis in some detail as a case study of the dangers and opportunities involved in implementing and interpreting alerts. During the Yom Kippur war of 1973, both the United States and the Soviet Union employed military alerts largely for diplomatic effect.

THE YOM KIPPUR WAR

During the Cuban Missile Crisis of 1962, the worldwide alert of U.S. forces was generally accepted as a wise precautionary move. Soviet ships carrying nuclear missiles were on their way to Cuba, and Kennedy had ordered a quarantine of the island. In Dean Rusk's memorable phrase, the two super-powers were "eyeball to eyeball," and one side or the other would have to blink. President Kennedy is said to have figured the chance of nuclear war as greater than one in three. In such a context of inevitable confrontation, a worldwide alert of American forces was almost preordained.

That was not the case in October 1973. There was little visible evidence of crisis outside the Middle East, and no public sign of an inevitable confrontation looming between the United States and the Soviet Union. Many American citizens openly wondered whether President Nixon's decision to alert U.S. troops was an effort to divert attention from his Watergate difficulties at home.

As the Yom Kippur war entered its third week, it became clear that Israel had gained the military offensive on the Egyptian front. Israeli forces had crossed the Suez Canal and advanced to within sixty miles of Cairo. Israeli Army units had also encircled the Egyptian III Corps, which included some of the best units in the entire Egyptian Army. The fragile cease-fire approved by the U.N. Security Council on October 22 had not held; Egypt accused Israel of continued violations and demanded a return to the original cease-fire lines.

The Soviet Union viewed these military developments with great dismay. Egypt had accepted a cease-fire on the basis of assurances from the Soviet Union. When the cease-fire failed to hold, the Egyptians felt betrayed by their Soviet ally. To ensure their own credibility, and to deter further Israeli advances, the Soviets felt compelled to take firm and decisive action to enforce the cease-fire.[5]

On the afternoon of October 24, Egyptian President Sadat proposed for the first time that the United States and the Soviet Union provide troops for a joint Middle East peace-keeping force. The United States responded with a fire but low-key rejection of the idea. About 8:00 P.M. that evening (Washington time), Secretary Kissinger received a note from Brezhnev which also suggested the possibility of a joint expeditionary force. Again the idea was politely rejected.

Three hours later another Brezhnev note was delivered to Kissinger. This was the communication which Senator Henry Jackson was later to characterize as "brutal and rough." In effect, the note declared, "We strongly urge that we both send forces to enforce the cease-fire and, if you do not, we may be obliged to consider acting alone."[6]

This escalation of Soviet diplomatic language was accompanied by an escalation of Kremlin military preparations. American communications intelligence revealed the presence of seven landing craft and two ships with troop helicopters in the eastern Mediterranean. Several thousand Soviet naval infantrymen were thought to be stationed in the Mediterranean and the Black Sea; U.S. officials were concerned that some of them might easily be moved into Egypt. In addition, American intelligence had observed an alert order to seven Soviet airborne divisions numbering well over 40,000 troops. On October 24 one division had been moved to a higher readiness condition, making it ready to move out on call.

More ambiguous signals were also detected. During the early stages of the war large Soviet transport aircraft had been used to ferry supplies from Hungary to the Arab states; now, suddenly, the planes were redeployed to bases in the Soviet Union. American officials suspected that such aircraft could be used to airlift Soviet troops to the Middle East. Another disconcerting bit of intelligence revealed that Soviet merchant ships might have begun transporting nuclear weapons to Egypt. The possibility was taken seriously only by a few military intelligence experts; nonetheless, it was another factor to consider in assessing Soviet intentions.

The Soviet diplomatic notes themselves were forthright and contained hints of unilateral action, but they were hardly as brutal or provocative as Senator Jackson implied. The military actions were also noteworthy, but in themselves were not particularly alarming. The Soviet military had called other alerts during the Yom Kippur war, and the naval activity in the eastern Mediterranean had not shown an alarming increase. In the week before October 26, the Soviets had added ten ships to their Mediterranean squadron. This brought the total number of Soviet ships in the Mediterranean to eighty, a significant but not astonishing rise from the average number of sixty.[7]

It was the combination of diplomatic notes and military activity that troubled U.S. officials. The Soviet words and actions caused Kissinger and Defense Secretary Schlesinger to consider for the first time that the Soviet threat might indeed be serious. The two officials moved quickly to develop an appropriate American response. First, the Soviet note was answered in the strongest possible terms. Kissinger flatly rejected the suggestion of a joint Soviet-American expeditionary force in the Middle East. He went on to say that the United States was even more opposed to the unilateral introduction of any military forces into that area. Second, the Soviet alert was countered by placing all U.S. military forces around the world on a "precautionary alert" or DEFCON 3. About 3:00 A.M., when these actions were accomplished, Kissinger called the President and informed him of the situation. Nixon approved Kissinger's actions, and the secretary went home for a few hours' sleep.

None of the top decision makers—not Kissinger, Schlesinger, or Nixon—anticipated the firestorm of domestic reaction which the alert created. Kissinger is said to have been astonished the next morning at the extent to which the alert totally dominated the news.

American officials saw the alert as an appropriate and measured response to prior Soviet actions, but many Americans and a number of allied governments were shocked and dismayed. A worldwide alert of U.S. military forces was reminiscent of the Cuban Missile Crisis of 1962, but this time the threat to the United States seemed vague and indirect. Many critics thought the U.S. government was engaged in a reckless display of nuclear machismo at a time when negotiation was a more appropriate response.

The worldwide alert had created more of a crisis atmosphere than U.S. officials had ever intended. At his press conference the following day, Secretary Kissinger repeatedly attempted to downplay the importance of the alert. '"We do not consider ourselves in a confrontation with the Soviet Union," Kissinger said. "We are not talking about a missile crisis-type of situation."

THE DIPLOMATIC USE OF MILITARY ALERTS

The military activity of the superpowers during the October War demonstrates the dangers involved in using military alerts to convey diplomatic signals. For the United States, the problem stems from its high state of defense readiness during normal peacetime conditions. Any alert which improves on an already high level of readiness runs the risk of being seen as a preparation for war. A high steady-state of readiness limits a nation's ability to convey diplomatic signals through military alerts. There are simply not many steps between peacetime preparedness and war.

For the Soviet Union the problem is precisely the reverse, and results from its relatively relaxed state of readiness. During a crisis the Kremlin will understandably take precautionary measures to enhance overall military preparedness. Such steps might not even be intended as signals, but because they represent such a radical departure from the standard practice, they may be misinterpreted by other nations. What would the American reaction be, for example, if three-quarters of the Soviet ballistic missile submarine fleet suddenly left port and went to sea?

In order to be successful, an alert must accomplish two functions simultaneously. It must convey a nation's seriousness of purpose while at the same time demonstrating restraint. The trick is to fashion a military alert which accomplishes both purposes. A properly designed alert will take the important first steps toward credible military action, but hold out the possibility of a political settlement by avoiding the final steps preparatory to execution.

Evaluated against this criterion, the Soviet alert during the October War should receive much higher marks than the American alert.

By late October, the Soviet Union had a specific policy objective in the Middle East: to see that both sides observed the original cease-fire lines agreed to on October 22. From the Soviet point of view, the ideal solution would be for the United States to persuade the Israelis to return to the original cease-fire lines. A less palatable option would be for the United States and the Soviet Union to mount a joint expeditionary force in the Sinai to enforce the cease-fire. Clearly the worst of all possible solutions would be the unilateral introduction of Soviet forces.

The problem for the Soviet Union was to come up with some means of inducing the United States to apply pressure on Israel. This was accomplished by suggesting the less attractive options of joint or unilateral intervention. But something more than a suggestion was needed. If the Kremlin had simply sent a note threatening to send forces into the Sinai, most U.S. officials would not have taken the possibility seriously.

The Soviet Union has never shown any particular appetite for intervention in nations outside the Warsaw Pact, and it is likely that Soviet leaders viewed the prospect of sending troops to the Middle East with almost as much distaste as did the Americans. Brezhnev could not admit it, but he probably had little quarrel with Kissinger's view that the United States and the Soviet Union should not "transplant the great-power rivalry into the Middle East, or ... impose a military condominium." In order to bring about a settlement in the Middle East, the Soviet Union had to make the threat of intervention credible, and that was achieved through the use of a military alert.

The ingenuity of the Soviet alert was that the military action which it suggested was credible but at the same time unwelcome to either side. It was evident to American officials that the Soviets did not want to intervene unilaterally in the Middle East. They would only do so as a final act of desperation. That realization encouraged all of the involved nations to seek a political settlement. Just how serious the Soviets were about carrying out their threat— just how close they were to deploying forces to Egypt—will never be known. That uncertainty is also consistent with the proper use of alerts as signals.

The American military alert served a somewhat different purpose. It was a response to the Soviet alert, and supported no specific policy objective other than to underscore American opposition to the idea of Soviet intervention in the Middle East. Kissinger and Schlesinger did not appear to give much thought to how a worldwide DEFCON 3 would be interpreted by the Soviet Union. What signal was conveyed to the Kremlin by an alert of all U.S. military forces around the world? What meaning could the Soviets possibly attach to the simultaneous alert of Marine divisions in Okinawa, Army forces in the Canal Zone, and nuclear submarines in the Atlantic?

The threat which the U.S. alert suggested was so extensive and so overwhelming in its potential that it lacked credibility. If the Soviet Union had actually deployed troops to the Middle East, would the U.S. response have involved American military forces around the world? Almost certainly, the answer is no.

A more appropriate American alert would have posed a more credible threat. The United States wanted to demonstrate that unilateral Soviet involvement in the Middle East would not be tolerated, and that if such action were attempted, it would be met by some undefined American response. That message could have been conveyed more accurately and less recklessly by moving several divisions of American troops in Europe to a higher state of readiness, perhaps even DEFCON 2.[8] Alternatively, airborne divisions in the United States could have been alerted and prepared for overseas deployment. Actions along these lines would have confirmed American opposition but at the same time limited a potential response to the convention level.

Even if a worldwide alert had been selected as an appropriate response, the United States could have demonstrated its interest in avoiding a strategic confrontation by exempting all strategic forces from the alert. A nation engaged in some future crisis might conceivably find it useful to employ a military alert in reverse. A *relaxation* of military readiness under some circumstances might help to defuse a crisis. Or a nation could alert some forces and relax others in order to convey a more precise diplomatic signal. Putting airborne divisions on alert and giving bomber crews the day off, for example, would be a clear signal that the contemplated military action was conventional and not strategic.

An alert which involves all military forces, whatever their mission and wherever deployed, is an unwieldy tool of diplomacy. In large part a worldwide alert suffers from the same limitations that afflicted the strategic doctrine of massive retaliation. A universal alert offers the threat of an overwhelming retaliatory blow as a means of deterring an opponent. At best such an alert lacks credibility; at worst it is an irresponsible means of nuclear diplomacy.

The United States gained little from its worldwide alert in October 1973. The Soviet Union was deterred from sending troops not so much by the American alert as by the U.N. Security Council resolution which authorized a Middle East peace-keeping force.

The Soviets were particularly galled that once the crisis had abated President Nixon took credit for having managed a successful piece of nuclear brinkmanship. Nixon called the aborted confrontation "the most difficult crisis" since the 1962 Cuban missile affair. Brezhnev's note, Nixon said, "left very little to the imagination of how we would react." This bit of braggadocio may have been necessary to justify the alert to the American people, but it infuriated the Soviets. It is an unfortunate precedent to establish in crisis diplomacy.

RECOMMENDATIONS

While the use of military alerts as a means of conveying diplomatic signals is inherently a risky venture, it need not be a foolhardy one. Several steps can be taken which will reduce the danger of unintended consequences. The five recommendations which follow are directed to the United States, but most of them have some application to the Soviet Union and other significant military powers.

The first recommendation is simply a plea for greater understanding of the use of military alerts. Senior government officials should develop a keener appreciation of the alerting process, the various defense conditions, and the likely problems to be encountered in implementation. Too often civilian leaders do not understand the implications of an alert. Frequently they assume the military services will immediately grasp the intended purpose of the alert and fashion an appropriate response. Unfortunately, many alerts look quite different in execution than they do in theory.

During the Big Four summit meeting of 1960, for example, Secretary of Defense Thomas Gates became convinced that the conference was about to collapse. As a precautionary move, Gates ordered a worldwide alert of U.S. military forces. Not being familiar with the military's defense conditions and alerting procedures, the defense secretary sent a message ordering the Joint Chiefs of Staff to call a "quiet" alert on a "minimum need to know" basis. Gates did not specify which defense condition he wished to have implemented. The Joint Chiefs, studying Gates's message, decided to go to DEFCON 3. They also followed the secretary's order about restricitng information. As news of the alert spread and became public, Pentagon spokesmen were unable to explain why it had been called. U.S. military preparations sent a diplomatic signal quite different from Gates's simple desire to have a "quiet" alert should the situation at the summit deteriorate.[9]

It is unwise to rely solely on military advisers to provide expertise about alerts. As we have seen, military predominance in the fashioning and executing of military alerts may have unintended diplomatic consequences. It would be advisable to have a specific senior official—the President himself, his secretary of defense or his assistant for national security affairs—assigned the specific responsibility of understanding alert procedures and acting as the direct supervisor of an alert during a crisis. Robert McNamara's detailed supervision of all aspects of the naval blockade of Cuba during the missile crisis is a useful precedent for future crises.

Some progress has already been made in this regard. During the transition between his election and inauguration, President Carter stated that one of his foremost tasks would be to study the military chain of command and mobilization procedures in order to be fully prepared should a crisis erupt during his first days in office.

The second recommendation concerns the general readiness status of American forces under peacetime conditions. The high level of readiness exhibited by U.S. strategic forces does not appear to be justified by current threats to national security. Readiness under noncrisis conditions can and should be relaxed significantly. Of the billions of dollars a year spent on strategic forces, many hundreds of millions are used to maintain forces at an unnecessarily high state of readiness.

Ten years ago B-52s used to fly continuous airborne alert missions. A number of bombers were actually kept airborne at all times, equipped with nuclear weapons and prepared to proceed to their targets if given the order. That practice was discontinued several years ago when the Defense Department realized it was wasting money on an unnecessary readiness luxury. Now bombers pull alert at the end of the runway and save a substantial sum of money. Similar cost-saving measures in other strategic forces should be investigated.

Is it necessary to maintain such a high percentage of nuclear submarines on station all the time? Do so many bombers have to be constantly on alert, ready to be launched within a matter of minutes? Significant savings could be realized by some marginal relaxation in strategic readiness, and defense dollars could be spent more productively in other areas.

The third recommendation, and a possible cost-saving device, is for the creation of a strategic reserve force. This could be accomplished by mothballing some fraction of the American ICBM, SLBM, and heavy-bomber forces. One estimate suggests that maintaining a third of U.S. strategic forces in an inactive status (from which they could be returned to the operational inventory in a matter of weeks) would save perhaps $600 million annually.[10]

In addition to saving money, strategic reserve force would offer other benefits. It would demonstrate U.S. satisfaction with the existing strategic balance and reflect confidence in the adequacy of the U.S. strategic deterrent. It would also permit more flexibility in designing strategic alerts. In a crisis the United States would then have two options: it could either improve the readiness of its operational forces or take steps to activate portions of the strategic reserve force. In some cases the latter step might convey a more dramatic, but at the same time less threatening, diplomatic signal.

The idea of a reserve force does not need to be limited to strategic nuclear forces. The creation of a conventional reserve force would realize many of the same benefits. One suggestion involves a change in U.S. naval deployment patterns. Traditionally, American naval policy has been to keep as much naval power as possible as far forward as possible. In the Mediterranean this has meant maintaining a large concentration of naval vessels, including two aircraft carriers, on assignment to the Sixth Fleet. Removing one aircraft carrier from the Mediterranean would reduce support costs somewhat, but, more important, it would build some slack into the system and provide the United States with a useful means of demonstrating its resolve in a crisis. Maintaining two carriers constantly on station in the Mediterranean might signal American vigilance;

keeping one carrier on station and supplementing it with another one when the next Middle East crisis erupts might provide a more dramatic signal of heightened U.S. concern.

A fourth recommendation is that the Defense Department undertake a comprehensive review of military alerting procedures and defense conditions. The number of steps between peacetime status and readiness for war should be expanded. The various defense conditions need to be kept distinct in militarily useful ways, but there is also a need for a variety of defense conditions which can offer greater diplomatic flexibility. Five DEFCONs are not enough, and there should certainly be more than one intermediate step between DEFCON 4 ("normal peacetime position") and DEFCON 2 ("troops ready for combat").

Soviet military forces have recognized the danger of inflexibility and recently revised their own alert procedures. In November 1975 the Soviet armed forces adopted a new order which would allow for a full mobilization of all Soviet forces except strategic nuclear forces. The military magazine *Voenny Vestnik* reported that the new defense condition, called "assembly," is specifically designed to permit the mobilization of large bodies of troops for immediate action while avoiding the brinkmanship which a full alert of strategic nuclear forces might entail.[11]

A final recommendation concerns the American use of military alerts in any future crisis. The United States is currently improving the accuracy of its strategic missiles; the Pentagon continually urges the development of new limited-yield nuclear warheads. The proposals advanced by former Defense Secretary Schlesinger—the so-called Schlesinger Doctrine—are aimed at developing nuclear war-fighting capabilities short of massive destruction. The effect of the doctrine is to emphasize the utility of nuclear forces, to focus thinking on the actual use of nuclear weapons. It also creates pressures to use alerts of strategic nuclear forces to send diplomatic signals.

This is a serious step in the wrong direction. No country should resort to an alert of its nuclear forces except in cases of vital national importance. For most crises a selective alert of conventional forces will not only pose a more credible threat to an opponent, but will also minimize the danger of misinterpretation. A worldwide alert is an appropriate military precaution only in the event of an extreme crisis.

So long as the national objectives and interests of the United States and the Soviet Union clash in various areas around the world, there will be crises. And so long as there are crises there will be military alerts and shows of force. Alerts will continue to be an important element of crisis diplomacy and will serve as the first step in the continuation of politics by other means. The two nuclear superpowers, and other nations as well, must recognize their obligation to understand the process by which alerts are implemented, the means by which they are interpreted, and the dangers they pose for international security.

NOTES

1. The use of military alerts as signals has received little scholarly attention. The general subject of diplomatic signaling is analyzed by Robert Jervis, *The Logic of Images in International Relations* (Princeton, N.J.: Princeton University Press, 1970). Other works more specifically on the subject of crisis diplomacy include Ole R. Holsti, *Crisis, Escalation, War* (Montreal: McGill-Queen's University Press, 1972); Charles F. Herman, *Crisis in Foreign Policy* (Indianapolis: Bobbs-Merrill, 1969); and Alfred Vagts, *Defense and Diplomacy* (New York: King's Crown Press, 1959).

2. See, for example, Barbara Tuchman, *The Guns of August* (New York: Macmillan, 1962); and Ludwig Reiners, *The Lamps Went Out in Europe* (New York: Pantheon Books, 1955).

3. Holsti, *Crisis,* pp. 199-200. This is also the argument of John D. Steinbruner, *The Cybernetic Theory of Decision* (Princeton, N.J.: Princeton University Press, 1974).

4. Quoted in Graham T. Allison, *Essence of Decision* (Boston: Little, Brown, 1971), p. 141.

5. Much of the following information on U.S. government decisions during the Yom Kippur war was collected by the author in off-the-record interviews with senior government officials who declined to be identified. Where possible, reference is made to press accounts which corroborate information gained in interviews.

6. See David Binder, "An Implied Soviet Threat Spurred U.S. Forces' Alert," *New York Times* (November 21, 1973): 1.

7. Drew Middleton, "Soviet Military Abilities Altering Power Balance," *New York Times* (October 26, 1973): 21.

8. Many American forces in Europe had been moved to DEFCON 3 very early in the Yom Kippur war.

9. David Wise and Thomas B. Ross, *The U-2 Affair* (New York: Random House, 1962), pp. 146-47.

10. Richard L. Garwin, Testimony prepared for the Senate Armed Services Committee, June 7, 1973.

11. Reported in the *Washington Star-News* (November 26, 1975): A-8.

COMMUNICATIONS, COMMAND, AND CONTROL:
THE NERVES OF INTERVENTION

Davis B. Bobrow

Discussions of the impact of new technologies on military matters in general, and military intervention in particular, tend to concentrate on weapons and their ancillary hardware. In effect, military systems are treated as unitary actors with an integrated and coherent nervous system, and military conflicts are treated as at most a series of set-piece battle engagements. Issues of communications, command, and control (C^3) and the pertinent technologies of information handling and dissemination are slighted, together with the impact of the pertinent equipment (satellites, computers, and signal transmission and encryption items). The result is a distorted image of the consequences and limits of military intervention now and in the foreseeable future.

While appropriate C^3 does not establish the merits of any particular military intervention, optimistic illusions about C^3 cannot help but inflate the expected value attributed to an intervention policy.[1] Such illusions endow policy makers with knowledge which they may well not have and gloss over manifest limitations on wise decision making.[2] They assume that tables of organization and weapon inventories provide the information to predict how the military will perform in practice.

Lack of attention to C^3 by national security experts in this country has resulted in chronic overestimation of the capacity of the U.S. to play military chess games and to a general lack of perception about the realities of intervention. It

AUTHOR'S NOTE: The views expressed in this paper are the personal opinions of the author and do not necessarily reflect those of any organization with which he is affiliated. Barry Goldman provided helpful research assistance. I am indebted to Oliver Boileau for helpful comments on an earlier draft.

leads to plans and outcome estimates which assume that Weberian notions of bureaucracy characterize the real working of national security organizations and the military. Alternatives are assessed as if perfect information were present à la economic rationality models, or at least as if the imperfections of information were known.

The purpose here is to provide a frame of reference for thinking about C^3 with respect to military intervention, illustrated by appropriate examples to the extent that the public record allows. The issues and their implications surely deserve serious attention from those who specialize in the behavior of people and large organizations. Unfortunately, although much wisdom has been displayed by many of the technologists and military professionals who have worked on C^3 problems,[3] social scientists have contributed little beyond general cybernetic theorizing and human factors engineering assistance.[4]

GENERAL CONTEXT FOR C^3

C^3 is usefully thought of as a collection of means (people, equipment, and procedures) to improve the performance of the participants in national security activities of intelligence planning, policy selection, and implementation. One source of improvement involves contributing to coordination with friendly foreign groups and signaling to hostile or ambivalent foreign groups. Any evaluation of C^3 is driven by judgments of the external international environment, the nature of the internal national security system, and the purposes for which military force can or should be used. These critical judgments are of necessity forecasts, because all the components of C^3—training people; developing, procuring, deploying equipment; and modifying procedures—have substantial lead times.

To convey the importance of general forecasts for C^3 analyses, one perspective will be provided on the shape of the international environment, the nature of warfare and military technology, and national decision-making processes. This may be treated as an invitation to substitute other views and trace their C^3 implications.

International Environment

We expect the U.S. to experience a further relative decline in military and economic power and to replace blanket obligational commitments to come to the military defense of others with specific assessments of the quid pro quo benefits and costs to this country. The U.S. military presence overseas will decrease further, and across-the-board notions of which nations are hostile or friendly will be replaced by perceptions of specific, selective, and rapidly changing areas of cooperation and opposition. An increasing number of governments and movements will be able to impose substantial damage and casualties on the U.S. should we engage in military intervention. Incidents treated as crises will occur in a wide variety of geographic areas and will involve a diverse range of issues and participants. In part because of their variety, crises will increasingly involve ad hoc coalitions rather than neat lineups established by formal alliances and treaties. The members of these coalitions will have different stakes in any given crisis, and accordingly will not want to depend fully on anyone else for their C^3. Crises will be salient issues with many possible ramifications and thus will stimulate the desire for centralized management at the national level.

The joint consequences of these developments bear centrally on the problem of military intervention. First, U.S. guarantees to use force in situations other than the direct defense of U.S. territory will have less credibility in the absence of specific, reinforcing military signals. Second, U.S. thresholds of value which must be crossed to warrant the use of any particular level of force or degree of military intervention will rise, and thus there will be a demand for more intermediate options. Third, there will be an increased need to have bargaining capability and latitude following any particular military step, and termination will be required as an always available option.

Some conclusions follow for desired C^3 performance. First, C^3 will have to make credible to U.S. and foreign decision makers the feasibility of selective military actions and pauses in the application of force. Second, it will have to be based on unilaterally controlled equipment available for use at will. Third, it will have to provide the highest national officials with a wide range of information about all of the parties involved in the crisis or potential intervention situation—including ourselves—and it must have the ability to guide our behavior in detail. Thus U.S. C^3 will have to enable unfiltered communication between the highest-level officials and the action elements of the military. Fourth, the capabilities will have to be global rather than area-bound. Fifth, they will have to allow for flexible, quick meshing, given uncertainty about the participants, issues, and U.S. organizations which may be involved.

Such integrative capacity is needed within U.S. forces, between U.S. forces and allies in a particular situation, and between central U.S. authorities and the leaders of all involved parties. On the U.S. side, our highest officials will be best served by a C^3 capability which links together elements of the U.S. government within and without the military at home and abroad. These properties are essential to the genuine availability of the option to pursue effective coercive diplomacy.

As George and his colleagues have argued, effective coercive diplomacy requires centralized management of intervention instruments and signals of intent.[5] It calls for speedy and accurate communication vertically through the institutional hierarchy and a high degree of compliance with central directives. Communication channels must be available and signals must be clear. If these requirements are met, it is possible to pursue the tactics of coercive diplomacy: appropriate demonstration, graduated escalation, and continuing diplomacy. The emphasis lies not on inflicting maximum damage, but rather on communicating that others may either modify their policy or face costs well beyond the likely benefits they will accrue from persisting in the confrontation. U.S. officials can pursue coercive diplomacy effectively only to the extent that U.S., allied, and adversary C^3 permit.

In addition, effective pursuit of coercive diplomacy carries with it a massive intelligence burden in terms of knowledge about C^3 and its distribution to U.S. decision makers. Three facets of intelligence information stand out: (1) indications and warnings of approaching confrontations, the withdrawal of third parties from a continuing or impending conflict, and the exploitation by adversaries of pauses; (2) estimates of the probability that particular signals will be received, interpreted, and responded to in particular ways, including the value attached to incremental coercive actions by the U.S. and its associates, and estimates of delay or failure to respond to coercive actions by adversaries (all of which imply intelligence about their C^3 systems); and (3) estimates of adversary and third-party perceptions of our and their C^3 capabilities with respect to the knowledge and control which effective coercive diplomacy entails. These intelligence requirements may themselves give rise to actions on our part whose consequences raise serious intervention, coercive diplomacy, and C^3 issues, e.g., attacks on intelligence collectors, such as the *Liberty, Pueblo,* and EC-121 incidents.[6]

Finally, the effective use of coercive diplomacy erases the well-entrenched bureaucratic distinctions between "strategic" and "tactical" resources. Situations with military intervention possibilities become matters of the highest importance to national decision makers, and strategic ends are played out through tactical actions. A C^3 system which reflects this fact spans bureaucratic territories, as must the intelligence provision discussed earlier.[7]

Warfare and Military Technology

Future warfare and military technology characteristics which bear on C^3 include: (1) the sheer volume of information; (2) the short time before substantial opportunity costs are incurred; (3) the need to coordinate operators of weapons systems, units of the same military arm, several arms and services, and cooperating national military establishments; (4) the geographic dispersion of relevant forces; (5) the feasibility of inflicting destruction with low collateral damage; and (6) the possibly disrupted decision environment of the adversary.

Those who manage and engage in military interventions, be they civilian or military, are increasingly exposed to massive doses of information. In part this reflects the increased use of reconnaissance satellites, drones, and remote-piloted vehicles (RPVs) to collect and transmit a wide variety of military intelligence information, to identify targets, and to serve as communications relays.[8] Another source of data in the information explosion lies in sensor systems associated with the image of the automated battlefield. Involving a number of technologies, they transmit observations directly or through relays to a decision point—which may be human, computer, or man-machine—to inform and focus the application of weapons.[9]

From a C^3 perspective, these innovations greatly increase the dependence of commanders on communications and pose massive problems of digestion, or the discriminating recognition of patterns or signatures. Reconnaissance and battle-field sensor observations improve military performance only when they can be interpreted accurately and meaningfully. To the extent that pattern recognition and interpretation tasks are delegated to computers, command and control quality depends critically on foresight about the diagnoses of patterns and on the reliability and perishability of the input and stored data and the stored software. It also depends in extremely critical ways on the discriminating power of sensors and pattern recognition software, so that we don't confuse the forces of adversaries with our own and neutral forces or with a decoy. As pattern recognition and interpretation are delegated to subordinates, command and control quality depends on their knowledge and acceptance of certain rules of interpretation and of engagement. These rules may not be stable throughout a military intervention. If they are changeable, still another communication requirement must be satisfied.

Information volume per se need not stress command and control if there exists ample time for digestion. The striking feature of evolving military technology is that information multiplies and the time available for effective action based on this information shrinks. The general nuclear attack problem which triggered advances in the principal C^3 technologies well illustrates this point. Concerns with deterrence and fear of incurring a first strike led to the proliferation of high-technology intelligence-collection means, transmission and analysis networks, and computer centers to provide strategic and tactical warning of such an eventuality. Yet at the same time advances in weapons technology reduced the period between beginning to prepare a launch and its impact. Information expands while other phenomena work to constrain the time for wise use of it. The problem applies to the conventional battlefield as well, with acceleration in the speed, reach, and rate of fire of major offensive and defensive systems and in the general rate of destruction in battle, e.g., the attrition rates in the Yom Kippur war. In effect, C^3 technologies are racing weapons technologies to provide the capacity for sound decision which the weapons technologies assume for their owner and work to take away from an adversary. These time-shrinking trends explain the technological emphasis on "real-time" information through almost instant communication. However, for C^3 we must also consider the time for interpretation, decision, transmission of orders and their implementation, and the status of each mode and action point.

Faced with the prospect of little time for analysis, choice, and implementation of decisions, one recourse is to prestructure sequences of interpretation and action, with heavy reliance on computers to apply the structure to incoming information and outgoing directives. However, prestructured sequences imply the ability to conceive of alternative situations which may arise and of preferred and feasible responses to those situations. The decision rules which underlie these conceptions must be clearly conveyed to those who write the relevant software and ought to pervade their product. Experience with complex computer programming raises questions about the level of consistency required even if we grant sufficient foresight.[10]

Another recourse in the face of time-poor and information-rich decision problems is decentralization and delegation. However, it may be unrealistic to assume stable decomposability, i.e., that relatively independent units or chunks of the problem can be identified well in advance and preserve their boundaries over time.[11] Also, national leaders may reject delegation in situations with great political and collective welfare stakes. Steps toward decentralization may moderate the time bind for command and control, reduce the information overload problem at the pinnacle of a command hierarchy, and lessen the communications needed to and from that pinnacle. However, even with stable decomposability, there is a somewhat offsetting requirement for numerous coordinating communication links among the decentralized command and control units.

The technology and the doctrine associated with advanced weapons make coordination and communication more complex and demanding. Doctrine envisions coordinated operations across service lines and, in military alliances, across national lines. These coordination expectations are only as valid as the C^3 capacity to turn them into realities. Technological requirements are that the communications systems be accessible and in some sense transparent to each other. There are also issues of electronic design and of language and codes. These matters are unlikely to be handled adequately without standardized communications technology among the parties expected to coordinate their actions.

Institutionally, coordination requires agreements on procedures and authority. Some of these agreements pertain to communications per se, e.g., message priorities and spectrum allocation. Others involve the central issues of autonomy and subordination across service and national lines. If these agreements are not reached in peacetime, it is wishful thinking to expect them to be reached quickly in the teeth of a major crisis or an active, intense war. And, most important, accessibility to and transparency of our C^3 implies a substantial element of trust and confidence in cooperative intent. Indeed, it can be argued that the failure to meet these C^3 requirements evidences distrust and somewhat shaky cooperative intentions. There is a tension between these issues and the very uncertainty of future international situations, with fluidity in the identities of allies, neutrals, and foes in possible military interventions. We might adapt by having multiple C^3 systems, some being widely accessible and transparent and others being unilateral and tightly held. However, that involves expense and, should it be a policy adopted widely, injects a serious element of uncertainty about the commitments of military parties to one another.

The geographic dispersion of military units relevant to most intervention situations compounds the coordination problem. We are far removed from the time when a commander could literally overlook his forces from some "commanding height." C^3 and its component technologies become the basis, then, for monitoring conflict situations—for monitoring our own forces, for selecting courses of action, and for directing forces. It is difficult to overestimate the dependency all this implies. Dependency suggests two other criteria to be considered in thinking about C^3: survivability and security.

Since effective military performance depends on C^3, it is only prudent to be concerned with the extent to which it will be there.[12] The hazards of man and nature to which it may be vulnerable include direct destruction, disruption through degradation by intentional human action (e.g., jamming, insertion of misinformation), poor performance due to unintentional human action (e.g., fatigue, distraction), and, finally, breakdowns due to weapons effects (e.g., electromagnetic pulse) or natural phenomena (e.g., earthquakes) or mechanical failure. While expensive, redundancy is perhaps the best protection against these problems. Any attempt to judge whether or not C^3 systems are redundant enough involves considering the problems of "end-to-end survivability" in the sense of technological or human bottleneck nodes in a communications and command network. And it is crucial to discard the premise that the most probable bottleneck nodes are the most technologically advanced parts of a C^3 system.

Survivability deals with the availability of our own C^3; security deals with making it unavailable to current or potential adversaries. The more that information to and directives from decision makers must be transmitted prior to military actions, and the greater the extent to which these officials must engage in electronically mediated conversation among themselves, the more opportunities adversaries have *ceteribus paribus* to interpret information and command messages and to foil them actively or passively. When communications security through countermeasures against penetration does not keep pace with dependence on communications, military effectiveness suffers. The exchange between information and coordinated action on the other hand, and granting an adversary advance notice and even opportunity for preemptive action on the other, cannot be calculated usefully except in specific situations. In principle it is always present, as the record of World War II and the Yom Kippur war demonstrate.

Another set of increasingly important C^3 problems arises from weapons that inflict destruction with low collateral damage, so-called precision-guided missiles (PGMs). Parenthetically, the issue of what is in normative terms low collateral damage merits careful examination, and it may well be that we are morally jaded to an undue extent by our visions of, and indeed use of, saturation killers. C^3

enters into how the weapons "find" their target and how we know what damage they have wrought. Certificates of accuracy and target proximity do not render these questions moot. Answers to them are key intervening variables which have serious implications for the consequences of military intervention and the limits on our ability to confine its scope and intensity. Target acquisition relayed to weapons systems and damage assessment after the use of PGMs are C^3 functions. Their quality depends on the extent to which C^3 systems are sound with respect to the considerations discussed previously.

It is important to recognize that the intervenor often will not have a monopoly of PGMs. The ability of small numbers of persons to operate some varieties of these weapons, and their diffusion throughout the world, raise a prospect of special vulnerability for our equipment and elements, in terms of their susceptibility of being located and locked onto by PGMs. C^3 facilities and equipment are always emitters of signals. If we are particularly dependent on vulnerable, fancy C^3, the diffusion of PGMs may work to our net disadvantage against a less dependent adversary. Finally, PGMs may increase the feasibility of attacks which disrupt or "behead" C^3 systems without the massive general damage to military forces or civilian targets needed to almost automatically trigger a massive response. The deterrence implications are clear, even if the proper solution is not.

National Decision Processes

National decision processes provide the third major elements of the context for C^3. While probable instances of future U.S. military intervention are not all crises, they are more likely to be so than they are to be extended conventional campaigns, general nuclear war, or prolonged occupation and peacekeeping situations. Accordingly, it seems useful to note some well-established properties of (at least U.S.) decision processes about military intervention in crises, and their implications for the C^3 that national security establishments will seek and use.[13] These features will suggest ways in which C^3 might help compensate for decision process weaknesses.

No national security establishment is unitary or homogeneous in the considerations which it seeks to satisfy through C^3. The C^3 that is developed, procured, institutionalized, and practiced will depend on specific configurations of bureaucratic and political power and interest. However, it is reasonable to assume that specialists and specialized bureaus seek the technology and procedures most conducive to their specialization and try to minimize compromises with other specialties. Communicators concentrate on message transmission in terms of volume, speed, reliability, and signal-to-noise ratios. Operational commanders concentrate on the ability to direct forces subordinate to them effectively and with minimum outside interference. Intelligence specialists concentrate on information about relevant others, supplying it to their own superiors and protecting their sources of supply. High-level military officials concentrate on the status of their own forces and on achieving military success along sanctioned lines of command through the execution of well-staffed-out and previously approved plans. Civilian officials responsible for defense matters concentrate on national policy options and military compliance with established policy directions. Civilian officials principally involved in bargaining with adversaries and third parties concentrate on the use of forces to signal intent and capability, and wish to be ensured that their control is absolute and detailed. The highest-level political officials give C^3 little attention except in periods of tension; but, if asked, they emphasize their need to know that strong actions are really necessary, their need to counsel with trusted advisers, their desire for many options and as much time as possible, their need to be intimately involved in the details of ongoing intervention in a highly public way, and their insistence on hedges against intervention getting out of hand and going beyond what they had in mind.

Three general points emerge about the C^3 posture that these tendencies generate in the absence of extremely strong countervailing influence. First, much more attention is paid to vertical C^3 within a hierarchy than to horizontal C^3 within or between hierarchies, or diagnolly across hierarchies. Second, everyone tends to pay much more attention to aspects of C^3 which are under their jurisdiction or involve support for their technology, information requirements, or command authority, than to aspects outside of their jurisdiction or which use their technology and information and exercise authority and restraint over them. This tendency would not matter if all the participants in military intervention paid equal attention to C^3 and had equal resources of money and human capital to pursue their concerns. That balanced situation does not prevail in complex national security establishments. The highest levels of decision makers probably pay the least ongoing attention, and their interests and needs are least likely to be well represented in the ongoing design of C^3 (other things being equal). Given a cultural set of preferences for technology, resources favor the most technological rather than the most human-intensive parts of C^3. Third, this situation results in substantial problems of C^3 balance and system coherence. Technologically, specialized hardware proliferates. In terms of information processing, overload occurs at postautomatic data processing points. As for communication, critical links are omitted.

There will, of course, be instrumental adaptations over time. Specific areas of unsatisfactory performance found through experience are corrected in piecemeal fashion. Systemwide alternatives go unexplored. For example, the need to use nongovernmental communication channels between the U.S. and the USSR leaders in the 1962 Cuban Missile Crisis provided impetus for the "hot line." Such adaptations are generally helpful, but they do not come to grips with the fundamental problem, which is that decision support systems are designed by some people for others who eventually find themselves asking questions, seeking alternatives, and issuing orders which no central design unit envisioned or turned into operating C^3 equipment and procedures. As the range of environmental problems that raise questions of military intervention increases, the more likely this outcome seems.

In real intervention situations, a number of behaviors occur with fair regularity. First, the sheer volume of information and messages which participants in the C^3 system generate increases enormously, and the importance attached by originators to any piece of those data rapidly inflates. Forwarding capacity becomes inadequate and major backlogs occur. The inflation of importance attached to given pieces of information defeats the purpose of precedence category systems. Second, the need for and attempts at coordination beyond narrow, vertical lines increase rapidly. If "official" C^3 systems do not do the job, participants at all levels seek ad hoc ways to accomplish what they feel is necessary and appropriate. Conferencing behaviors are one adaptation where the conferees set aside considerations of communication security. At high levels, executives turn to trusted advisers, whether or not these advisers have the benefits of the information that advanced C^3 systems purportedly supply. Third, the involvement of high-level, nonspecialist officials increases rapidly. Accordingly, the information sought from, and action alternatives to be executed through, C^3 change from those expected by lower-level specialists. Fourth, because of information overload and unexpected questions, much of the data in the C^3 system are unused, and those variables that are used are rarely reexamined as frequently as they can be updated. Information actually used often is too old to provide feedback on the consequences of the last action or decision before the next step must be taken. Fifth, command alternatives seem less constrained by what high-level officials can know and stipulate than by the habitual modes of thought and operation of those who must implement them. The inevitable detailing out of command directions seems to drift toward previous practices in the "system." The eventual actions may be ones which, if known to central decision makers when they issued their general command, would have led them to different choices.

As the intervention or near-intervention unfolds, conflicts of goals and priorities become exacerbated. Participants place different priorities on bringing situations within some tolerable range or achieving very focused, preselected outcomes, or on such matters as U.S. domestic political support or adversary perceptions or military victory in the theater of engagement. As military stresses and the intervention drag on, the C^3 system degrades in terms of the fidelity of information sent upward and compliance with commands downward. Central political authorities will not wish to continue the intervention indefinitely while it takes lives, consumes materiel, and threatens escalation and reprisal. They will seek to use C^3 to signal cooperative as well as hostile intent, to indicate interest in terminating the conflict.[14] As a result, the control they exercise may become strained and the information they receive from those caught up in hostilities distorted in numerous ways.

C^3 can be designed to ameliorate or to intensify certain pervasive tendencies in decision processes. Students of crisis management have observed decreases in the number of options considered, in the ability to invent new options, and in the consideration of information which contradicts prior premises. They emphasize the prevalence of conformist thinking, subjective foreshortening of the time available for decision, reversion to historical analogies that are not thought through, increasingly negative stereotypic thinking about the adversary, and inattention to various possible outcomes from the decision makers' own actions. The information storage, processing, and presentation elements of C^3 systems can exacerbate these tendencies or help to curb them. We can imagine a C^3 which presents options with regard to indications and warnings, facilitates dynamic planning and reprogramming, and provides salient information counter to established conclusions. We can imagine more objective calculations of the opportunity cost of delays in decisions (or the range of probable costs), similarity-checking routines which compare current decision situations with suggested historical analogies, alternative models of adversary decision processes and constraints which explicate their behavior, and causal path displays to show a variety of paths from a given action choice into the future. Alternatively, we can imagine funnel-like C^3 systems which filter out options, present impossibility conditions, for minority views, suppress contradictory information, and create a compulsion for immediate decisions.

The impact of C^3 systems on these matters depends more on their "soft" than on their "hard" ingredients. We know that people often make a number of errors in estimating the present and the future. It is easy to imagine subroutines in computer programs and sections in information display formats which would show officials the implications of their biases and raise questions about the importance of such biases in their judgments. For example, intervention planning is prone to conjunctive optimism, or overestimation of the probability of success. The success of individual steps may be quite probable (especially of the first step), but the overall probability of success with a large number of steps can be rather low. Assessments of the risks of intervention are prone to disjunctive pessimism, or underestimation of the probability of failure. The probability of each unwanted event occurring may be quite low (especially of the first event), but the probability of the intervention plan breaking down if there are a large number of unwanted events can be rather high.[15] Instead of surfacing these biases and showing their implications, C^3 systems can ignore them, thus exacerbating their effects because of inaccurate perceptions that elaborate information technology and modern information displays are especially objective.

In sum, the decision process context suggests these criteria to evaluate C^3: (1) the extent to which it is the product of normal bureaucratic processes; (2) the extent to which participants in military intervention situations resort to informal "patches" on the extant systems; and (3) the extent to which the "soft" components of C^3 systems exacerbate or ameliorate well-known problems in decision making and estimation.

SOME OBSERVATIONS ON U.S. C³

The public record on U.S. C³ (consisting of congressional testimony, committee reports, and major statements by high officials in the Department of Defense) provides a general sense of the existing and planned systems, priority problems in official eyes, and management arrangements.[16]

Institutions

On May 21, 1970, Deputy Secretary of Defense David Packard established the Office of Assistant to the Secretary of Defense (Telecommunications). Before that time there was no unified management center in the office of the secretary of defense, and this action held promise even if it was confined to only one "C"—telecommunications. Subsequently retitled several times, by February 1974 command and control had been added to its charter under the banner of director, telecommunications and command and control systems. While the previously existing Defense Communications Agency (reporting to the JCS) had been responsible since 1960 for establishing a Defense Communications System (DCS), it had and has little control over tactical communications, which remain under the control of the military departments. In 1971, even the 25% of Department of Defense communications included in DCS was composed of personnel and facilities belonging to the military departments. In February 1975, the Special Subcommittee on Defense Communications of the House Committee on Armed Services concluded that there was still no effective central authority over defense telecommunications and that the services continued to protect jealously their prerogatives.

This institutional history suggests that it is purely fortuitous if deployed U.S. C³ facilities, technology, and equipment complement one another. Given a procurement lead time of a good ten years, we have some sense of the limitation on synergy in the U.S., C³ system. The institutional roots of C³ are overwhelmingly in the military departments rather than in the domain of elected authority, the office of the secretary of defense, the JCS, or the Commander in Chiefs. The inheritance of C³ runs counter to centralized high-level management of military intervention and of our forces in general.

Systems and Plans

The chosen instrument to remedy these shortcomings is the World Wide Military Command and Control System (WWMCCS). Under the authority of the WWMCCS Council, it is intended to bring high-level policy perspectives and coherence to Defense C³. Two charts will clarify WWMCCS. The first shows the core systems of WWMCCS in an illustrative network of U.S. military C^3.[17] Two points merit notice—the nuclear emphasis, and primary governance limited to the systems of the Unified and Specified Commands.

Chart I suggests that there are in effect three realms of communications equipment and procedures to handle the four types of missions which U.S. C^3 should support: strategic or limited nuclear war; intense short crisis; prolonged conventional military operations; and routine military functions. The chart suggests that WWMCCS has the scope to integrate C^3 for nuclear missions but lacks governance over the set of C^3 involved in the most likely situations of intervention and near-intervention—intense, short crises, and prolonged conventional military operations. The integration-effective C^3 required for those situations supposedly will happen through what are ubiquitously called interfaces. In Chart II some interfaces are shown schematically. The core of WWMCCS is the National Military Command System (NMCS) and the directly related "national" command centers, whether ground-based or airborne.

Chart I: Worldwide Military Command and Control Network[17]

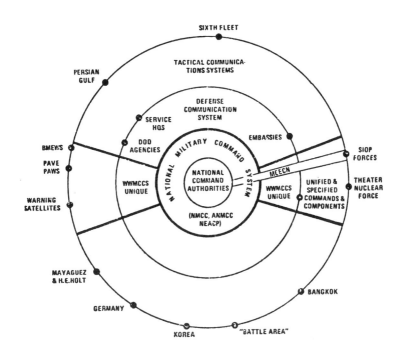

Chart II: WWMCCS Schematic

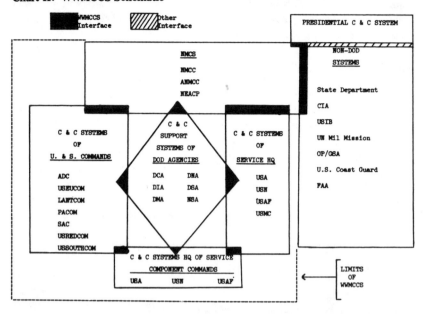

Chart II gives some sense of the linkage problems but does not display the variety of interface modes with very different probable performances in terms of survivability, reliability, and speed. At one extreme is interoperability, where linked technologies move messages quite smoothly; at the other are message centers with numerous human steps required. At one extreme, conferencing and skip-echelon arrangements allow for direct communications from the President to a military field unit and direct simultaneous communication among geographically and hierarchically scattered parties; at the other, messages move serially through command levels. Clearly one requirement for strong, effective linkage is compatible automatic data processing (ADP), given communication volumes of many megabits. Major efforts have been reported to ensure compatible ADP at the heart of WWMCCS, but that leaves the complex, extended periphery. The quality of the linkages critically affects the performance that can be expected of U.S. C^3, since bottleneck nodes degrade the performance of a network.

WWMCCS deserves to be assessed as a system, but not assumed to be one simply because it is called a system in official directives and tables of organization. A man-machine system exists when the component elements not only emerge from research, development, test, and evaluation, but are deployed and built into the standard operating procedures of the relevant institutions. We should distinguish between the system as promise and the system as reality. To estimate the time to fulfill the promise, two sorts of information need to be considered. The first is the time required for the components being developed to be internalized into the national security establishment. The second is the extent to which there is a valid, coherent system architecture driving development of hardware and the soft elements of future U.S. C^3. Without such an architecture, the whole may well be less than the sum of the parts.

The public record suggests that at this time WWMCCS is largely a paper system. Priorities for realizing a working system relate to the nuclear forces. In part this stems from the realization, reflected in Secretary Schlesinger's statement several years ago, that our nuclear weapons are more survivable than the C^3 related to them.[18] In part, it reflects the extremely complicated and critical C^3 implications of the policy of flexible nuclear response options. Major development and procurement programs are under way to support nuclear C^3 including the Advanced Airborne National Command Post (AABNCP), the Minimum Essential Emergency Communications Network (MEECN), more survivable Air Force Satellite Communications (AFSATCOM II), and Extremely Low Frequency (ELF) communications with the nuclear submarine force. Other programs concern C^3 for theater nuclear forces, especially in NATO. Many of these programs are expected to continue well into the 1980s before full procurement and deployment are achieved.

For the nonnuclear situations in which military intervention may be more likely, we find an even wider gap between the abstract term "system" and the reality of severe performance limitations. This domain is that of the Defense Communications System and the tactical communications rings in Chart I. There are substantial problems of capacity, security, and reliability. The first phase of efforts to improve the transmission system in Europe are not programmed for completion before 1980. Within the services, message handling and processing is still largely manual, and while there are five-year automation plans, we are only at an early stage of those five years, even according to plan. The Defense Satellite Communications System (DSCS), which is essential to the WWMCCS crisis management capacity, requires a set of Phase II satellites to have global coverage, but there have been a number of launch failures and the set is not scheduled for launching until well into 1978. The Joint Tactical Communications Program (TRI-TAC) is critical if there are to be effectively coordinated tactical operations by elements of several of the U.S. military services which are not easily accessible to adversary electronic intelligence (as our communications were in Vietnam).[19] The TRI-TAC program was supposed to have provided an all-digital system to be in operation by the mid-1980's with the first production switch delivered to the field by 1976. The production switch, the pacing item, will now not be delivered until late 1979, with the full system operational date slipping at least into the late 1980's.[20] High Frequency (HF) radio, on which the Navy relies, has not provided the accuracy, capacity, or all-weather availability which effective intervention performance tends to assume. The solution, the Fleet Satellite Communications System (FLTSATCOM), was supposed to be available by 1976, but that projection has now slipped to 1979, though interim technologies are being used. As for the Army's Ground Mobile Forces, DSCSII (as shown in Chart I), even when available, will not provide the wartime C^3 that military plans and operations call for. A program of satellites and terminals for that purpose was approved for development in early 1974.

For these future operating systems to enhance C^3 as much as their technological capacity allows, they must be fitted together effectively from end to end of a heterogeneous information-collection/decision/implementation process. The framework for that should exist before major equipment investments and acquisitions. To illustrate the complexity of the architectural task, we note the kinds of questions whose answers have strong implications for C^3 systems. For some envisioned set of national security situations, what functions will the C^3 system have to support? Possibilities include indications monitoring, initial crisis assessment, response planning, action selection, execution, operations monitoring, threat assessment, resource analysis, damage assessment, and adjustments to degradation in the C^3 system itself. Who will have to coordinate and communicate with whom? Beyond the possibilities within U.S. military forces, interagency and intergovernmental coordination may be involved. How current must information, including commands, be? What is the dependence of each relevant actor on different sorts of information? What precedence should different messages have, based on the acceptable time for them to be developed, transmitted, and received in intelligible form by their audience? What mode of communication is most desirable (voice, data, graphics)? What volume of communication will be required? How secure must that communication be?

Answers to these questions reflect and embody positions on the basic issues of who should control force, toward what ends, and on the degree of valid foresight that is possible on international futures. They demand some position on the continuing controversies about command and control: centralization versus decentralization; automated versus manual systems; direct versus serial information flow; and ad hoc versus formal contingency planning. The public record suggests that major efforts at WWMCCS architecture have continued to lag behind major satellite and ADP investments, even though those investments may not have resulted in a great deal of deployed technology. The public record does not suggest that the philosophy embodied in the architecture has been or is being worked out by high civilian authorities, including elected officials, to safeguard against (1) institutionalizing distributions of authority and definitions of utility they do not accept; and (2) omitting ones they take for granted.

Performance

Historical situations of intense, time-sensitive crises and of military actions in prolonged conventional military interventions illustrate poor C^3 performance. Some may believe otherwise and cite the lack of disastrous consequences from the U.S. military alert in October of 1973, with its overwhelming reliance for signaling, on the part of both the U.S. and the Soviets, on electronic reconnaissance communicated to national decision makers.[21] I believe that some cautionary experiences with instant-crisis C^3 merit our attention:

1. Four messages ordering that the U.S.S. *Liberty* be moved away from the coasts of Israel and the United Arab Republic, were directed to that ship on June 7-8, 1967. The first of those messages was released by the sender about thirteen hours before the ship was attacked, while the last was released for transmission three and one-half hours before the attack. None of them reached the *Liberty* prior to the attack. Two messages were misrouted and went to the Pacific rather than to the Mediterranean. One of those, upon being retransmitted to the Pentagon, was then missent to Fort Meade. The other was not placed on Fleet Broadcast until nine hours after the attack on U.S.S. *Liberty*. One copy of a message was lost in a relay station and never relayed. All experienced inexcusable delays for in-station processing.

2. On January 23, 1968, two messages were dispatched from the U.S.S. *Pueblo* with a Pennacle designation. That designation denoted a message of major significance and required immediate delivery to national command authorities. As a result of delays for processing, these messages required two and one-half and one and one-half hours, respectively, before they were delivered to national command authorities in Washington.

3. Three messages, reporting that an EC-121 aircraft was being tracked by North Korean aircraft, were dispatched to the Joint Chiefs of Staff from Korea on April 15, 1969. Those messages required one hour and sixteen minutes, three hours, and a half-hour, respectively, for transmission to Washington.

4. Analysis of Navy message traffic in the Mediterranean during the Jordanian crisis of September 1970 . . . revealed that outgoing traffic experienced the following delays: Flash, thirty-three minutes; Immediate, three hours, sixteen minutes; Priority, nine hours, fifty-eight minutes; Routine, fifteen hours, thirty-six minutes. . . . In fact, the overall performance of the system in the Mediterranean in September 1970 was not significantly improved over its performance in June 1967.[22]

The examples up to this point are all more than five years old. Let us turn to the *Mayaguez* seizure of May 1975. There are substantial indications of numerous and serious C^3 failures, including: (1) lack of knowledge as to whether the seizure was authorized by the Cambodian government; (2) inability to communicate with the Cambodian government; (3) inability to quickly receive communications from the Cambodian government at a sufficiently high U.S. level of authority to interrupt authorized military actions; (4) inability to ensure that U.S. forces in the area did restrain themselves in line with the intent of central authorities; and (5) inability or unwillingness to terminate conflict without further escalation once the demands with no precise deadlines had been met.[23]

The historical cautions also apply to instances of prolonged military intervention that involved bargaining to achieve some resolution short of elimination of adversaries. For example, the failure of the U.S. military in Vietnam to comply with damage-limiting instructions regarding bombing and the treatment of civilians raises important reservations about command and control performance.

CONCLUSION

Estimates of the consequences and limits of intervention need to be realistic about U.S. C^3 performance. Expectations which will not be fulfilled can have no positive result. To treat promised systems as if they were operating systems and to downplay critical human elements in C^3 can only foster dangerous illusions. With regard to military intervention, there seems little reason to assume that its context, consequences, and limits are fully controllable even with regard to our own behavior. There is little wisdom in striking political-military postures and proclaiming doctrines of coercive diplomacy unsupported by a C^3 capability. That can only lead to unnecessary risks of three kinds: (1) self-delusions about the ability to fine-tune military intervention; (2) preemptive or, at best, highly vigilant, threat cycling behaviors by adversaries who may suspect that U.S. C^3 does not enable the rapid, limited, controlled use of force enunciated by policy; and (3) domestic political attacks on administrations which do not engage in military interventions, since these would be "surgical" and "clean."

Effective C^3 does not guarantee wise policy. It helps provide some necessary conditions for the efficient execution of chosen policy. If crisis management and military intervention have had disappointing results in retrospect, the mere presence of poor C^3 does not provide a sufficient base for deciding what should be done differently in the future. Surely fighting the wrong war, in the wrong place, at the wrong time, for the wrong reasons is the ultimate failure of intelligence, authority, and restraint no matter how well what we formally define as C^3 systems perform.

NOTES

1. The relationship between improvements in C^3 and the projection of military power is hardly new. See H. A. Innis, *Empire and Communications* (Oxford: University Press, 1950).

2. For a stimulating theoretical treatment of maladaptive foreign policy, see James P. Bennett, "Foreign Policy as Maladaptive Behavior," *Papers of the Peace Science Society (International)* 25 (1975): 85-104.

3. Over the years my understanding of the technologies and policy issues involved in C^3 has benefited enormously from many experts (none of whom may agree with anything in this paper), including Arthur Biehl, Eugene Fubini, Charles Herzfeld, Kenneth Jordan, Dorothy Pavkov, Kenneth Plant, Eberhart Rechtin, and Howard Yudkin.

4. On the general perspective, see Karl W. Deutsch, *The Nerves of Government* (New York: Free Press, 1963). For a discussion of the evolution of command and control in the 1960's and a useful bibliography on materials published during that period, see Judith A. Merkle, *Command and Control* (General Learning Press, 1971).

5. The seminal treatment is that of Alexander L. George, David K. Hall, and William E. Simons, *The Limits of Coercive Diplomacy* (Boston: Little, Brown, 1971). My thinking about the perspective has benefited greatly from discussions with Steve Chan.

6. For analyses of these cases with respect to communications, see U.S., Congress, House, Armed Services Investigating Subcommittee of the Committee on Armed Services, *Review of Department of Defense Worldwide Communications, Phase I,* 92d Cong., 1st sess., May 10, 1971.

7. The need to cut through the strategic/tactical distinction does not find expression in the legislation establishing the new Senate Intelligence Oversight Committee, or in President Ford's Executive Order 11905 (February 18, 1976) on the control and direction of U.S. foreign intelligence. The need to bridge the gap is recognized explicitly by Secretary Rumsfeld in his discussion of C^3 in *Report of the Secretary of Defense, Donald H. Rumsfeld, to the Congress on the FY1977 Budget and its Implications for the FY1978 Authorization Request and the FY1977-1981 Defense Programs* (January 27, 1976), p. 175.

8. For useful summary discussions of reconnaissance, see Ted Greenwood, *Reconnaissance, Surveillance and Arms Control,* Adelphi papers no. 88 (London: International Institute for Strategic Studies, 1972); *World Armaments and Disarmament: SIPRI Yearbook, 1974* (Cambridge, Mass.: M.I.T. Press, 1975), pp. 287-302; and *World Armaments and Disarmament: SIPRI Yearbook, 1975* (Cambridge, Mass.: M.I.T. Press, 1976), pp. 339-401.

9. For an overview of the automated battlefield, see Frank Barnaby and Ronald Huisken, *Arms Uncontrolled* (Cambridge, Mass.: Harvard University Press, 1975), pp. 49-73.

10. On the problems of complex software, see Ralph E. Strauch, "Information and Perception in Limited Strategic Conflict," RAND P-5602 (Santa Monica, Ca.: Rand Corp., Feb. 1976); Joseph Weizenbaum, "On the Impact of the Computer on Society," *Science* 176 (May 12, 1972): 609-14; Morton Gorden, "Burdens for the Designer of a Computer Simulation of International Relations," in *Computers and the Policy-Making Community,* ed. Davis B. Bobrow and Judah L. Schwartz (Englewood Cliffs, N.J.: Prentice-Hall, 1968), pp. 222-45.

11. On the general properties of the cybernetic paradigm for policy systems, see John D. Steinbruner, *The Cybernetic Theory of Decision* (Princeton, N.J.: Princeton University Press, 1974).

12. For some informed discussions of computer and telecommunications interdependence and dependence, with a view toward consequent vulnerabilities, see Ithiel de Sola Pool, "The International Aspects of Computer Telecommunication," *Research Program on Communications Policy, Report No. 15* (Cambridge, Mass.: M.I.T., February 4, 1975); and "The Vulnerable Computer Society," Secretariat for National Security Policy and Long-range Defense Planning, Ministry of Defense, Sweden, 1976, p. 4.

13. Some particularly helpful works are Charles F. Hermann, ed., *International Crises,* (New York: Free Press, 1972); Irving L. Janis, *Victims of Groupthink* (Boston: Houghton Mifflin, 1972); Graham T. Allison, *The Essence of Decision* (Boston: Little, Brown, 1971); Raymond Tanter, "Crisis Management across Disciplines," The Bendix Corporation Applied Science and Technology Division (Ann Arbor, Michigan: August 1974); Cristine Candela, "Decision-making during Crisis," The Bendix Corporation Applied Science and Technology Division (Ann Arbor, Michigan, August 1974); Avi Shlaim, "Failures in National Intelligence Estimates," *World Politics,* 28 (April 1976): 348-80; Howard B. Shapiro, "Crisis Management," Human Sciences Research, HSR-RR-75/3-Cr (March 1975); and Howard B. Shapiro and Patricia L. Cummings, "Problems in the Use of Ad Hoc Structures in DOD Crisis Management and Implications for Change," Human Sciences Research, HSR-RR-76/1-Nr (March 15, 1976).

14. Some empirical evidence of the attention to cooperative as well as hostile behaviors is presented in Linda P. Brady, "Explaining Foreign Policy Behavior Using Transitory Qualities of Situations," CREO Publication no. 51, Mershon Center (Columbus: Ohio State University, 1975).

15. On the pertinent psychological research, see Amos Tversky and Daniel Kahneman, "Judgement Under Uncertainty," in *Benefit-Cost and Policy Analysis—1974,* ed. Richard

Zeckhauser, et al. (Chicago: Aldine, 1975), pp. 66-80. On some implications for international policy systems, see Davis B. Bobrow, "Policy Attention and Forecast Bias" (Paper prepared for delivery at the meeting of the International Studies Association, Toronto, February 25-29, 1976).

16. For detailed discussions, there is little substitute for the testimony in House and Senate over the years by the director of the Defense Communications Agency and, since 1970, the incumbents of the OSD offices—called at different times, assistant for telecommunications to the secretary of defense, assistant secretary of defense (telecommunications), and, most recently, director, telecommunications and command and control systems. For more policy-oriented overviews, the posture statements by Secretaries of Defense Schlesinger and Rumsfeld are especially useful, and it is important to look both in the sections dealing with nuclear forces and in those explicitly titled "Communications, Command and Control." Reference has already been made to the House report titled *Review of Department of Defense Worldwide Communications, Phase I*, and there are two useful follow-up reports: U.S., Congress, House, Special Subcommittee on Defense Communications of the Committee on Armed Services, *Review of Department of Defense Worldwide Communications, Phase II*, 92d Cong., 2d sess., October 12, 1972; and U.S., Congress, House, Special Subcommittee on Defense Communications of the Committee on Armed Services, *Review of Department of Defense Worldwide Communications, Phase III*, 93d Cong., 2d Sess., February 1975. Finally, a useful overview of new technologies from an official point of view is that of Thomas C. Reed, "Command & Control & Communications RDT & E," *Signal* (October, 1975): 6 ff.

17. *Report of the Secretary of Defense, Donald H. Rumsfeld*, p. 173.

18. *Report of the Secretary of Defense, James R. Schlesinger, to the Congress on the FY 1975 Defense Budget and FY 1975-1979 Defense Program* (March 4, 1974), p. 74.

19. *Review of Department of Defense Worldwide Communications, Phase II*.

20. *Review of Department of Defense Worldwide Communications, Phase III*.

21. *New York Times* (November 21, 1973): 1 ff, and (November 22, 1973): 1 ff.

22. *Review of Department of Defense Worldwide Communications, Phase I*, pp. 3-4; *Review of Department of Defense Worldwide Communications, Phase II*, p. 16501.

23. U.S., Congress, House, Committee on International Relations and Its Subcommittee on International Political and Military Affairs, *Seizure of the Mayaguez, Part I: Hearing*, 94th Cong., 1st sess., May 14-15, 1975.

NEW WEAPONS TECHNOLOGY AND ITS IMPACT

ON INTERVENTION

James F. Digby

SOME QUESTIONS

Over the past few years considerable attention has been focused on a new generation of nonnuclear weapons. At their best, some of these promise to make the more traditional weapons—which would be less cost effective and quite vulnerable—obsolete. But as discussion continues, a number of points have been raised which identify serious shortcomings in the practical use of these new weapons and which indicate that they are not likely to be used at their best as military mass meets military mass.

This paper will touch on arguments on both sides of this discussion, and will cover some technical aspects of new weapons, especially precision weapons. It suggests some ways in which the new kinds of weapons may make the forces of the smaller states more powerful in a military sense, but also mentions aspects in which these forces are not miniatures of superpower forces. It raises points which argue against unquestioned acceptance of the belief that the diffusion of technology is a destabilizing influence—but suggests some future uses of precision missiles which are likely to be destabilizing. It explores the prospects for the industrial nations' exercising some restraint over recipient states—but sees little hope of actually turning off the flow of arms to rich, less-developed countries. It discusses how the new technology—at its best—may help the United States to

AUTHOR'S NOTE: Parts of this paper draw on a forthcoming study for the California Seminar on Arms Control and Foreign Policy on the implications of the spread of new nonnuclear weapon technologies.

carry out its security obligations within increasingly stringent economic constraints. And finally, it suggests that prospects are not entirely bleak for arms limitations and for restraints in the use of weapons. But before discussing these matters which relate to immediate policy choices, it is appropriate to get some perspective on the relation between technical means and political behavior.

Raymond Aron, looking back at two world wars, pointed out that the availability of technical excess had caused nations to replace definite war aims with "sublime—and vague—principles," and he discussed the consequences in *The Century of Total War.*[1] A few years later, in 1956, Aron wrote a brilliant essay on war, *De la Guerre,* which is just as much worth reading today as it was then. Following a discussion of the views of those optimists who felt the atomic weapon was so diabolic that it would put an end to war, and those pessimists who heralded the approach of the apocalypse, Aron declared himself a "realist" and said:

> Optimists and pessimists are concerned with the future. Only the realists deal with the present—that is, with a world in which two states have the means of destroying one another and are therefore condemned to suicide or coexistence. In this present which must be measured in years, perhaps in decades, politics do not radically change; they do not exclude violence within nations or in the relations between states. Neither alliances nor revolutions nor traditional armies have disappeared. Frontiers are not unchangeable, transfers of sovereignty have not abated. More than ever, the diplomatic field is a jungle in which "cold-blooded monsters" are at grips with each other. More than ever, all possible means are resorted to—all except one, the use of which might well be fatal and which nevertheless profoundly influences the course of events, just as the British fleet used to assure the freedom of the seas, while anchored at its bases.[2]

Thus, it might be said that we are still in Aron's "present," that it has, in fact, lasted for decades, that the monsters stalking the world jungle have used increasingly powerful means—all except one—and that it is necessary to explore the mechanics of the new means and the limits of their use. While the nature of politics has not changed radically, the military moves available to political leaders are more varied and are open to more players.

This leads me to four sets of questions which suggest why it is important to understand the new generation of weapons:

1. Is military power becoming more divisible? It appears that many of the new precision weapons are well adapted to being used in small packets. Thus, can small states increasingly dispose of military power in significant degree?

2. Is military power—with the new weapons—becoming more usable? If so, this has both its good points and its perils, from the American point of view. While the new weapons might help the United States to back its political moves with a more credible threat, there might be an increase of confrontations—with or without American involvement—which reach the stage of actual combat.

3. Will military power—in use and threat of use—be applied more precisely? Military intervention *can* increasingly be threatened with means that are tailored to objectives.

To what extent will nations actually be restrained? (Their aim should be to get their way without needless risk.)

4. Will there be a trend toward more precise political objectives? The overhanging threat of nuclear intervention should serve as a great incentive to antagonists in nonnuclear war to avoid vague and grandiose goals which might widen the conflict.

The next section of this paper details the mechanics of the new weapons, and later parts discuss the increasingly varied ways they might be used. Understanding these more technical matters is a prerequisite to full consideration of the four sets of questions raised as well as to exploration of the limits of the use of these new weapons and of the limits of military intervention.

ENGINEERING EVOLUTION AND DESCRIPTION OF THE NEW WEAPONS

There are a variety of advances in weapons technology—new kinds of tank armor, new submarine hull designs, automated test equipment, to name just a few. However, the focus here will be on a set of developments which seem central to the topic of precise application of military power, for they have resulted in a new generation of precision-guided weapons and remote-piloted vehicles.

Some Definitions

Elsewhere I have defined precision-guided munitions (PGMs) this way:

A guided munition whose probability of making a direct hit on its target at full range (when unopposed) is greater than half. According to the type of PGM, the target may be a tank, ship, radar, bridge, airplane, or other concentration of value.[3]

This definition includes a wide variety of weapons, with the term "munitions" indicating that they are designed to impact on their target. Thus the increasingly important category of cruise-missiles is included.

A related and overlapping class of weapons includes remote-piloted vehicles (RPVs). Many of this class are designed to be recoverable and are used primarily to carry reconnaissance equipment or devices such as laser designators. Others, designed to impact on the target, qualify as PGMs. An RPV may be defined this way:

A vehicle which is piloted from a remote location by a person who has available much of the same piloting information he would have if he were on board.

Table 1: Examples of Precision Weapons

Designation	Developed by	Range	Guidance	Comments
Anti-Aircraft				
SA-7 Grail	Soviet Union	2.3 miles	Aimed optically; then infrared homing	Portable infantry weapon; shoulder-fired
Rapier	Britain	3.5 miles	Optically tracked; radio commanded	–
Hawk	United States	25 miles	Homes on radar reflection	Long deployed on NATO Central Front
Surface-to-Surface				
Sagger AT-3	Soviet Union	2 miles	Optically tracked; wire-guided	Antitank missile in wide service
TOW MGM-71A	United States	2+ miles	Semiautomatic optical tracking; wire-guided	Antitank missile; 100,000 produced
Harpoon	United States	60 miles	Radar homing	Antiship missile. Can be launched from surface ships, aircraft, or submarines
Tomahawk sea-launched cruise-missile	United States	1,400 miles	Navigates by terrain comparison	Launched from surface ships or submerged submarines
Air-to-Surface				
Pave Way	United States	Free fall	Homes on laser spot	Based on 1,000-lb. or 2,000-lb. standard U.S. bomb
Rockeye	United States	Free fall	Homes on laser spot	Antitank bomblets, carried in dispenser
Maverick	United States	– –	TV-guided; locks on and homes on target	Antitank missile
Martel	Britain/France	35 miles	TV-guided or homes on enemy's radar or radio emissions	– –

Source: *The Economist* (March 27, 1976): 3-5.

Table 2: Examples of Remote-Piloted Vehicles—All U.S.

Designation	Weight	Comments
Praeire	75 lbs. (dry)	Miniature recoverable aircraft carries reconnaissance devices and laser designator; under development.
Walleye II	2,000 lbs. (approx.)	Free-fall bomb guided from remote TV picture; used in 1972.
Condor AGM-53A	2,130 lbs.	Antiship missile for late 1970s. Various forms; can be remotely steered from TV picture
Compass Cope	14,000 lbs. (approx.)	High-flying, carries reconnaissance devices; recoverable.

Source: *Aviation Week* (March 17, 1975): 83-97.

Some people are considering RPV techniques for tanks, submarines, or other vehicles, but in its most common use the term refers to aircraft.

Tables 1 and 2 show examples of PGMs and RPVs from a number of countries. Walleye and Condor, listed as RPVs, are also PGMs.

Technical Bases

Three technological advances have greatly facilitated the development of these new weapons:

1. The capability to produce practical transmitters and receivers which use much higher frequencies than those used in the past. These high frequencies have made it possible to obtain angular accuracies approaching those obtained with visual telescopic sights.

2. Progress in microelectric circuit designs which permit quite complex signal processing and storage to be handled in small, reliable, relatively rugged devices.

3. Progress in the design of nonnuclear warheads. These new designs permit much smaller weapons to have the capability of destroying targets that formerly required much heavier warheads.

Perhaps the most important aspect of PGMs—if they are used under the conditions for which they were designed—is described in the following statement:

Accuracy is no longer a strong function of range; if a target can be acquired and followed during the required aiming process, it can usually be hit. For many targets hitting is equivalent to destroying.[4]

This statement also gives some clues as to what might go wrong. For example, actual experience in the 1973 war in the Middle East showed that acquiring targets, and then recognizing which were hostile and important, was a very difficult job. That war also showed that it was possible to evade relatively slow PGMs, such as the Soviet-supplied Sagger antitank missile, during their fifteen to twenty-five seconds of flight. Israeli defenders quickly learned to take Sagger crews under fire while they were guiding their missiles. Finally, there are a number of ways of interfering with the seeing process. For some of the earlier missiles which use visual sighting, such factors as darkness, battlefield smoke, or ground fog may prevent seeing. (Later systems using long-wave infrared will considerably expand the conditions when seeing will be possible.)

Manpower Needs

An important question to ask about all new systems is what impact they have on manpower requirements. Some of the PGMs require very little training. For example, with TOW, the American-made wire-guided antitank missile, crews are considered trained after a week of instruction, including just one day of actually firing the weapon. But TOW has a semiautomatic feature, requiring only the target to be tracked. Others, like the Sagger and the British Swingfire, require that the crew fly the missile into the target. Thus the crew must track both the missile and its target. This job is significantly harder and imposes substantial additional requirements on training—an observation which was borne out by reports from the 1973 war on the selection and continual retraining of Egyptian missile crews. There are also longer-range PGMs which appear likely to require very substantial efforts in crew training. Nonetheless, the point should be noted that Egyptian, Syrian, and North Vietnamese crews gave a good account of themselves in handling various Soviet-made guided weapons.

Maintenance

The impact of new systems on maintenance needs must also be taken into account. Again taking TOW as an example, experience has shown that its design, which calls for the missile to be left in the container in which it was shipped from the factory until it is used, has worked well. Maintenance is required principally with respect to the tracking equipment and training gear. But others of the new systems which contain many functions—such as Condor—are likely to impose quite severe maintenance requirements, comparable to those being experienced with the highly integrated multipurpose systems of several modern aircraft. Small powers will need to be very cautious in listening to the sales arguments for high-performance but trouble-prone systems.

IMPLICATIONS FOR MILITARY POSTURE, WITH EMPHASIS ON THE SMALLER STATES

This section examines some implications of the new generation of weapons, with particular reference to those aspects which would permit their use in relatively small packages, especially by the smaller powers.

First, both in superpower use in a major engagement and in small-power use in lesser combat situations, the nature of the new weapons is likely to encourage tactics which employ small independent units, perhaps mobile squads with two or three men each. Even such small squads could be quite powerful if equipped with five or ten precision weapons. Weaponry for self-protection might also be carried by some squads, with antiaircraft missiles and antipersonnel weapons as well as the antiarmor weapons which are likely to be primary armament. Besides being quite powerful, these small units would have the advantage both of being more concealable and of permitting the distribution of forces in a way which would tax the target acquisition and the command-control systems of the opponent. It might be expected that both sides would sooner or later break up their forces into these small groupings.

Naturally there are some counterarguments, among them the strain which the control of many independent units would place on command systems and the fact that larger groupings of forces could enjoy more of the benefits of mutual support. But to the extent that this small-unit trend occurs, a small portion of a battlefield occupied by a superpower might bear substantial resemblance to a battle arena occupied by a smaller power. Many of the ingredients of force would be just the same, many of the tactics would be the same, and the ability to hold ground or take it over a limited area might be about the same. Two exceptions will be noted below, when the uses of combined arms and of the supporting structure for PGMs are discussed. In particular, the smaller states are not likely to be able to make efficient, coordinated use of large numbers of aircraft—even if they possess them. Moreover, all military moves will take place in the shadow of superpower nuclear capabilities. So, while smaller states may dispose of locally capable forces, they are different in structure from superpower forces and in the ways their use can be threatened.

Second, it is likely that forces employing the new weapons could be much more easily moved about than traditional forces. Clearly it is easier to move enough TOW missiles over substantial distances (these weigh forty pounds) to counter an armored division than it is to move enough defending tanks. A decade from now, when PGMs and RPVs having a range of several hundred kilometers may be available to support an offensive thrust, it is likely that these weapons can more readily be moved into launch position than the forces for a more traditional offense. This enhanced mobility would seem to affect both lateral deployment—moving forces along a front—and deployment from a central reserve.

A third point has been widely noted: the current generation of PGMs is likely to be effective for forces tactically on the defensive. This is clearly true for those current weapons which are specifically designed for antitank or antiaircraft uses. In one respect this may be true much more generally: the important task of target acquisition is more readily handled against a force which is moving over unfamiliar terrain, as an offense usually must, than it is against a defending force which can be stationed in previously prepared emplacements and provided with a substantial degree of concealment. Note, though, that having a good defense at the tactical level may support an offense at the strategic or campaign level, since an efficient defense would permit a concentration of forces for a thrust. In addition, future postures are likely to include PGMs and RPVs of substantially longer ranges that are capable of functions generally associated with offensive thrusts.

While the taking of ground in the traditional way may not be appropriate to the new weaponry, there may be substituted a kind of leapfrog tactic whereby desired objectives are initially attacked by suppressing their defenses, secondarily attacked by airdrop or by helicopter-borne forces, and finally defended heavily with the attacker's own defensive PGMs. Thus it would be premature to say that the acquisition of PGMs will uniformly add to the stability of those Third World areas to which they are transferred.

Sales pressures for precision weapons are likely to come from many companies in numerous countries. The development and production processes for many current systems are relatively easy, and production is, in fact, under way in a number of industrial countries. As longer-range PGMs become more numerous, there will probably be an increasing tendency to develop guidance and payload packages separately from vehicles. It will still require the huge industrial firms of the large nations to build complex, multipurpose, penetrating-weapon systems, where each part is tightly integrated into the vehicle, but many sensible designs will be producible by smaller companies. While hardly approaching the level of a cottage industry yet, the production of significant numbers of the simpler precision weapons or payload packages by factories in Third World countries may be not many years off.

Despite all these newly feasible ways to use precision weaponry, small and medium powers will still need to allocate a fraction of their defense funds to traditional weapons. There are certain situations which call for tanks, not PGMs. Moreover, a conservative approach would call for concern about a number of difficulties with the new weapons. Some of these are being worked out by the larger powers and arms suppliers; others are too formidable for early solution.

For example, it has already been noted that the early-generation PGMs, which use visual guidance, are subject to such simple countermeasures as smoke and camouflage, and they cannot work in the presence of heavy dust, bad weather, or darkness. Later kinds of guidance systems cope with some of these problems, but as this class of weapons becomes increasingly important to success, so the efforts to counter its effectiveness will become both more vigorous and more ingenious.

This points up an aspect of using the new weapons which may put small powers at a relative disadvantage compared to medium-sized powers: the value of using the new weapons as part of a combined-arms strategy. The Soviets have developed this sort of strategy to a high degree, and some of the more successful Arab attacks in the 1973 war followed Soviet precepts. On the other hand, when Israeli tanks thrust into the Sinai without infantry support they encountered exceedingly high losses, a matter which was later rectified as Israeli infantrymen took Arab antitank missile crews under fire while they attempted to guide their weapons.

An even more important aspect of fully exploiting PGMs has been relatively neglected until recently: the supporting structure. Many analysts have emphasized the great technical improvements which give PGMs almost a "one shot, one kill" capability in one-on-one engagements. But in a large-scale conflict, the characteristics of individual weapons, taken one-on-one, could be dominated by the way thousands of weapons of several types were made to work together in a mutually supportive way and applied effectively to thousands of targets.

This supporting structure has several elements: (1) the advance reconnaissance which localizes targets; (2) the target acquisition system which identifies individual targets right up to trigger-pull; (3) the command function which allocates and marshals the new weapons to the place where they are needed most (each weapon represents substantial military power which a defender would not wish to leave where it would see no use); (4) the transport (perhaps laterally) of the new lightweight but powerful weapons systems; and—most important—(5) the network which replenishes expended weapons.

The importance of this supporting structure can be appreciated when one considers that a brigade commander in World War II might do his job from a situation map that showed where ten enemy infantry battalions and three tank companies were located. In 1980, he and his subordinates might need to keep track of 500 to 1,000 individually moving and independently powerful squad-size units. To fully exploit his PGMs, each of these targets would have to be acquired on an individual basis.

For a large-scale war, along NATO's Central Front, for example, or along the Sino-Soviet border, a decisive aspect might be the destruction of the enemy's supporting structure. Thus each of the five elements named would need to be as survivable as possible, and not easily disrupted. For instance, NATO commanders would need to ensure that replenishment supplies of antitank missiles would continue to arrive at resupply points during battle, and that the quantities on hand and the pathways for resupply were designed to hold up under the attacks that would undoubtedly be pressed against them.

For a small-scale war, where the numbers of targets presented per day were in the tens rather than the thousands, the single-shot kill probability or one-on-one weapon performance might be the dominant factor.

But there is an intermediate case of considerable interest, in connection with the consequences of arms transfers to the nonindustrial countries, where recipients might acquire hundreds of the weapons but be incapable of dealing with all elements of the supporting structure. Another war in the Middle East might well be of this intermediate size. As a part of U.S. policy on arms transfers to the Middle East, it is important to consider the extent to which our government could exercise some continuing control over their large-scale employment, through controlling reconnaissance or replenishment functions essential to the full exploitation of the weapons. It is equally important to consider just how a limited supporting structure may serve to restrict the size of military intervention by any of the newly armed smaller powers.

NEW WEAPONS AND INTERVENTION: THE SUPERPOWERS

There seem to be two pathways to weapons acquisition in the U.S. One path stresses the new precision weapons, which are generally small in size, are relatively cheap in many cases, and (because they are equipped with terminal guidance) tend to have a performance not greatly influenced by the conditions of launch or the type of platform which carries them to the launch point. This last property allows them to be designed independently of their platform, and permits an updating of weapon payload without necessarily changing an adequate and proven vehicle. The weapon and vehicle can obsolesce at different rates. In general, these weapons would be needed in great number.

The other path includes the more traditional weapons, many of which are increasing in size, in complexity, in failure rate, and especially in unit cost. By and large the weapons systems given the highest priority by the services are all of these things, in part because they have multiple functions. Typically, each weapons systems is an integral, interwoven part of a vehicle intended for use directly in the combat area. Such systems include deep-penetration fighter bombers, new tanks, and nuclear-powered guided-missile-cruisers. (Current examples of these systems have unit costs, in FY 1975 dollars, of about $13 million, $1.05 million, and $370 million, respectively.)

There is, of course, a middle ground between the two paths. Successive U.S. directors of defense research and engineering have called for a "high-low mix," that is, for the building of some relatively cheap systems and some more expensive ones. This policy is aimed at the procurement of sufficient numbers of systems to man the necessary locations, but without sacrificing the knowledge obtained in the course of developing the more complex equipment. Another kind of middle ground comes about when the large penetrating platforms are made to carry the simpler and cheaper precision weapons. However, recent experience shows that the "high-low mix" is more an exhortation than an actual policy supported by the services and the Congress. For example, the Army's highest priority for development goes to the "Big 5": the XM-1 tank, the MICV mechanized combat vehicle, the AAH armed attack helicopter, the SAM-D air defense missile, and the UTTAS utility helicopter. Even Admiral Elmo Zumwalt, when he was chief of naval operations, could not gain much support for his proposition to procure a greater number of medium-sized ships in place of fewer large, nuclear-powered ships.

In the United States many complex cost-effectiveness analyses have been made comparing postures heavy in the traditional weapons with those emphasizing new weapons; none is likely to be entirely believable until a great deal more empirical data have been collected. My own view, based on several years of analysis of the relevant pieces, is that those postures heavily emphasizing precision weapons can do an adequate job ten years from now for less money than the traditional weapons would require. Correspondingly, I think that postures relying primarily on the traditional systems, given the current trends in their costs and vulnerabilities, indicate they can hardly be afforded unless U.S. defense budgets increase greatly.

The Soviet policies on weapons procurement are clearly different, and like most Soviet policies their basis is not well understood by Americans. One thing is clear, however: the Russians believe in grinding out multiple copies of the same weapons system in great numbers, as though from a series of sausage factories. The existence of the flow seems a goal in itself. In submarines, in small surface vessels, in artillery, in fighter interceptors, and in tanks, the numbers continue to increase; and the new models are often added to field dispositions without retiring the old. While a decade ago many Soviet designs seemed outdated to Westerners, recent weapon types have combined substantial sophistication with procurement in great numbers.

Until the mid-1960s most new Soviet weapons systems were incremental improvements based on well-tested predecessors. More recently, they have deployed both incremental improvements and quite novel systems, the latter including the mobile SA-6 antiaircraft missile, the ZSU-23-4 optical-or-radar-directed gun, and the important new armored combat vehicle, the BMP. Their precision air defense missiles are quite advanced and they have long had sea-based guided-cruise-missiles of varying degrees of sophistication; however, their great production of wire-guided antitank missiles has been of rather unsophisticated models. Their progress in air-to-surface PGMs and laser-guided bombs appears to be well behind that of the United States. While much of the Soviet debate over how much emphasis to place on the new technology and how to exploit it remains hidden, there does appear to have been a period of doctrinal turmoil.[5]

The continuing Soviet buildup and the availability of new types of weapons have not only led to the current debate on the adequacy of American defenses, but have also raised the complex question of how the United States budget should be allocated between traditional systems and the new classes of weapons. It is the latter choice that bears most directly on the questions of usability and precision of objectives which were raised at the outset of this discussion. Now let us assume that the two classes are (by some measures) equally effective per dollar spent. We would still expect some differences in their usability and in the way they would be deployed. The trend to fewer weapons with high unit costs might encourage a policy of keeping these weapons in a central reserve—mainly in the United States—from which they would not be moved lightly. Nor would deploying this reserve be very easy in a physical sense. On the other hand, sea-launched cruise-missiles, air-launched cruise-missiles, and many of the anti-tank and air defense missiles could be deployed peripherally and could be moved to a new deployment with relative ease, if not in terms of political considerations, at least in terms of physical and strategic ones.

With larger, more expensive weapons, we might expect that prudence would dictate less of a tendency to risk them, since each loss would be so significant. The smaller precision weapons, on the other hand, might seem more usable to national authorities, both because the minimum quantum of arms risked would be low and because the military damage done could be more precisely controlled. For those precision weapons of short range, there is the added factor that their use would more likely be seen as reactive than aggressive. They might be more usable in small numbers because their totality would seem less threatening in an aggressive sense.

Not all classes of PGMs would always seem nonaggressive, however. Consider some of the limited nuclear options so often discussed by former Secretary of Defense James Schlesinger. Some of those options *could* be carried out by nonnuclear missiles, most notably cruise-missiles. The usability of such weapons would appear to exceed that of nuclear weapons of similar range, but still the total sequence of events following such use could never be predicted with much confidence. Whether such a *capability* would lead to substantial changes in stability is hard to say, given the present level of understanding of these matters. In any event, these chains of events can hardly be considered outside the framework of specific contexts, a matter too ambitious for the present discussion.

What can be said is that if a country decided that such a capability looked attractive from a strategic point of view, cost considerations would be unlikely to stop its acquisition and there would be no requirement for a great industrial infrastructure. Many countries will be able to afford from 50 to 500 long-range cruise-missiles by the end of the 1980s. Deterrence, for a time almost the exclusive province of the Americans and Russians, may be "parceled out."[6]

Summing up on this point, I believe that the new precision weapons make an adequate defense posture for the United States more affordable. They also make both American and Soviet military power more usable. They may reduce the superpower monopoly on deterrence—with some unknowable effects on stability. I am not prepared to say that all of this is good, but I am prepared to say that it is different, and that significant military power is going to spread among more national actors.

LOWERING RISKS THROUGH ARMS LIMITATION AND RESTRAINT IN WEAPONS USE

This final section will discuss the new weapons in respect to three matters: (1) the effect of dispersing powerful weapons to the smaller states, and prospects for the control of this dispersal; (2) some prospects for holding down arms purchases by the superpowers themselves; and (3) prospects for restraint in weapon use.

The shift of economic power from the established industrial nations toward those rich in resources has created so great a market for arms, with such diverse buyers and sellers, that curbing sales is impossible, and even modulating them is difficult. The trends we have seen with respect to the oil-producing nations may be a precursor to more general shifts, which will include the exploitation of ocean areas in newly claimed zones (with all sorts of designations). The potential value of ocean areas which will be claimed by states like Panama or the People's Democratic Republic of Yemen will not usually be proportional to present land resource values. These new riches will evoke the invidious behavior of neighbors as well as of local factions, so that rulers will have incentives to buy arms at the same time that they have the means.

What options are open to the present industrial powers to affect these arm buildups? There are at least five avenues to explore:

1. Attempting to shift purchases from tanks, fighter bombers, and Pershing-type missiles to highly effective, shorter-range precision weapons.

2. Endeavoring to retain—to the extent possible—superpower control over the "supporting structure" which is so necessary if precision weapons are to be used effectively in *large-scale* combat.

3. Maintaining tight controls over the export of guidance technology for longer-range missiles such as Pershing II and the sea-launched cruise-missile.

4. Reducing the initiative for nuclear weapons acquisition by encouraging the substitution of precision nonnuclear weapons, while at the same time making the ingredients for a deliverable nuclear weapon capability difficult to obtain.

5. Encouraging restraint and precision in the application of miliatary power. (More will be said below about restraints in the use of weapons.)

None of these avenues has been very thoroughly explored; if adopted by the United States, all have within them the seeds of risk. They deserve a great deal more attention before actual moves can be taken.

The second matter—an understanding between the superpowers to hold down arms purchases—draws on a solid, but sometimes neglected, incentive for arms control: saving money. The large traditional weapons are becoming more expensive, more vulnerable to precision weapons, and more susceptible to being replaced by smaller weapons. (This is not to say that the newer systems have no problems, nor that tested weapons should be abandoned before there is confidence in the alternatives.) In addition, there seems a good chance that several decades from now there will be a much greater separation of weapons from their platforms, and that the tightly integrated systems will increasingly seem inefficient. So the question arises whether there might be sufficient mutual advantage to the Soviets and the Americans to form the basis of an agreement to limit certain traditional classes of arms. To the most ardent advocates of arms control, this might seem too modest an anticipation of the inevitable. On the other hand, such anticipation could save hundreds of billions of dollars over the decade of the 1980s, money which might be put to more productive uses.

The third matter is an even more neglected aspect of arms control: the limitation of damage through restraint in the *use* of weapons systems. While the best way to avoid damage is to avoid conflict, we live in an imperfect world. Thus it is important to consider restraint in use, a restraint which would be greatly facilitated by the new precise weapons and by current tendencies in both Washington and Moscow to treat the battlefield use of nuclear weapons as less and less inevitable. The point is that it is now possible to lower damage done to unintended targets, while efficiently dealing with intended targets.[7] Civilian casualties could be minimized. Military forces could be very efficiently used. And, most important, a military commander could convey a more precise signal while the military damage was taking place, a matter of great importance when a nonnuclear war is being fought under a threat of escalation.

SOME CONCLUSIONS

This paper is intended mainly to introduce a number of arguments relating to the four questions raised at the beginning and not to provide answers. But it does seem to be the case that military power is, in fact, becoming more divisible. Many of the new weapons systems seem to be more readily usable, and in smaller packages, than the traditional systems. It is questionable whether military power will be used more precisely or whether political objectives will, on balance, be set forth to friend or enemy with a correspondingly greater specificity.

In spite of the potential importance of the new kinds of weapons, it is not likely that their impact will be revolutionary. This is true for several reasons, among them the fact that deployed weapons are likely to have technical deficiencies for some years to come (for example, some will not work at night, or in bad weather); they will be subject to an increasing array of countermeasures, both tactical and technical; and military establishments will change slowly from traditional tactical patterns to those which exploit the new systems. But the important thing now is to understand the potential values of the new systems, because changes are inevitable and will occur in the lifetime of procurements and strategies now being decided on.

A number of trends seem likely over the long run. There will be a decrease in the funds allocated to the procurement of large, expensive, penetrating-weapons systems. Tactical units will be smaller and very mobile. The data gathering and processing systems which allocate and support these units will receive emphasis. In Europe, plans for conflict will envisage a much higher rate of consumption and destruction of military materiel. Replenishment, and attacks on replenishment networks, will be of great importance.

Some of these trends will be destabilizing, but those elements which make for a better chance of defending friendly territory are stabilizing. The greatest instabilities would arise if one side felt that the other had not thought through the necessary new tactics or had only begun to acquire an effective modern posture or had not prepared for the intensity and suddenness of war. Some of the trends will run against arms control objectives, and some will help achieve them. Agreements which count on the old labels like "strategic," "tactical," and "forward-based systems" are likely to be defective. The concealability of very powerful new weapons will strain "national means of verification." On the other hand, there are new opportunities to save money, to shift arms transfers to weapons best used in the defense of territory, and to arrive at agreements which would constrain weapons use and limit damage caused to civilian targets.

Thus, while there are many promises in the new technology, there are also dangers. In particular, there are the dangers of less inhibition in starting combat and of the addition of more military actors, including some who may not seek stability. Military intervention can be tailored to more precise goals; it has a new and more flexible arsenal; and its students have new and serious responsibilities to probe the consequences.

NOTES

1. Raymond Aron, *The Century of Total War* (Garden City, N.Y.: Doubleday, 1954).

2. Raymond Aron, *On War*, trans. Terence Kilmartin (Garden City, N.Y.: Doubleday, 1959), p. 16.

3. This definition is slightly modified from James Digby, *Precision-Guided Weapons*, Adelphi Paper No. 118 (London: International Institute for Strategic Studies, 1975).

4. This is slightly modified from Digby, *Precision-Guided Weapons*, p. 4.

5. Some aspects of the debate are treated in Phillip A. Karber, "The Soviet Anti-Tank Debate," *Survival* (May/June 1976): 105-11.

6. See Johan J. Holst and Uwe Nerlich, eds., *Beyond Nuclear Deterrence: New Aims, New Arms* (New York: Crane, Russak, 1976). See especially chap. 14 by Holst, and chap. 7 by Digby.

7. Henry Rowen and Albert Wohlstetter call this the "dual criterion." See their chapter 11 in Holst and Nerlich, *Beyond Nuclear Deterrence*.

PART III. CHANGING MILITARY OPERATIONS

AIRLIFT AND MILITARY INTERVENTION

John R. Pickett

Over the past twenty-five years, the U.S. military has intervened repeatedly in support of allied governments. Whether such activity will continue in the future will depend on many factors; some of them are obvious, and some of them cannot be defined or predicted in advance. It is not the purpose here to construct a case for or against U.S. intervention in future crises or conflicts—the cases will be established and the decisions reached by policy makers. The reality remains, however, that the United States has a number of mutual security arrangements, formal and informal, with other nations throughout the world. If these agreements are to remain credible, it is essential that the United States maintain a viable and perceivable *capability* to intervene whether or not we elect to exercise it in any particular situation.

Given these conditions, it is necessary to examine the U.S. experience in military intervention and note the critical role that strategic air mobility has frequently played. There is no reason to expect this role to diminish. To the contrary, if one reviews those areas of the world in which armed conflict is most likely to occur in the present period, it can be argued that air mobility can provide an effective option should the United States choose to intervene. More important, under certain sets of circumstances, air mobility may offer the only effective means of military intervention.

This study seeks to consider the changing nature of the military structure, including the complex balance of nuclear and conventional forces, declining manpower levels, a shrinking base structure, and the effect of advanced technology. It then outlines a set of plausible criteria under which air mobility would be the only means of intervention and assesses current strategic airlift capability by examining the logistics resupply of Israel during the 1973 war. Finally, it

AUTHOR'S NOTE: This paper reflects the opinion of the author and does not necessarily constitute the official policy position of the Department of the Air Force. I greatly appreciate the valuable assistance of Ray Carlson, Lindsey Parris, and Deborah Barnhart.

considers some of the ramifications of modern aircraft technology in light of the lessons learned from that conflict.

THE CHANGING SHAPE OF THE MILITARY

The military structure is being shaped by a number of circumstances, some of which are external to the influence of either the military establishment or the U.S. government. An examination of several important factors and some of their more explicit manifestations is necessary to an appreciation of the requirements, capabilities, and limitations of strategic air mobility.

First, of course, one must consider the continuing shift in the strategic nuclear balance. Where once there existed an acknowledged U.S. strategic superiority, this nation and the Soviet Union now have perceptibly equivalent strategic nuclear power. The results of the shift have been many and pervasive; but, in the present context, the principal effect has been continuing emphasis on forces designed for conventional warfare.

Having achieved parity, and perhaps aiming toward superiority, in the strategic forces, the Soviet leadership may regard a U.S. nuclear response to less intense activity as so unlikely that, in the absence of strong conventional U.S. forces, they will chance specific military interventions. The U.S., without adequate conventional strength to deter or defeat such efforts, may be faced with the choice between accepting continued losses or resorting to use of nuclear weapons. These ideas were summarized in 1976 by former Undersecretary of State Joseph Sisco:

> But strategic forces are not enough. World peace in the present circumstances of rough strategic equivalence is more likely to be threatened by shifts in local or regional balances—in Europe, the Middle East, Asia, Latin America or Africa—than by strategic nuclear attack. Thus, it is more important than ever to maintain and improve forces that can be used for local defense in support of our allies and to help maintain regional stability.[1]

A serious obstacle to our ability to react fully with conventional military power is the pradoxical decrease in size of the armed forces. The number of active-duty personnel in uniform has declined from 2,687,000 in 1964 (before the SEA buildup) to just over two million in 1975—a reduction of over one-half million.[2] This decline in numbers has been prompted by a number of factors; the most prominent is the rising cost of personnel.

In an effort to offset declining numbers, the force planners have attempted to substitute technology for manpower, and have thus been driven toward seeking higher and higher unit effectiveness with fewer and fewer units. This too has not been without its penalties in increasingly sophisticated equipment, a greater and more complex logistics "tail," and increasing size and weight of combat equipment.

A further constraint on effective use of conventional forces is the continuing decline in the U.S. base structure. In 1958 there were 280 Air Force installations worldwide, 173 located in the continental United States and 107 abroad. By 1975 this number had been reduced by one-half, to 140 total bases, and only 29 were overseas installations. While the overseas installations tend to be somewhat clustered in Western Europe, adequate facilities exist in other areas for worldwide operations in peacetime. The events of the 1973 Arab-Israeli conflict showed clearly, however, that existence in peacetime and availability in the political turmoil that may surround military intervention are not synonomous.

The constraints on manpower and bases, as well as political and fiscal factors, have led to a search for ways to achieve greater efficiency through flexibility, diversity, and locating combat resources centrally. The greater efficiency attainable through such centralization is evident; however, credibility in a worldwide context can be achieved only through adequate and responsive mobile forces capable of moving these resources rapidly from their centralized locations to trouble spots. While a major portion of our forces are procured, maintained, and earmarked for Central Europe, it is clear that the capability to respond militarily in other areas should also be of concern.

MOBILITY FORCES: TYPES AND ROLES

To perform this function, the military maintains both air and sea strategic mobility forces. Sealift dominates airlift in terms of cost per ton and volume of supplies deliverable over a sufficiently long interval. Even during the war in Southeast Asia, sometimes characterized as an air-dominated war, over 95% of the supplies were transported by sea. However, there are types of conflicts which possess characteristics that virtually dictate reliance on air mobility, at least in the initial phase.

Figure 1 illustrates the relationship between the air and sea delivery modes of supplies as experienced during the 1973 Middle East resupply operation. Of particular interest are the speed of response and shallow slope of the volume-constrained airlift forces and the sharp upward slope of the sealift curve during the last half of November 1973.

First, by definition, a war of intervention (or limited war) is likely to be a war of limited objectives and limited application of force by the intervening nation to attain those objectives. Second, it is likely to possess some characteristics of an emergency. Third, the shock value of rapid employment of force, which is likely to have as great an immediate impact as the military effects of that force, will decay rapidly with time. Thus, it is incumbent upon the national leadership

Figure 1: Israeli Resupply Airlift/Sealift (85,108 Tons)

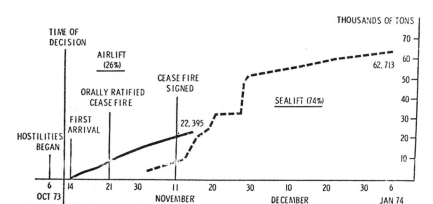

to commit adequate forces to attain specific objectives rather quickly. Fourth, these conditions impart specific requirements to the military response to be employed. For example, if ground forces are to be employed, they should be largely self-contained or supportable by air, since there probably will not be enough time to establish long sea or land supply lines.

It is not necessary to believe that all military intervention would possess these characteristics; it is necessary to acknowledge that an important subset can be so described. Under these conditions, the successful conduct of military operations will depend on air support.

STRATEGIC AIRLIFT FORCES AND MEASURES

The primary strategic airlift forces consist of 234 C-141s and 70 C-5s assigned to the Military Airlift Command (MAC). The C-141 and C-5 aircraft provide complementary capabilities in the strategic airlift mission; the C-141 is used primarily to deploy troops, general cargo, and smaller equipment, while the C-5 carries the largest items of equipment.

The C-141 can lift payloads of over 32 tons and can carry most equipment possessed by the Army; however, it is not, as of 1976, equipped for in-flight refueling. The larger types of Army equipment which fit into the C-141—the current armored personnel carriers, 2½ ton trucks, and M-551 light tanks—are categorized as oversize cargo.

Cargo too large or too heavy for the C-141—such as self-propelled howitzers, shop vans, engineering vehicles, and M-60 tanks—is defined as outsize cargo and must be carried by the C-5, which can lift more than 100 tons. While the C-5 was built with air-refueling capability, MAC crews were not trained in this technique until after the 1973 Middle East resupply operation.

In addition to this primary force of military aircraft, the civilian air carriers, through the Civil Reserve Air Fleet (CRAF), provide another source of strategic airlift. As of 1976, aircraft committed to the CRAF include 140 long-range cargo aircraft, of which 25 are wide-body aircraft capable of carrying oversize equipment. The other 115 aircraft are the narrow-body design and thus are limited to carrying only the bulk type of cargo, consisting of small items which can be loaded individually or in small groups. These aircraft can be mobilized only following a declaration of national emergency. However, the U.S. has frequently relied on contract civilian airlift during worldwide operations, including operations in combat zones. No civil aircraft are capable of air refueling.

The U.S. tanker aircraft is the KC-135. This is an early version of the Boeing 707 jetliner initially procured as the primary tanker for support of bomber operations by the Strategic Air Command (SAC). Currently, over 600 such aircraft are assigned to SAC; however, a portion of this force is routinely used to support tactical and logistics operations.

Tactical airlift aircraft, principally the C-130, would also be available. These aircraft are smaller and jet-prop driven, as distinct from their longer-range, pure jet-powered counterparts in the strategic airlift inventory. The distinction between tactical and strategic airlift forces has basis not only in differing performance characteristics but also in the past practice of divided operational control by two different major air commands. However, this distinction will have blurred after the consolidation of the operational control of all airlift in the Military Airlift Command in 1975. It will undoubtedly become even less pronounced if a wide-body, pure-jet successor is procured to replace the C-130. Here, however, we will deal primarily with the introduction of military forces and equipment into a theater as opposed to subsequent operations within the theater. While the tactical airlift force would be very important in the latter, the relatively short range and lack of air-refueling capability, along with reduced cargo capacity, would limit its utility in the former. In those areas in which the C-130 can play an intertheater airlift role, the constraints on its use will be about the same as for the strategic airlift aircraft.

Jet-powered airlift aircraft—primarily the C-5 and C-141—offer significant improvements over their propeller-driven predecessors in reliability, range, speed, and cargo capacity. The most common standard measure of transportation capability for strategic airlift is the amount of weight transportable over distance over an increment of time—usually ton-miles per month. The criteria necessary to compute this measure are range, speed, cargo capacity, and utilization rate. Thus ton-miles per month is a measure of potential. From 1965 to 1975, the number of cargo aircraft was reduced by about half. Nevertheless, cargo potential, because of the introduction of more capable aircraft, increased twofold as measured by ton-miles per month. However, as will be shown later, this measure, while analytically convenient, fails to take into account a number of relevant operational considerations. Further, these constraints are most likely to be operative—in fact, may be the driving consideration—in the context of limited military intervention.

MILITARY INTERVENTION: TYPES AND LOCALES

To assess the utility of airlift forces in plausible military intervention, an examination of other factors is necessary. Most notable among these factors are the types of military intervention and the most likely locations for such operations.

Military intervention may take many forms. For example (to be considered in more detail later), such involvement may take the form of logistics support, as in the 1973 Middle East war. In this case, the combatants were engaged in a highly capital-intensive conflict which used the most modern Soviet and U.S. weapons. As noted earlier, modern U.S. weaponry tends toward complexity and largeness, which makes the Israeli resupply effort worth examining in greater detail because of the mass and variety of equipment transported. Further challenges were presented by Israel's remoteness and the somewhat dire straits of the Israelis when the decision was made to intervene. Unlike some other types of intervention, the one in Israel did not involve large-scale deployment of personnel; however, of the resources that may require air deployment, personnel are among the least constraining. When all forms of airlift are considered, there is an abundance of capacity to transport people.

Other types of military intervention may involve only air support for indigenous forces, or, alternatively, the introduction of ground forces, as in Lebanon in 1958 and the Dominican Republic in 1965.

A most demanding requirement, and the one that is traditionally used to assess the adequacy of mobility forces, would be a conventional conflict in Central Europe. Most U.S. conventional forces are structured and maintained for employment in the defense of Central Europe against conventional attack by the Warsaw Pact nations. Mobility planning is predicated on rapid reinforcement of forward-deployed U.S. and allied forces. The mobility workload required is enormous, consisting of 2-2/3 Army divisions with equipment pre-positioned in Europe and 5-2/3 divisions with equipment and support elements to be deployed along with personnel.[3] One can quickly get a feel for the scope of this task by considering that one infantry division and its support equipment weigh about 77,000 tons—nearly 800 times the maximum load of a C-5. Obviously, not everything is earmarked for delivery by air; most personnel would deploy by air, while the bulk of the equipment would be transported by sea.

Of course, airlift is by far the most expeditious mode of transportation and, given the current Warsaw Pact numerical advantage along the Central Front, more rapid mobility is being emphasized through a variety of airlift enhancement programs. Included among these are higher utilization rates (additional crews and spare parts to increase aircraft availability) modification of wide-body (747/DC-10 class) aircraft in the civil airlines to permit carriage of oversize equipment, and the addition of air-refueling capability to the C-141. These combined initiatives have the potential to double the current ton-mile capability in a European conflict without the procurement of additional aircraft.

Since the reinforcement and resupply of a conventional conflict in Central Europe would involve virtually the entire U.S. military establishment, it is usually viewed as the "worst" case. That is, mobility forces which can cope with that situation are assumed to be adequate in less intense conflict. Certainly, in terms of volume, an appealing case can be made for such a view. But in terms of aerial port facilities, fuel supplies, runways, and distance from the U.S., Europe represents one of the least severe scenarios.

CHARACTERISTICS OF AIR MOBILITY

Airlift offers the benefits of speed and access to locations not accessible by either land or sea transportation; but these attributes are not without cost. Aircraft are expensive to procure and to operate in terms of the quantity of cargo that they can deliver. Further, strategic airlift aircraft require elaborate and extensive aerial port facilities—runways, loading and unloading equipment, and refueling facilities, including extensive fuel reserves.

This last point cannot be overemphasized. Airlift is unalterably a fuel-intensive mode of transportation—a factor which has changed remarkably little over the past years. During the Korean War, four tons of aviation fuel were required en route or at the terminus for every ton of cargo airlifted to Korea. For every ton airlifted to Europe, one ton of fuel was required in Europe for the return trip.[4] The advent of large, jet cargo aircraft has not significantly altered the equation. For every ton of cargo delivered during the 1973 resupply effort, a ton of fuel was taken out of Israel.[5]

The principal difference between the European/Korean experience and the Israeli effort stems from two other factors. First, the enormous increase in the cargo requirement and the compressed timing in the Middle Eastern case escalated the fuel requirement proportionately. Second, since most nations of the world are equipped with jet aircraft, jet fuel itself is now an essential commodity of war. The confluence of these circumstances was best summed up by Vice Admiral Thomas R. Weschler, former director of logistics of the office of the Joint Chiefs of Staff:

It's worth noting that our great airlift capability can also cause problems as the Israelis were soon to find out. When the USAF transports began operations in support of Israel, the question of fuel came up. The Israeli officials assured us that they had sufficient fuel reserves—not to worry about it. However, after we were well into the airlift and they learned that *it took more fuel to support the C-5s than to support the entire Israeli Air Force,* they did a double take and rechecked their reserves. Fortunately, they were sufficient for the time frame involved.[6]

Fuel availability is not the only constraint on current airlift operations. Except for Central Europe, there are very few destinations outside the Western hemisphere that can be reached with significant payloads without the use of en route staging facilities. Refueling with the current KC-135 tanker can extend the range of the C-5 somewhat; but the range/payload characteristics of the tanker are such that operation from overseas facilities would be required in many likely cases. Thus, again, the operation would become dependent on access to overseas locations.

Further, when en route staging is required, the staging facilities rather than destination facilities may well become more important in determining the rate of flow. In many instances, a review of the physical, geographical, and political circumstances will quickly narrow the choices to a single base. Thus an entire operation can hinge on the availability of one overseas base subject to the vagaries of weather, accidents, and sabotage. While these factors have always been present, political restrictions on the alternatives may well elevate them to playing a decisive role in determining the outcome of a conflict.

Another characteristic of airlift stems from the ponderous size of the aircraft and the rather limited number of ways to protect them. Since the area of transport operations is small and known, the possibility of a direct attack on the resupply effort exists. A large cargo aircraft such as a C-5, C-141, or 747 is an easy target for even the most antiquated of jet fighters. This, again, is not an observation that came suddenly with the advent of jet power—it has been ever thus. Yet through the Berlin airlift, Korea, Vietnam, and numerous less intense operations where there was both motive and opportunity, there have been no overt attacks by enemy aircraft against a transport aircraft or air transport facilities.

There are no simple answers as to why there has been such restraint, but there are factors which militate against overt attack. An overt attack against shipping—air or sea—signals an escalation of conventional conflict to near its highest levels; i.e., there are few remaining stops. Thus if the intervening nation possesses a clear advantage in power, the perceived assurance of commensurate response constitutes a deterrent against such attacks. To test this deterrent exposes the attacker to retaliation on a larger scale—a price he may not be willing to pay unless he feels he can severely cripple the airlift operation. Future situations in which we do not possess a clear preponderance of power, or where our commitment is judged to be equivocal, may invite a departure from this pattern.

Overt attack, however, is no longer the only option. The appearance of effective, but small, man-portable surface-to-air missile systems such as the Soviet SA-7 Strella and the U.S. Redeye provide a means for both effective and anonymous attack. Again, cargo aircraft are very vulnerable to such attacks during takeoff, landing, and periods of low-altitude flight.

Experience in Southeast Asia, as well as at international airports worldwide, would seem to indicate that security procedures in the immediate vicinity of the airport can be effective. Portable surface-to-air missiles were available to the North Vietnamese and were used against tactical aircraft in a number of situations with varying degrees of success. However, security procedures—and air traffic procedures designed to exploit them—were apparently successful in preventing attacks on airborne craft in the vicinity of airports.

In a broader sense, arguments about attrition almost surely will not be critical in assessing the utility of air mobility in military intervention. Considering the very real political risks that are bound to surround such a decision, it seems unlikely that a forthright decision to proceed in this environment would be contravened by the prospect of some losses. It also seems unlikely that the rate of losses expected in the context of limited intervention would be sufficient to impair the effort given the resolve to proceed. Nevertheless, as the subsequent examination of the Israeli airlift will demonstrate, the criticalness of a single facility can be such that detailed planning and specific action to protect both the facility itself and the air traffic may be important parts of an operation.

THE 1973 MIDDLE EAST RESUPPLY OPERATION

The war began when Egyptian armed forces crossed the Suez Canal on October 6, 1973. Six days later, on October 12, President Nixon directed the Department of Defense (DOD) to begin an immediate airlift to Israel, and the C-5 and C-141 aircraft of the Military Airlift Command began to operate. The operation was complicated by severe restrictions, such as no overflight, staging, or landing rights in the relevant nations of Europe, the Mediterranean, and Africa. Lajes AB, Azores, was the only available refueling or staging base between the U.S. and Israel. Beginning on October 13, 1973, an around-the-clock operation was maintained, with a peak flow of six C-5s and 17 C-141s per day. When the airlift terminated on November 14, 1973, a total of 566 missions had delivered about 22,400 short tons of cargo. The 145 C-5 sorties accounted for 10,750 tons, and 421 C-141 missions delivered 11,650 tons.

Although a success by most standards, the airlift operation confronted the U.S. with new set of perceptions concerning the political-military aspects of military intervention. Some of our staunchest NATO allies denied support, or even the appearance of support, under the threat of economic sanctions by the Arab states. In this regard, the airlift to Israel in 1973 is perhaps typical of what we must be prepared for in the future. Neither alliances, nor historic ties, nor ideology will necessarily represent accurate or reliable predictors of how each nation will react. Perhaps no other recent event points more clearly to the consequences of the emerging military, political, and economic interdependence in the world and the necessity of assessing framework against the more traditional ones.

Portugal did not deny the U.S. the rights to the long-time MAC facility at Lajes AB, Azores. Oddly enough, this facility, essential in earlier times of shorter-range, propeller-driven transatlantic operations, was viewed by some as an anachronism in the jet age. This tenuous thread, which was the difference between success and failure, is not of sturdy enough fabric to be used to support the fate of future operations—considering the current political situation in Portugal.

How essential was Lajes to this operation? Without its facilities, and with the other sanctions in effect, the C-141 could not have flown to Israel at all, and the C-5 would have been restricted to payloads of about 33 tons. And it is doubtful whether the C-5, even empty, could have returned nonstop to the U.S., because of the prevailing westerly winds. Had we attempted such an operation with the C-5 alone, 670 sorties with the restricted payload would have been required to move the equivalent amount of cargo. At the C-5 utilization rate actually used, this operation would have required over 1000 days.

The fact that the crews were not trained to use the air-refueling capability of the C-5 bears testimony to our inadequate preparation for conducting this sort of unilateral effort. (The C-141 is not equipped for air refueling, although such a modification has been proposed.) If the C-5 could have refueled from existing KC-135 tankers, the allowable load could have been increased significantly. However, the KC-135 tankers would have had to operate from Lod Airport, which might only have complicated the situation. If 747-class tankers had been available, full cargo loads could have been carried and the equivalent workload completed by 220 C-5 sorties without access to Lajes or without fuel at Lod.

Despite the apparent success of the operation, it is necessary to consider it further before extrapolating the results of this air resupply effort to other settings. While political restrictions and a lack of operational preparedness were severe complications, at least two favorable factors contributed heavily and perhaps decisively to the final outcome.

First, both Lajes and Lod are large, well-equipped airports which routinely support high-density traffic consisting of large, modern jet aircraft. Although Lajes was the only base available, in terms of fuel capacity and refueling facilities, it is unlikely that many airports in the world could have performed as well. It was decided to restrict the traffic flow through Lajes to 6 C-5 and 36 C-141 eastbound movements a day, and the actual peak load was only 6 C-5s and 17 C-141s per day. The initial restriction represented the MAC-computed capacity of Lajes, considering ramp congestion, en route support, and refueling.[7] The lower number was a restriction imposed by the secretary of defense on the number of aircraft that could land at Lod each day.[8] Thus, even with good facilities, the flow was kept far below its maximum ton-mile capability; in fact, no more than 24% of the MAC aircraft were ever used.[9] Yet, in terms of intervention scenarios, the facilities at Lajes and Lod airports should be considered far above average.

Perhaps an even more serious problem was one alluded to earlier. For every ton of cargo delivered to Israel, a ton of jet fuel was taken out. The success of the operation hinged on the fact that Israel has one of the most modern jet air forces in the world and that her adversaries could not or did not disrupt' the fuel-storage facilities. There are very few nations in the world that could have supported an effort of this scale, particularly while simultaneously waging an intensive air war.

AIRLIFT ENHANCEMENT

The capability to intervene militarily in the most likely locales will not be enhanced by increasing volume and rate measures alone. In fact, with the possible exception of Central Europe, there are virtually no other settings in which ton-mile potential is a relevant measure of capability. The Achilles' heel of airlift operations is the present need to rely on en route and destination facilities and fuel supplies, a vulnerability made more tender by a reduced overseas base structure and changing political perceptions around the world.

The enormous range/payload potential of modern, wide-body jet aricraft is such that operations in most parts of the world could be conducted without reliance on en route bases. For example, the C-5 (and the C-141, if it is equipped for air refueling) can reach most areas of possible involvement nonstop when supported by tanker aircraft operating out of the United States or Puerto Rico (see figure 2). Moreover, if refueling support were provided by wide-body tankers, the airlift craft could, with multiple refuelings, operate in these areas without taking fuel from either destination. The attractiveness of these aircraft is further enhanced by the fact that there is a logistics network to provide contract support in most areas of the world.

As noted earlier, a number of programs have been proposed to enhance the capability of strategic mobility forces. Most, however, are typified by the proposal to convert civilian wide-body jets in the CRAF to handle oversize cargo and to purchase additional parts and aircrews to increase the utilization rate of the C-5. Advocates of these and similar programs justify them by citing the mobility requirements for an intensive conventional war in Central Europe. The procurement of new 747/DC-10 aircraft is currently being considered as the

Figure 2: C-5 Unrefueled, and With One Refueling by Various
         Tankers Payload: 90 Tons

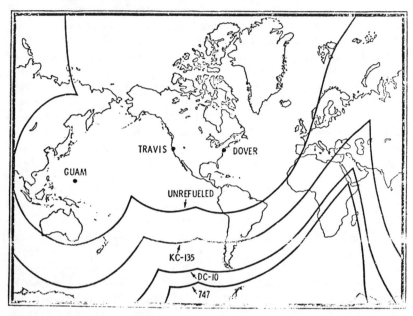

Advanced Tanker Cargo Aircraft (ATCA) program, which would provide an
enormous increase in tanker capability while retaining the inherent cargo capability of these huge aircraft. However, the future of the ATCA is far from
assured, because it is a less cost-effective addition to the resupply potential to
Central Europe, in which en route fuel and facilities problems are minimal and
rapid movement of large amounts of equipment is vital. The U.S. preoccupation
with that aspect of our defense commitment tends to detract from the appeal of
a more capable tanker for support of conventional forces in other less intense,
but in many respects more demanding, circumstances. The question, therefore, is
whether the United States is willing to invest in the capability to intervene in
perhaps more likely conflicts worldwide as well as (perhaps at the expense of)
our ability to provide maximum support to Europe.

CONCLUSION

The ability to promote regional stability in remote areas of the world through
the credible threat of military intervention continues to draw support from both

the Department of Defense and the Department of State. The problem of maintaining the credibility of this capability has been compounded by shrinking force and equipment levels. Attempts to alleviate this quantitative decline by more and more advanced weapons have resulted in larger and more complex equipment as well as an increased requirement for logistics support.

In many circumstances, only strategic airlift offers the robustness and speed of response required in the crisis atmosphere that is likely to surround a decision to intervene militarily. However, strategic air mobility may currently be thought of as a process whereby military forces are transported from one location to another and exchanged for an equal or greater quantity of jet fuel—another vital commodity of war. The rate at which military forces can be introduced depends on the rate at which this conversion can be accommodated—which in turn depends on the adequacy of aerial port facilities.

While these seem to be self-evident truths of long standing, our preoccupation with the "Central European worst-case" philosophy tends to obscure them. While there can be little doubt that the European setting is the worst instance in terms of quantity of things to be moved, it is among the best in terms of facilities and fuel supplies. Increases in analytically convenient measures of potential, such as ton-mile per month, may persuade us that our airlift capability in a worldwide context is also expanding. In fact, the events of 1973 illustrate clearly that any coupling between the two is tenuous at best. Of the various proposals to enhance airlift, most focus on increasing ton-mile potential. The addition of refueling capability to the C-141 and the procurement of the Advanced Tanker Cargo Aircraft would offer much-needed improvement of current air mobility forces in the context of worldwide operations in less extensive conflicts.

NOTES

1. U.S., Congress, House, Subcommittee on International Political and Military Affairs of the Committee on International Political and Military Affairs of the Committee on International Relations, *The Department of State and National Security Policy,* testimony by Joseph J. Sisco, April 29, 1976, pp. 637-40.

2. James R. Schlesinger, *Annual Defense Department Report, FY 1975* (Washington, D.C.: Dept. of Defense, 1975), p. 172.

3. U.S., Congress, House, Subcommittee on Department of Defense, House Appropriations Committee, *Department of Defense Appropriations for 1975; Hearings,* General Paul F. Pateh, 93d Cong. 2d sess., pt. 7, Procurement, p. 1114.

4. Norman Precoda, *Logistic Support in Limited War,* RM 58TMP-32, Technical Military Planning Operation, (Santa Barbara, CA: General Electric Company, December 31, 1958), p. 7.

5. Edgar Ulsamer, "New Look in USAF's Strategic Airlift," *Air Force Magazine* (February 1975).

6. Thomas Weschler, Speeches before the National Defense Transportation and Logistics Forum and Exposition, Las Vegas, Nevada, September 24, 1974 (italics added).

7. General Accounting Office, *Airlift Operations of The Military Airlift Command During the 1973 Middle East War* (Washington, D.C.: Comptroller General of the United States, April 16, 1975)

8. Ibid., p. 9.

9. Ibid., p. 16.

CHANGING NAVAL OPERATIONS AND
MILITARY INTERVENTION

Michael MccGwire

Navies have long been a means of bringing military force to bear in distant parts of the world; the purpose of this study is to consider the influence of contemporary developments on this traditional instrument of Great Power policy.

In a naval context, military intervention can include a cocktail party in Mombasa, a show of force in the Caribbean, naval interposition off Iceland, carrier air strikes on Hanoi, or the landing of Marines in the Persian Gulf. This discussion will concentrate on the application of force, as opposed to the display of force, for two reasons. First, our understanding of the processes underlying political influence building is still unclear,[1] and becomes even more so when we introduce the diffuse concept of "a naval presence."[2] And second, to the extent that a naval presence *does* have any political influence, this must stem from the ultimate possibility that the force involved will actually be used.

Although this paper discusses military intervention both at sea and by sea, it stops short at the beachhead; military activity on land is addressed only to the extent that it is relevant to maritime operations. Similarly, although the political costs of naval intervention are touched on, the more general question of the political utility of military force is not addressed, since it comes within the purview of the more general, theoretical discussions.

However, so many assumptions about the contemporary role of force at sea stem from past centuries that it is worth spending a moment on the pertinent changes in the international environment. Mahan, who chose the term "sea power" for its evocative ring rather than its usefulness as an analytical term, saw it as one of three interlocking circles, the other two being colonies and commerce. His theories about sea power and command of the sea derived from a historical analysis of the years 1660-1783, the height of mercantalism and monopoly trade, and were thought to have been validated by what Graham terms "the illusion of Pax Britannica" in the nineteenth century.[3] But British naval power was not the sole or even the most important reason for the Pax Britannica, which resulted from a combination of various factors. Of these, the most important was "Britain's industrial supremacy, which made possible a phenomenal commercial development."[4] The period of the Industrial Revolution provided both the means and the stimulus for Western nations to establish more or less effective dominion over a world which seemed to lack viable political entities. The process was accompanied by the spread of a Western administrative infrastructure (part governmental, part commercial) throughout much of the world, and was supported by a belief in "la mission civilatrice" and "the white man's burden," as well as Victorian ideas about child rearing and colonial government. Important factors were the will to empire, the readiness of the imperial authorities to use force, and the knowledge by their subject people that resistance would lead to certain retribution, even if delayed. God was white; and to spare the rod spoiled the child.

Navies were prime instruments of imperial retribution, and in those days of coal-fired ships and manually operated gun mountings, sizable bodies of well-armed men could be landed at short notice, while the warship lay virtually invulnerable offshore. As recently as the Boer War, it was still practical to dismount naval guns and drag them by oxcart to the battlefront.

By World War I, attitudes toward empire were already changing, and the Western imperial tide had begun to recede. But even in the 1930s it was thought unexceptionable to bomb villagers in the Aden Protectorate as a form of collective punishment; and on the shores of the Malaysian Archipelago and the China Seas, villages were razed to discourage piracy.

Since World War II, attitudes and circumstances have changed radically. Of the latter, the most significant would seem to be the proliferation of nation-states and their membership in the United Nations. The corollary of this has been the progressive dismantling of the infrastructure of colonial occupation which played such an important role in bringing imperial retribution to bear. There has also been a change in general attitudes toward the acceptability of coercive force. The circumstances in which long-range intervention is likely to be acceptable have been progressively circumscribed; in the last thirty years, large-scale coercive intervention by major powers has been successful only within their respective contiguous national security zones, where power gradients and political commitment are both high. Effective intervention overseas now requires an initial favorable balance of political forces in the "host" country, as well as sufficient weight of sustained response. But even if attitudes had not changed, warships would no longer be able to serve as the autonomous wielders of graduated retribution. The specialized demands of modern warfare mean that naval units now lack the military flexibility of the prewar general-purpose cruiser, with its numerous guns and comfortably large ship's company.

Meanwhile, the proliferation of sophisticated weapon systems means that no longer are warships necessarily invulnerable when lying offshore. Sensors may have to be manned continuously, weapons may have to be at standby alert, and it may be difficult to spare a landing party without hazarding one's ship. The modern equivalent of the cruiser with its landing party is the carrier task force and its Marine battalion landing team. But while the political effects that each could achieve may be comparable, the political stake is obviously very different.

None of this means that military intervention by sea is no longer likely or possible. But it has placed constraints on the almost casual use of force which used to be the norm. And it does mean that the economic and political costs are likely to be very much higher, and that the chances of a successful outcome are far smaller. However, while the utility of coercive force is increasingly in question, the threat of such force remains a powerful diplomatic weapon. Whether or not it ultimately achieves its goals, coercive intervention is an unpleasant experience for the target country, and a credible threat is likely to introduce some element of deterrence to its political considerations.

There are two separate calculations involved in assessing the level of capability required for a successful intervention overseas. First, there is the level and type of force which is to be brought to bear on the target ashore, whether it be naval bombardment, carrier air strike, or men and tanks. Second, there is the capability required to get such a force to the target area by sea, and to sustain offshore operations as necessary. Here we are concerned only with the second category, which includes the possibility that passage may be deliberately obstructed, and the use of force may be required to secure such passage. The policy maker will want to know the political costs of such ancillary operations, and how they compare with the political costs of such ancillary operations, and how they compare with the political benefits that the major intervention is supposed to achieve.

Maritime intervention is a complex subject, and therefore a discussion framework, which allows us to consider the level of capabilities and the types of cost involved, will first be developed. We will then look at the major operational developments and their likely effect on military intervention by sea, before turning to review the different types of intervention and why they could occur. Finally, we will consider certain differences between the Soviet and the U.S. approaches to oversea intervention.

THE USE OF THE SEA–A THEORETICAL FRAMEWORK

The sea's strategic quality derives from the access it provides to nonadjacent areas. Maritime strategy is therefore about the *use* of the sea–using it for one's own advantage and preventing its use to one's disadvantage, in peacetime as well as in war. This navigational use of the sea breaks down into two main categories: (1) the conveyance of goods and people; and (2) the projection of military force against targets ashore.

The first category of use covers seaborne trade, which in a strategic context spells maritime communications. It also covers the movement of military cargoes in merchant ships, although this shades into the second category, particularly when a war is actually in progress. The shading is inevitable, since the military and commercial uses of the sea form a continuum. While we can identify what is purely military, there are few commercial cargoes which have no military value. For analytical purposes, therefore, it is impractical to distinguish between military and nonmilitary uses of the sea, except in the broadest terms, whereas the projection of force, and the conveyance of goods and people, are functionally distinct.

The second category has two forms: (1) the traditional one of bringing military force (actual or latent) to bear on coastal states; and (2) the deterrent form of targeting distant land areas with nuclear weapons. We are here concerned only with the traditional form. This may involve the landing of troops or may be limited to standing offshore and striking targets with shipborne weapons such as guns, missiles, or aircraft.

There is also an instrumental category: (3) the deployment of naval forces in order either to *prevent* or to *secure* the two main categories of use. We all know that certain types of naval units also embody the capability for projecting force ashore, but the analytical distinction between categories (2) and (3) is worth preserving. It serves to emphasize that maritime strategy is wholly about the *use of the sea* and only incidentally about the *use of force* at sea. Naval forces are necessary to the use of the sea only if attempts are being made to prevent it.

The ease with which use can be prevented depends on maritime geography and the type of use involved. A waterway (defined as any stretch of sea used for passage) can be described in terms of its geographic characteristics, lying somewhere on the continuum between narrow, shallow waters and the deep ocean. Narrow waterways, where ships must pass close to shore-based weapons, are relatively easy to obstruct, particularly if they are shallow and hence minable. It is far more difficult to prevent passage across an ocean waterway, out of range of land and with opportunities for evasive routing. By the same token, different types of use involve different capabilities and lengths of time at risk. It is usually easier to interrupt a flow of merchant shipping than to prevent the passage of a naval task force.

As a general rule, it is also easier to prevent the use of the sea than it is to secure such use. This is partly because the means of *preventing* use are not limited to naval forces, and in narrow waters they include the simple blockship, the mine, and a whole range of shore-based weapons. Naval forces are more important on the ocean waterways, the submarine being the most universal long-range weapon, but even here the task of preventing use can be shared by land-based strike aircraft and supported by satellite and shore-based surveillance systems.

However, *securing* the use of the sea against opposition remains a predominantly naval task—or at least the military means are primarily naval. There are, of course, other ways of securing use, including diplomatic pressure and economic sanctions.

We are now in a position to draw a box diagram, plotting the type of waterway against the type of use; and in each box we can show the minimum capability needed to *prevent* the use of the sea in such circumstances. We are not able to show the level of capability needed to *secure* the use of the sea, since this will also depend on the type and scale of opposition, which will vary among cases. However, we can show the *type* of costs which will be incurred in using military force to secure the use of the sea against opposition.

These costs can be economic, in the sense of increased demands on the domestic economy for defense expenditure; or they can be political, in the sense of adversely affecting relations with other states. The type of cost is determined by the strategic quality of the waterway. In the case of narrow waters, it is geopolitical, in that it stems from a combination of geographical configuration and the political control of the adjacent coasts. A military response to an attempt to prevent passage through narrow waters therefore cannot avoid political costs, and these will tend to be heavy, because the response will usually require attacks on national territory.

The strategic quality of ocean waterways is primarily military, and stems from the reach and geographical distribution of maritime forces and their relative capabilities in the encounter zone. The costs of the military response to an attempt to prevent passage across the ocean are primarily economic; and, in the international context, the response can usually be contained politically, unless it has become essential to attack shore-based support facilities.

Between these two extremes lie those waterways which traverse open seas within range of land-based weapon and surveillance systems, where the strategic quality will be some mix of military and geopolitical, and the costs part economic and part political.

In the same context of securing use, there is a distinction to be made between the "terminal" and the "passage" legs of a waterway. Obviously, the terminal of one voyage can be the passage of another, and the distinction will lie in the mind of the user. But it is somewhat akin to the distinction between ends and means; and, depending on which applies, it influences the relative ease with which use can be prevented, the range of options open to the user, the costs of securing use, and the levels of political commitment.

The point of immediate interest is that very rarely is the passage leg the only route between two terminals. It is therefore usually possible to divert around obstructions to narrow waterways; and although ocean waterways are more difficult (because the obstructions are mobile), some form of evasive routing is often practicable. This means that there is usually an alternative to insisting on passage, and consideration can be given to the relative costs.

The extra distance involved in accepting diversion can be expressed in time and money, and this also will translate into economic and political costs. But in this case, the political costs will reflect lost opportunities to influence events, or the inability to meet an important commitment. Political costs of this type will be incurred only when time is an issue—for example, if the deployment of military force in response to a sudden crisis is involved, or the supply of a distant battlefront by sea at the outbreak of a war is necessary.

Our diagram is now complete (see p. 154). The boxes for trade in the terminal area have been left blank to show that in most cases the coastal state will be concerned to secure rather than to prevent such use of the sea. Where local conflict prevents such use, trade and military supply would have the same indices. The political costs of securing use in terminal areas are not shown, since they cannot be separated from the larger costs of the military intervention.

The diagram shows the *minimum* level of military capability needed to prevent use in the different situations. The assessment is intuitive, and military capability has been arbitrarily divided into six levels, reflecting both the range and the degree to which violence can be projected. Level I (the highest) implies the capability for sustained attack on naval forces in midocean, and is possessed only by the U.S. and, in certain sea areas, by the Soviet Union. Level II implies a lesser capability, which could attack a strong naval force but not sustain an engagement. Britain has this capability in much of the Atlantic, and China is moving toward it in the Asian Pacific. At the bottom end of the scale, Level VI implies the ability to prevent the passage of merchant ships through narrow shallow waters, perhaps using contact mines laid by junks or dhows, and protecting them with field artillery from being swept. Level V would be able to prevent passage through less constricted waters and might include torpedo and

Minimum Capability Needed to Prevent Use: Cost of Securing Use

Types of Waterway \ Types of Use	The Conveyance of Goods and People		The Projection of Military Force	
	Trade	Military Supply	Stand Off Strike	Land Ashore
Ocean	II : e		I : e	
Narrow	VI : p		IV : p	
Diversion	e	e/p[a]	e/p[a]	
Open	–	V	III	IV
Narrow	–	VI	IV	V

[a]Political costs are incurred only when timeliness is a critical factor
Note: Level of Capability = I(high) to VI(low)
      Cost: e = economic, p = political

gun-armed coastal patrol craft. Levels IV and III lie between these two pairs. Level IV could cover broader, deepwater straits and would include missile-armed craft and coastal installations, plus a measure of shore-based air support. Level III implies a greater offshore capability, including either submarines or else reasonably effective surface forces, backed by shore-based air strike.

These descriptions are deliberately vague, because military forces tend to be unbalanced and do not lie tidily along a smooth continuum of capability. The levels do, however, give some idea of the leverage provided by maritime geography, and the extent to which passage can now be controlled by coastal states in general, and by straits states in particular.

OPERATIONAL DEVELOPMENTS

Turning to the operational factors affecting maritime intervention, we find that there have been significant developments in four main areas: advances in weapons technology, the dispersion of weapon systems among nonindustrialized states, the Soviet Navy's shift to forward deployment, and international attitudes toward the rights of maritime passage. The last of these is of a different kind than the other three, and will be disposed of first.

Erosion of Rights of Passage

Since the first two U.N. Conferences on the Law of the Sea in 1958 and 1960, there has been a remarkable shift in world opinion concerning the balance between exclusive and inclusive use of the sea. In 1958, the "traditional maritime powers" were still fighting for a three-mile territorial limit; the South Americans' claim for 200 miles was seen as preposterous. In 1960, the compromise proposal for a six-mile territorial sea, with an additional six-mile exclusive fishing zone, failed by one vote to get the necessary two-thirds majority. And yet, by 1974, most nations, including the major maritime powers, had come to accept the much broader concepts of a twelve-mile territorial sea and a 200-mile exclusive economic zone, and argument focused on the scope of national jurisdiction within that zone. This tendency has been reinforced by claims that archipelagic seas should be considered as internal waters, and that marine pollution could threaten the security of a coastal state. The dominating principle of "freedom of the seas" has now been seriously eroded, and specific claims have undermined both the concept and the right of "innocent passage" through territorial waters.

A new regime of "transit passage" may yet emerge, but the net effect of these developments has been to make it more likely that, in the future, coastal states will challenge, or even deny, the right of passage to certain categories of ship through waters coming within their various jurisdictions. It is also likely that such action will be seen as legitimate by many other countries, including perhaps the hundred or so members of the Group of 77. Passage through the Suez Canal and the Straits of Tiran was denied to Israel in the past; this could serve as a precedent.

Advance in Weapons Technology

Such challenges to passage will be all the more threatening because of advances in weapons technology and the dispersion of sophisticated systems among coastal states. The former have made quantum jumps possible in such fundamental weapon characteristics as range, accuracy, payload, and systems reliability. These have been matched by an exponential increase in the capabilities of sensor and surveillance systems.

By depriving the seas of their capacity for concealment, the improved surveillance systems have simplified the problems of ocean interception by warships. They can also provide the target-location data which allow long-range weapon systems to be brought to bear. Tactical systems with ranges from 300 miles (cruise-missiles) to 1,500 miles (aircraft) have been in service since the end of the 1950s, but the emerging ability to strike moving targets with ballistic missiles at intercontinental ranges is introducing a new dimension to maritime warfare. As long ago as 1972, the Soviet Union claimed that "naval groupings" were targeted by the Strategic Rocket Forces,[5] and we know that they are developing a homing reentry vehicle for a medium-range ballistic missile.[6] We are now moving into an era where maritime warfare will be fought as much by land- as by sea-based weapon and sensor systems, and it is becoming necessary to distinguish between the "reaches" of different systems and to think in terms of "global" and (for want of a better term) "local" systems. In the middle ranges, such distinction will be somewhat arbitrary, but it becomes clearer if we allow that "reach" covers response time as well as range. Thus an IRBM would come within global systems, while a medium-range bomber would be at the high end of the local systems. Perhaps more important is the concept that "global" systems are of a kind that can be launched from national territory (or from a strategically located submarine) to strike without warning at maritime targets in distant sea areas, across intervening seas or territory, whereas "local" system implies a more direct relationship between adversaries. Global systems will be extremely sophisticated and expensive, and in the main they are likely to be limited to the superpowers. Several components for such systems are already in service, and it seems clear that the Soviet Union (at least) intends to adopt an integrated "all arms" approach to maritime warfare.

While the global systems introduce a new dimension, improvements in local systems have been equally dramatic. The main instrument has been the terminally guided cruise-missile, which allows a patrol craft to pack the punch of a battleship, and which can be fitted to aircraft, surface ships, submarines, or coastal defense installations. As important as the accuracy and payload of this weapon is its range, which extends a coastal state's reach to seaward. In addition, the greater the range, the smaller the number of weapon platforms needed to cover a given sea area or stretch of coast.

The homing cruise-missile can be a deadly weapon against an undefended or unalerted target. But once the threat was properly assessed, it was appreciated that in many ways the cruise-missile simplified the defense's problem. Early missiles were transsonic and provided a reasonably homogeneous target which, within the existing states of the art, could be shot down or seduced. In many ways this compared favorably with the previous situation, where the weapon was a torpedo, shell, or bomb whose flight could not be arrested. Effective defense was therefore predicated on the destruction of the weapon platforms (submarine, surface ship, or aircraft) prior to weapon launch—a very demanding requirement. The weakness of these systems had been their inaccuracy; but, in the case of bombs and shells, this can now be overcome by the use of precision-guided missiles (PGM) that home on the designated target. Of course, the terminally guided cruise-missile remains a serious threat, and later generations are supersonic, harder to detect, and more difficult to decoy or shoot down.

So far, only strike systems have been referred to, but there have also been considerable advances in counter-strike or "protect" systems. These include electronic countermeasures (ECM), image masking, and so forth, as well as weapons designed primarily for shipboard self-defense. We have here the classic contest between attack and defense, and up to now it has been a fairly even match. But the advent of the tactical ballistic missile, and the prospect that it may be mounted on surface ships, submarines, and ashore for use against maritime targets, raises the requirements for shipboard self-protection to new levels which will be difficult to attain. These ballistic strike systems will be expensive and therefore reserved for high-value targets; but their existence does prompt the question of whether traditional surface warships will be able, in the future, to survive in a hostile maritime environment.

Dispersion of Weapon Systems among Nonindustrialized States

These technological developments relate mainly to confrontations between the two superpowers in the context of general war. But, since 1955, the industrialized powers have provided a steady supply of sophisticated weapons to emerging nations. Whatever the motives behind this, the effect has been to increase the ability of these nations to defend themselves against external intervention and, in several cases, to prevent the use of their coastal seas. As an indicator of the latter capability, by 1976 about twenty-three nonindustrialized states had been supplied with missile-armed surface units (or missile systems for retrofitting), ten by the Soviet Union and thirteen by the West; fourteen such states had been supplied with submarines, four by the Soviet Union and ten by the West—six of the latter being in South America.[7] These by no means constitute the only type of weapon which can be used to prevent the use of the sea; besides other naval forces like torpedo boats and gun-armed surface units, there is the whole range of shore-based systems such as aircraft, missiles, and coastal batteries, and fixed obstructions such as mines. And all these weapons are being progressively upgraded. When the supplies are from the West, this is largely for commercial reasons. When they are from Russia, this is a by-product of her economic system, which allocates a fixed share of resources to weapons procurement, resulting in the periodic replacement of all equipment by improved versions. In this context, the Soviet SS-N-3 300-mile surface-to-surface antishipping cruise-missile will be superseded by the end of the 1970s and may become available for selective supply to client states for coast defense purposes.

The supply of weapons is one thing; their effective use is another. This is why maritime geography plays such an important role in determining a coastal state's ability to prevent the use of its waters. It requires an experienced submarine commander to bring a diesel boat within torpedo range of a target in open waters. And while range is not so great a problem to missile-armed patrol craft, these craft are very susceptible to counterattack when away from the cover of land, and the state of the sea affects their operational performance. Mines are a cheap and simple way of preventing use, but they can be laid only in relatively shallow depths, and are effective only if they cannot be circumvented or swept, factors which depend largely on the breadth of the waters.

There is also the complex matter of what a nation needs to maintain and operate the weapons it possesses. We have the example of the buildup and decline of Indonesia's Navy, and the limited effectiveness of the Egyptian force; both are nations with a seafaring tradition. The rapid deterioration of the Indonesian Navy was mainly a failure of maintenance, and the lack of spare parts was a subsequent cause; this underlines the problems of keeping complex equipment operational, particularly in hot, humid climates. When this factor is coupled with such evidence as the apparent superiority of Israeli pilots over their Egyptian opponents, one begins to ask whether a country requires some minimal technological base in order to make effective use of the latest weapons. On the other hand, North Vietnamese air defense units inflicted heavy casualties on the latest American aircraft, which suggests that perhaps it is as much a matter of priorities and commitment as of innate capability. Meanwhile, the trend in weapon design appears to be toward increasing internal sophistication, matched by a greater simplicity in operation and maintenance; and this may come to compensate for the technological constraints.

The Soviet Navy's Shift to Forward Deployment

The fourth major development has been the Soviet Navy's shift to forward deployment. Although this has received the most publicity, in practical terms it seems to have had little real effect on either the capability or the willingness of the West to use their navies in support of military intervention overseas. If anything, in the last ten years there has been an increase in such activity. The presence of Soviet naval units in distant sea areas must obviously introduce a complicating factor to U.S. plans and impose costs in terms of higher states of readiness and increased surveillance requirements. But it has certainly not restrained America from active naval intervention, as we saw in the Jordanian crisis in 1970, the Indian Ocean deployments in 1971 and 1973, two Arab-Israeli conflicts, and throughout the war in Vietnam. Commentators who insist to the contrary tend to disregard the rise of nationalism, the Western withdrawal from empire, and the diminishing utility of coercive intervention; they ascribe the results of these historical trends to the presence of a few Soviet warships. Given their opportunities, the Sovets have made remarkably few gains.

It is now generally accepted that the primary determinant of the Soviet decision that their Navy should shift to forward deployment was the sharp acceleration in strategic weapons procurement ordered by President Kennedy on taking office, and the marked increase in the emphasis on sea-based systems. These factors generated a Soviet requirement to deploy a counter against this threat to Russia from the "maritime axes," and resulted in the radical restructuring of the Soviet Navy.

The carrier threat, which had been the Soviet Navy's primary concern since 1955, yielded precedence to the threat from Polaris, and, since 1961, antisubmarine warfare (ASW) has received top priority in research and development and in warship design. Between 1957 and 1967, naval new construction entering service was heavily oriented toward the antisurface role, with SSM as the primary weapon. Since 1967, the emphasis has swung sharply to ASW; additionally priority has been given to self-protection weapon systems on the larger surface ships. Except for one class of four ships (the rump of a cancelled program), all new construction major surface units which have entered service since 1962 are designated by the Russians as large antisubmarine ships; the Moskva and Kiev classes are called antisubmarine cruisers. Two older classes of SSM-armed surface ships have undergone major conversion and been redesignated as large antisubmarine ships. U.S. officials now refer to both Moskva and Kiev as "ASW carriers," and they have also acknowledged that the missile launcher tubes in Kara (called a cruiser in the West) carry antisubmarine weapons and not SSM, as had previously been thought. This probably also applies to the other three classes of new construction large antisubmarine ships which have entered service since 1966.[8]

Despite the shift to forward deployment, the Soviets are still building a navy for a narrowly defined, defensive mission, tailored for general war. If anything, this tendency is likely to increase as they continue striving to develop an effective counter to Polaris, Poseidon, and then Trident. The construction of distant-water surface warships proceeds at a modest pace—about two cruiser-size and two destroyer-size large antisubmarine ships a year, and an ASW carrier every two years, and one has the impression that they are an interim expedient, while the final answer to the problem is being developed. Submarines are a different matter, and nuclear construction proceeds remorselessly at ten units a year, while a new diesel program is also under way. The Soviet submarine force now constitutes the primary antisurface capability, and SSM-armed submarines operate in company with Soviet surface forces. They make a powerful team, but its capabilities lie at the high end of the spectrum of force, and it lacks any projection capability.

Although the presence of Soviet naval forces in distant sea areas increases the possibility that they can be used to hamper Western military intervention, the past ten years provide evidence of Soviet caution on this score. Of greater significance is the future role of the new global weapon systems, and their potential as a deterrent to such operations.

The overall effect of these developments in law of the sea, advances in weapon technology, and proliferation of sophisticated weapon systems has been to make the sea a much more complex and potentially hostile operating environment. Attempts to prevent its use have been more likely, and the capability to do so is much more widespread. The near-monopoly of naval power enjoyed by the West during the first two postwar decades has been steadily eroded. The reach of coastal states is being progressively extended, and regional navies are beginning to emerge in such areas as the Arabian and China Seas, and the western South Atlantic. These developments do not imply that the U.S. Navy will lack the capability to project military power in distant parts of the world, or to secure the use of the sea for such purposes. Its ships were designed for war with Russia and should be able to operate in the face of Soviet hand-me-downs and suboptimal Western systems. But the developments do mean that the deployment of naval forces will need to be less an instinctive reaction and will have to take more factors into account, including the possibility of losses. They also mean that self-protection systems will need to be given higher priority in each ship's weapons outfit.

THE COSTS OF MILITARY INTERVENTION BY SEA

Military intervention can be coercive or supportive.[9] The distinction is not entirely clear-cut, since, in the case of supportive intervention, the other party can claim he is being coerced (e.g., North Vietnam), and in a coercive intervention a third party may be supported indirectly (e.g., Pakistan in the 1971 Bangladesh war). The distinction is useful, however, because of the different levels of capability required for the different types of intervention, both on land and at sea.

The proximate aim of maritime intervention is either to secure the use of the sea or to prevent its use. *Preventing* use is a relatively simple concept; we have as examples the U.S. blockade of Cuba in 1962, the mining of Hanoi in 1972, and Britain's Beira patrol aimed at Rhodesia. These were all coercive. A supportive intervention of this type is the Guinea Patrol, established by the Soviet Navy in November 1970, to discourage further seaborne attacks on Conakry. Except for the Cuban blockade, all these interventions were by nonadjacent powers.

The Terminal Area

The concept of *securing* the use of the sea is more complex, raising the question of "use for what?" and sending us back to the categories in our box diagram. Focusing first on the projection of force ashore in the terminal area, we need to distinguish between coercive and supportive intervention, and to know whether ground forces are involved. In *coercive* intervention, the maritime environment will be hostile; where troops have to be landed and kept supplied by sea, it will be necessary for the Navy to secure command of the offshore zone and to be responsible for air superiority, until airfields are established ashore. In constricted waters, the need to cauterize possible threats and and forestall a surprise attack will inevitably incur additional political costs, particularly if other states are close set, as, for example, in the Persian Gulf. However, if coercive intervention is limited to "punishment" by strikes from ships lying offshore, effective force defense systems may be all that is necessary, unless a strong opponent and unfavorable geography are present.

Supportive intervention is a very different matter, involving much lower risks and costs, even when ground forces are engaged. The presence of a friendly coastline and the availability of shore facilities for coastal surveillance systems and air support are important assets. When ground forces are not involved, the Navy's role is to bring prepackaged firepower to bear on the area of conflict. At present, this mainly involves airborne systems, and these can be used in various ways, ranging from air defense to reconnaissance and close ground support, with the carrier serving as an offshore airfield. But the advent of precision-guided weapons and rocket-aided shells may mean that gunfire support from surface ships will gain a new lease on life.

Involvement by three or more parties in the terminal area is becoming increasingly likely. When support is being given to one side in a local conflict, the temptation for the other side to attack the intervener is very strong. Whether this temptation is resisted will depend on the other side's capability for effective action, fear of the consequences of attack, and any external political constraints which may exist. Western "sanctuary" theory has never been very persuasive; and the spread of potent weapons, the existence of leaders like Qdaffi and Amin, and, where submarines and missiles are concerned, the difficulties of pinning down responsibility, all combine to make it unwise for major powers to assume that smaller nations whose interests are threatened will not dare to retaliate. Outside powers who are not parties to the local dispute may also become involved. For example, the emerging regional powers may react against external intrusion in an area where they themselves are competing for influence. But the more interesting instance is involvement by other superpowers, and the prospects for this type of confrontation, and its consequences, are discussed in the following section.

So much for the terminal area. But to intervene, one must first get there in time to achieve one's purpose, and then if necessary sustain the operation by sea. This brings us to the question of securing passage.

Securing Passage

Narrow waters or straits offer the best opportunities for obstructing passage; ignoring the question of plausibility for the moment, we can consider what ought to be done to secure use in such a case. Ideally, the solution should stem from a comparison of the political costs and benefits of the possible courses of action. We start with the political *gains* that are supposed to accrue from the main military intervention in the terminal area. Against this we set the political *costs* of insisting on passage through the narrow waterway against the wishes of the littoral state(s), which may involve a subsidiary military intervention. And if there is an alternative way of getting to the terminal area, we assess the political and economic costs of accepting such a diversion.

The political costs of forcing passage must depend on the particular circumstances, but to some extent they will reflect the bloodiness of the battle. This will stem from military factors such as relative capabilities, distance from land, length of time within range of attack, capacity for point defense, depth of water, the likelihood of third-party intervention, and the type of land-based weapons available to the littoral state. There is also the type of use. It is one thing to burst through deep-water straits with a carrier group; it is another to laboriously sweep a passage through mined waters within artillery range of land. To secure a continuous flow of shipping through hostile narrow waters is very difficult and probably requires that key points on the coast be occupied. One can postulate a general relationship between the costs of forcing a passage in peacetime, and the depth and width of the waterway and the time in transit. To force a long passage through narrow, shallow waters is likely to have high political costs that stem mainly from the need to take action against the national territory of the littoral states.

Accepting Diversion

If questions of "prestige" and "precedent" are set aside, the costs of accepting diversion will depend on the extra distances involved. They can be expressed in time and money, and will translate into economic and political costs. In most instances, the costs will be predominantly economic (although these may have domestic implications), but external political costs will be incurred in a situation where time is crucial. Russia would be faced with such a situation in the event of war with China, since she would almost certainly have to supply her Far Eastern front by sea. The length of the delay before the regular flow of supplies began to arrive in the Far East would be directly related to the length of passage, and Russia has a vital interest in ensuring that the shortest route (Suez Canal and Malacca Straits) is not obstructed. The next shortest route (via Panama) is half again as long. In the case of the U.S., it is more likely to involve the reactive deployment of a carrier force from the Pacific into the Indian Ocean, in circumstances where the fate of a client regime depends on support's arriving within a limited period of time. But in this example, the political costs can be translated into economic costs in the longer run. If it were essential to be able to intervene in both the Indian Ocean and the western Pacific, extra carriers could be procured and deployed on both sides of the archipelagic barrier.

In all other circumstances, time and distance can usually be translated into dollars and cents straight away. In preplanned military interventions, the extra distance can be covered by anticipating and sailing earlier. Cyclical deployments like Polaris patrols can be handled by increasing the number of units, reducing time in rest and maintenance, or changing crews in the forward area. Continuous flow operations like logistic support and military supply can be performed by placing additional bottoms in the shipping pipeline.

We cannot rule on the comparative cost-benefit balance without knowing the particular circumstances. But it would seem that, when time is not a problem and when an alternative route exists, even if it is twice as long, the costs of accepting a diversion while negotiating the use of a waterway are likely to be considerably less than those incurred in forcing passage. Even when time is critical, the costs must be weighed carefully against the benefits to be achieved at the far end.

For the same general reasons, the denial of passage to commercial shipping will rarely justify the costs of military intervention. Not only can the merchant ships usually be diverted, but it is also possible to send the goods by other means, such as pipeline, rail, or road. Where shipping continues to be used, it is the *relative* increase in distance which is important—and its effect on shipping costs as a share of the final price of the product. It is hard to generalize about this, because, although there is a direct relationship between the length of passage and the cost of providing shipping services, the extent to which the price of shipping actually reflects these costs varies between trades. However, shipping represents a comparatively small proportion of the total cost of imports, and as a general rule, the effects of making a major diversion are likely to be no greater than the effect of normal fluctuations in commodity prices and charter rates. For example, if we postulate that all the straits through the Indonesian Archipelago are closed, and all shipping from the Indian Ocean has to pass south around Australia, and then make the worst-case assumptions about freight rates, this would raise the cost of living in Japan by less than 1%.[10] And yet 40% of Japan's imports normally pass through these straits, including 80% of her oil. There would, of course, be some dislocation of supplies while the first ships steamed the longer routes, but there are numerous examples of how rapidly international trade adapts to new circumstances; dislocations are likely to be temporary.

OBSTRUCTIONS TO PASSAGE

How likely is it that littoral states would seek to prevent the use of narrow waterways? In most cases, they have a vested interest in the continuous flow of trade and shipping through these waters, and their economies would be damaged by a prolonged diversion. The closest precedent is the blocking of the Suez Canal by Egypt in 1956, but this was in response to an Anglo-French assault. Littoral states may wish to use their monopoly power to extract rent from a geographical asset, and might threaten various restrictions if their demands are not met. But so far their position in this regard has been moderate, reflecting reasonable concerns for the dangers inherent in the passage of very large crude carriers and comparable ships through narrow waters, and the devastation that could be brought to their shores. In this they can expect a fair amount of international support. But there would be little support for a general toll on all types of cargo, because most countries now have a vested interest in lower shipping costs. An unprovoked attempt to hold the international community to ransom by preventing use of such waterways would inevitably leave the littoral states worse off than they started, and undoubtedly they appreciate this.

Provocation is another matter. Newly emergent nations are so sensitive about national sovereignty that any infringement on it would be perceived as due cause by many of these countries, even if their consequent actions damaged their immediate interests. For this reason, the passage of warships, amphibious forces, and military supplies falls into a different category than normal trade, particularly when the forces are intended for use against some friend of the littoral state, or in support of some enemy. We have seen the use of the oil weapon to bring pressure on Western nations during the Arab-Israeli war, which had tactical as well as strategic consequences. Denial of passage through strategic waterways could be used in the same way. Whether it would is another matter. Turning off the oil did no damage to the supplying countries; rather the reverse. But a littoral state which sought to prevent the passage of U.S. forces would have to assume that its territory would be attacked. While it is true that not all states speak the language of interest, and that when international passions are roused reactions tend to be unpredictable, it would still be a heavy price to pay in support of a distant state and the diffuse aims of a loose ideological bloc.

The degree of political commitment is central to the use of force, which is why attempts to prevent the passage of military supplies are more likely in the terminal area. The absence of such attempts in the past probably reflects a lack of capability rather than the will to make the attempt. In Vietnam, it seems likely that the Soviet Union did not wish to jeopardize her maritime supply line to Haiphong, lest Hanoi be forced to rely on overland support from China. However, the U.S. mining of Haiphong has now "legitimized" a whole new range of actions in the terminal area, and in future conflicts the client state may be provided with the means to interfere with the shipment of military supplies.

This leads to the question of whether military intervention is likely against the ocean waterways. To start with the more general, international trade, it is sometimes argued that, because the West is so dependent on the shipment of oil from the Middle East, the Soviet Union will be tempted to attack the line of supply; such argument is a modern variant of the more venerable bogey that because Europe depends heavily on imports, it would be in Russia's interests to initiate submarine commerce war in the North Atlantic. This is a classic example of the fallacy that what hurts oneself must help one's enemy, and can be shown to be implausible for a whole range of reasons. Outside the circumstances of world war, it is nearly impossible to identify circumstances in which it would be in the Soviet Union's interests to initiate commerce war, least of all in the Arabian Sea. The reasons range from comparative military capability to political and economic costs and alternative instruments of policy, and include Russia's own interest in maritime stability and freedom of the seas, which still remain largely within the gift of the West.[11] In general, the diffuse nature of international seaborne trade is its own best protection, since most nations have an interest in the principle of safe passage for merchant ships in peacetime. Meanwhile, as the number of national merchant fleets grows, so too does the extent to which all ships are hostage to one another.

The shipment of military supplies is a different matter. So far, the convention has been observed that attacks on the lines of supply have been limited to the territory and coastal waters of the primary belligerents or client states. With the growing number of states possessing submarines, it is not certain that this convention will hold. The U.S. came close to breaching it during the Cuban Missile Crisis, but this could be justified by the nature of the Soviet initiative, and on the grounds that Cuba was within the American national security zone. But the latter justification can be claimed by China in its adjacent sea areas, and it now has a force of more than seventy submarines. While the midocean interdiction of military supply lines remains unlikely, the probability is increasing that these lines will be liable to attack or other forms of interference as they near the terminal areas.

MARITIME INTERVENTION AND THE SUPERPOWERS

The United States

Russia and America have somewhat different approaches to overseas intervention, both in their historical experience and in their current assessments. The American case will not be explored in depth. Suffice it to say that she was both the offspring and the inheritor of Western attitudes, experience, and tradition in this area, and subsequently made her own contributions. Since the end of the nineteenth century, the U.S. Navy has been an important instrument of policy, whose potential was vastly increased by its development during World War II. America ended that war as the world's paramount power, with a Navy second to none, and soon found herself at the head of a Western maritime coalition which had a virtual monopoly of seapower; this was used to some effect in following decades. The U.S. Navy includes an organic air force which for a long time was the third largest in the world (after the USAF and the Soviet force), and a Marine Corps which is larger and better armed than most national armies. The "peacetime" employment of naval forces has been a dominant consideration and has generated its own substantial force requirements. During the past thirty years, there has probably been a greater use of navies in this way than in any comparable period.

The Soviet Union

Russian naval history goes back to a time when America had not yet gained her independence. But, traditionally, the Navy has been seen as an expensive necessity rather than as an instrument of worldwide policy. From the first half of the nineteenth century, Russia's naval policy was increasingly dominated by the requirement of defending four widely separated fleet areas against maritime powers who could concentrate their forces at will. This same attitude persists in the present-day Soviet Union, where the defense establishment is dominated by ground-force officers and where there appear to be considerable doubts about the value of military intervention overseas. This is reflected in the shape of the Soviet Navy, which lacks a distant-water intervention capability and is structured for the war-related task of posing a permanent counter to the West's seaborne strategic delivery systems. The primary maritime instrument of foreign policy is the merchant fleet, which carries trade, aid, and arms supplies to client states and other countries, and whose well-disciplined crews project the Soviet presence ashore.[12]

The Overseas Role of a Soviet Military Presence

It would, however, seem that, between 1969 and 1973, there was a sustained debate within the Soviet Union about the use of armed forces in support of international goals.[13] The causes and the results of this debate are still obscure, but it appears that in 1969, under pressure of the rapidly deteriorating situation in Egypt, the political leadership agreed to commit Soviet armed forces overseas, thus taking the first step down the road of a traditional Western-style policy toward the projection of military power. This major policy decision was followed by the deployment of Soviet air defense systems to Egypt in the spring of 1970. It seems, however, that as events unfolded and as the costs and implications of such involvement became clearer, the arguments of those who opposed the original shift in policy were strengthened, until they were able to reverse the deployment decision. However, the final policy on the role of a "Soviet military presence" had yet to be agreed, and it seems that the debate continued for a further twelve to fifteen months until a compromise was reached. By May 1973, it was apparently decided that direct Soviet involvement overseas would be limited to the provision of advisers, weapons, and strategic logistic support; the combat role would be delegated to the Soviet-equipped forces of "revolutionary" states such as North Korea, Vietnam, and Cuba.

The outcome appears to be a policy which gives the Soviet Union the best of both worlds; namely, being able to affect the outcome of an overseas conflict with direct battlefield support, while ensuring that political commitment and liability remain strictly limited. This is achieved by *(a)* facilitating the arrangements and providing the lift to bring cobelligerent forces to the zone of conflict; *(b)* ensuring that the client state or regime receives adequate military supplies in the course of the battle; and *(c)* remaining silent about Soviet involvement until success is assured. Of course, a corollary of such a policy is that it allows only the supportive use of Soviet military force; the coercive use must be achieved through proxies.

In terms of force projection, the major instruments of this policy appear to be the merchant fleet and the military and civilian air transport fleets. The Soviet Navy has made some contribution—for example, the sea lift of Moroccan troops by landing ship to Syria in April and July 1973, the use of landing ships to ferry military supplies from the Black Sea to Syria during the October 1973 war, and the use of the landing ships based on Berbera to move supporters of the Dhofari rebellion to Oman. This naval contribution is marginal in comparison with men and supplies shipped by other means, and the emphasis on the peacetime employment of Soviet naval forces is in other directions.

The Navy's Peacetime Role

The 1967 Arab-Israeli war, which gave the Soviet Navy its much-needed access to Egyptian shore facilities, also marked the start of the second and more distant phase of the shift to forward deployment, as Soviet naval forces moved out into the Caribbean, off the west coast of Africa, and into the northeast quadrant of the Indian Ocean. Thereafter, political exploitation of the presence of Soviet warships in distant sea areas steadily increased. In 1970 there was a marked change in the trend, with naval detachments being deployed specifically for peacetime (as opposed to war-related) tasks, but this activity leveled off in 1972-1973. Soviet pronouncements refer to the Navy's peacetime role in general terms as "defending (or securing) state interests," a nebulous formulation whose scope has yet to be systematically researched. While not losing sight of the all-encompassing scope of this phrase, it is useful to discuss Soviet naval activity in terms of four major categories: establishing a strategic infrastructure; countering "imperialist aggression"; increasing prestige and influence; and protecting Soviet lives and property.

The first and most important category covers the task of establishing the physical, political, and operational infrastructure required to support two quite distinct war-related tasks, namely, posing a permanent counter in peacetime to Western sea-based strategic delivery systems, and securing the safe and timely arrival of military supplies to the Far Eastern front, in the event of war with China.[14]

The geographical extent of the first requirement can be seen by drawing 1,500 nm and 2500 nm circles centered on Moscow, which show the arcs of threat from the Polaris A-2 and A-3 missiles. The smaller circle takes in the south Norwegian Sea and the eastern Mediterranean and explains the heavy pressure brought on Egypt, from 1961 onward, to provide base facilities to support the Soviet Navy's forward deployment.[15] The larger circle takes in the eastern half of the Atlantic and much of the Arabian Sea, running from the tip of Greenland to cut the west coast of Africa abreast the Cape Verde Islands, and crossing the Indian Ocean between the Horn of Africa and Bombay. This explains the Soviet Union's persistent interest in the politically insignificant West African states, and her initial move into Somalia in 1969, despite the latter's talent for acquiring political enemies both in Africa and on the Arabian peninsula.[16] Meanwhile, Cuba gives access to the departure ports on the East Coast of the U.S., and (with West Africa) covers the sea lines of communication with the Mediterranean.

The second strategic requirement, to secure the sea lines of communication with the Far East front, explains the increased involvement in Somalia which followed after Marshal Grechko's visit in February 1972. Concern about the Chinese threat in the Far East began to crystalize after the 9th Congress of the Chinese Communist party in April 1969; this saw the emergence of what the Soviets perceived as a military-bureaucratic elite which was basically antagonistic to Russia. Following the series of incidents on the Ussuri River, the Soviet Union increased the buildup of its forces in the border region of China; presumably this would have prompted a review of the arrangements for logistic support in the event of war. Reliance could not be placed on the Trans-Siberian Railway, and supplies would have had to be shipped by sea. The reasons the Soviets shifted their focus from Egypt to Somalia are probably similar to those which prompted the British to start constructing a major base in Kenya in the late 1940s, as an alternative to the existing one in the Canal Zone. The decision to build up the Somalian facilities was taken at least six months before the withdrawal from Egypt, and it seems likely that Sadat's request suited the Soviets' purposes.[17]

Turning to the second category of "countering imperialist aggression," we should note that in the Soviet lexicon "imperialist aggression" includes the deployment of U.S. sea-based systems within range of Russia. Because of the very different type of political commitment involved, it is important to distinguish between the war-related task of posing a permanent counter to such systems, and the peacetime task of opposing/challenging Western military intervention against "progressive states" and "national liberation movements." In areas such as the eastern Mediterranean, where additional naval forces were deployed during the 1967, 1970, and 1973 crises, this peacetime task is upstaged by the more important war-related task of countering the U.S. carriers' nuclear strike potential; until the dangers of escalation were past, Soviet naval units unmistakably had this as their only priority during the first two crises. During the 1973 crisis, in addition to the carriers, they targeted the Sixth Fleet's amphibious forces, and this may have been intended to deter the U.S. from committing ground forces to the battle ashore. There is, however, an equally plausible war-related explanation. The Soviets plan to seize the Black Sea exits at the outbreak of a major conflict, and their Mediterranean squadron has the additional task of preventing the Sixth Fleet from reinforcing the defense of the Turkish Straits.[18] The primary mission during the 1973 crisis therefore remains uncertain.

The first clear example of the peacetime task of "countering imperialist aggression" was the establishment of the "Guinea Patrol" in December 1970, apparently to deter further Portuguese-supported seaborne attacks on Conakry. The next example was the dispatch of Soviet naval detachments to the Indian Ocean in December 1971, in reaction to the deployment of British and U.S. carrier task forces prior to and during the Indo-Pakistan war. The most recent example was during the Angolan affair, when a Kresta-class large antisubmarine ship was deployed south of Guinea; on the basis of past practice, the assumption would be that it had SSM-armed submarines in company. This placed the detachment in a blocking position between Angola and U.S. naval forces in the North Atlantic.

The other two categories are of lesser interest for this discussion. The task of "increasing Soviet prestige and influence" assumed a new dimension in 1972, when the Soviet Navy undertook port-clearing operations in Bangladesh; it was also used to sweep the southern approaches to Suez in 1974. The Navy's role in "protecting Soviet lives and property overseas" is best exemplified by the landing ships which take up station off Syria and Egypt when war breaks out between them and Israel, and off Angola in the 1976 conflict; it appears that their task is to evacuate Soviet personnel if defeat is imminent. The only other example is the deployment of three warships to Ghanaian waters in 1969, which may have helped effect the release of two Soviet trawlers that had been held for over four months on conspiracy charges.

Any particular operation may further the objectives of more than one of these four peacetime tasks. The continuation of the Guinea Patrol after the Portuguese threat evaporated in 1974 suggests that its primary justification may in fact have been to "establish the geostrategic infrastructure" by securing access to base facilities on the west coast of Africa. The same general objective may also have prompted the Ghanaian episode in 1969 and the politically timed visit to Sierra Leone in 1971.[19]

Political Commitment to Peacetime Tasks

It can be seen that the Soviet Navy's war-related task and its three main peacetime tasks are all intended to promote the two primary objectives of Soviet foreign policy. In order of priority, these are: (1) to ensure the security of the Soviet Union; and (2) to increase the Soviet Union's share of world power and influence. It is useful to dichtomize the peacetime employment of Soviet naval forces in this manner, because it clarifies the level of political commitment behind different types of interest and operation.

It is quite evident from their pronouncements, from the output of their defense production programs, and from their pattern of naval operations that the Soviet Union gives high priority to the task of countering Western sea-based strategic delivery systems. To support this task, they have been willing in the past to accept new political costs and commitments. Many of the paradoxes in the Soviet-Egyptian relationship since 1961 can be explained by perceiving that the Soviet Union had a near vital interest in gaining access to shore facilities to support her counterforce naval deployment in the eastern Mediterranean. It is possible that there may now be somewhat less willingness to accept large political costs on this score: partly because of SALT-generated changes in Soviet perceptions of the threat of nuclear war; partly because war with China is now the more likely contingency; and perhaps partly because the new global all-arms weapon systems will soon be entering service and will relieve the dependence on shore support in the forward operating areas. But the task still exists, and since it contributes to the security of the Soviet Union, the level of political commitment to securing the necessary geostrategic infrastructure will be of a different order than other types of overseas involvement.

"Countering imperialist aggression" is a different matter, and the level of political commitment to this has never been very clear. Certainly it is not worth risking war with America, which would violate the priority objective of ensuring the security of the Soviet Union. The Soviet perceptions of the dangers of escalation may have been modified by the SALT negotiations, increasing their readiness to risk confrontation at sea, in pursuit of overseas goals. And this brings us back to the possibility and risks of involvement by the second superpower, in a military intervention initiated by the first. The later stages of the Angolan affair provide an example of one kind of situation. This was an overt, supportive intervention, initiated by the Soviet Union, using proxy forces and shipping a large volume of military supplies by sea. The U.S. Navy certainly could have imposed a stop-and-search blockade on Angola in order to prevent this flow of supplies, but in fact it took no action. Presumably to discourage any such interference, the Soviets deployed a Kresta and one or more cruise-missile-armed submarines in a blocking position. Certain points can be made. First, the nature of Soviet interests in Angola were not such as to justify the sinking of a U.S. warship on the high seas, particularly a carrier; and a blockading force could have sailed through the Soviet patrol line with impunity. Second, the long-term political costs to the U.S. of imposing such a blockade would have been very high. It would have demonstrated to the Soviet leadership that Gorshkov was right when he argued that a powerful general-purpose fleet was the essential foundation of an independent overseas policy; and it would have encouraged a shift in the allocation of resources in favour of increased naval building programs, and the construction of a large, balanced surface fleet, including aircraft carriers. Such costs could hardly be justified by the U.S. interests at stake. And third, in order to shape the Soviet Union's future expectations, the U.S. could ostentatiously have dispatched a force of ships to sail through the Soviet patrol line, and it could then have reversed its course and returned home, thereby having shown that it was not intimidated. As it happens, the Atlantic Fleet was engaged in other operations and was instructed to ignore the Soviet deployment; this was the next best thing, but still a long way short of optimal.

Soviet-U.S. Confrontation at Sea

But, besides political commitment, there is also the question of effective military capability. The deployment of a U.S. carrier task force to the Indian Ocean in December 1971 during the Indo-Pakistan war may have been counter-productive in political terms, but at least the force had a demonstrable military capability, which could be used if wished. Not so in the Soviet case, despite the missile armament of their surface ships and submarines. Under what circumstances would these units have been ordered to attack the carrier? As soon as it readied its aircraft for takeoff—to an unknown destination with an unknown weapon load? Or perhaps only *after* the aircraft had struck some target ashore? Perhaps the Soviet Union could claim they got some political mileage out of this operation, although they certainly risked being exposed as paper tigers. But their next deployment, in response to the mining of Haiphong, was both militarily and politically pointless; a fairly substantial force of surface ships and sub-marines sailed to the South China Sea, hung around for a few days, and then returned home. There was nothing effective that they could do.

I am not persuaded by the suggestion that there now exists a set of tacit "rules" for the peacetime employment of naval force that apply equally to the Soviet Union and the U.S.[20] The two powers have different levels of naval capability and very different interests and types of commitment. Special account must be taken of Soviet interests in those areas of geostrategic importance to the security of the Russian homeland. But in most other circumstances, I consider that Soviet action at sea is largely conditioned by their estimate of U.S. reactions, and as a general rule, the low level of Soviet commitment to "countering imperialist aggression" does not justify risking confrontation.

The Soviet impulse to "counter imperialist aggression" is a long-standing one, as can be seen by the pattern of Soviet arms supply in the 1950s and 1960s. So too is the Western impulse to react against the emergence of left-wing regimes. And, for many years, the situation could be described crudely in terms of the West conducting a dogged rearguard action against change, while the Soviet Union was the natural ally of historical trends. But we are now thirty years down the road; there are few colonial territories left; and whatever their political complexion, the newly independent states have national interests and wills of their own. The old ideological reasons for military intervention by the two superpowers have largely evaporated, and it now becomes a question of picking sides in a traditional civil or interstate war. Given the transitory nature of political alignments, this would seem hardly worth the risks and costs involved. In the future, we may find that the main role of superpower intervention is to protect smaller states from the hegemonical tendencies of the emerging regional powers.

There remains, however, the problem of Southern Africa. Although the West is unhappy with the dominant white regimes, kith-and-kin and cultural factors constrain the type of support it is willing to afford the movement towards Black liberation, an ambivalence which provides excellent opportunities for Soviet influence-building. The possibilities for their involvement are manifold, ranging from the supply of arms to mounting a naval blockade to enforce a United Nations' resolution on mandatory sanctions. Given that the area is remote from both Russia and the U.S., and allowing that the Soviet Union may have downgraded the risks of escalation to general war, the pressures for an assertive policy will be strong, increasing the possibility of serious East/West confrontation.

OVERVIEW

The maritime aspects of military intervention are too diffuse a subject to draw together in a few well-chosen words, and to discuss the problem without having addressed the prior question of the utility of military force is like describing the mechanics of a religion without referring to its god. Certain points, however, can be made.

The most obvious is that we now have a situation which is infinitely more complicated than that facing Palmerston in the heyday of gunboat diplomacy. For a start, the maritime environment is much more complex. We have the diffusion of sophisticated weapon systems; the increased "reach" of coastal states; a change in international attitudes toward the rights of passage and the ownership of the sea; and the appearance of new "global" weapons for tactical use.

The political environment is also much more complex. We have just passed through thirty years of radical change that saw the dismantling of the Western colonial empires and an ideological competition for the favor of the newly emerging nations. We are now faced with an international system whose structure is hard to discern, with a change in the nature of usable power and its distribution, and with a range of threats to human survival that are altering national and international priorities and goals. Attitudes about the use of coercive force by the Great Powers have altered fundamentally, and new states do not "respond" to the threat of violence in the formerly accepted fashion.

Missiles don't know their mums, and the proliferation of modern weapons means that an increasing number of coastal states have some ability to prevent the use of their seas by both superpowers; narrow, shallow waterways are particularly vulnerable. The change in political attitudes means that maritime powers can no longer count on being able to use the seas for maritime intervention, unhindered and the terminal legs of the sea lines of supply are now vulnerable to attack. Meanwhile, the political costs of forcing a passage through narrow waterways are likely to be so high that it is usually better to take an alternative route, where one exists, except when major interests are engaged and time is an issue. The economic costs of such diversion are generally lower than would be expected.

The utility of *coercive* intervention is increasingly in doubt, except for short, sharp, small-scale rectifying operations, and possibly at the other end of the spectrum of violence, where the scale of operations changes "intervention" into "overseas war." *Supportive* intervention has a better record, but the increasing costs and risks raise the question of whether navies are necessarily the most effective instrument for such purposes. Aircraft carriers have an unmatched capability for bringing flexible firepower to bear in distant areas, but their high political symbolism and their need for sea room places constraints on their unfettered use. Meanwhile, the Russians have shown what can be done with merchant ships and airlift, making use of facilities in the host country.

Many of the attributes which in former times were the monopoly of naval forces, and gave them their special value as instruments of foreign policy, have now been dissipated or are shared by other instruments. The international news media and satellite surveillance mean that knowledge of warship movements is no longer in the flag state's control, to be released (or not) as circumstances indicate. Naval units can no longer deploy the graduated range of violence that used to be at their disposal; the level of force needed to achieve comparable results is very much higher. Violence (punishment) at the high end of the spectrum can now be inflicted on nonadjacent areas by aircraft and missiles, as well as by ship. In fact, the air is often a viable, alternative means of gaining access to distant areas, and the response time is of quite a different order. Modern communications allow heads of state and other ministers to transmit their concerns, interests, and intentions to their opponents in carefully chosen language; this compares favorably with the crude signaling of naval deployments. And the explicit language can now be backed by latent force emplaced ashore.

The latter is perhaps one of the more interesting possibilities which lie ahead. The advent of global systems which can deliver tactical weapons opens up new ways of preventing the use of the sea or of providing direct support in distant parts of the world. In practical terms, there is not much difference between sinking a carrier with a salvo of torpedoes, a 300-mile SSM, or a 3,000-mile terminally guided ballistic missile. It is illogical to be concerned about two of these possibilities and to ignore the third; the difficulty of countering the ballistic missile makes it the much more potent threat.

Despite these constraints and complexities, in the foreseeable future there will continue to be situations where the sea will be the most appropriate means of bringing traditional military force to bear in distant areas of the world. Changing circumstances will encourage progressive developments in the size and characteristics of naval units employed in this capacity, with particular emphasis on reducing the vulnerability and political salience of individual units. While making it less likely that such units will be disabled, this will reduce the political costs if they are, and hence increase the general usefulness of the naval instrument.

These changes in hardware will probably be easier to achieve than the even more necessary changes in traditional attitudes toward the role of naval force as an instrument of peacetime foreign policy. "Send a gunboat" can now do as much harm as good; the advantages of timeliness must be weighed against the political costs inherent in forward deployment. The Soviet presence in distant sea areas, such as the Indian Ocean, demands a careful evaluation of the costs and benefits of matching such deployments, compared with those of doing nothing and using the Soviet presence as a stick in the psychological competition for world influence. There is an urgent need for more selectivity in the type of naval force deployed and the occasions on which it is deployed. Carriers, which will continue to be operational thorugh the turn of the century at least, are likely to be reserved for use in major planned interventions, involving substantial forces and political commitment. Their more general role will be to contribute to the worldwide naval balance as a capability in being.

Military intervention by sea will persist as an instrument of Great Power policy, but there are likely to be considerable changes both in its character and in its relative importance.

N O T E S

1. The difficulties are emmense, as can be seen from Alvin Rubinstein, *Soviet and Chinese Influence in the Third World* (New York: Praeger, 1975), which represents a concerted attempt to address the problems of political influence-building. See particularly his chapter, "Assessing Influence as a Problem in Foreign Policy Analysis." See also his "The Soviet-Egyptian Relationship since the June 1967 War," in Michael MccGwire, et al., eds. *Soviet Naval Policy Objectives and Constraints* (New York: Praeger, 1975).

2. What seems likely to be the most substantial work in this field for some time to come is Ken Booth, *Navies and Foreign Policy* (London: Croom-Helm, 1977). Edward Luttwak addresses the question in *The Political Uses of Seapower* (Baltimore: Johns Hopskins University Press, 1974), although the context is rather restricted. For a pioneering, but not entirely successful, attempt, see James Cable, *Gunboat Diplomacy* (London: Chatto & Windus, 1971).

3. G. S. Graham, *The Politics of Naval Supremacy* (Cambridge: At the University Press, 1975). This compact book contains much wisdom about the role and influence of navies; see esp., the final chapter, pp. 96-125.

4. Ibid., p. 119.

5. A. A. Grechko, "A Socialist, Multinational Army," *Krasnaya zvezda* (December 17, 1972).

6. SS−NX 13 . . a submarine-launched ballistic missile with a range of 750 km. and with mid-course guidance and terminal homing. Norman Polmar, "Thinking about Soviet Naval ASW," *U.S.N. Institute Proceedings* (May 1976): 126. For a full discussion of Soviet naval weapon developments, see my "Soviet Naval Programmes," in Michael MccGwire and John McDonnell, eds., *Soviet Naval Influence: Domestic and Foreign Dimensions* (New York: Praeger, 1977), pp. 337-63.

7. These figures are extracted from tables in H. S. Eldredge, "Non-Superpower Sea Denial Capability. Paper prepared for the Conference on Implications of the Military Build-up in Non-Industrial States, Fletcher School of Law and Diplomacy, May 6-9, 1976. Eldredge concentrated on presenting a global picture of the distribution of submarine torpedoes and surface-to-surface missiles fitted in surface ships.

8. MccGwire, "Soviet Naval Programmes," in MccGwire and McDonnell, eds., *Soviet Naval Influence*, pp. 350-53.

9. There could also be a third category, "mediatory," but this is subsumed under "supportive."

10. For a summary description of the factors underlying these assertions, see Michael MccGwire, "The Geopolitical Importance of the Strategic Waterways of the Asian-Pacific Region," *Orbis* (Fall 1975): 1058-77.

11. For a summary statement of this argument, see Michael MccGwire, "The Submarine Threat to Western Europe," in J. L. Moulton, *British Maritime Strategy in the 1970's* (London: Royal United Service Institute, 1968), which was based on a longer, unpublished study.

12. For a discussion of the various maritime instruments of foreign policy, see Michael MccGwire, "The Navy and Soviet Oceans Policy," in MccGwire and McDonnell, *Soviet Naval Influence*, pp. 133-50.

13. See Michael MccGwire, "The Overseas Role of a Soviet Military Pressence," in MccGwire and McDonnell, eds., *Soviet Naval Influence*, pp. 31-60.

14. See Michael MccGwire, "The Soviet Navy in the Seventies," in MccGwire and McDonnell, eds., *Soviet Naval Influence*, pp. 626-28.

15. See G. S. Dragnich, "The Soviet Union's Quest for Access to Naval Facilities in Egypt prior to the June War of 1967," in MccGwire, et al., eds., *Soviet Naval Policy*, pp. 237-77. After gaining access to these facilities, year-round deployment was achieved for the

first time, the number of combatants on station rose by a factor of 2-3, and air support became available.

16. For the evidence underlying this geo-strategic argument, see Annex A of MccGwire, "The Soviet Navy in the Seventies," in MccGwire and McDonnell, eds., *Soviet Naval Influence,* pp. 653-57.

17. See MccGwire, "The Overseas Role of a Soviet Military Presence," in MccGwire and McDonnell, eds., *Soviet Naval Influence.*

18. This task prompted the basing of Soviet submarines on Valona in Albania from 1958 until they were ejected in August 1961. The present Soviet squadron, when not trailing Western units, spends most of its time at anchorages covering the Mediterranean approaches to the Aegean and Dardanelles.

19. See Michael MccGwire, "The Evolution of Soviet Naval Policy," in MccGwire, et al., eds., *Soviet Naval Policy,* pp. 525, 528, and notes 55, 63-66.

20. J. McConnell and A. Kelly, "Superpower Naval Diplomacy in the Indo-Pakistan Crisis," in Michael MccGwire, ed., *Soviet Naval Developments: Context and Capability* (New York: Praeger, 1973), pp. 449-51. This article provides an excellent analysis of the 1971 developments, but in going on to postulate the emergence of certain "rules of the game," I consider that McConnell commits the error of crediting the Soviet Union with interests which are comparable to those of the U.S. and makes insufficient allowance for the marked disparity in worldwide capability.

TECHNOLOGY, MOBILITY, AND CONVENTIONAL WARFARE

Lewis S. Sorley

This discussion seeks to outline the characteristics of emerging forms of high-intensity conventional warfare in the context of the contemporary system of nuclear deterrence, and to assess the impact of projected technology and mobility means on the prospective utility of conventional forces. The focus is on the perspective of United States forces in relation to the forces of the Soviet Union.

The central argument is that United States conventional forces retain both deterrent and war-fighting utility, but that contemporary realities mandate important changes in their organization, equippage, and employment. The case to be made will postulate an increased advantage for defensive forces (stemming from the nature of precision-guided missiles) and a decrease in the duration of conflicts (owing to higher rates of attrition in battle). Among the changes viewed as necessary are increased attention to the readiness of forces in being, acquisition of precision-guided missiles as a first order of business, restructuring of the active force to exploit reduced requirements for heavy-tonnage munitions resupply, and substantial revision of the role contemplated for reserve forces.

THE INTERNATIONAL CONTEXT FOR CONVENTIONAL FORCES

The central strategic question of the nuclear age concerns the continuing utility of the use of military force. Now, some three decades after the introduction of nuclear weapons in warfare, we are still just beginning to come to grips

AUTHOR'S NOTE: The views expressed in this paper are those of the author and do not necessarily represent those of any agency of the United States Government.

with the impact of the existence of such weapons on conventional warfare.

It is easy to understand how, in the initial, almost overwhelming, impact of the fateful technological marriage of nuclear weapons and then intercontinental missiles as a means of projecting them, an instinctive reaction might well have been that the use of force could no longer be contemplated. Even with subsequent qualification of the reaction—that no *responsible* state could any longer contemplate the use of force—it might still appear that the capability of such devastating power would inhibit any actions that could lead to escalation and the unthinkable nuclear exchange.

Such views were short-lived, of course, even in the era of United States monopoly and then preponderance of nuclear weapons. It quickly became clear that in many cases of contention, including those most likely to occur, the disparity between the ends sought and the nuclear means of applying force was simply too great for the threat or actuality of employment of nuclear weapons to be credible or contemplated. While "massive retaliation" was articulated as the centerpiece of United States strategic policy, it did not constitute a workable comprehensive response to military challenges; in fact, while massive retaliation was for a time apparently the nation's declaratory policy, at least in the shorthand articulation of it, it never became the action policy. The gap between what was at hazard and the means of defending it was simply too great for those means to be used.

Situations arose in which the use of military force was considered or actually undertaken, but where the application of nuclear weapons was clearly inappropriate, or appeared unlikely to beneficially influence the outcome, or both. Korea was one such case, perhaps the most illustrative of the less than universal usefulness of the war-fighting aspects of strategic nuclear weapons. With it went the hope that the threat of nuclear war would serve to dampen conflict at lesser levels. Whether the existence of such weapons served to restrain or moderate those lesser conflicts, either during the period of United States nuclear monopoly (as in Korea) or later (Suez and Lebanon, for example), is less clear; but certainly in the case of the Cuban Missile Crisis the preponderance of United States strategic power (as well as the locus of the confrontation) appears to have greatly influenced the outcome.

An additional element which inhibited use of nuclear weapons arose when the Soviet Union, in particular, and then several other states acquired their own nuclear arsenals. Now there was added to the inappropriateness, in many cases, of nuclear response the threat of retaliation, eventually to be regarded as a certainty between the superpowers, and one against which there was no defense. Assured mutual destruction, or at least the prospect of it, has exerted a powerful influence on the United States for a number of years.[1]

In the nuclear age, it is necessary to continue to assess the interplay of military consequences and the political utility of conventional forces. There is an evident and plausible connection among the existence of conventional forces (including the context of events), the operating logic of authorities to employ military force, and the resulting political effects. This causal relationship is evident across the entire scale from internal domestic influence to global power.

In terms of the viability of domestic governments, legal structures, and social fabrics, the existence of military force provides the necessary utlimate sanction of governmental authority. This is true not only in states where a repressive and unpopular regime relies on military force to maintain itself in power; it is also the essential element in the most open of governments, the more so as they incur certain vulnerabilities as a consequence of the very freedoms they seek to perpetuate. The capacity for ultimate resort to military force undergirds such governments' capacity to protect the rights of individuals, enforce the provisions of law, and reinforce where necessary the power of civil authority to deal with illegal acts. It is only rarely that elements of airborne divisions need to be stationed at public schools to protect individual rights and prevent illegal interference with judicial injunctions. However, if there were no such forces to meet this need when called upon to do so, the viability of the society and its representative government would be threatened. The political utility of military power in this domestic sense is apparent and immediate.

In international affairs, such political utility is equally operative, although the connection is often more remote, more tenuous, more conjectural. As former Deputy Secretary of Defense Robert Ellsworth once pointed out:

> Other states, whether adversaries or allies, will mold their own policies and behavior upon their expectations with regard to U.S. actions. Those expectations are based partly on estimates of the capability of America's military forces in being, partly on assessments of the trends between ourselves and the Soviets—and partly on estimates of our readiness to act.[2]

The political utility of those forces which both the United States and the Soviet Union have stationed abroad are prominent cases in point. The continuing presence of American troops in Western Europe has achieved more than to provide the United States with a greater voice in the affairs of the region, a pervasive influence through custodianship of theater nuclear weapons, and guaranteed involvement in repelling any aggression against that area. It has also made possible the continuing assurance that the Federal Republic of Germany, emerging from the status of conquered nation to that of full and perhaps even preeminent (European) member of the North Atlantic alliance, remains a non-nuclear power. This political impact of conventional forces has been of incalculable value. It is problematical in the extreme whether the NATO alliance could accommodate a nuclear-armed FRG, to say nothing of the fears this would engender in the Eastern bloc. Yet it is equally hard to imagine Germany's willingness to forgo nuclear weapons without the contribution in both potential war-fighting capacity and manifestation of commitment represented by the presence of American troops. The political utility of those troops, which have not had to be committed to combat in the more than three decades they have been stationed in postwar Europe, is both evident and enormous.

Soviet forces in Europe have also had pervasive political utility, although this was marred by their having been used for war fighting on a number of occasions when the impact of their potential employment proved insufficient to achieve their objectives. Unquestionably these concrete examples of willingness to actually employ forces, as in Czechoslovakia in 1968, have in turn enhanced their subsequent political utility. Maintenance of the preferred governments in power, direction and control of Warsaw Pact forces, and influence (if not domination) in East European economic and political cooperation with the Soviet Union have all been enhanced by the magnitude, disposition, and potential for employment of Soviet conventional forces.

Clearly, neither superpower has wanted a nuclear war. And yet neither has wanted to lose the influence it previously enjoyed in the world. Faced with frustrating inhibitions on the use of their great power, both have sought alternative means of bringing force to bear, means that lessen the risk of superpower confrontation. Alliances became a primary means utilized by the United States. The Soviet Union often used proxies, or provided support to revolutionary movements seeking to overthrow established governments. And, although they arrived at it by quite different courses, both superpowers came to view foreign aid as a means of attaining influence without the hazards of direct confrontation in the ear of nuclear stalemate. The "reliance upon economic instruments by the United States and the USSR [was] based in part upon the fear of the consequences of competition on the military plane in a nuclear age."[3]

These measures, while sometimes availing, have also been less than fully effective. It is unwieldy, slow, and self-limiting to have to deal through a surrogate, and it is frustrating not to be able to bring one's own tremendous power to bear. Maneuvering in the strategic nuclear realm by one or both superpowers might, of course, result in developing capabilities which could unlock the nuclear stalemate. These could range from a truly effective (which is not to say totally effective) antiballistic missile defense to a usable, disarming first-strike capability. Developments in warning, in hardening, in accuracy, in mobility, and perhaps later in exotic new systems could conceivably unbalance the strategic equation. All would have dramatic impact on the context of conventional warfare as well.

Meanwhile, given the overwhelming unwillingness of both major powers to enter into nuclear war under present conditions, we could expect to see a great deal of cunning and ingenuity devoted to maneuvering political and military situations so that the opponent is the one faced with the decision of whether to escalate the conflict to the nuclear level. In such a case, it would be surprising indeed if the nation suffering the disadvantage decided to initiate strategic nuclear war rather than experience far less serious losses. Only if the alternative also amounted to massive destruction could we expect the lower to opt for nuclear devastation.

Under such circumstances, the concept of the "nuclear umbrella," or extension of the protection of one nation's nuclear retaliatory capacity to protect an ally against aggression by another nuclear state, seems shaky indeed. The context in which this is usually discussed is that of Soviet aggression against a Western European ally of the United States, or against Japan. It is at best problematical that in such an event U.S. leadership would choose to initiate theater nuclear war, much less strategic, to counter aggression not directly threatening the American continent.

What is not so often considered, and ought to be given more careful thought is the range of symmetrical circumstances in which the United States might put the Soviet Union in the untenable position of contemplating the initiation of nuclear warfare without having been directly threatened itself. While such a situation might never come to pass, or even threaten to do so, it is possible for the sake of illustration to imagine a range of situations, from intervention in the Middle East to neutralization of Cuba, which could force the Soviet Union to make such a fateful choice.

The critical point is that the opponent must not be capable of defeating our initiative by the use of conventional forces alone; if he can, then we are left with very restricted options. If he cannot, then we have the opportunity to influence events where necessary, and the Soviet Union, not the United States, would be faced with having to decide whether to opt for nuclear war, a choice we can no more imagine its making (again, it must be emphasized, under present conditions) than it can imagine us doing.

Thus, it is assumed that the conventional warfare capability of a state is overwhelmingly important in maintaining its capacity to influence world events and in keeping the nuclear threshold at the highest possible level. A state which is unable to resist aggression by using conventional means has but two choices: escalate to nuclear warfare (if it has the means), or suffer defeat. With adequate conventional forces, it can prevent the opponent from winning conventionally, and can place on him the burden of deciding whether to escalate. By realistic standards of self-interest or rationality, the opponent would choose to desist rather than to initiate nuclear war, simply because a nuclear exchange would guarantee far greater disadvantage than could conceivably result in any other way.

POWER PROJECTION

It is critically important, in considering what can and cannot be accomplished at an acceptable price, to recognize that what can be accomplished is in large measure a function of who wants to interfere with the accomplishment. For the United States, in the contemporary world, this means preeminently the Soviets. One can accomplish certain objectives with given conventional forces, provided the locus of conflict is favorably situated with regard to the location of those forces, the distance from their base of supply, the vulnerability of the lines of communications thus relied on, the opponent's means of interdiction and his willingness to enlarge the conflict, and these same factors as they impact on his forces. Thus the two crucial elements in determining what can be done, or, alternatively, what is required to achieve some specific objective, are the location of the conflict and the opponent. The practical basis for the concept of spheres of influence is simply the recognition that overwhelming advantages in the application of power accrue as a result of location.

In determining the size, stationing, and equipping of United States forces, therefore, it is essential to take into account the kinds of things they might be called on to do, where these things are likely to take place, and who is likely to provide opposition. Given the extreme difficulty of predicting the full range of possible future conflicts, it is necessary to design "general purpose" forces having wide applicability. But the primary determinants of the design of those forces are of necessity the capacity of potential opponents and the probable locations of conflict; and this means, at present and for the foreseeable future, the Soviets and those places where their interests and ours are at odds.

The determination of what those interests are and where they must be protected is of course central to the design and deployment of military forces. There has not yet emerged, at the time this is written, anything that could be described as a new consensus on which to base a coherent force rationale for U.S. general purpose military elements. Yet, clearly, only the United States possesses the capacity to pose an effective counter to Soviet strength and ambition in the contemporary world. Clearly, the future hopes of many other peoples depend on the effectiveness of the United States in filling that role. And, clearly, the future prosperity and well-being of the American enterprise are dependent on such action.

Countering Soviet strength does not, of course, mean solely or even primarily military action. Nor does it mean determining events, for influencing them is all any one nation can hope to do in an uncertain world of competing interests and ideologies. It means, rather, demonstrated leadership in bringing to bear—across the whole complex of economic, diplomatic, political, and military issues—the most constructive and purposeful example.

In the military aspect of this complex, what are the elements of the ability to project power? First, of course, there is the possession of forces in being. Then, they must be deployable, or pre-positioned, so as to be able to bring influence to bear. This entails forward basing, or strategic mobility, or both. Next, they must be sustainable for the necessary duration of the conflict, which implies war reserve stocks, pre-positioned supplies and equipment, and the strategic logistics capability to accomplish resupply. These capacities may be enhanced through judicious use of security assistance and military aid, and through means of an effective system of alliances. These latter are not without their drawbacks, as we have come to realize sharply since the oil embargo, but they can markedly enhance the projection of power in appropriate circumstances. Availability of staging areas, overflight rights, port facilities, and the like strongly influence the ability to project power, as can the denial of such assets to an opponent.

With regard to the availability of bases, particularly staging areas such as airfields for refueling, and overflight rights, some consideration might well be given to the circumstances under which such facilities are required. While most discussion of bases centers around negotiations and agreements for their use, it should be recognized that in situations of sufficiently pressing need the United States could, and might be forced to, seize, defend, and utilize key strategic ports or airheads—and not confine its actions to those facilities belonging to the opponent. Furthermore, nations reluctant to commit themselves in peacetime to allowing the United States to use such facilities in the event of war might assess the situation differently when war actually occurred. Others might be unwilling to be viewed as having agreed to such use, but acquiesce if it appeared that they were forced into it. Thus, realistic contingency planning might well take into account bases not actually possessed, but potentially available for emergency use. Naturally, consideration of Soviet capabilities requires the evaluation of similar prospects for contingency use by their forces.

The Soviets are apparently impressed by the flexibility of United States general purpose forces and weapons and their capability for the projection of military power. In thinking of power projection, it is useful to consider the complementary but different roles of *projecting* power and of *interfering* with the projection of it. In the context of use of the seas this problem is a familiar one: it is generally recognized that it is far more difficult and demanding to *control* the seas, thereby guaranteeing unimpeded use of them, than to *deny* their use to others. The latter, "spoiler's," role is one that concerns us greatly, for many of our important allies and interests are separated from us by the oceans, and sea control would be important to us in cases where we needed to maintain support for them. Thus greater consideration of the opportunities which the sea denial role offers us, especially in an era of expanding Soviet interest in the projection of power, seems likely to be productive. Forces trained, equipped, and deployed to enforce a quarantine of a theater of conflict could play an important and essentially peaceful and stabilizing role in a number of potential conflicts.

What, then, are the several missions which conventional forces must be prepared to accomplish in the future? In addition to the customary requirements to be able to project power at a distance, to control use of the seas, to seize and hold territory, to defend against hostile attack, and to lend support and assistance to allies, the new missions may well prove more difficult yet. Means of countering terrorism, for example, seem likely to become more necessary in the future. Dealing with potential or actual proliferation of nuclear weapons, but without resort to their use in the process, will pose severe challenges for conventional forces. And performance of the traditional missions in the contemporary environment will be conditioned by new or increasingly important factors. An increasing vulnerability of strategic mobility means to cheap and widespread interdiction systems, the complexity of problems posed by conventional arms proliferation, the potential penetration or neutralization of computer-based command and control systems, and other even more futuristic challenges in the offing guarantee that the lot of force planners in the future will not be dull.

THE NATURE OF THE CONFLICT

There has been, in the renewed attention to the prospects and problems of high-intensity conventional war which has characterized the period of waning preoccupation with the problems of Vietnam, much discussion of "winning the first battle of the next war." There is a great deal of common sense in this outlook, although it has often been misunderstood or distorted in subsequent commentary. Simply put, concern about winning the first battle of the next war stems from the view that there is likely to be little time for preparation, the conflict will probably be intense and especially costly in terms of materiel losses, and thus such traditional strengths as an expandable industrial base, mobilizable reserve forces, and the like are not as important as they once were, since there would not be time to bring them to bear.

There are clearly limits to such a formulation. For one thing, it draws heavily on the data derived from study of the 1973 Middle East war, where major equipment loss rates were the highest ever recorded. However, this experience may not necessarily be repeated in future conflicts involving different opponents or taking place in different environments. More particularly, it cannot be said with any assurance that it will invariably apply to possible future United States interventions. And while high loss rates might well deplete the arsenals of combatants more quickly than in the past, determined opponents could undoubtedly find means of fighting on, even if more primitively, if their losses were roughly symmetrical.

Given a situation in which equipment assets had been rapidly and heavily depleted, such capabilities as battlefield logistics and repair could prove even more important than formerly; thus the recent trend in American ground forces of drastically reducing the combat service support in favor of a greater preponderance of combat elements could turn out to be highly counterproductive. And if the fighting continued, even at less sophisticated levels, there could well be time for traditional mobilization to take place and to influence the outcome.

In the service schools the time-honored method of dealing with such unavoidable uncertainties as the outcome of the interplay of all these complex factors is to observe that "it all depends on the situation." In more theoretical circles the assertion is often made that such cases are "extraordinarily scenario-dependent." It amounts to the same thing: where it is not possible to be reasonably certain in advance which contingency will arise, it is prudent to prepare for as general a case as possible. The aspect of the winning-the-first-battle strategy which seems most certain is this: it is important to survive the first battle as a viable fighting force, and this means, if not winning, at least not losing decisively. Therefore the forces in being, capable of being employed in the opening stages of a conflict, assume tremendous importance. The United States has traditionally depended on its industrial strength and capacity to field and equip a mobilized army when necessary. It has also depended on others to keep the conflict from being lost irretrievably and to buy the time needed for such mobilization. But unless the forces in being are capable of sustaining the conflict through the period until mobilization can be effected, there may not be time in a future conflict for this capability to have any bearing.

There is no validity to the argument, sometimes made, that it is *enough* to win the first battle. Nor can it be asserted categorically that future battles, even high-intensity ones, will *necessarily* be of short duration. Given the hazards of escalation to nuclear conflict, major opponents might very well be content to continue a conflict for an extended period at the conventional level. Unless one side were markedly superior to the other, even heavy losses could provide no assurance that the conflict would be brief. Certainly it might be diminished in sophistication and technological emphasis, but continue nevertheless. Under such circumstances the side better able to reconstitute its forces, to sustain them, and to perpetuate their viability as an effective fighting force might well find that capability the decisive factor.

The deterrent effect of conventional forces, in contrast to their military intervention function, has received substantially less attention than that of strategic nuclear forces, yet it may be a question of nearly comparable significance. This is true first of all because of the connection, previously discussed, between the adequacy of conventional forces and the nuclear threshold. The maintenance of insufficient conventional forces is not only improvident in terms of the ability to counter hostile conventional attack; it also increases the likelihood of having to face the agonizing dilemma of resort to nuclear weapons or acceptance of conventional defeat. The stronger the conventional forces a nation maintains, the less likely it is to have to face such a dilemma. For a nation such as the United States, whose objectives are nonaggressive and defensive in character, this is an ideal posture, since it entails no initiation of situations which pose the dilemma; only their own aggressive acts could put aggressors at such hazard, and they would have the additional option, not available to peaceable defenders, of simply ceasing the conflict with no further loss to themselves.

A crucial component of conventional deterrence, as well as of its strategic counterpart, is a nation's willingness to employ the forces at its disposal. It seems correct to represent the deterrent as resulting from the product of two factors: military capacity and the resolve to employ it. If either factor is zero, the product is zero; if either is minimal, the result is very low; if both are high, then the deterrent effect is also very great. In modern times, it is possible to know quite a lot about the real capability of another nation's armed forces, especially its conventional forces, and particularly in the case of an open society such as ours. Thus the factor in the deterrence product which the state of the forces represents is not only fairly easy to determine and assess, but also to manipulate. The size of the forces, their equipment, their state of readiness, where they are stationed, the scope and frequency of the exercises in which they engage, and other such tangible factors can be enhanced, and are concurrently quite visible to potential opponents. A wise strategy will recognize not only the contribution to deterrence, as well as to war-fighting capabilities, of such aspects of conventional forces, but also the return on the investment which this represents.

Furthermore, vigorous efforts to enhance and maintain such conventional force capabilities are viewed as evidence of the other factor in the deterrence product, that of national resolve to employ the forces when necessary. The nature and intensity of the public and governmental discussion of the use of force in various international events is also a factor in communicating national resolve, but one that is often skewed by the vocal expression of minority views which may not be representative; the state of the forces in being is a more reliable and tangible signal of what the people in general want and are willing to support in terms of conventional forces and the disposition to employ them. And while that willingness is notoriously variable, especially when other nations come to be viewed as exploiting or taking advantage of the essentially peaceful outlook of the United States, the generation of the forces to implement a willingness to use them is far more time-consuming than a shift in intention. Forces in being need not be employed; but forces which do not exist cannot be employed, no matter how urgently they are required. No prudent policy can be based on the absence of a capability.

What, then, given some willingness to maintain forces, are the determinants of success in conventional war? This question is very much bound up with that of winning the first battle, or at least not losing it, in order to be around to win the last battle. It also has to do with concern about whether future warfare will more likely involve a short or a long campaign, which in turn poses many crucial questions concerning the structure, location, and size of forces in being and reserve forces, if any, as well as the relevance of industrial capacity to national power in such a context.

It is possible to articulate any number of factors contributory to military success in various historical or hypothetical situations. Among those that seem most enduringly important are the following: surprise, by far the greatest multiplier of combat power; tactical skill, and effective means of command, control, and communications to bring it to bear; mobility means, both strategic and on the battlefield; sustainability of forces; location of the conflict; ability to concentrate a preponderance of force at the critical juncture (far more important than overall superiority in numbers); morale of the forces (particularly important to the armies of a democratic state); and domestic support for the prosecution of the conflict. With regard to this last factor, it is critically important that we develop and organize support for a coherent and consistent policy to guide both the military endeavor and those aspects of great importance in supporting it, which should include political, diplomatic, economic, and psychological initiatives and programs.

THE NATURE OF THE FORCES

Conventional forces are, or ought to be, almost continually in a state of flux, as new technology, changes in the world environment, and institutional maturation dictate necessary changes. Response to these stimuli is often delayed or incomplete, providing opportunities for advantage to potential opponents, and indeed it might be argued that the essence of strategy is the early recognition of and reaction to meaningful change.

American conventional forces at present pose a number of problems. In October 1975 the Army chief of staff observed that he was "not satisfied with the quality, the quantity nor the affordability of our equipment."[4] There will probably be changes in our forces, and to determine what those changes should entail we look to the impact of new technology and to the developments in Soviet forces.

Genuinely revolutionary developments are taking place in the technology of conventional warfare. In terms of those developments which are known and extant, and thus will make a substantial difference in the next few years, none is more dramatic or challenging than the change in guidance for conventional munitions. The difference can be stated simply: throughout the history of warfare, when a gun, a bomb, an arrow, or any other projectile was aimed at an enemy, it was expected to miss; now it is expected to hit. It is virtually impossible to overstate the impact of that fundamental change. In the past, the accuracies of guns and bombers were such that a large number of shells or bombs had to be delivered in order to have reasonable assurance that some would hit the target. Artillery barrages showered shells on the enemy so as to achieve a mathematical probability that the target would be hit; the probability that any one shell would hit the target was much less than the probability that it would miss. Until now.

While it is easy to overestimate the potential influence of technological innovations and expect them to provide the perfect solution, the impact of the improved conventional munitions and precision-guided missiles is demonstrably revolutionary. The Thanh Hoa bridge in North Vietnam is a good illustration. This bridge, a vital link in both road and rail communications leading down the

North Vietnamese panhandle, was attacked by hundreds of sorties during the bombing campaign extending from 1965 through 1968. It was hit many times, but was never neutralized, although there were many losses of attacking aircraft. But when the tactical air assault against the North resumed in May 1972, the aircraft which struck the bridge were carrying laser-guided bombs as well as 500-pound bombs, and the bridge was left unusable. The new technology made it possible to do in one day what it had not been possible to do in three previous years.[5]

With the advent of precision-guided missiles, it has become fashionable to assert that any target which we can see we can hit, and any target we can hit we can destroy. While there is an element of overstatement in this formulation, it does help to illustrate the changing nature of the problems of battlefield survival, mobility, and effectiveness. These weapons are, it must be remembered, being developed by both adversaries. To gauge the probable effectiveness of weapons systems in land warfare, it is necessary to envision them amidst the interplay of numerous weapons, troop dispositions and movements, terrain and meteorological conditions, intelligence and logistical impacts, and other contributory and complicating factors. To cite one very simple example, the performance of an infantry-delivered weapon on a test range pitting antitank against tank, or even against several tanks, will produce one set of results; the results will be very different when overhead artillery fire, close air support, chemical or flame weapons, darkness, fog, even partisan terrorism—or some combination of them— is added to the calculus of battle. However, the outcome could well be tipped the other way by swampy terrain, reduced visibility, or lack of supporting fire or accompanying infantry; these factors and others can make tanks more vulnerable. Thus, in making the difficult assessments of relative combat effectiveness, the danger of single-factor analysis must be avoided and the total combat environment taken into account.

To illustrate further, a photograph accompanying an article on the impact of battlefield guided weapons displayed two infantrymen, clad in arctic overwhites, each with a man-portable antitank weapon, prone and alone in the midst of a vast snowfield. What would be their prospects of survival under preparatory artillery fires? Or, more pressing yet, how long could they lie like that and still remain combat effective? Even if they were packing a superbly crafted antitank missile, they must remain alive and functioning in the face of enemy action and the elements long enough to bring that combat power to bear.

The implications of the new accuracy in weapons are profound, and they extend from probable equipment and personnel casualty rates to grand strategy. Taking the European case as an example, the viability of a conventional defense by NATO forces would seem to be substantially enhanced by the advent, even if the capability were acquired by both sides, of precision-guided missiles. Such weapons would seem inherently to favor the defender. If what can be seen can be hit, and what can be hit can be destroyed, then the necessity for the attacker to expose himself in the advance would become even more disadvantageous than in the past, while the defender's use of prepared positions, built-up areas, and natural cover would offer even more of an advantage than formerly.

What developments in tactics and weaponry would the need to counter this increased defensive advantage be likely to engender? The answer would appear to lie with weapons which do not depend for their effectiveness on being able to see the target, which would presumably be concealed and under cover. It does not take much imagination to link the chemical, biological, and radiological protective capacity built into the Soviet equipment which appeared on the Middle East battlefields to this perceived need.

The impact of the new technology on logistical considerations is also very important. In World War I the British are said to have shipped more fodder than ammunition to the front: some 5,500,000 tons of oats and hay.[6] The passing of the hay-burner from the battlefield changed only the nature of the fuel that had to be shipped, but the advent of precision-guided missiles could affect by orders of magnitude the amount of munitions that have to be manufactured, stocked, maintained, and shipped. Where before masses of shells had to be fired in order to gain reasonable assurance that a few would find their targets, now we are dealing with weapons which will probably hit what they are aimed at, and it would seem that ammunition inventories could be radically reduced. Those elements of the support force formerly engaged in trucking, guarding, caring for, and issuing that ammunition could be converted into additional combat power or support forces responsive to the greater lethality of the battlefield, with no concomitant increase in force levels.

On the strategic level, reduction of the need for Atlantic transshipment of large quantities of one of the heaviest commodities could save shipping, free storage facilities in the combat theater for pre-positioning of other needed supplies, and even reduce the critical dependence on maintaining the seaways during the initial stages of a conflict.

Countervailing factors may emerge which will diminish or negate one or more of the apparent impacts of this new technology, but the basic point remains clear: radical changes in available technology present planners with both opportunities and vulnerabilities, and successful response involves thinking through the full range of implications and making necessary adjustments.

The pace of technological change continues to increase, but some lines of development prove to be of transitory utility. The high-water mark of the viability of the helicopter on the battlefield was reached and passed by the late 1960s, a realization which has yet to come to all those responsible for planning and fielding our forces. Even before the advent of man-portable air defense missiles, with heat-seeking and other sophisticated guidance systems, the helicopter was becoming restricted in its survivability over the battlefields of Vietnam, where the opposition had no airpower at all. The enemy's deployment of the .51-caliber machine gun pushed U.S. helicopters from flying levels of 2,000 feet up to 3,000 feet to avoid ground-fire casualties, with the alternative of flying the nap of the earth (minimum altitude) a distinctly inferior protective measure owing to the degradation of command and control, artillery direction, and other common missions which such a flight profile entailed. It does not seem likely that we will ever again see the stacks of commanders' helicopters, describing endless circles at successive elevations, above a battle in progress on the ground which were so typical a feature in Vietnam. More to the point, the prospect of armed helicopters playing a major offensive or defensive role is unlikely to be realized on future battlefields. Important, if severely restricted, roles for helicopters in future combat can be envisioned, but these would be largely behind friendly lines: evacuation of wounded, high-priority resupply, command liaison. Certain limited offensive roles might persist against inferior or widely scattered opponents, especially in very fluid situations; these could involve raids, flank surveillance, and the like. But, as a central element of combat power, the helicopter has had its day.

While most enthusiastic helicopter pilots would not be happy to hear it, they have been supplanted (at least in the Soviet forces) by squad leaders in armored infantry combat vehicles. This is somewhat hard to understand for those who think of such a capability in terms of the lumbering steel box which has been for so long (and still is) the U.S. version of the armored personnel carrier. In contrast to the less effective U.S. equipment, the Soviets have been fielding, since the late 1960s, the BMP, a genuine armored infantry combat vehicle which features, among other things, two antitank missile systems (also useful against helicopters), provisions for the crew to fight from within the vehicle (U.S. infantrymen must leave the shelter of their carrier to fight), and extensive built-in protection against biological and chemical warfare agents (lacking in both current and developmental U.S. versions). Far less vulnerable than a helicopter, it has impressive ground mobility, protection, and striking power, and is battle-tested and in service with forces in the field.

The example of the armored personnel carrier raises a more general issue. While the United States has for decades claimed the superiority of its research and development and industrial production capacities, the confidence one might have that these strengths translate into usable battlefield superiority should today be much tempered. For while it is true that in many, perhaps most, realms the United States retains the capability to field superior weapons systems, in practice that capability is diminished because in many instances the superior technology, while potential opponents have not only developed but produced comparable or better systems (tanks, armored infantry combat vehicles, and field army air defense systems are cases in point).

In designing systems for the emerging battlefield, it seems likely that there will be a significant advantage to the side which, subsequent to an initial high-intensity, high-attrition engagement, can reconstitute and maintain the continuity of combat effectiveness of its forces. Intrabattlefield mobility—the capacity to rapidly disperse, concentrate, reorient, or redeploy forces in response to evolving tactical developments—is likely to be of great significance. Communications, transport, bridging and breaching capacity will be important. Intelligence, both of the battlefield and of broader compass, will be essential to the effective manipulation of forces. Surprise will continue to offer important and possibly decisive advantages and, with the enhanced intelligence capabilities which both sides will enjoy owing to satellite and communications technology, deception (never an American forte) may well decide the outcome. Given the lethality of the battlefield, supporting arms (infantry, artillery, air defense) must be able to accompany the tank/antitank force and survive in the same environment if they are to be effective.

With the increased importance of forces in being, force readiness becomes more critical than ever, both as it contributes to war-fighting capability and in terms of its effect on deterrence. A visible high state of readiness can improve the deterrent aspect of conventional forces. Some aspects of readiness, such as availability of repair parts and trained logistical support specialists, are not readily visible in and of themselves. They can be made visible, however, by means of demonstrated performance of the combat elements engaged in maneuvers and exercises, including those which involve moving substantial distances, showing the mobility and reliability of the equipment. Since such readiness contributes to both war-fighting capability and deterrence, it is advantageous to advertise high states of readiness whenever they can be achieved.

We have, by way of frequent references to the comparative sizes of forces and to their equipment inventories as indicators of relative military strength, helped to create a perception of the critical importance of the quantitative aspects of forces. But qualitative factors can also be extremely important, perhaps in some cases decisive. These include such force characteristics as readiness, training, discipline, morale, leadership, flexibility, and sustainability. Such factors are difficult to measure and assess, especially in a complex interaction analysis, which probably accounts for the insufficient attention they have received. But they are also areas in which United States forces are frequently thought to enjoy substantial advantages. With the use of some imagination in terms of exercise design and other means of demonstrating force capabilities, this edge in qualitative aspects of conventional forces could be made more visible while being enhanced. The result would be a net gain in both the deterrent effect and the war-fighting capabilities of the forces.

The prospect of high-intensity conventional warfare requires a restructuring of the reserve forces. What that structure should be has been a continuing unresolved question. There is, on the one hand, the residual influence of the Minute Man image, with its attendant implication that the citizen soldier can turn away from his fields, take up his musket, and defend the republic on a moment's notice. Reinforcing this bit of folklore is what amounts to a powerful lobby in favor of maintaining (although not necessarily employing) substantial reserve forces. On the other hand, there is the generally unsatisfactory experience of the very limited mobilizations of reserve forces at the time of the Berlin crisis (1961) and late in the Vietnam War (1968). Reinforcing the general pessimism of many, in the wake of these events, is a more general impression that it is simply not feasible, even as frequently as once or twice a decade, to mobilize reserve units whose members must customarily earn their livings at civilian pursuits which are often difficult to leave at unexpected times for indeterminate periods. This view holds that mobilization is a feasible response only to a very large, sustained, and widely acknowledged threat, and that what is needed in the reserves is a cadre and training establishment to support such a general mobilization, rather than units for inefficient, politically difficult, and problem-plagued partial mobilizations in a succession of lesser crises.

The utility of reserve forces as a recurring source of additional equipment for active forces could also, given such an approach, be explicitly recognized, and a more efficient custodial arrangement than dispersing the gear through a number of tactical units could be devised. Were such a rational and potentially useful restructuring of reserve forces into a training and mobilization establishment and equipment repository to take place, it would of course be necessary to retain in the National Guard those forces and units needed for domestic roles.

Reserves, it is time we recognized, are difficult to mobilize and deploy, especially for recurrent crises in which the physical security of the United States itself is not threatened; there are political difficulties in calling them up, and practical difficulties for those who are called, their employers, and of course their families. Should a crisis of major proportions and extended duration occur (such as the deterioration and prolongation of an initial high-intensity conventional conflict), the reserve establishment could serve far more usefully if it were prepared and equipped to commence the immediate training of large numbers of recruits for expansion or augmentation of the active forces, than if it deployed a limited number of units of varying degrees of readiness, willingness, and utility. Even in crises of lesser dimensions which nevertheless required additions to the standing forces, mobilization of reserve forces to provide the training base would prove far more feasible and palatable than mobilizing them for deployment.

MAINTAINING A VIABLE CONVENTIONAL FORCE POSTURE

The calculus of the application of general purpose forces is a complex one, far more difficult to analyze and assess than the strategic nuclear balance. It entails the complicated interplay of alliances; intertheater and battlefield mobility; time and distance factors; strategic and tactical surprise; intelligence and deception; sustainability of forces; mobilization potential and the time available to bring it to bear; political intentions and resources to maintain forces, and to deploy and commit them when necessary; and, in the event, the skillful command, concentration, maneuver, and employment of the resultant forces to achieve success. While ground forces play the central combat role (along with tactical air forces, but to a lesser and possibly precipitously declining extent now than in the past), important contributions are also necessary from naval general purpose forces (both ships and aviation, especially in the projection of power), possibly some elements of the strategic forces (such as bomber aircraft), and mobilized civil elements such as the merchant marine.

The range of situations in which conventional forces might be employed, or in which their existence might have a positive political impact, is impossible to specify in detail before the fact, and is fraught with what Dante called "horrid perhapses." It is too late, when forces are needed, to set about procuring them. Also, it is not necessary, for a capability to be worth having, that it be viable under all the worst-threat conditions. In seeking answers as to the conventional forces demanded by a prudent policy, the instrumental questions include the following: What could be expected to happen if military force was not available? Could military force achieve the desired objective, or any significant part thereof? Could it do so at an acceptable cost, broadly defined in terms of manpower, casualties, money, diversion of resources, opportunity costs, domestic impact, and the like? Can the use of military force cause something to happen? Can it prevent something from happening? If the answer to these questions is even a qualified yes, then the penalties of failing to maintain adequate military forces in a world in which others are not so inhibited promise to be very severe indeed.

The imperatives for maintaining a viable conventional force posture in the future derive from the complex of national interests, potential adversaries, technological impacts, and political considerations which define likely conventional conflicts. They include in particular the following:

• A high premium on forces in being, and especially on those which are based at or within easy reach of potential conflict locations.

• Essentiality of equipping forces with the best available in precision-guided missiles, and devising doctrine and deployment schemes which maximize their effectiveness.

• Need for means of mobility, both strategic and intratheater, maintained in a state of readiness comparable to that of the forces to be lifted.

• Necessity of not losing decisively the first battle of a conflict, which dictates the size and location of the forces in being.

• Requirements for extended sustainability of forces in being, and for their rapid augmentation or expansion when required.

It is apparent that there is much to do to enable United States conventional forces to meet these requirements. But they can be met, and with a resultant force that will be more effective, more efficient, and quite probably more economical.

NOTES

1. The idea that a stable balance (one in which the Soviet Union and the United States share a common interest in nuclear stalemate and a common belief in the desirability and reality of the stability fo their relationship) has genuinely been achieved is not persuasive to me. On the contrary, I believe that the Soviets seriously contemplate the possibility of nuclear war, and intend to be in a position (in strategic weaponry, civil defense of their population and industrial capacity, and psychological preparation) to win such a war. From their viewpoint I understand winning to mean emerging from the conflict with a still viable society and economy and a residual force superior to that of any potential challenger. I do not believe that they have achieved this posture as yet—hence their continuing caution with regard to nuclear war.

2. "Military Force and Political Influence in in Age of Peace," *Strategic Review* 4 (Spring 1976): 10.

3. Robert S. Walters, *American and Soviet Aid: A Comparative Analysis* (Pittsburgh: Pittsburgh University Press, 1970), pp. 4-5.

4. As quoted by Eric C. Ludvigsen in "Weapons and Equipment, 1975," *Army* (October 1975): 117.

5. Richard H. Ellis and Frank B. Horton III, "Flexibility—A State of Mind," *Strategic Review* 4 (Winter 1976): 28-29.

6. Bernard and Fawn Brodie, *From Crossbow to H-Bomb* (Bloomington, Ind.: Indiana University Press, 1973), p. 17.

PART IV. POLITICAL-MILITARY AFFAIRS

MILITARY DEMONSTRATIONS: INTERVENTION
AND THE FLAG

M. D. Feld

THE CULTURAL CONTEXT

The act of showing the flag is an original European contribution to the procedures of international relations. It emerges as a conventional practice at the end of the fifteenth century, a ceremonial component of the process of exploration and conquest culminating in the recently ended European hegemony. As a symbol of cultural aggression and of imperial expansion, it epitomizes the attitudes and impulses which led to the control by Christian societies of virtually every part of the earth.

Showing the flag thus has its origins in religious conflict, in the struggle between Christianity and its rivals. At the end of the Middle Ages, Western Europe was in a virtual state of siege, hemmed in on the south and east by its Islamic enemies and on the north and west by inhospitable and apparently limitless seas. The discovery of new routes and new worlds was the result of an effort to break this blockade, to acquire fresh resources and new allies. Given the fact that the Ottoman state was the greatest military power of the age, an attempt to break out along the line of the Mediterranean or of the Russian steppes was impractical. The most promising theater of action lay along the sea barriers, where new tactics of navigation and techniques of shipbuilding held out some promise of success.[1] It was in this direction that efforts were accordingly concentrated. The emergent European ascendancy was intimately linked to the ability of its naval forces to penetrate every part of the globe.

The lead in this process, or indeed campaign, was taken by Spain and Portugal. Students of this period have noted the fact that these two pioneer exploring states were also the two most successful and persistent crusading ones. In an era of virtually uninterrupted Islamic victories and conquests, the Christians of the Iberian peninsula had progressively defeated Muslim armies, destroyed Muslim kingdoms, and even crossed the Mediterranean and estab- lished a foothold in North Africa. The awareness of the unique nature of their achievement—accomplished at a time when Constantinople had fallen, the Balkans had been lost, and the Turks had gained a foothold in southern Italy—led the Spaniards and the Portuguese to regard themselves as the militant and singularly successful champions of Christianity and European culture. It also endowed them with an unusual degree of aggressiveness and self-confidence.

These facts are not simply historical background. They are essential to an understanding of the social and ideological factors that gave a new dimension to sea power and made it for the first time a creator of international systems. Spain and Portugal had a dual mission: to break the ring of the European blockade, and to establish a new and more advantageous pattern of interstate relations. They were seeking to establish contact with the kingdoms of East Africa and the empires of the Far East, areas believed to be sympathetic to Christianity.

This expansion by European crusading impulse was made possible by a series of apparently fortuitous technological discoveries which for the first time made ocean-going expeditions possible. Fifteenth-century developments in navigation and shipbuilding are notable in themselves. But the ends to which they were directed are even more remarkable.

Hispanic naval forces represent one of the earliest cases of that application of technological processes to political ends that was to become a salient characteristic of Western ascendancy. The combination of the compass, the adjustable mast, and the large metal gun resulted in the earliest model of that unique European contribution to international and even interplanetary rela- tions, the self-guiding, self-propelling missile platform. It was a device whereby the mode of communication was given political significance. These seagoing fleets were securing new audiences for the sovereign voice of the nation that sent them forth. The discovery of such audiences was regarded as an extension of national authority.

The message carried was essentially a religious one. The powers that sent forth the fleets were the secular armies of Christianity, with the obligation of maintaining and advancing that faith. Religion inspired the early explorers. Religion guided them in dealing with the problems they encountered. Religion also colored their perceptions of the situations with which they came into contact.

Two distinct possibilities were recognized: the lands discovered had already been exposed to Christianity, or they had not. In the first case it was reasonable to expect them to accede to revealed truths and to present themselves as fellow believers and natural allies of the Europeans. Their failure to do so could only be interpreted as the reaction of willful sinners, subject to the full penalties of lawful war. If they could not be presumed to have had any prior knowledge of Christianity, they were by virtue of that fact natural wards of the respective crowns of Spain and Portugal and their commissioned representatives. The latter had the duty of preparing and administering their peaceful conversion.[2]

The seriousness with which these alternatives were taken, and the effect they had on the approach tactics of the explorers, can best be illustrated by quotations taken from first-hand accounts of two of the earliest confrontations: one with the presumably ignorant Indians of Mexico, the other with the presumably knowledgeable Indians of Asia.

> The flagship hoisted her royal standards and pennants, and within half an hour of anchoring, two large canoes came out to us, full of Mexican Indians. Seeing the big ship with the standards flying they knew that it was there they must go speak with the captain; so they went direct to the flagship and going on board asked who was the Tatuan which in their language means the chief.[3]

> On the following morning, which was Monday, 28th May, the captain-general set out to speak to the king, and took with him thirteen men of whom I was one. We put on our best attire, placed *bombards* in our boats, and took with us *trumpets* and many *flags.*[4]

The passive approach of Cortez stands in contrast to the aggressive landing of da Gama. Cortez, assuming Christianity to be unknown in Mexico, had no idea what to expect. As Diaz del Castillo makes clear, he had hopes that the process of Christian revelation would smooth his path. Da Gama, on the other hand, came equipped with a protocol for dealing with rulers, who insofar as they were not Muslim must be Christian. Both of them left open avenues of accommodation. The Spaniards, upon landing in Mexico, erected a cross and an alter. The local Indians were given the opportunity to acknowledge the truth of Christianity and the sovereignty of Spain. The Portuguese in India interpreted Brahmin practices, i.e., the absence of Islam, as those of a primitive or proto-Christian sect. That being the case, they had grounds for establishing formal relations.

Even at this early stage, the aggressiveness of European powers is remarkable. Sailing into foreign waters and showing the flag was not in their eyes a hostile act. It was, rather, a simple statement of fact. They were there, and their traditional enemies were not. The authority of Christian rulers was then demonstrated. In the bipolar world of early exploration, physical presence in and of itself was an act of conquest. It provided a justification for the standards of law and authority under which the newly contacted societies could enter the community of nations. It was the rejection of these standards on the latter's part that constituted the act of war.[5]

In their very beginnings, acts of flag-showing were thus representative of the asymmetrical relationship that Europeans assumed to govern their contacts with non-European societies. It was the Westerners who had the capacity to establish the new relationships, and not the other way around. It was accepted without question that a successful voyage would result not in an exchange of trading fleets, but rather in the establishment of a one-way European monopoly. A Spanish ship showing its flag on the coast of Mexico, a Portuguese ship doing so on the coast of India, took that very fact as proof of its inimitable cultural superiority and divine guidance. Whatever the religion of the natives might be, it was obviously of a lower order than that of the Europeans. The societies to whom the flag was shown, even though they were obviously complex and presumably very wealthy, were demonstrably incapable of reciprocal behavior.

The asymmetrical nature of flag-showing operations affected the political status of the flag-shower. He was more of a missionary than an entrepreneur. But his missionary credentials could only be validated by the success of enterprise, proof of divine guidance. Until his mission succeeded, he had few if any claims on the state. Success, in effect, confirmed his commission and ratified his privileges. If he failed, he was exposed as an imposter. Witness Columbus, set back in chains for his failure to find gold; and Cortez, honored for his mutiny by the expectation of large amounts of looted treasure.

From its very beginnings, therefore, the act of flag-showing intervention was defined by the normative and territorial limits of Christianity. It took place when agents of the sovereign moved out of the areas where European conventions were in force and moved into areas where no such conventions held. The absence of such conventions had a twofold effect. It left the status of the discovered area undefined. It also gave the discoverers a broad mandate.

Sovereign authority, as Europeans knew it, had little or no significance outside of Europe. The expeditionary commander's powers were as negotiable as the beads he exchanged. He was there to get something for nothing. No agreement he made could in any way impair the basic authority of his sovereign. An unfavorable outcome automatically canceled his credentials. On the other hand, he was in no way bound to respect any of the institutions and practices of the societies with which he had now come into contact. Their legitimacy was measured entirely in terms of their conformity to his crusading ends, i.e., whether or not they contributed to the spread of Christianity and the accumulation of treasure. Expeditions were staffed by the most expendable members of society: younger sons, discharged veterans, impressed vagrants. They were sent to regions Europeans had never before seen, and where therefore they had nothing to jeopardize. The losses could be written off. The profits were windfall in nature.

From its very beginnings the act of flag-showing was a sort of negative image of European society. It was staffed by social outcasts. It took place in areas where neither the agents nor the symbols of European sovereignty functioned as part of an established system. Within Western Europe itself there was no need to show the flag. The upper-class aristocrats who represented the sovereign were readily recognizable. They were masters of the common language and protocol that governed interstate relations. But outside Europe the firing of cannons and the sounding of trumpets were akin to the behavior of a tourist who shouts in his own language at uncomprehending natives.

THE EVOLUTION OF THE CONCEPT

The elementary act of flag-showing thus implied the absence of any real possibility of communication. In this form it still persists for use in extreme cases, such as the ascent of Mt. Everest, the arrival at the North and South Poles, a landing on the moon—cases, in short, where the conquest of distance is the major achievement, and where the political and social conditions of the attained region are of minimal importance. The earliest explorers viewed the globe in a bipolar context, Christianity and Islam. Societies affiliated with neither camp were, by definition, political vacuums and, therefore, the legitimate spoil of whoever happened to discover them.

Flag-showing was thus based on the premise that native culture could be ignored or, at most, colored with the political and ideological assumptions of the exploring powers. The simplicity of this approach was destroyed by two emergent factors: the undreamed-of possibilities of wealth offered by the newly found areas, and the development of a competitive European system of nation-states. These last two developments forced the Western societies into explicit and programmatic relations with the natives of the new-found areas.

In their initial phase the European expeditions had the limited mission of establishing diplomatic and commercial relations with their natural, non-Islamic allies. but the apparently inexhaustible supplies of gold, silver, and spices in these territories, and their demonstrated vulnerability to European military technology, changed the picture. Exploratory expeditions were transformed into agencies of forcible expropriation and systematic exploitation. Relations with non-European, non-Islamic societies were governed not by the prospects of political support but by the existing mechanisms of economic development. The system of extra-European international relations created was one which sought to minimize the expenditures and maximize the profits of the expeditions involved. The fabled wealth of the Indies, moreover, promoted a frantic competition to obtain control of its sources. By the mid-seventeenth century the new worlds had become an extension of the European arena.

This development, apart from anything else, served to accentuate the asymmetrical nature of the relations between Western and non-western societies. The political ordering of the non-European world was viewed in terms of inter-European conflicts. Colonial enterprises were designed to implement the resources of European states in the waging of continental wars. For Europeans, the non-European world was notable as a source of tremendous windfall profits, as an area where uninhibited exploitation offered the possibility of unprecedented returns. The resultant international network was, in European terms at least, economic rather than political in nature. It was, moreover, an economy that was entirely European in its orientation.[6]

Symptomatic of this is the fact that, throughout the seventeenth and eighteenth centuries, relations between Europe and the rest of the world were carried out not by diplomatic missions but preponderantly through the agency of chartered trading companies. These marginal instruments carried the flag but only indirectly represented the sovereign. They subjected societies and created empires without directly involving the sovereign they claimed to represent.

Theory covered up for practice. Francisco de Vittoria, the sixteenth-century Spanish founder of modern international law, declared contacts between nations to be based on the universal right of peaceful trade.[7] This doctrine covered the form, if not the substance, of the Spanish conquest of a large part of the Western Hemisphere. It also set the tone for the global behavior of Europeans.

The impulse to trade was, however, one-sided. It could be stimulated only by the presence of European armed forces. The monopoly of armed force being an essential characteristic of the European nation-state, trade invariably followed the flag. The connection, thus established, made the commercial enterprises of Europeans with the non-European world an exercise in the selective extension of the state's authority. The practices and standards enforced in Europe had little if any relation to those encouraged abroad. At home, the destruction of the private armies of the domestic nobility was the basis of national reconstruction. The licensing of the private armies of the entrepreneurial bourgeoisie was the basis of overseas expansion. The fact that the middle classes were still politically marginal minimized the risks in this procedure. Their instruments of aggression were not official arms of the sovereign, and there was little likelihood of those arms being employed at home.

With the Industrial Revolution and the post-Napoleonic consolidation of the European nation-state system, showing the flag intervention entered a new phase. Within the North Atlantic political complex there arose a new class of intellectuals and public officials whose status and authority rested not on their social affiliations but rather on their relationship to the state. These groups took upon themselves the role of inspiring and directing both the rationalization of the state's control of its domestic territories and the widest possible extension of its influence abroad. Just as the power of the state was extended to regulate and adjust the conflicts of competing social groups at home, the authority of the state was extended to regulate and adjust the conflicts of competing commercial groups outside Europe. The nineteenth-century state suddenly took upon itself the direct responsibility for protecting the claims and markets of its merchants and bankers in the non-Western world.[8]

In part, this tendency was a response to the revolutionary improvements in the technology of transportation and communication. In part, it was a response to the fact that the middle classes now had regular representation at the highest decision-making levels of government. Whatever the underlying reason, the fact remains that the acquisition of colonial possessions ceased to be an absent-minded and fortuitous occurrence and became a debated and programmatic policy.

A third factor was the narrowing of the scope for overseas enterprise. By the nineteenth century the broad outlines of the terrestrial portion of the globe had been more or less charted. The remaining "open" portions of the non-European world were not so much undiscovered as unclaimed. While discovery could be the act of an enterprising surrogate, establishing a claim had to be a deliberate political act. The appropriation of discovered areas could be presented as a divine reward for opening new areas to the practices of Christianity, but the expropriation of already known regions could only be justified on the basis of the introduction of the higher standards of European political economy: the unimpeded development of natural resources and the regular payment of debts.[9]

With this coalescence of political and commercial interests, the great globe itself became an extension of European frontiers. Rival expeditions stumbled over one another in their anxiety to be first to plant the flag. The politicization of colonialism, however, created a self-regulating system of arbitration. Territorial claims were no longer determined by the armed conflicts of rival trading groups, but by conferences in the European capitals. The rationale of international law gave way to an open declaration of Western hegemony. The North Atlantic powers became, in effect, a club, organized to divide the rest of the world. "The Concert of Europe" and the Monroe Doctrine were conventions granting imperial status to states satisfying European political criteria. Societies and territories that did not meet these criteria were parceled out among them.[10]

From the European point of view, the scramble for colonies was a model of international arbitration. Competition in non-European areas did not result in European wars. Credit for this must be given to the retention of the original principles that armed forces employed outside of Europe should be ancillary in return. A sharp distinction was maintained between national armed forces and the forces responsible for establishing and maintaining an empire abroad. The former were conscript forces, representing the nation-in-arms. Colonial units, of which the French Foreign Legion was perhaps the most celebrated, were made up of mercenaries and volunteers—individuals without votes, families, or parliamentary representatives. They could be employed with a minimum of domestic repercussion. Their operations could be encouraged or repudiated without too great concern for the honor of the state or the impact of such decisions on the structure of domestic politics. There is room for melancholy reflection in the fact that the pre-World War I colonial conflicts of the Western powers were all successfully (from the European point of view) regulated. The armed forces employed were, from the diplomatic aspect, rationally controlled. In intra-European disputes, on the other hand, the use of armed forces introduced an uncontrollable element. The social and political significance of conscript armies as a symbol of the nation-in-arms made them an uncontrollable instrument. Once unleashed they had to be permitted to run their full course.

The politicization of nineteenth-century European imperialism was accompanied by a shift in the intellectual perception of the distance and differences between the European and the non-European world. Before the French Revolution, the two worlds were separated by the physical obstacles to communication. The existence of such barriers did not prevent—and even encouraged—eulogies of the Noble Savage and glorifications of the "enlightened monarchies" of Persia, China, and Japan. In the post-Napoleonic era, the difficulties in physical communication began to melt away and the barriers of space were replaced by a psychological and cultural gap. The Noble Savage gave way to the benighted native. Former "enlightened monarchs" were now described as corrupt and slothful despots.

The notion of physical distance placed its emphasis on the establishment of regular communication. Space was the barrier to be conquered. Now that space had been conquered, the cultural differences between European and non-European societies were placed into sharper relief. This emphasis on cultural and psychological distance made political intervention seem a natural and justifiable act. In a one-sided but growing process, Europeans and "natives" were being brought into sustained and regular contact. Yet the intellectual attainments of Europe were so superior that any communication between equals was out of the question. It was unreasonable to expect natives to comprehend such advanced standards. These could only be imposed by force.

PRESENT TRENDS AND FUTURE PROSPECTS

Showing-the-flag interventions, then, have been characterized by asymmetrical European initiatives and by an awareness of physical and psychological distance, and have been regulated by the use of ancillary military forces. Do these conditions still exist? In what form? And what kind of role can they be expected to play in the future?

Each of these factors has been transformed, if not eliminated, by contemporary conditions. The notion of distance has been replaced by a sense of proximity; the increasing speed of transportation and communication make us all one world. At the same time the heightening pressures for social integration within Western societies have eliminated the former distinction between regular and ancillary forces. Societies no longer permit themselves the luxury of officially designating significant numbers of their members as expendable. Units with quasi-sovereign significance, made up of individuals with something less than full civic status, no longer exist. To the degree that societies attain the advanced industrial stage, they appear to become incapable of generating the attitudes and instruments that formerly made showing-the-flag interventions possible.

This is not to say that forces are no longer sent abroad to establish national presence. That obviously still takes place. But there has been a crucial change. The units sent are flawlessly regular. The places they are sent to are not regarded as being far off. Rather they are those areas most closely bound to the home base. Both the United States and the Soviet Union maintain sizable military commitments on the territory of their closest allies. The units involved represent the full sovereign commitment of the governments they represent. Showing the flag as practiced today is not a gesture of asymmetrical involvement. It is rather an assertion of mutual support.

In a related conceptual reversal, international community has replaced alienating distance as a justification for aggressive overseas acts. Cuba, for example, recently felt free to send its armed forces to Angola in support of the MPLA, legitimating that act with a declaration of anticolonial revolutionary solidarity. The United States and the other Western powers, lacking any such patent ideological tie, were deterred by distance in space and perception from intervening directly in this area. They were thereby obliged to respond in a covert and ineffectual fashion. Cuba, on the other hand, cited the physical distance as evidence of the revolutionary solidarity that bound it to Angola.[11]

What we are obviously dealing with here is a new notion of military intervention, similar in effect but different in content from the traditional one. The original notion of showing the flag, as outlined above, was based on a state-of-siege mentality that drew a sharp boundary between encircled Europe and the world that lay outside. This picture of the world, originally rooted in a sense of physical isolation, was transformed by success into one of cultural superiority. The concept of physical distance was replaced by that of cultural distance. The rationale of forcible intervention changed from the assertion that the areas in question were too far from Europe to have any notion of its conventions to the assertion that the areas in question were too benighted to have any understanding of its norms.

Now we have the notion of a natural international community whose fulfillment is impeded by a barrier of reactionary exploitation. The new concept of military intervention evokes the claim of ideological distance, of a scattered international underground separated from one another by the agents of their oppression and reaching out hands in mutual aid.

Military intervention today cannot be treated as a casual imposition on some remote society. Ideological orientations divide and unite areas in patterns of their own. Distance has become a function of politics, a projection of internal structures of power. Albania is closer to China than it is to Greece. Yugoslavia vacillates between East and West.

By outright declaration, we intervene to preserve or create a society similar to our own, and the distance is perceived in terms of such kinship. As public acceptance of the claim of South Vietnam to be a representative democracy diminished, the perceived distance between Saigon and Washington grew greater and greater. Eventually it became so great that the presence of American forces could no longer be presented as an assertion of "free world" influence, but was regarded as an act of asymmetrical intervention. The same shift in perception caused a rift in the armed forces between those elements who considered themselves to be part of a citizen army and those who considered themselves to be professional fighting men.[12] The culturally based inability of the United States to draw a line between colonial and metropolitan armies undermined the effectiveness of its fighting forces. Citizen armies could not be employed in an "unpopular war."

European political developments over the past century have contributed to the elimination of the factors of geographical and cultural distance. The claim of national self-determination has become the paramount factor of legitimate sovereignty. A social system that claims independence on such terms effects, by that very act, a significant bond of political community with established Western states. For influential groups of the latter, it becomes a society similar in structure and related in motivation to the nations of the West. Thus, cultural distance is eliminated, and with it support for acts of intervention. A threat to the principle of national self-determination in one particular area is presented as a threat to the greater community of nations.

In this matter, the West labors under the handicap of having criteria of influence and intervention that are much less refined than those employed by the Communist bloc. In terms of the liberal ideology, any assertion of popularist national self-determination is an affirmation of legitimate sovereignty. A society has achieved independence when it has a government staffed, more or less, by indigenous personnel. National movements against particular instances of Western colonialism thus create a heightened sense of community between the areas in question and the general NATO bloc. Recognition and concrete offers of assistance follow almost immediately.

In communist theory, national self-determination can take place only in the context of a reaction against the West. There is no such thing as legitimate anti-Soviet self-determination. Reactions against Soviet imperialism, as in the cases of Hungary and Czechoslovakia, increase the sense of ideological distance between the Soviet Union and the areas in question, and justified armed intervention follows, while the West, because of its awareness of the proximity of these areas, passively observes.[13]

It is ironic that the cultural triumph of the West has turned its own weapons against it. "The criterion of the truth," Vico, a father of modern social science, observed, "is to have made it."[14] The political rhetoric of nineteenth-century Europe has become an international lingua franca. The European nation-state has, as a result, become an ideological patron of every state emerging from colonial tutelage. In the case of Rhodesia, for example, Great Britain supports the native societies against the English settlers, an act formerly inconceivable. For the Western nations, self-determination has become the hallmark of legitimacy for the governments of their former possessions. The acceptance of Western political rhetoric creates "true" states. Its rejection overrides all other considerations.

The irony is even more striking if we dwell on the coincidence that the Soviet Union, breaking out of what it considers to be a Western-imposed blockade and encirclement, should first establish new contacts in Cuba, Angola, and Mozambique, almost exactly the same areas where Spain and Portugal almost five hundred years ago established way-stations in the process of shattering the Islamic siege of Europe. This striking historic parallel provides us with some clues as to why the Communist bloc appears to have so much more flexibility and so much more success than the West in flag-showing intervention projects.

The Soviet Union and its allies have conditioned themselves to a state-of-siege mentality. They are surrounded by ideological enemies. Any penetration beyond the sphere of Western-oriented states represents, so to speak, a great leap forward, a bursting of hostile barriers and the attainment of a nonaligned and, therefore, exploitable political terrain. The consciousness of this image creates the conditions of physical and psychological distance that make flag-showing interventions ideologically justified.

The West, on the other hand, with its self-assumed role of universal mentor and guide, lacks the ideological motivation for open intervention in contested areas. The assertion of goodwill toward every self-determining society, and of special tutelary responsibilities toward those less advanced industrial states, argues against any use of regular armed forces. It lends itself, accordingly, to clumsy efforts of paramilitary subversion. The recent CIA efforts in Chile and Angola are examples of the limitations and costs of an interventionist attitude deprived of the sense of psychological distance and therefore incapable of proceeding in a direct fashion. Equally striking were the abortive arguments in 1974-75 for American armed intervention in the Arab oil-producing areas. In an effort to create the necessary preconditions for such an act, its advocates postulated an extreme degree of estrangement and distance between the Arab sheikhdoms and the United States. The imaginary nature of this argument was one among many reasons why their proposals could not be taken seriously.

MEANS AND ENDS

Naval forces, as is self-evident, have been the traditional vehicles of flag-showing intervention. Command of the sea has been the historical prerequisite for asserting a national presence in an alien environment. The sailor, moreover, is the prototype of someone who willingly withdraws himself from the domestic stage. Throughout history, the seas have been the great physical barrier. The fifteenth-century European shattering of the Islamic blockage was brought about by a clear-cut naval superiority at a time when their land forces were markedly inferior to those of the Ottoman Empire.

This tradition is still in force. Current strategic discussions place naval policy in the context of maintaining effective instruments of intervention. The presence of naval units, backed up by local base structure, is regarded in many quarters as the fundamental requisite of national influence in distant areas. However, the seas are no longer regarded as a barrier but rather as a vital medium of communication. A strong navy, it is thus argued, is essential if we are to maintain our influence in areas of critical strategic importance.

The argument of this paper notwithstanding, historical analogies can be dangerously misleading. Influence and intervention may not be adjacent terms on a spectrum of strategic reaction, but rather polar opposites. With the seas regarded as a means of regular communication rather than as a barrier to it, the function of naval units is transformed. Distance is no longer the obstacle, but rather culture and ideology. Ships are no longer employed to create the national presence in unexplored areas; they are, rather, an instrument for maintaining normal traffic along regular channels of communication. The scope of naval strategy is thus determined by the nature of the societies with whom regular communication must be maintained.

The societies in question, as we have already seen, can be regarded as benighted or equal. If benighted, they must be rendered subject to European political control. If equal, they are to be considered as bound in a web of alliances. But the notion of benighted sovereign states has, in the post-World War II world, become a contradictory term. All sovereign states are equal and, theoretically at least, natural allies. Alliances are cemented by the provision of port facilities, which are both a token of and an argument for the necessity of maintenance of mutual dependence. Naval presence thus runs counter to the asymmetry that is the basic condition of showing the flag.

It can be argued that the stationing of naval forces in distant waters narrows rather than expands a nation's range of options. A nation becomes more closely bound to the ally controlling its terminal port. The existence of a naval base at the Piraeus, for example, was the most common argument for American support of the patently disastrous colonels' regime in Greece. Similar considerations now color the relations of the United States with Turkey and its official perception of the Cyprus issue. As for the Russians, it can be argued that they lost the necessary leverage in Egypt the moment they established a naval base at Alexandria. The appearance of Soviet naval units off Africa and in the Arabian sea have an impact out of proportion to their combat capabilities, largely because they are a free-floating factor, with no existing commitments to defend.

This development was foreshadowed in the late nineteenth century. British naval supremacy transformed the oceans into domestic waterways. The Royal Navy had the mission of maintaining British influence throughout the globe. Its acts of intervention were almost accidental and forced upon it, as in the case of the Boer War, by the impertinent behavior of some minor state. With the sun never setting on the British flag, intervention was no longer necessary.

The emergence of the Imperial German Navy was accordingly perceived as an act of aggression. A threat to imperial communication was being created. If Great Britain's control of the waves was no longer absolute, the legitimacy and indivisibility of its empire was placed in question. Any impediment in communication increased the distances between Britain and its empire and undermined the sovereign status of its presence abroad.[15]

A surface navy of the modern kind is, therefore, not an instrument of intervention but a token of dependency. It operates in terms of mutual interests rather than of perceived barriers. It is most effective in asserting support of the policies of friendly powers.

Theoretically, of course, a navy can be transformed into an instrument of intervention and used as a covering force for landing troops. But how often has this been done? The areas in which we operate most comfortably are those where we assert a close similarity in internal politics as well as in foreign policy. Any evidence of divergence, particularly in the former, leads to pressure for withdrawal of American forces. Moreover, the more sympathetic the ally, the more reluctant it is likely to be to serve as a staging area for American intervention elsewhere.

It is in this context that Soviet naval forces are regarded as expansionist. The novelty of the instrument, rather than its apparent capability, colors our appreciation of its significance. An impressive Soviet surface naval force is an act of intervention because its mere existence shatters a host of strategic presuppositions. It complicates the process of communication between allies. What was practically a domestic waterway again takes on some of the elements of an uncharted sea.

Though it observed in horror, the West could assess with equanimity the brutal Soviet repression of popular movements in Hungary and Czechoslovakia. What happened there was accepted as the maintenance of the status quo. On the other hand, much more ambiguous Soviet penetrations in Africa, Latin America, and the Middle East were considered as creating areas of political conflict. Yet, in a literal sense, the Russians were intervening in Central Europe, i.e., asymmetrically interfering. In the non-European areas, the Soviet Union was behaving in a notably more legitimate manner, i.e., responding to the invitation of a recognizable authority. Moreover, the Politburo knew it was intervening in Central Europe. It treated that act as an extreme reaction forced upon it by circumstances beyond its control. In the non-European parts of the globe it justified its presence as conventional behavior of a recognized superpower. Soviet intervention in Eastern Europe was perceived as cementing the existing and legitimate political structure. Its expansion into the non-European world was regarded as part of a process of tearing that structure apart.[16]

This peculiar perception framework can perhaps be attributed to the physical contours of NATO military deployment, and particularly of its American components. The forward positions of American units in West Germany and the Mediterranean constitute a frontier defining the Western world. But it is a frontier created in symmetrical fashion; it is the product of mutual agreement. The psychological distance, therefore, does not exist. The limits are of our own creation; they are not forced upon us. The Mediterranean base structure of the Sixth Fleet defines a naval preserve. It is a zone of friendly ports of call. In terms of such parameters, Soviet behavior on the farther side of the iron curtain was legitimate. The frontier was as much ours as theirs. Their appearance within the Mediterranean is, however, a quasi-aggressive act. They are creating frontiers where none previously existed. It is this matter of who is creating what that determines our perception of our true interests. Central Europe is peripheral to the West, while Egypt and Angola are part of its heartland.

It all boils down, perhaps, to the manner in which distances and boundaries are drawn. The Western style is essentially geometrical. It is based on open and direct awareness of communication. Underlying this is the belief that wherever we are free to move our rhetoric will take root and flower into a sympathetic ideology. In renouncing this kind of communication with Eastern Europe, the West has tacitly placed such areas beyond its reach.

The Soviet perception is essentially organic. There are two kinds of societies, popular and capitalistic. As a society approaches popular fulfillment, its solidarity with other popular societies—particularly the Soviet Union, the most fully fulfilled one—grows correspondingly greater. Between popular societies there are no real boundaries, only varying degrees of submersion under capitalist oppression. The boundary pierced by Communist intervening forces is, therefore, neither cultural nor geographic. It is the superimposed capitalist system that prevents the popular forces from coalescing into true international unity. Communist forces, when sent abroad, are not agents of particular national policies but are instruments of "moral, political, diplomatic and other kinds of support."[17] The target of their intervention is not the space their forces wish to control but the social and political system that divides the world into Communist and non-Communist blocs.

This difference of perception leaves the Western bloc with the outline and the Soviet bloc with the substance of a global strategy. The forms of Western intervention, as in Chile or Angola, are now invariably covert. They seek to maintain a respectable mask for their verbal and material experts. They do not show the flag. They operate behind the scenes. To intervene openly would undermine the self-determining legitimacy of their allies. For the Soviets, on the other hand, the ability to operate openly, as part of the Communist system, is an index of political maturity. Thus the United States can provide facilities to train civil and military bureaucrats, but with an emphasis on expertise, not on ideology.

It is therefore pointless, at the present moment, to speak of American military forces as potential instruments of intervention. Whatever their overseas station may be, their primary mission is that of defending themselves, of placing, in effect, the onus of intervention on non-Western powers. They also have the symbolic mission of representing Western influence and its alliance structure. The existence of freely granted overseas bases is a token of some kind of partnership. Whether this partnership is a form of privilege or one of inhibition is a matter open to debate.[18]

It is in all probability likely that during the next decade the Soviet Union will broaden the scope of its non-European interventions and that the Western powers will progressively constrict the range of their military demonstrations. This is not an altogether disastrous course. The embarrassments and frustrations of the Atlantic powers may force them to reconsider the relationship between their strategic posture and their cultural and political pretentions. Some stock-taking of this sort may lead them to an awareness of what is unique in their values, and to an understanding of the incompatibility of these values with their present role of universal model and mentor. With some conscious notion of the distance between themselves and other kinds of societies, they will perhaps be in a better position to assess the rationale and costs of military intervention.

NOTES

1. J. H. Parry, *The Age of Reconnaissance: Discovery, Exploration and Settlement, 1450-1650* (New York: Praeger, 1969), pp. 19-127.

2. Ibid., pp. 303 ff.

3. Bernal Diaz del Castillo, *The Discovery and Conquest of Mexico*, trans. A. P. Maudslay (New York: Farrar, Straus & Cudahy, 1956), p. 69.

4. Alvaro Velho, *Vasco da Gama's First Voyage*, trans. E. G. Ravenstein (London: Hakluyt Society, 1898), p. 29 (italics added).

5. Bernice Hamilton, *Political Thought in Sixteenth Century Spain* (Oxford: Oxford University Press, 1963), p. 102.

6. J. H. Parry, *Trade and Dominion: The European Overseas Empires in the Eighteenth Century* (New York: Praeger, 1971), p. 273.

7. Ibid.

8. L. H. Gann and Peter Duignan, "Reflections on Imperialism and the Scramble for Africa," in *The History and Politics of Colonialism*, ed. Gann and Duignan (Cambridge: Cambridge University Press, 1969), pp. 116 ff.

9. Maurice Collis, *Foreign Mud: Being an Account of the Opium Imbroglio at Canton & the Anglo-Chinese War that Followed* (New York: Alfred A. Knopf, 1947); and William L. Neuman, *America Encounters Japan: From Perry to MacArthur* (Baltimore: Johns Hopkins University Press, 1973), pp. 30 ff.

10. Patricia Wright, *Conflict on the Nile: The Fashoda Incident of 1898* (London: Heinemann, 1972); and Ima Christina Barlow, *The Agadir Crisis* (Chapel Hill: University of North Carolina Press, 1940).

11. Speech given by Carla Rafael Rodriguez at Planning Session of Fifth Summit Conference of Movement of the Nonaligned Countries, *Granma.* (August 29, 1976): 7:2.

12. John Helmer, *Bringing the War Home* (Glencoe: Free Press, 1974), pp. 170 ff.

13. Robin Allison Remington, *The Warsaw Pact: Case Studies in Communist Conflict Resolution* (Cambridge: M.I.T. Press, 1971), pp. 109 ff.

14. Isaiah Berlin, *Vico & Herder; Two Studies in the History of Ideas* (New York: Viking, 1976), p. 17.

15. Robert Art, *The Influence of Foreign Policy on Sea Power: New Weapons and Welt-Politik in Wilhelminian Germany* (Beverly Hills: Sage Publications, 1973).

16. State Department Summary of Remarks by Helmut Sonnenfeldt, *New York Times* (April 6, 1976):4:4 n.

17. Soviet in U.N. Defends Its Angola Intervention, *New York Times* (March 31, 1976): 3:7.

18. Pertinent recent discussions of U.S. naval strategy on which these remarks are based can be found in the following: Barry M. Blechman, *The Control of Naval Armaments: Prospects and Possibilities* (Washington: Brookings Institution, 1975); Edward N. Luttwak, *The Political Uses of Sea Power* (Baltimore: Johns Hopkins University Press, 1974); and George H. Quester, ed., *Sea Power in the 1970's* (New York: Dunnellen, 1975).

U.S. MILITARY ASSISTANCE TO NONINDUSTRIAL NATIONS

Caesar D. Sereseres

Since the termination of World War II, military assistance has been portrayed by official Washington as playing a vital role in maintaining national security, the strategic balance, and constructive relations with foreign governments. However, despite the continued belief in some circles that the provision of military hardware and services is crucial as a basic instrument of foreign policy, we have yet to reach a consensus on how to evaluate the costs and the benefits, short range and long range, of a specific security assistance relationship or of the military assistance program in general. Furthermore, the proliferation of nations and their respective defense needs, usually unrelated to the strategic balance, has become enmeshed in U.S. national security rationales and views about the proper course of events in the nonindustrial world.[1] Regardless of rationales, however, the transfer of military equipment, the provision of military training, and engagement in supportive military services are forms of military intervention.

Thus, an appropriate focus for analysis is the link between such programs and U.S. national interests in the nonindustrialized world. More specifically, how do security assistance programs relate to the specific interests of the U.S. in a particular region or country? Is U.S. *security* enhanced or *influence* provided via a particular security assistance program? How much political leverage does military assistance provide the U.S.? Further, if we have the analytical capacity to determine if such arms have made a difference, do we have the same capacity to ascertain which U.S. interests were affected by the outcome of the events? One analyst has warned that "unless and until scholars and statesmen alike are prepared to do justice to the complexities of military assistance programs and their relationship to the strategic milieu in particular areas, the debate as to what effects weapons transfers have upon these areas will continue to be couched primarily in ideological terms."[2]

The purpose of this discussion is thus to examine the policy of security assistance to the nonindustrial areas of the world, and, in the process, *question the notion that the United States increases its control of events by supplying arms.* The focus will be placed on two issues concerning security assistance: (1) To what extent do such programs enhance the national security of the United States? (2) To what extent do such programs become instruments of influence for United States foreign policy? In pursuing answers to these questions, the possibility is strong that military assistance programs may in fact do all that both their supporters and critics claim. The uncertainty and ambiguity of military assistance is reflective of a larger phenomenon: the uncertainty and ambiguity of events throughout the world and the inability of the U.S. to manage such events. Further, the political benefits of a military assistance relationship can be temporal in nature, and its economic, political, and psychological costs unexpected and long range. Lastly, military assistance may be only one aspect of a broader relationship consisting of economic and financial assistance.

THE UNITED STATES-NONINDUSTRIAL WORLD MILITARY ASSISTANCE RELATIONSHIP: THE NIXON DOCTRINE IN THE POST-VIETNAM PERIOD

One of the chief characteristics of U.S. foreign policy since the end of World War II has been the use of materiel and technical resources as diplomatic tools. The resources of the American economy and military forces have been used in the foreign policy process to provide decision makers with options in the pursuit of national objectives. It is in this regard that economic, financial, and military assistance programs have been utilized to foster the type of military, economic, and political development that Washington believed to be in the interest of the United States.

The Southeast Asia war forced a reexamination of American global security policy as well as of the cold war era belief that radical changes in Africa, Asia, and Latin America constituted a threat to U.S. national interests. We have long accepted the assumption that the United States is the only nation that can prevent countries from "falling" into Soviet/Chinese/Cuban spheres of influence. Despite such an assumption, it remains a virtual impossibility to ascertain the value to U.S. security of changes in the status and orientations of a particular country outside the industrial world. Without this capability it is most difficult to objectively consider the type of commitment in resources and credibility that the U.S. should provide a country. Finding the "worth" of a country vague and uncertain, despite the claims of some policy makers, the *bottom line* in U.S. foreign policy is best characterized as "preventive (or pre-emptive) intervention aimed not simply at restoring or preserving anticommunist authority, but more broadly at maintaining or creating a dependable, advantageous stability."[3]

The inescapable conclusion is that American reactions to world events have rested on analogies to the "loss" of China and Cuba and to the perceived "threats" to Greece and Turkey in the 1940s. These cases remain to this day as the basic rationalization for military assistance and as "models" of international Communist behavior. The extent to which the U.S. can avoid the pitfalls of such experiences and "lessons" of history in the post-Vietnam period may well rest with the manner in which the Nixon Doctrine provides new insights and criteria for security assistance relations. As Guy Pauker of the Rand Corporation has pointed out: "The 'loss' of some countries may be cheap compared with the cost of 'holding' them."

The Nixon Doctrine and Self-Reliance

Under the Nixon Doctrine, military assistance programs become a substitute for a direct American military presence in a country. At the core of the doctrine is the belief that the U.S. must continue to honor old obligations, continue to support "allies," and at the same time reduce the possibility of using American (especially ground) forces in regions such as Asia, Africa, and the Persian Gulf. President Nixon, in an April 1971 message to Congress, explained the intent of the doctrine by stating that "we must help to strengthen the defense capabilities and economies of our friends and allies ... so that they can increasingly shoulder their own responsibilities [and thus] reduce our direct involvement abroad."

One interpretation of the doctrine suggests that there are three key operational factors to consider: "total force planning," "regionalism," and "self-reliance."[4] With very few exceptions, the concept of total force is virtually meaningless in the nonindustrial world. The thought of including the military forces of a Third World nation for the protection of U.S. interests has serious flaws, especially if the operational approach focuses on U.S. air and sea power and Third World ground forces. In the attempt to seek a new division of labor between the U.S. and some of its security assistance "allies," questions are raised about whose blood in whose interest. That is, while the U.S. may be prepared to provide air and sea combat support (emphasizing technology and minimizing American casualties), allies must be prepared to provide the fodder for ground combat.[5]

Regionalism, the second operational concept of the doctrine, seeks to place considerably more responsibility on certain countries to encourage regional security cooperation. Military assistance that contributes to this goal is said to reduce the likelihood of the need for U.S. troops in local or regional conflicts.

However, rather than considering regional cooperation as a vehicle for managing conflict and repelling Communist efforts, the U.S. has defined regionalism more in terms of "regional caretakers" such as Brazil in South America, Zaire in Southern Africa, Iran and Saudi Arabia in the Persian Gulf, and Indonesia in Southeast Asia.

Perhaps the most important aspect of the doctrine is its call for the promotion of "self-reliance" as a primary objective of security assistance. At the core of this objective is the belief that each nation must provide the manpower for its own defense and rely on the United States only for the necessary military hardware, training, and support services. Analysts who have examined the doctrine suggest that the underlying concern is to minimize (if not terminate) the client relationship in military assistance. A militarily self-sufficient nation (although still undefined) is to be preferred to one that is dependent on the U.S. for continual resources. Thus, the message from Washington is that "political albatrosses" will no longer be acceptable in the aftermath of Vietnam.

Whether in fact the intent of the Nixon Doctrine is actually being implemented can be debated. The extent to which the ideological predispositions of American foreign policy makers and institutions can be attuned to the principles of self-reliance in development and security, as well as in a reduction of the U.S. presence and involvement throughout the world, remains to be seen. Such an effort would require a radical break with a traditional global view and perception of threat to the national interest.[6]

Aside from the instrumentality of the Nixon Doctrine, it appears that basic to U.S. security interests is the necessity to prevent an internal or regional conflict from evolving into a strategic conflict between the U.S. and the USSR. *Indirect* military intervention in these internal and regional conflicts via military assistance programs underlines the political and diplomatic importance of transferring arms to the nonindustrial nations. The diplomatic nature of military assistance, however, will come under increasing manipulation by recipient countries. As the hundred odd nations of the nonindustrial world increase their economic and technical capacities, seek national symbols of modernity and prestige via military weapons, attempt to manage regional balancing, and pursue an independent and flexible foreign policy, U.S. security assistance will increasingly serve purposes other than American national security needs. *The extent to which the U.S. proves capable of selectivity in its security assistance relationships will largely determine the costs as well as the benefits incurred in the use of arms as an instrument of American foreign policy.*

Security Assistance

Whether such selectivity is possible in the post-Vietnam period—given the political turmoil and uncertainty of world events—remains to be seen. As recently as 1976, Henry Kissinger could offer little hope when he observed that

[The] era of American predominance has given way to strategic parity at a time when nuclear capability proliferates and festering regional conflicts imperil global stability ... we have no choice but to help contain these disputes ... no equilibrium can long be maintained without our active participation. And many countries of consequence to us will measure our will and capacity to perpetuate a constructive involvement in [regional] balances of our efforts to help others develop a more self-reliant defense position.[7]

To help foster military self-reliance, the U.S. has extended military assistance to numerous countries in the nonindustrial world. Since 1972, the executive began to present military assistance requests to Congress under the term "security assistance." Under this caption, all security-related assistance coming under the authority of the foreign aid bill was brought together: the military assistance program (MAP), foreign military sales credit, excess defense articles, security supporting assistance (defined as economic assistance to countries making extraordinary military efforts to meet threats to their security), and, beginning in 1976, the military assistance training program. Security assistance thus provides, through grant, credit, and sale, new and used military equipment, parts, ammunition, services, training, and economic support for defense-related activities.

Through its various types of military assistance the U.S. has provided some $32 billion dollars in arms, equipment, and support during the 1965-74 period— of this, nonindustrial regions received 78%. (See the appendixes for comparative data on the major suppliers of arms to these regions.) The most significant change within military assistance has been the shift from a grant- to a sales-oriented program. Sales averaged about 23% in the 1950s, 68% in the 1960s, and has now gone over 90% in the mid-1970s. For example, of a $2.2 billion program in 1967, sales accounted for 44%, while in 1975, sales made up 94% of the $10 billion program.

The U.S. withdrawal from Vietnam, the 1973 Israeli-Arab war, the oil embargo, and the lessening of restrictions in the selling of arms all contributed to these trends in military assistance. As table 1 indicates, several types of military assistance are heavily concentrated in particular regions (actually a handful of countries worldwide). The so-called forward-defense countries have obtained significant portions of grant military assistance (MAP) and excess defense articles, while the Persian Gulf and Israel account for 69% of foreign military sales (FMS). Israel alone accounted for 55% of all FMS credit for the 1973-75 period.

In assessing the *magnitude* and *significance* of military assistance dollar figures, it is important to consider the 47% inflation factor between 1967 and 1975 and the purchases of sophisticated military equipment which contributed to the rapidly rising dollar value of arms transfers. In addition, 40% to 45% of the dollar value of "arms transfers" was for military weapons and ammunition, the remainder being for vehicles, construction, training, and technical assistance. For example, until 1976, 80% of Saudi Arabia's "arms program" was for

Table 1: United States Security Assistance Program, 1973-75
(billions of dollars and percentages of aid)

	MAP	FMS Orders	FMS Credits	Commercial Sales	Excess Defense Articles
Worldwide	$1.98	$24.688	$2.695	$1.466	$.540
Industrial countries[a]	1%	19%	0%	60%	8%
Israel	0	14	55[e]	15	0
Persian Gulf[b]	*[d]	55	0	13	0
Latin America	2	2	12	4	3
Forward Defense countries[c]	47	8	28	4	72
Other countries	49	2	5	4	17

Sources: **Foreign Military Sales and Military Assistance Facts,** Data Management Division, Defense Security Assistance Agency (Washington, D.C., 1975); and **International Security Assistance and Arms Export Control Act of 1976,** Report of the Committee on Foreign Relations, United States Senate (Washington, D.C., 1976).

[a]Includes twenty-three countries.
[b]Iran, Kuwait, Saudi Arabia.
[c]Greece, Indonesia, Jordan, Korea, Philippines, Taiwan, Thailand, Turkey.
[d]Less than 1%.
[e]Excludes $1.6 billion of nonreimbursable financing.

construction and a variety of defense and nondefense services primarily provided by the U.S. Army Corps of Engineers. Further clarifying the dollar value of military assistance is the fact that 69% of the $25 billion in FMS orders for the 1973-75 period was attributed to four countries: Israel, Iran, Saudi Arabia, and Kuwait.

By 1976, worldwide military assistance relations reflected a distinct pattern. Security assistance relations were based on a $4 billion foreign aid bill and a growing military sales program. However, half of the security assistance program was accounted for by Israel; and four countries (Israel, Iran, Saudi Arabia, and Kuwait) accounted for 70% of worldwide FMS. Furthermore, eight countries (Korea, Jordan, Turkey, Greece, Philippines, Thailand, Indonesia, and Ethiopia) accounted for 90% of grant military assistance; seven countries (Israel, Greece, Turkey, Korea, Jordan, Taiwan, and Brazil) accounted for 87% of the FMS credits; seven countries (Israel, Egypt, Jordan, Syria, Portugal, Greece, and Zaire) accounted for 99% of security supporting assistance; and six countries (Greece, Turkey, Thailand, Korea, Philippines, and Ethiopia) accounted for 77% of excess defense articles deliveries. Only the foreign military training program reflected a wider regional distribution of resources: of the $30 million programmed for 1976, Latin America received 38%; East Asia and the Pacific, 27%; the Near East and South Asia, 12%; Europe, 15%; and Africa, 8%.

The dollar figures on security assistance can be reasonably "deflated" by accounting for the special case of Israel and the arms-purchasing binge of the Persian Gulf states. Aside from these countries, a handful of nations absorbed the lion's share of U.S. military assistance. This is not to suggest that smaller amounts of assistance are insignificant, but to illustrate that the reaction of critics to the "arms problem" needs substantial clarification and qualification. In addition, the quantitative and qualitative characteristics of military assistance tell us little about the significance of these military goods and services to U.S. national security and diplomatic influence. A squadron of F-5s or a million dollars in support services and training are not easily translated into "influence" and "security." The analytical, as well as policy, challenge is to link the provision of arms and services to expected results that are based on explicit U.S. security interests. Unfortunately, the likelihood of determining a cause-effect, cost-benefit relationship is clouded by psychological and ideological predispositions which afflict the assessment of American foreign policy activities.

THE MILITARY ASSISTANCE CONUNDRUM: JUDGING THE SUCCESS OR FAILURE OF ARMS TRANSFERS

In examining numerous cases of arms transfers, the most consistent pattern that appears is the temporal nature of a diplomatic benefit and the uncertainty of the consequences of providing arms. In assessing a security assistance relationship one is struck by the fact that there are aspects of both "failure" and "success." The evaluation of security assistance as a foreign policy instrument is most aptly described as a conundrum—a riddle with no real answer. The riddle: what is the efficacy of transferring arms and providing military services *as an instrument of influence in the pursuit of American security interests?* Few concrete examples of the benefits to U.S. national security and even fewer examples of "influence" derived directly from the transfer of arms exist in the available literature. This does not rule out the possibility that military assistance has been "successful" in some instance; but there exists a conundrum when it comes to evaluating the "worth" of security assistance programs.[8]

If such worth is assessed in terms of the number of military missions abroad, base rights, security assistance programs, and the increasing dollar value of military equipment and services—especially in the Middle East and the Persian Gulf—the conclusion could be that military assistance efforts of the U.S. have been quite successful. However, if it is measured in terms of enhancing national security and providing for an active instrument of influence, there is considerable doubt. It has been all but impossible to provide precise criteria for calculating the political or military returns of military assistance.

The Persian Gulf and Middle East regions provide examples of the limitations of security assistance. In the case of Iran, it appears that "dependency" on the U.S. for modernizing the Shah's armed forces has meant little in terms of lower oil prices for the U.S. In fact, while the flow of arms into Iran is said to contribute to the stability of the area (and thereby permit the continued flow of Persian Gulf oil to the West), in the long run the arms buildup could contribute to a conflict which would disrupt oil supplies. There are some thoughts that initial arms sales to Iran contributed to the decision by OPEC to increase the price of oil. When the Shah of Iran desired to continue both a domestic development plan and a military modernization plan, his only solution was more financial resources—i.e., increasing oil revenues. While arms sales to Iran may enhance our ability to maintain access to oil and prevent the Shah from seeking military assistance elsewhere, there is also the possibility that the U.S. could become the unwilling participant in a local conflict. If in fact, as some experts suggest, the Iranian armed forces (at least those units utilizing sophisticated American military equipment) could not actively engage in combat without the logistical and maintenance support of the U.S., it might very well become impossible to separate the vital interests of the U.S. from those of Iran.[9]

Likewise, Saudi Arabia (with the highest reserves of oil in the world) has sought a greater responsibility for its own defense. As the U.S. develops the military capabilities of the Saudis, the Israelis will be forced to consider these Persian Gulf military forces as possible parties to a conflict in the Middle East. The extent to which U.S. security assistance to such Persian Gulf countries as Kuwait and Saudi Arabia affect Israel's perceptions of potential threat will mean additional financial and political costs to the U.S. for support of Israel. Unfortunately, there is no way of ascertaining such a likelihood. Under the circumstances it has been difficult to assess the "success" or "failure" of arms transfers to the Persian Gulf.

While arms transfers to the Persian Gulf may result in uncertain as well as possibly unsettling consequences, it is also possible to point to a successful use of arms as a diplomatic instrument. An example was the U.S. pursuit of a Sinai agreement in 1975. The settlement hinged on keeping negotiations going, and to accomplish this the United States drew upon military and economic resources to remain in control of the diplomatic process. To this end, American security assistance to Egypt, Syria, and Israel (and the encouragement of West European countries to sell arms to Sadat) played a vital role not only in bringing the contending sides together on a Sinai agreement but also in breaking the Soviet Union's monopoly as the supplier of weapons to Egypt.

The evolution of arms as a diplomatic instrument reflected changing attitudes in Washington regarding the Middle East. For example, the objective of arms transfers to Israel shifted from a total support for military superiority vis-à-vis the Arabs to using arms and support assistance to influence Israel to negotiate.[10] One commentator who observed the Middle East negotiations pointed out that the essence of the approach was to utilize every "manipulative capability" available to pursue the dual objectives of the containment of the Arab-Israeli conflict and the promotion of U.S. technology (including military) as a means of buying time to cope with the first objective.[11]

The efforts to establish a quasi-military relationship between the U.S. and Egypt with a symbolic transfer of C-130 transport aircraft was only the beginning of the "manipulative" usage of arms as a diplomatic instrument to bring about a settlement between Israel and Egypt. It was also the first step toward replacing the USSR as the major military supplier for the Egyptians. Despite the warnings of Israeli Ambassador Simcha Dinitz that "a military supply relationship between Washington and Cairo would be a dangerous course of action that could lead to a dangerous imbalance in the Middle East," Washington was prepared to utilize a security assistance relationship with Egypt as an inducement to the antagonists to negotiate a peaceful solution to the Middle East conflict. A danger in this form of diplomatic venture is the extent to which the U.S. will be willing (or forced) to assist in the "Westernization" of the Egyptian armed forces as a means of maintaining Sadat in power and his moderating position as a viable domestic policy. If Sadat will require $7 billion for a ten-year arms aid program to phase out Egypt's Soviet weapons, then the U.S. must decide the "worth" of such a policy in pursuit of peace in the Middle East.[12] Congressional action, as well as Israeli reaction, via American domestic politics will undoubtedly play the major role in determining the possibility of using an arms modernization program for Egypt as a vital diplomatic tool for Middle East negotiations for the remainder of the decade.

If the United States strategy in the Middle East can be considered a qualified, short-range "success" (at least from the perspective of American interests), then the most unqualified long-term success in military assistance in the region has undoubtedly been Jordan. Over the past two decades Jordan has been able to survive two wars with Israel and three major political crises. Security assistance to Jordan contributed significantly to the maintenance of King Hussein's regime: it has helped to retain the loyalty of the armed forces, it has demonstrated a U.S. commitment to Hussein which has deterred neighboring Arab countries, and it has contributed to Jordanian military self-confidence and war reserves for combat operations. But, while American diplomatic actions and "shows of force" have augmented military assistance to Jordan, the "success" of this security assistance relationship must also be attributed to the political acumen of King Hussein. While military assistance has allowed Jordan to maintain a large, well-equipped, standing army, much of the credit belongs to King Hussein, who has provided effective leadership, benefited from the personal loyalty of Bedouin military combat forces (that recognize the legitimacy of the monarchy), and demonstrated an ability to avoid complete isolation in the Arab world (and at the same time not risk losing the support of the United States).[13]

The Jordanian experience suggests a major theme in most of the security assistance "successes": namely, that *while U.S. military assistance may be necessary for the maintenance of a particular regime or the control of insurgencies, the assistance itself is not sufficient to guarantee such results.* To understand the "successes" in military assistance, it is not enough just to count up the number and type of weapons and training provided a country; far more important are the domestic political conditions and institutional arrangements of the society.

A further example of this theme can be found in the region of Latin America. During the 1960s and early 1970s, the "successes" of the Latin American armed forces against rural and urban guerrillas were frequently attributed to U.S. military assistance. Success in Guatemala, Venezuela, Colombia, Peru, Bolivia, and Uruguay has often been attributed to "military" victories based on the use of sophisticated intelligence equipment, modern armaments, and large combat forces. However, a case-by-case examination suggests that this was not the total story. In most Latin American countries there was not a strong correlation between a recipient's military capabilities and the failure of an insurgency. In other words, military considerations were less important than domestic political conditions in determining the outcome of the conflicts.

In Bolivia, the Guevarista insurgency failed primarily because it attracted no popular support from the conservative peasants of the Altiplano. In Columbia, the various guerrilla movements failed primarily because they generated little popular support beyond their traditional enclaves, and because government institutions were strong and officials increased communication with the rural areas. In Peru, revolutionary insurgents were denied prospects for peasant support in La Convencion Valley when the government linked the areas into the national economy by building a road and instituting a mild land reform program. The same can be said for Venezuela, where guerrilla groups failed basically because the government institutions were relatively strong, and because the political and organizational skills of President Betancourt and his party attracted popular support. In Guatemala, guerrillas failed because they lacked popular support, because civilian groups formed to act as counterinsurgent forces, and because the central government officials began to pay attention to the pressing needs of the rural population.

In each case, the insurgents failed not because of military measures alone, but rather because of political conditions and government policies taken in collaboration with the armed forces. In Latin America, the primary factors in successful counterinsurgency were the domestic political conditions and policies, to which U.S. military assistance made little effective contribution. Military assistance has had little relationship to the outcome of insurgencies, the absence of local military conflict, military participation in politics, resistance to regional military organizations, or curtailment of governmental policies (including military governments) directed at the nationalization of American investments. With few exceptions, military assistance provides very little insurance for American interests—despite the allegations of military dependency. Providing arms and military training to the Latin American region is best understood in terms of military modernization and the institutional development of the armed forces.

In focusing on the "success-failure" conundrum, a significant factor for consideration in military assistance relationships is frequently ignored. A phenomenon in nonindustrial nations which will present a greater challenge to

American interests (although not necessarily security) than Soviet involvements is the increasing rate of military intervention and overt military rule. Such activities have contributed significantly to the bureaucratization and militarization of government in the nonindustrial world. If such a trend continues into the 1980s, the U.S. must be prepared to assess the consequences for the U.S., since security assistance, regardless of its uncertainties as an instrument of influence, does in fact contribute to the modernization, centralization, and institutional growth of the armed forces. In the case of Latin America, the growth of military regimes has not prevented the takeover of American investments and properties. Indeed, there is an increasing reluctance, on the part of Latin American militaries, to accept at face value the apparent benefits and to ignore the probable liabilities of "business as usual" with the United States.[14]

In summary, there is substantial evidence to suggest that, with sufficient time, military assistance to nonindustrial countries can result in improving the quality and performance of the recipients' armed forces. However, the provision of security assistance is not apolitical; in fact, with few exceptions, the United States does not exercise much control over the political consequences of military assistance. Furthermore, the influence and security derived are seldom commensurate with the military assistance provided. Unfortunately, it is virtually impossible to determine the costs of *not* providing security assistance.

The assessment of ongoing and future military assistance relationships must take into account not only a realistic determination of what is attainable, but also an evaluation of the unintended political consequences—including undesirable involvement in domestic and regional politics and unwanted identification with "unsavory" regimes. Whether the United States has the capacity or the will to seek a more selective arms policy is to be decided by the psychological perspectives of policy makers toward the peoples and events of the nonindustrial, nonwhite regions of the world. Because of the persistence of the military assistance conundrum, decision makers (critics as well as proponents of an American arms program) continue to regress to positions and solutions largely determined by ideological predispositions.

INFLUENCE, DEPENDENCY, AND SECURITY

As has been suggested above, the link between the provision of arms and U.S. national security is vague and ambivalent. Unless we assume that "stability," base rights, access to raw materials, and contact with local militaries are by definition enhancing the national interest and a reflection of influence, then we must be prepared to critically examine the military assistance conceptual framework. It is still necessary to raise the question: arms for what? To view assistance as a diplomatic tool for *influence,* considerably more knowledge is necessary concerning the decision-making processes of recipient countries. The uncertainties and complexities of events in the nonindustrial world, plus the lack of an agreed-upon criterion to evaluate the consequences of security assistance, make an assessment of the degree of influence that the U.S. gains from the transfer of arms highly suspect.

Ideally, it would be necessary to know the extent to which a recipient (or potential recipient) country takes U.S. security assistance into account in the making of a specific decision that is commensurate with the preferences and interests of the United States. Defining, as well as actually identifying, cases of influence as a direct result of a military assistance relationship is difficult and often misleading. For example, the influence of small allies in a security assistance relationship is often overlooked—often to the detriment of U.S. interests. Despite the appearance of influence, crucial limitations exist. In noting the dilemmas facing the U.S. in Vietnam, Robert Komer has stated that:

> Perhaps the most acute dilemma was the perennial question of stability vs. potentially destabilizing change. The more we became entangled in Vietnam, the more concerned we were over the risks to our growing investment if the regime we were supporting should collapse. Constantly facing U.S. policymakers was the dilemma of whether, if we pushed too hard, we would end up collapsing the very structure we were trying to shore up.[15]

The experience of Vietnam suggests two limitations in military assistance: influence may decline as U.S. involvement increases, and a recipient's weakness—despite its military dependency—is quite often an effective leverage on the U.S. Certainly, U.S. concern for regime maintenance, at least within the executive branch, limits American willingness to pressure governments in such countries as Korea, Turkey, Greece (during the military government), Iran, Ethiopia, Brazil, and Chile.

Although the notion of influence is necessary to the debate, the belief that security assistance can contribute to a *dependency* relationship is just as important in ascertaining the consequences of arms as a diplomatic instrument. A fundamental premise that needs examination is that sophisticated weapons make the recipient dependent on the U.S. for the needed technical services to maintain and operate the equipment. An arms relationship, it is argued, generally tends to tie the recipient politically to the U.S. because of the need to maintain military effectiveness. In the words of one U.S. aviation corporation executive: "When you buy an airplane, you also buy a supplier and a supply line—in other words you buy a political partner."[16] Such comments, however, appear to be directed at the U.S. government as further justification for arms transfers and not as a reflection of the likelihood that military dependency will result in accommodating political partners. Both the Soviets and the U.S. have often found this dependency to be costly in military and political terms, and in many instances not commensurate with the benefits obtained.

The concern for seeking influence via a military dependency relationship raises a further conceptual problem—namely, the extent to which military assistance should be based on *valid military requirements* or on the concern for *political influence and leverage.* The debate over criteria is not insignificant—especially if we are concerned with the consequences of the provision of American weapons and support equipment. In many cases the U.S. appears to be considering the phychological needs of a particular regime and/or military institution, regardless of the merit of the military requirements for assistance. The concern for *political good will* thus takes priority in the provision of arms. In such a situation, there exists the opportunity for a country to influence the U.S. by assuming a posture that argues for arms (or more, as the case may be) by saying that either the United States does not understand the importance of the country or does not care enough!

Given the propensities for the need of more foreign assistance in the military development of the armed forces in nonindustrial nations, it is difficult not to imagine countries attempting to play upon the security concerns of the U.S. in order to seek a military assistance relationship— regardless of the military requirements. The U.S., it would thus seem, in constantly caught in *the dilemma of wanting to provide arms and military support services to assist in the development of militarily self-sufficient nations* (in accordance with the Nixon Doctrine), *while at the same time desiring to maintain leverage with aid recipients by making them militarily dependent on the U.S. for continued arms and logistical support.* Further complicating the military self-sufficiency goal of U.S. foreign policy is the necessity to link self-sufficiency with valid military requirement criteria. The concern to maintain or establish political good will with a regime is often predicted on ignoring so-called valid military requirements. In other words, a preemptive arms transfer policy will most likely take precedence over the concern for military self-sufficiency. The extent to which this may adversely affect, in the long run, U.S. interests or the defense capabilities of the recipient is a question that is generally left unanswered, mainly because of the appearance of a short-term gain.

Irrespective of the justification provided—political stability, regional balance, base rights, raw materials, contact with local militaries—the bottom line (with a few possible exceptions, such as Israel) focuses on the preemptive concern of the U.S. The *preemptive* rationale consists of the following assumptions: (1) if the U.S. refuses to respond to a military request, the USSR, or other countries, will provide the military assistance; (2) the Soviets are more effective than the U.S. in utilizing an arms supply relationship to enhance their interests at the expense of the U.S.; and (3) nonindustrial countries are vulnerable to Soviet pressures and intrigues, and are not capable of protecting their national interests. Defenseless Third World countries, once exposed to Soviet military hardware, training, and advisers, are seen as adversely affecting U.S. security interests either in a particular region of the world or in the strategic relationship between the U.S. and the Soviet Union. However, the experiences of the USSR with such countries as Syria, Iraq, Ghana, Cuba, and Indonesia suggest otherwise. In each of these cases, the military assistance relationship produced gains for the Soviet Union that were marginal at best, and in areas that were of little consequence to the arms recipient. The characteristic that stands out has been *the adaptability of the Soviets to yield to the preferences of the recipients rather than the reverse.* [17]

The connection between a preemptive policy of military assistance and U.S. influence and security has not been clearly established. The premises that need exploring are as follows: (1) military relationships between nonindustrial countries and arms suppliers such as the Soviet Union and West European countries adversely affect the general relationship with the United States; (2) the absence of an arms supply relationship between the U.S. and a country lessens potential influence in matters of interest to the U.S. because of the lack of dependency on maintenance and logistic support; and (3) it would be a diplomatic "failure" for the U.S. if it did not take the opportunity to establish a security assistance relationship with a country at the expense of the Soviets, or if the Soviets responded to a request for military assistance after the U.S. had refused to provide such assistance.

Under such a conceptual cloud the link between a preemptive policy of arms transfers and the enhancement of U.S. national security is more clearly seen in terms of the *psychological* dimensions of the U.S.-USSR strategic relationship. The increasing ability of nonindustrial countries to play upon the strategic concerns of the superpowers means that military assistance is being used less and less for the promotion of U.S. security interests. For the remainder of the decade, *U.S. military assistance will be directed less toward defending against shared threats and more toward just protecting U.S. military access and possible assets in a particular country.* There are, of course, exceptions to this. But the trend appears clear: the U.S., in most cases, is being confronted with a "buy-elsewhere" bargaining strategy. As long as the U.S. perception of the strategic worth of many of these nonindustrial countries persists, it will be difficult to argue against the logic of a preemptive policy. How far such a security assistance policy can take the U.S. will be determined largely by the "world view" of the national security managers and by the efforts of the Congress to play a more active role in the making of American foreign policy.

U.S. MILITARY ASSISTANCE AND FOREIGN POLICY: THE LIMITATIONS ON FUTURE INVOLVEMENTS IN THE NONINDUSTRIAL WORLD

The dominant "world view" in Washington in the post-Vietnam period has hinged on the apparent relationship between the U.S.-USSR strategic balance and the geopolitical balance within regions. The vagueness and frequent confusion that link the two types of balances to U.S. national security have a common theme: the desire to maintain internal and regional stability beyond America's borders. The unsettling effects of instability—which frequently turn into "targets of opportunity" for U.S. adversaries—become a primary concern of foreign policy decision makers. Whether a framework can be developed to provide the U.S. with a basis for selective involvement in response to attempts by other nations to exploit "targets of opportunity" in the nonindustrial world is highly questionable.[18]

Regionalism and Stability

The belief in the relationship between the strategic and geopolitical balance and the concern for minimal direct U.S. military involvement in nonindustrial regions led to a shift from a reliance on formal alliance and traditional security relations to one of focusing on "regional powers" such as Iran, Saudi Arabia, Indonesia (the ninth-largest oil producer), Brazil, Zaire, and perhaps Egypt in the near future. More and more it appears that the U.S. is willing to rely on close relations with regional powers throughout the world. Politically, most have had relatively strong, stable government institutions, and economically these countries possess and produce important energy and other raw materials upon which the U.S. and its traditional allies appear increasingly dependent. Militarily, these countries are developing into major regional forces as well as major recipients of U.S. military assistance.

While there are advantages to supporting and establishing close security assistance relationships with a handful of regional powers—such as helping to reduce U.S. involvement abroad, contributing to the stability of a particular region, and expecting these countries to act as proxies in preventing Soviet, Cuban, or Chinese intervention—the costs may also be high if such relations jeopardize those with other countries in the region. Such a situation exists in the case of Brazil, especially after the signing of a "formal agreement" in 1975 which called for economic and political consultation between the U.S. and Brazil. With half the total population of the continent and an obviously growing economic, political, and military potentiality, Brazil will heavily influence the future direction of South America, at least in the eyes of the U.S.—a view not joyfully shared by the other South American countries.

Aside from the more obvious examples of Iran and Indonesia, Saudi Arabia, by the mid-1970s, had also sought to become an active regional power in the Persian Gulf. The Saudi strategy was unique: it literally attempted to "buy" the USSR out of the area. The Saudis established a policy of utilizing petro dollars, in combination with the purchase of U.S. arms, to push the Soviets out and induce military and political cooperation from regimes in the Persian Gulf. Such efforts apparently succeeded well in North Yemen—where the Saudis agreed to finance the purchase of $100 million of American arms—and to a lesser extent in

South Yemen in 1976. In addition, the "bankrolling" strategy would have been directed at Somalia—which permitted the establishment of Soviet missile and naval bases at the mouth of the Red Sea—if U.S. support had been provided. Thus, while the Soviets could ill afford to get into a bidding war with Saudi Arabia, the U.S. was benefiting not only from increased arms sales but also from the decreasing Soviet military presence in the Persian Gulf. However, mutual interests between the U.S. and a regional power are seldom that clear-cut, nor are the costs so minimal. The cases of Brazil and Saudi Arabia, nevertheless, suggest a clear pattern in military assistance policies for the next ten years. The focus on regional powers as criteria for selective assistance will become a necessity as Congress evolves an increasingly restrictive foreign policy.

Congressional Restrictions

As a direct result of Vietnam, Congress has come to demonstrate an assertive role in American foreign policy. In the 1975-76 period it successfully opposed the President on security assistance-related issues when it prohibited military support for Angola, voted an embargo on military aid to Turkey, suspended grant and credit assistance to Chile, and blocked the sale of Hawk missiles to Jordan. By the mid-1970s military assistance became increasingly affected by the disillusionment in Congress with foreign assistance and with efforts to gain more control over the making of American foreign policy.

As early as 1966 Congress showed its displeasure with U.S. security assistance policy, particularly the shift from grants to sales, as nonindustrial countries began what Congress described as the "pursuit of illusory prestige." Since that time efforts have been made to examine the financing, control, and consequences of military assistance. However, at the heart of the debate between Congress and the executive (at least for the more articulate critics) is the extent to which basic American political values should be reflected in foreign policy. In the words of one observer: "America, once the arsenal of democracy, increasingly has become just the arsenal."[19] The real challenge to military assistance may well rest in the following question: *Is there the possibility of a comfortable fit among domestic ideals and values, humanitarian concerns, violence and instability abroad, and U.S. involvement in the affairs of other countries?*

The conflict between Congress and the executive over foreign policy is well illustrated in the International Security Assistance and Arms Export Control Act of 1976. At the time, President Ford stated that the legislation contained unprecedented restrictions that would "seriously inhibit a president's ability to implement a coherent and consistent foreign policy." Restrictions contained in the act included a ceiling on total military sales in a fiscal year, the termination by 1978 of grant assistance and military assistance advisory teams, the prohibition of security assistance to a country found in serious violation of human rights or practicing discriminatory policies, and the subjection of all arms sales over $25 million to congressional approval.

One observation was made that the "chief values of [these restrictions] is that they impose some constraints on the Pentagon and thus require choices among arms recipients based on American national interest in place of the policy, aimed primarily at economic gain, of selling as much as possible to almost all comers."[20] However, the actual results of such "legislative vetoes" in military assistance cause more dislocation and uncertainty than more selectivity. In seeking to gain a measure of control over security assistance relations with some seventy-one nations, the Congress established unmanageable mechanisms. In subjecting military assistance to congressional "politics," it undoubtedly undermined the executive's ability to utilize weapons and military support as a diplomatic instrument. The uncertainty of congressional reaction becomes a dominant factor in negotiations with other countries. In the case of the violation of human rights and discriminatory practices, it becomes easier for ethnic and religious groups in the United States (as well as those affected in the respective countries) to act through Congress to influence an ongoing or pending security assistance relationship. The example of the Greek-American effort to gain an arms embargo against Turkey, in the aftermath of the Cyprus invasion, is a case in point. Furthermore, in terms of the practicality of enforcing the legislation on human rights, the Congress may end up penalizing only those regimes that are "inefficient" in their violations.

Do such congressional efforts in fact provide the U.S. with a more discriminatory policy in military assistance? While the Nixon Doctrine sought to provide guidance on who should receive military assistance, congressional restrictions provide the executive with guidance on who should not be a party to a security assistance relationship. The trend that stands out is the effort by Congress to minimize (if not terminate) military relationships between the U.S. and the nonindustrial world. The goal of terminating grant assistance and military assistance advisory teams, gradually limiting military training, and eventually doing away with credit assistance can only be seen as the *attempt to disrupt formal relations with military institutions abroad.*

Finally, congressional concern for human rights abroad is in keeping with U.S. efforts in the 1960s to suspend assistance and/or recognition for the purpose of influencing a regime to maintain liberal democratic practices. However, these paternalistic measures proved to be relatively ineffective. This experience suggests that the curtailment of military assistance will also have little or no impact on a regime's tendency to violate human rights. In practice, most of the restrictions will be easiest to implement against less important countries and most difficult to apply to such countries as Brazil, Iran, South Korea, and Indonesia. Such dilemmas bring into question the capacity of the U.S. to apply its resources productively and with discrimination. Military assistance programs expose American foreign policy as somewhat indiscriminate reactions by the executive or the congress to perceived threats—be they Soviet expansion, regional instability, or repressive regimes that violate human rights.

The Future Limitations of Military Assistance

It would appear that military assistance programs, while highly effective in some cases as *instruments of diplomacy* (on a short-term quid pro quo basis), contribute marginally to basic U.S. national security. If all base rights, intelligence facilities, and the like were forced out of Third World regions, to what extent would U.S. national security be endangered? If such a change meant increased vulnerability for the U.S., then these bases and facilities abroad are a representation not of strength but of weakness. If our national security is so dependent on the cooperation of weaker allies, then our national defense posture abroad needs a close reexamination.

As has been seen in such places as Ethiopia, black Africa, and Southeast Asia, as well as in many of the military regimes in nonindustrial countries, security assistance and modernized military institutions are no insurance against the more compelling social processes taking place in much of the developing world. One conclusion is that the issues associated with military assistance policy, as well as the costs and benefits of such assistance as an instrument in foreign policy, are much more political than military or economic. Another conclusion is that the American concern for maintaining credibility and prestige in the nonindustrial world is questionable. The United States is too large and economically powerful, regardless of the arms it provides, to be ignored by other countries. "Prestige" may be an altogether meaningless and costly issue. Lastly, the limits of U.S. military assistance often go unrecognized because of the failure to realize the extent to which American resources and military presence can be used by local political actors. The American government has often overlooked (if not deliverately ignored) the manipulation of U.S. resources and presence for local ends. Many countries have been able to manipulate American commitments in order to acquire increased military and economic aid and to develop a U.S. interest in, and ultimate responsibility for, the regime's very survival.[21]

Despite the increasing unmanageability of the world, the U.S. has continued to believe in the need for continuity and consistency in world affairs. It is an unsettling fact that countries in the Third World experiment politically and economically to solve national development problems. Some choose nondemocratic and noncapitalist forms of political and economic systems; however, the U.S. should not consider such events as a threat to national security, or, for that matter, as "defeats" for the West. The U.S. must be prepared to accept, as well as tolerate, disorder and instability as the experimentation and frequent failure at social change and development continue. A military assistance policy focused on the goal of "stability" in such a world environment is fraught with the seeds of failure.

The security rhetoric utilized to justify military assistance is a major contributor to the weaknesses in policy analysis. Too often, military assistance as a lever of influence and the malleability of events and processes abroad are overestimated, while the guile of the leadership in nonindustrial countries in using military assistance as an influence lever vis-à-vis the U.S. is underestimated. With few exceptions, nonindustrial countries have demonstrated the ability to "create" a U.S. security interest when one need not have existed. What is called for is a case-by-case evaluation when considering questions of political influence, military dependency, and national security. Generalizations will be virtually impossible, and dangerous—even if applied to countries in the same region. Of significance is the fact that the *learning process* of local leaders and the particular character of the institutional growth of government, particularly the armed forces, will have more to do with the outcome of security assistance relationships than most other "military" or "security" factors. More often than not, military assistance becomes a placebo, that is, it provides for the satisfaction and gratification of the recipient. The danger for the U.S. derives not from providing the placebo but from confusing the "gratification" of the recipient with the resolving of the political and economic maladies that are prevalent throughout the developing world.

Once a security assistance relationship is established, the illusion of influence and security becomes readily apparent. The expectations and hopes of policy makers and administrators are dimmed (and then usually ignored) as knowledge of the local conditions and circumstances that limit U.S. efforts become known. Without doubt, *the risks involved in a security assistance relationship derive mostly from the absence of a management capability to control, monitor, and modify military assistance as the effects on the political and social system of the recipient country are determined.*

Furthermore, the risks associated with military assistance come from the emphasis placed on the military aspect of security and stability rather than on the recognition of the dependence of military capabilities on the political institutions and environment of a nation. There exists the necessity to inquire into the *political premises* of military assistance in order to better understand its consequences and limitations. Lastly, there is an inescapable conclusion that as the U.S. becomes more deeply involved in the military affairs of Latin American, African, Middle Eastern, Perisan Gulf, and Asian countries, there will be a declining ability to manage the military assistance relationship as an instrument of influence—despite the increasing investment in military development and regime stabilization.

NOTES

1. Although there are serious shortcomings to the concept of the "nonindustrial world" (just as with "Third World"), the term will be used in a geographical sense to encompass the regions of Latin America, Africa, the Middle East/Persian Gulf, and all of Asia (excluding Japan). As will be pointed out in the text, the distinctions between regions and between countries in the same region—in terms of historical and institutional development, ideological perceptions of the international environment, and the patterns of civil-military relations—are critical in assessing the limits and consequences of U.S. military assistance programs.

2. Geoffrey Kemp, "Conflict in the Third World: The Effects of Military Assistance Programs," Memorandum prepared for the Senate Foreign Relations Committee, *Views on Foreign Assistance Policy*, U.S. Senate, 93d Cong., 1st sess., 1973, pp. 197-207.

3. Melvin Gurtov, *The United States Against the Third World: Antinationalism and Intervention* (New York: Praeger, 1974), pp. 201-2. Gurtov goes on to describe the American compulsion that sees an inevitable involvement in the security and stability of the entire world, which in effect suggests a responsibility for the affairs of other societies.

4. For a critical assessment of the characteristics and significance of the Nixon Doctrine, see Stephen P. Gilbert, "Implications of the Nixon Doctrine for Military Aid Policy," *Orbis* (Fall 1972): 660-81; Guy J. Pauker, et al., *In Search of Self Reliance: U.S. Security Assistance to the Third World Under the Nixon Doctrine* (Santa Monica: Rand Corporation, 1973); and Earl D. Ravenal, "The Nixon Doctrine and Our Asian Commitments," *Foreign Affairs* (January 1971): 201-17. The confusion regarding the significance of the Nixon Doctrine as a policy is suggested by Ravenal when he states that "While pledging to honor all existing commitments, the [U.S.] has placed them all in considerable doubt. While offering promise of avoiding involvement in future [Third World] conflicts, [the doctrine] has biased the nature of our participation."

5. If the United States plans to provide air power and, if need be, sea power for local conflicts while Third World nations provide ground troops, then security assistance programs would of necessity place emphasis on the modernization and buildup of ground forces. However, this has not been the case, and it might be presumed that the air forces in industrial countries would not appreciate such a policy. The Nixon Doctrine has also contributed to the internal U.S. naval debate on the need for aircraft carriers. Critics argue that every $2 billion investment in Nimitz-type carriers detracts from the capabilities of the U.S. Navy. Secretary of the Navy Middendorf has noted that "the survival life of a ship will be measured in minutes in high threat areas" in a confrontation with the Soviet Union. In the words of one observer, the U.S. is "building a Navy second to none in its ability to project power ashore against Third World countries. The odds are much better in using the carrier against Third World countries or proxy wars. This is where the Nimitz is most likely to see action." This debate is reported by Michael Krepon, "Navy: Does the U.S. Now Rule the Waves?" *Los Angeles Times* (May 9, 1976).

6. The fact that such views will be difficult to overcome is illustrated in a recent editorial comment by former Secretary of Defense James Schlesinger, "The Military Balance," *Newsweek* (May 31, 1976): 9. Schlesinger contends that "Given the disappearance of U.S. strategic superiority, the growing significance of conventional forces, and the adverse balance in those forces ... [the U.S.] military mission is more complex and demanding than that of the Soviet Union. The U.S. must be able to project its own power into the Eastern Hemisphere ... to support deterrence and defense structures protecting nations on the margins of the main power of the Soviet Union. Everywhere there exists serious vulnerabilities for the coalition of nations led by the U.S."

7. The testimony and discussion that followed can be found in U.S., Congress, House, Committee on International Relations, *International Security Assistance Act of 1976: Hearings*, 94th Cong., 1976, pp. 1-6.

8. Satisfactory conclusions have not been reached regarding military requirements, or the relationship between security assistance programs and regional stability, influence, access to raw materials, keeping the Soviets out, and the protection of American interests. The following are only representative of the ongoing debate: Luigi R. Einaudi, et al., *Arms Transfers to Latin America: Toward a Policy of Mutual Respect* (Santa Monica: Rand Corporation, 1973); U.S., Congress, House, Committee on Foreign Affairs, *Persian Gulf, 1974: Money, Arms, and Power*, 93d Cong., 2d sess., 1974; U.S., Congress, House, Committee on International Relations, *United States Arms Sales to the Persian Gulf*, 94th Cong., 1st sess., 1975; U.S., Congress, House, Committee on International Relations,

Suspension of Prohibitions Against Military Assistance to Turkey, 94th Cong., 1st sess., 1975; U.S., Congress, House, Committee on International Relations, *Proposed Sales to Jordan of the Hawk and Vulcan Air Defense Systems,* 94th Cong., 1st sess., 1975; and U.S., Congress, House, Committee on Foreign Affairs, *U.S. Policy and Request for Sale of Arms to Ethiopia,* 94th Cong., 1st sess., 1975.

9. A critical insight into this question is provided in U.S., Congress, Senate, Committee on Foreign Relations, *U.S. Military Sales to Iran,* Staff Report, July 1976.

10. During the most crucial period prior to the cease-fire, the ammunition that Israel was expending late in the day had arrived only that morning from the U.S. Under these circumstances, a refusal to comply with the U.S. request was totally out of the question. In short, the Israelis were *compelled* to accept the cease-fire demands—despite their eagerness for a total military victory over the Egyptian Third Army in the Sinai. The relationship between Israeli military dependency on the U.S. and the Israeli decision to accept a cease-fire is covered in Matti Golan, *The Secret Conversations of Henry Kissinger* (New York: Quadrangle, 1976); and *The Yom Kippur War,* by the Insight Team of the London Sunday *Times* (New York: Doubleday, 1974).

11. Edward R. F. Sheehan, "How Kissinger Did It: Step by Step in the Middle East," *Foreign Policy* 22 (Spring 1976): 3-70.

12. Drew Middleton. "Sadat Seen Asking U.S. for 10-Year Arms Aid," *New York Times* (October 22, 1975).

13. Stephen S. Kaplan, "United States Aid and Regime Maintenance in Jordan," *Public Policy* 23 (January 1976): 189-217.

14. For an example of this perspective, see Irving Louis Horowitz and Ellen Kay Trimberger, "State Power and Military Nationalism in Latin America," *Comparative Politics* 8 (January 1976): 223-44.

15. Robert W. Komer, *Bureaucracy Does Its Thing: Institutional Constraints on U.S.-GVN Performance in Vietnam* (Santa Monica: Rand Corporation, 1972).

16. As quoted in Michael T. Klare, "How to Trigger an Arms Race," *The Nation* (August 30, 1975): 137-42.

17. Alvin Z. Rubinstein, ed., *Soviet and Chinese Influence in the Third World* (New York: Praeger, 1975).

18. For many observers, Angola became the first post-Vietnam "test" of American will. Secretary of State Kissinger warned that "it cannot be in the interest of the U.S. to create the impression that, in times of crisis, either threats or promises of the U.S. may not mean anything because our divisions may paralyze us." Angola, however, was not so much a "test case" as was suggested by both sides to the debate. Entering into the final outcome was the more general conflict between Congress and the executive, the historical role of the Soviets in supplying arms to Angolan liberation movements, Cuba's desire to extract military resources from the USSR, and the reelection concerns of California Senator John Tunney, who used Angola as an opportunity to establish "liberal" if not dovish credentials needed to withstand the strong challenge of antiwar activist Tom Hayden. The complexity of the Angolan case is illustrated in the following sources: Colin Legum, "A Letter on Angola to American Liberals," and Robert Morris, "The Proxy War in Angola: Pathology of a Blunder," *The New Republic* (January 31, 1976): 15-23; Gerald Bender, "Angola: A New Quagmire for U.S.," *Los Angeles Times* (December 21, 1975); and Edward Gonzalez, "Castro and Cuba's New Orthodoxy," *Problems in Communism* 25 (January-February 1976): 1-19.

19. Early concern for the issue is to be found in U.S., Congress, Senate, Committee on Foreign Relations, *Arms Sales and Foreign Policy,* 90th Cong., 1st sess., 1966. An excellent critique of the conflict between American democratic values and foreign policy necessities is presented by Thomas L. Hughes, "Liberals, Populists, and Foreign Policy," *Foreign Policy* 20 (Fall 1975): 98-137.

20. These comments are to be found in an editorial in the *New York Times* (May 7, 1976).

21. For example, see Robert O. Keohane, "The Big Influence of Small Allies," *Foreign Policy* 2 (Spring 1971): 161-82. Keohane suggests that the nature of the American political system and the perception of Soviet, Chinese, and Cuban challenges shared by many foreign policy managers and congressmen give allies a degree of influential access to American decision making and decision makers far out of proportion to their importance. Thus the American "world view," combined with the fact that elements of the U.S. government and domestic groups have special foreign interests, enhances the bargaining power and influence of weaker allies. The "big influence of small allies" is an unplanned but natural result of an active, worldwide foreign policy that includes military assistance relations with some seventy countries.

Appendix 1: Total Arms Transfers of Major Suppliers, 1965-74
(millions of current dollars and percentage of transfers)

	Total	U.S.	USSR	France	Great Britain	China
World Total	$64,404	$31,563	$18,793	$2,826	$2,089	$2,119
Industrial	28%	22%	29%	31%	38%	1%
Nonindustrial	72	78	71	69	62	99
Regions						
Middle East/						
Persian Gulf	21%	18%	30%	16%	29%	1%
Latin America	4	3	2	16	13	0
Africa	4	1	4	24	12	4
Asia	32	46	22	1	7	76
Other Developing Countries	11	10	13	12	1	18

SOURCE: U.S. Arms Control and Disarmament Agency, **World Military Expenditures and Arms Transfers 1965-1974** (Washington, D.C.: Government Printing Office, 1976).

NOTE: Arms transfers represent the international transfer under grant, credit, cash, or commercial sales terms of military equipment including weapons, parts, ammunition, support equipment, and other commodities considered primarily military in nature. Training and technical services are not included.

Appendix 2: Types of Equipment and Services Obtained via Security Assistance

FMS-MAP-MASF TOTAL	Cumulative FY 1950-1975	FY 1975
Weapons/ammunition[a]	40%	44%
Supporting/equipment[b]	19	13
Spare parts	17	21
Supporting services[c]	24	22

SOURCE: Department of Defense, Defense Security Assistance Agency, Office of the Comptroller, **Analysis of Foreign Military Sales Orders, Military Assistance Programs, Military Assistance Service Funded Programs by Types of Defense Articles and Services** (Washington, D.C., July 1975).

[a]Includes fighter aircraft, bombers, destroyers, submarines, tanks, artillery, machine guns, rifles, and missiles, and all ammunition.

[b]Includes trainer and cargo aircraft, tankers, tugs, barges, trucks, trailers, radar and communications equipment, and other equipment and supplies.

[c]Includes construction, supply operations, training, technical and administrative services.

NATION BUILDING, COUNTERINSURGENCY

AND MILITARY INTERVENTION

Lawrence E. Grinter

Following the Communist takeovers in Indochina in the spring and summer of 1975, the Soviet- and Cuban-supported Communist victory in Angola in the spring of 1976 drew repeated warnings from senior spokesmen in the Ford administration. While noting that the United States had failed to block Russian and Cuban intervention in Angola, Washington warned both Moscow and Havana that the Ford administration would not acquiesce to further Communist military intervention in the developing countries.[1] All this poses a clear quandary for future U.S. policy. If new Vietnam or Angola types of war occur, and an American government does decide to intervene, will we have the capabilities—doctrine, programs, and command structure—to operate effective nation-building and counterinsurgency programs? That is the main question that will be discussed here.

This study examines the capabilities which the United States and its allies brought to bear in the Vietnam War and attempts to draw broad future-oriented lessons from that experience. The study uses the Vietnam experience as a model *not* for how the next war may be fought, but for how U.S. agencies involved in any counterinsurgency/quasi-conventional war in a developing country will be likely to perform. A prognosis for the future concludes the discussion.

It would be unrealistic to assume that the next conflict in which the U.S. intervenes will resemble Vietnam. Vietnam was unique: a revolutionary war where nationalism and communism were often indistinguishable; an insurgency which gradually changed into a quasi-conventional war; a conflict of marked asymmetries on both sides (the Communist use of ground sanctuaries, U.S. use of air power); a long war—fifteen years of important American involvement peaking at 550,000 men; and a televised war where big-unit military operations of one side were shown nightly, while nothing of the other side's activities, political or military, was screened. Nevertheless, even allowing for its special characteristics, Vietnam is instructive because it tells us a great deal about how the American government and its agencies performed, and how they may well perform again. We must not take one observer's advice: that "our policymakers may best meet future crises and dilemmas if they simply blot out of their minds any recollection of this one."[2] One of the worst disasters of the Vietnam experience would be to put our heads in the sand—strong tendency anyway.

The Vietnam War was a major test of American limited-war doctrine and operations (counterinsurgency and conventional war) and it remains an appropriate case study for predictions about the style of future U.S. intervention, direct or indirect, in Third World situations. Recall that in Vietnam we saw: (a) an oligarchical regime under attack by a Communist opponent; (b) both government and adversary critically dependent on outside support; (c) significant casualties among noncombatants; and (d) the world imputing stakes to the war which far transcended the geopolitical confines in which it was fought. These characteristics appear in numerous revolutionary situations around the world today and will do so in the future.

As a kind of signpost, or preliminary set of propositions, about the future effectiveness of U.S. military intervention in the Third World, three observations from the Vietnam experience are offered.

First, the success or failure of future American-assisted stability operations in the Third World will depend greatly on the character and capabilities of the regimes or factions which the U.S. elects to assist—the instruments through which we will work. This was always the case in Vietnam, although, in our impatience to apply resources and find solutions, at times we almost completely eclipsed the Saigon government's efforts.

Second, in addition to the influence of the type of regimes we assist, future American attempts at nation building and counterinsurgency will be successful to the degree that they address the actual nature of the challenge on the ground. Understanding the dynamics, causes, and grievances on which insurgent movements feed is very difficult for America—as Vietnam proved. It will be imperative that we coldly evaluate host governments' strengths and weaknesses—and their actual motives. "Progress reports," that inevitable bureaucratic symptom, greatly undermined accurate understanding of what was really going on in Vietnam.

Finally, the success of future U.S. military intervention in the developing world will be significantly influenced by which agency or agencies obtain predominant custody of the resources and programs. Give the armed services (or any agency of government) a mission, and once their prestige becomes involved they will argue that they are doing their best. All bureaucracies tend to equate effectiveness with effort, favored resources with relevant measures. These kinds of incentives and blinders, unless understood and controlled, will skew comprehension and rational decision-making.

NATION BUILDING AND COUNTERINSURGENCY IN VIETNAM: HOW BUREAUCRACY SHAPED STRATEGY

In a Rand Corporation memorandum published in August 1972, as North Vietnam was taking major American retaliation for its Easter invasion of South Vietnam, Robert Komer, a retired U.S. deputy ambassador to South Vietnam, asked why, with a cumulatively enormous U.S. input over the years—550,000 troops at peak, thousands of aircraft and ground-force operations, and $150 billion of expenditures on top of South Vietnam's own great effort—the war continued on such an intractable course with such ambiguous results. Komer's study is an enlightened analysis of numerous motives, constraints, and weaknesses in the U.S. and South Vietnamese decision-making process and the performance of various agencies.[3] Komer and several other serious analysts of the Vietnam War have been pointing out, for several years now, how conventional American (and South Vietnamese) thinking and performance inhibited us from adapting well to the challenge in Vietnam, and how the agencies often became trapped through their own institutional traditions and blinders. I propose to delineate some of the related results of those institutional constraints by examining and comparing the validity and relative effectiveness of the actual strategies and programs which the Americans and the South Vietnamese implemented in the field. The general applicability of these strategies to other Third World situations will then be assessed and their implications for future U.S. military intervention gauged.

Competing and contradictory political-military doctrines and strategies were legion in the Vietnam War. A large part of Saigon's and Washington's problems stemmed from the very multiplicity of recommendations and advice about the war. Upon review, we find that the prescriptions come down to six particularly prominent doctrines and strategies:[4]

1. The social mobilization and organization-building plus armed action approach (the Communist strategy, later advocated in part by the CIA)

2. The power concentration and authoritarian control appraoach (Ngo Dinh Diem's style of government, later adopted and modified by Nguyen Van Thieu)

3. The power limitation and democratic institution-building approach (the liberal American prescription; publicly advocated by the State Department and USIA)

4. The stability operations plus economic development approach (the Rostow doctrine)

5. The military occupation/search and destroy approach (The U.S. Army's strategy, but with French roots)

6. The administrative approach (British in origin)

The Communist Challenge in Vietnam: Social Mobilization and Organization Building plus Armed Action

Viet Minh strategy, and subsequent North Vietnamese and Viet Cong activity in South Vietnam, built upon both Lenin's organizational weapon and Mao's approach to revolutionary warfare. As adopted and refined by Ho Chi Minh, Vietnamese Communist strategy began with a small, clandestine, highly trained revolutionary party appartus. The party fashioned a comprehensive view of revolution as a stage-by-stage social process designed to preempt the government's contact with the people by motivating roughly ten times more manpower at the local level through policies of indoctrination, sociopolitical control, armed forces, and the redistribution of power, status, and wealth. Strategically it was a multidimensional Marxian approach; revolution was seen as an unfolding process of social and class conflict. Victory would come when a decisive superiority in the overall balance of forces, based on actions which dramatized grievances and employed armed violence, had been achieved.[5] Beginning in 1928, when he founded the Indochinese Communist party, Ho Chi Minh used this strategy against Vietnamese nationalist groups, the Japanese, the French, and then against Saigon and the Americans. Carefully adapting to and then becoming the champion of local grievances and issues, the Communist insurgent organization threw a net of social, political, economic, and military associations around the people. The use of terror was controlled, selective, and frequent.[6] The Communists' organizational capabilities, their comprehensive approach to revolution, the causes they championed, and their ability to develop and structure political and military participation in South Vietnam's fractured, personalistic society gave the Communist revolution great momentum.[7]

Distinct from their political prowess, however, Communist military fortunes in Vietnam were not so consistent. Hammered by US/ARVN "search and destroy" operations from mid-1965 onward, the Communists switched military strategy in mid-1967, and temporarily shelving main-force big-unit war, moved into massive attackes against South Vietnam's cities with southern Viet Cong cadres as the spearhead during Tet 1968. But then, with their forces shattered by the ARVN and American defense of cities (85,000 NVA/VC troops killed or permanently disabled in nine months),[8] Hanoi had no choice but to let the war slide back toward guerrilla patterns, with periodic military "high points" as a sop to the hard-liners in the Politburo. By 1971, sensing defeat in the southern countryside in the face of the GVN's resurgence into the villages after the 1968 attacks, Hanoi switched strategy again. With the full knowledge and assistance of the Soviet Union, Hanoi staged its Russian-equipped, conventional invasion of South Vietnam in March 1972. But this force also was beaten back and the North Vietnamese homeland wrecked under massive American and South Vietnamese reprisals.[9] The interim period, from the January 1973 Paris Accords through late 1974, allowed Hanoi to legally refit and resupply its shattered expeditionary force in the South and proceed to develop a lavish network of base camps, airfields, logistic routes, and antiaircraft screens in preparation for a return to all-out regular warfare, probably planned for mid-1976.[10]

But then, in early 1975, as the Saigon armed forces' spare parts and ammunition dwindled under U.S. congressional cutbacks, Thieu ordered the ARVN, at that point facing relatively light NVA pressure in the Central Highlands, to abandon the territory, and the whole defense effort collapsed in panic. Hanoi's divisions swept in to an easy, unexpected final victory.[11]

In late 1964, analyzing the revolutionary political and administrative work of Communist cadres in southern villages, American CIA officials concluded that if Saigon was ever going to win it would have to employ local socioorganizational tactics similar to the Communists'. As a corollary to U.S. military strategy, CIA doctrine in Vietnam advocated counterorganization of the villages and emphasized pacification and territorial security. By 1966 CIA influence on GVN/U.S. doctrine and programs was apparent in the Revolutionary Development Cadre program:[12]

> Successful pacification is essentially a problem of counter-organization. Current Pacification/Development strategy, with its emphasis on the revival of strong village communities, is aimed toward that end. The overriding objective of the village development effort is to confront and supplant the enemy's political/military organization in every village with a deadly rival—a "friendly infrastructure."[13]

While the CIA had an important influence on the Revolutionary Development program, we must recall that the resources going into those local pacification and security efforts were *minuscule* compared with resources invested in conventional air and ground operations. The emphasis in U.S. doctrine, from the very start, was conventionally military. That tells us something about why U.S./GVN responses to the multileveled Communist challenge proved relatively inflexible, and often ineffective, even in the face of later regular force battles.

The Saigon Government's Preferred Response: Power Concentration and Authoritarian Control

Since CIA influence on strategy in Vietnam, and on the Saigon leaders, was low compared with that of the Army and other DOD elements, it is hardly surprising that the Saigon governments did not seek to challenge Communist revolutionary warfare by counterorganizing the people. Instead, with their armed forces molded, shaped, and equipped in the American military image, the Saigon regimes (generally traditionalist military juntas from November 1963 onward) largely operated from doctrines of political authority that reflected both the legacy of the Ngo Dinh Diem regime and their own personal inclinations. While sheer expediency characterized much of the activities of Minh, Khanh, Khiem, Ky, and Thieu, their actions also reflected traditional Vietnamese and Chinese concepts of government. They were, essentially, power concentration and authoritarian control proponents. Power concentration advocates saw the purpose of government to be the maximization of the central authorities' influence. Power was to be concentrated at, and protected by, an elite stratum. It was believed that the key to success at the mass level lay in maintaining stable public attitudes and behavior through sociopolitical control. In Vietnam, the myth of the power concentration approach was that the central authorities would enjoy a "mandate of Heaven" if they set a superior moral example. This was Ngo Dinh Diem's formula and, with some inevitable modifications by Nguyen Van Thieu, it was the favored approach of most of the Saigon governments which followed Diem. In actual practice, however, the Vietnamese who held power in Saigon and in Hanoi believed that a key to power lay in manipulating rivals, not in morality. Competitors were neutralized or jailed. Deception was the mark of effectiveness. The use of force was expected. Douglas Pike described it as follows:

> The world of organizational infighting is fluid and dynamic, in constant flux. One must keep running simply to hold his own . . . . The world should never know precisely where one stands. . . . The best leader is paternalistic, sly, skilled at intrigue, master of the deceptive move, possessor of untold layers of duplicity, highly effective in the world in which he moves. Sagacity in the follower consists in knowing whom to join and when, for timing is all important. It is no accident that the Vietnamese hold the professional magician in particular awe.[14]

Toward the population at large, Saigon's approach was designed to "keep people from endless scheming about life and calculations about how to improve one's lot. Good government should train people to keep their stations and to accept the structure of society."[15] Ngo Dinh Diem's application of power concentration and authoritarian control drew on the trappings of Communist ideology and technique. But there was little substance to it, and Diem's system collapsed overnight when the Ngos fell in November 1963. After mid-1968 the governments of Nguyen Van Thieu operated with a more flexible approach to power concentration, combining it (albiet belatedly) with more relevant measures which decentralized power and emphasized local security and economic welfare. But over the long run Thieu was not able to link the center to the population in a mutually reinforcing, beneficial way; ultimately he failed to fashion a political community in South Vietnam.[16]

Power Limitation and Democratic Institution Building

Conventional thinking about the Communist insurrection in Vietnam was not restricted to the Saigon regimes or the U.S. Department of Defense. It was also evident in Department of State, White House, and congressional prescriptions about South Vietnam's need for a Western style of constitutional democratic government. Western liberal doctrines of political authority, when grafted onto

South Vietnam, equated effective government with restrictions on government. Unlike the power holders in Hanoi and Saigon and the more realistic U.S. officials, power limitation proponents argued that the purpose of government was to maximize personal freedom, not to centralize authority. In their view, governments which were dictatorial or resistant to reform invited rebellion. A "social contract" existed between the people and the authorities. Because the people had granted power and legitimacy to the government, if officials acted arbitrarily, the people had the right to withdraw their grant of power. In general, government was the political equivalent of the marketplace, and competitive pluralism was its dynamic. As Theodore Lowi explained it:

> The system is not fragmented and decentralizing. It is fragmented and self-correcting. It represents classical economics applied to the political system. Bargaining among directly conflicting interests is the basic pattern of politics, and the "power structure" is dynamic as well as rational. ... But there is no center of the system, no elite, no meaningful order below the order of the system itself.[17]

Democratic theorists argued that the cause of the Vietnamese rebellion was in popular grievances. To head off the insurgency, Saigon had to reform itself and then share power with the rebels. As President Kennedy said in May 1961:

> No amount of arms and armies can help stabilize those governments which are unable or unwilling to achieve social reform and economic development. Military pacts cannot help nations whose social injustices and economic chaos invite insurgency and penetration and subversion.[18]

The American Department of State and its affiliate, the U.S. Information Agency, publicly equated "political development" in South Vietnam with democratic structures and limitations on the central authorities' power. As a 1968 Department of State publication argued:

> The vast majority of the people of South Vietnam are determined to build their own future under institutions and leaders of their own free choice. ... [They want] to formulate a democratic constitution ... including an electoral law ... and to create, on the basis of elections rooted in that constitution, an elected government.[19]

The democratic approach to politics and pacification, always apparent in our public justifications of our presence in Vietnam, became operationally prominent in the summer of 1965 when Ambassador Henry Cabot Lodge and Major General Edward G. Lansdale were reappointed to Saigon. The formula was emphasized at the February 1966 Honolulu Conference and the next year at the Manila Conference. During this time the Saigon government, under a military directorate headed by Generals Thieu and Ky, held ostensibly contested elections and published an American style of constitution. But the power limitation and democratic institution-building approach to politics was never taken seriously by Vietnamese authorities—in either Saigon or Hanoi.

The Rostow Doctrine: Stability Operations
plus Economic Development

In the early 1960s, advisers in the Kennedy administration, in particular the economist Walt Rostow, argued that insurgency was a manifestation of the larger modernization process—and a challenge which American economic, social, and military programs and technology could and should meet. "Bringing the Third World through the modernization process" was spoken of. Under Rostow's guidance, this far-ranging theory of modernization and America's role, what we call here the "Rostow doctrine," became the primary ingredient of American policy toward the developing areas and the principal rationale for U.S. intervention in Vietnam. The Rostow doctrine combined cold war toughness with Western-style economic development. Rostowians saw the world locked in a Communist-capitalist struggle whose outcome would be decided in the developing areas.[20] South Vietnam was the test case in the struggle. The road to modernization was fraught with risks, particularly Communist-supported guerrilla warfare. As Rostow told the officers at Fort Bragg:

> It is on the weaker nations—facing their most difficult transitional moments—that the Communists concentrate their attention. They are the scavengers of the modernization process. ... Communism is best understood as a disease of the transition to modernization. ... We are determined to help destroy this international disease.[21]

To guide the developing areas, Rostow and other intervention-prone technologists recommended a wide range of American programs—economic, military, psychological, and social. Not surprisingly, State, Defense, AID, USIA, and CIA all found something in the doctrine. But it was the armed services, the most technical elements of the American bureaucracy, that became the principal advocates of the Rostow doctrine. As Lieutenant General Arthur Trudeau, chief of army research and development, told an audience in March 1962:

> Our whole civilization is on trial today. Forces are loose in the world that would destroy all we hold dear. These forces stem from a malignant organism that grows and thrives on human misery—which reaches out its long tendrils in every field of human endeavor, seeking to strangle and destroy.[22]

And General William Westmoreland, the senior American commander in South Vietnam from 1964 until 1968, said in 1967: "If we had not met [the Communist challenge in Vietnam] squarely it could well have been the precedent for countless future wars of similar nature."[23] In addition to Westmoreland, the most forceful advocates of unrelenting military pressure on Hanoi and the Viet Cong were Rostow, who became President Johnson's national security adviser, and General Maxwell Taylor, the retired Army chief of staff, later chairman of the Joint Chiefs of Staff, whom Johnson appointed ambassador to South Vietnam.

The Military Occupation/Search and Destroy Approach

As the Rostow doctrine was applied in South Vietnam, its principal operational formulae were designed and executed by the U.S. armed services, particularly the Army. But French and Vietnamese military influences were also apparent. Originally employed by France in its colonies, the military occupation approach relied on taking physical control of an area and expanding control outward. Early French pacification campaigns in Indochina and Africa were military affairs. French soldiers, "colons," and small businessmen went out to the colonies and, after taking up a more or less permanent residence, directly administered local areas. At the core of French pacification methods was the "oil-stain" *(tache d'huile)* technique first developed between 1892 and 1896 in the Tonkin region of Vietnam under Colonel Joseph-Simon Gallieni.[24] (Some American planners would later advocate similar techniques in South Vietnam, calling them "clear and hold.")

Despite early successes, later French pacification campaigns failed. From 1957 to 1962 in Algeria the French Army's Special Action Squads applied oil-stain and other techniques, but politically France could not hold Algeria. During the 1947-54 Indochina war the French had neither the resources nor the patience to counter Viet Minh organization efforts. In South Vietnam from 1954 to 1956, Prime Minister Diem, with Brigadier General Edward Lansdale advising, launched a series of oil-stain types of pacification campaigns, but they were inconclusive. During 1962 and 1963, the Diem regime had the resources to carry out a population protection campaign, but Diem and his brother Nhu were completely insensitive to the political and administrative requirements. In the summer of 1964 the Khanh government began a clearing operation around Saigon ("Hop Tac"). It failed to pacify the area but probably prevented the Viet Cong from taking the city that year.

Beginning in mid-1965 the military operation approach became transformed under the U.S. Army's influence. Following the entry into South Vietnam of regular North Vietnamese infantry in late 1964, and the near collapse of the Saigon government, American armed forces began to occupy the RVN en masse. Escalation begat escalation, until by early 1968 over 1,300,000 allied forces, principally South Vietnamese, American, and South Korean, were arrayed against 250,000 to 300,000 Communist forces, mostly North Vietnamese (regular combat troops on both sides, however, were much fewer). U.S. Army strategy, under Westmoreland's direction from 1964 to 1968, and significantly influenced by his original deputy for operations, Brigadier General William De Puy, sought to encircle, engage, and destroy large Communist units—hence the term "search and destroy."[25] While "clear and hold," "oil-spot," and "enclave" area control/occupation approaches were less in accord with the general Army doctrine of seizing the initiative, "search and destroy" (which had many tactical variations) became the preferred military doctrine from 1965 through the Tet offensive of 1968, magnetizing press attention.[26] Following Tet 1968, General

Creighton Abrams dropped the term "search and destroy" and employed smaller-unit operations and a more consistent level of military pressure, although preemptive tactics were still very much in use.[27]

While the Westmoreland big-unit strategy, and Abrams's subsequent modification to smaller-unit operations, did spoil many Communist offensives (except Tet 1968 and Easter 1972), and did provide something of a shield for protection of paramilitary efforts in the villages, they did not break the Communist effort. Moreover, the attrition strategy proved enormously costly—both in dollars and in adverse side effects. Ammunition, fuel, logistic and equipment expenditures necessary to the strategy may have constituted the majority of the $150 billion the U.S. spent on the war.[28] And massive American and ARVN air and ground firepower also brought major damage to the society, seriously jeopardizing civilian socioeconomic rehabilitation efforts.[29]

The Administrative Approach

Another, final important doctrine and strategy which appeared in South Vietnam was largely British in origin, although it was also adopted by some American and South Vietnamese proponents. Administrative approach theorists argued that political development was essentially a problem of efficient government: the "administrative capacity to maintain law and order efficiently and effectively and to perform governmental output functionally, rationally and neutrally."[30] Ideology and politics were deemphasized; when insurgency occurred, it was due to a breakdown in rural administration.

In their colonies the British relied on an indirect, usually civilian, approach to government; the army played a less prominent role than in French operations. Effective government was seen as a problem of devising more efficient public administration rather than conciliating interest groups or mobilizing the masses. Richard Clutterback described Sir Gerald Templer's formula in Malaya during the 1948-58 Emergency:

> Templer was . . . impatient with the idea of "independence before breakfast." He realized that, for the people in the villages, self-government was less important than good government. He was determined to bring self-government to Malaya, but not until the independent government could be strong enough to prevent racial violence (as had occurred in India) and the people were no longer in a state of insecurity and poverty.[31]

Above all, this doctrine assumes that it is the restoration of governmental authority, administrative control, and "law and order" that counts. Sir Robert Thompson, formerly Malayan defense minister and head of the British Advisory Mission to South Vietnam during 1961-65, states:

No communist insurrection has got off the ground where the rural administration hadn't broken down beforehand. . . . Before you can get all the aspects of democracy or whatever [the] forms of political government may be—economy, etc.—you must have an administrative machine that works right down to the village.[32]

Following efforts of American public administration advisers in Saigon from 1955 to 1961 (chiefly the Michigan State University Advisory Group), British specialists with Thompson reemphasized the administrative formula. In 1962 the Diem government began a massive new population regroupment and internal security program ("strategic hamlets") with American material support and British advice.[33] The scheme failed because of conceptual weaknesses and disastrous implementation. In subsequent years American public administration advisers continued to press for an administrative strategy. The administrative approach had one thing in common with the Communist social mobilization and organization-building approach: a belief in organizational skills. But the British saw bureaucracy as a politically neutral mechanism for carrying policies to the villages. The Communists saw bureaucracy as an organizational weapon for cutting the villages away from the government in order to build an alternative power structure.

ANALYSIS: HOW VIETNAM WAS LOST

The Communist approach to revolutionary warfare in Vietnam was a stage-by-stage preemptive social strategy braced by military action: what we have labeled social mobilization and organization building plus armed action. Against this challenge, two U.S./GVN doctrines and strategies proved generally irrelevant or often counterproductive: the power limitation and democratic institution-building approach, and the military occupation/search and destroy strategy. Two other allied responses contained both relevant and wasteful elements: the power concentration and authoritarian control approach, and the Rostow doctrine. By contrast, the administrative strategy and the CIA's version of social mobilization and organization building were highly applicable to combating Communist revolutionary warfare in Vietnam. It was the misfortune of the allied effort that, until the 1968 Communist Tet offensive, Saigon and Washington emphasized combinations of these six approaches which were largely irrelevant to the Communist challenge and meaningless or damaging to the society. The trend reversed after the Tet attacks and a more appropriate strategy was devised. This later effort put increased emphasis on population protection, local organization building, political participation, and economic reform. It provided considerably more security to the local people, decentralized some power to reorganized villages, laid more stress on attacking the Viet Cong infrastructure, and set in motion a broad-based land reform effort. Hanoi's Russian-equipped invasion of South Vietnam in April 1972 skewed GVN/U.S. strategy back toward high-technology military warfare. But when the invasion petered out, the Thieu regime returned to elements of its earlier post-Tet strategy, continuing them with mixed success until the long slide began in mid-1974.

Power limitation and democratic institution building were not pertinent to the problems of South Vietnam. And, as a political recipe, they have little relevance for Third World countries where traditional regimes are combating revolutionary insurgent movements. Successful political development and counterinsurgency require that power must be created, concentrated, and stabilized *before* it can be shared. In addition, Western democratic institutions and procedures at the national level were not salient for the Vietnamese, nor do they apply to most developing countries. The military occupation/search and destroy strategy in Vietnam, while an appropriate response to some of the conventional aspects of the war, was an outgrowth of the U.S. Army's traditional military doctrine. Relying on mobility and massive firepower, the Army strategy still could not prevent the adversary from controlling his losses, or U.S. operations from damaging the society they were trying to protect. Despite their many valiant sacrifices, discrimination in their operations was not something at which American forces excelled. The size, clumsiness, and firepower of regular American and South Vietnamese units often proved significantly counterproductive. Hanoi and the Viet Cong regularly exploited this, goading U.S. and ARVN forces into overreactions. The effect was to multiply popular grievances against the Saigon governments. Not until after Tet 1968 were more resources allocated to the territorial militia units and the people's self-defense forces, and was serious attention paid to retraining the South Vietnamese armed forces.

The Communists' use of power concentration at the elite level, social mobilization and organization building at the mass level, and continuous military pressure year after grinding year was responsible for much of their success. When Ngo Dinh Diem tried to apply power concentration and authoritarian control from 1954 to 1963, it became a charade of elite manipulation and mass indoctrination. And the military cliques which immediately followed Diem had little concept of government.[34] But by mid-1967 Nguyen Van Thieu had moved to solidfy his influence in the Army and the newly created legislature. Pressures from the 1968 Tet offensive drove Thieu to modify his earlier political-military approach, and he took some resources and power away from the Army and bureaucracy and redistributed them to the villages, with a salutary effect on the GVN's overall position.

Like the power concentration approach, the Rostow doctrine had both useful and counterproductive elements. Its advocates were right in believing that a combination of efforts was needed to combat the Vietnamese Communist challenge. But it was the fundamental error of those who embraced the Rostow doctrine to assume that the ultimate source of South Vietnam's problems lay in

North Vietnam. By concentrating massive resources against infiltration from the North rather than focusing on the political and administrative decay in the South and Saigon's reluctance to address it, Rostow doctrine advocates and their principal agents in Saigon—MACV and the 7th/13th Air Force advocates—missed the central processes and dynamics by which the revolution endured.

The administrative approach was a necessary (although not sufficient) precondition to combating revolutionary warfare in Vietnam. The Diem regime inherited and then perpetuated an administrative and political vacuum in South Vietnam which no number of French, Vietnamese, or American soldiers and advisers could fill. Power vacuums invite insurgent organizational efforts. When a developing country is experiencing incipient insurgency, invariably the rebels emerge out-administering the government, not outfighting it. Diem, the generals who followed him, and the United States all made the mistake of assuming that a large army and conventional military occupation operations could substitute for effective penetration and organization of the population. Unlimited injections of economic aid and military resources were seen as replacing indigenous sources of participation and support, administrative talent, and organizational skill.

The social mobilization and organization-building approach, when supported by military action, was an effective insurrection strategy for the Communists and would have been a potent counterstrategy for the government—if it had been given enough priority. Executed with sophistication by Hanoi and the Viet Cong, it went to the heart of the matter: penetrating the villages; adapting the organization to local conditions; mobilizing people; and giving or forcing them to take a part in the revolution. During 1966 and 1967, and in a dramatic fashion after the January-February 1968 Tet offensive, Saigon adopted or amplified elements similar to those used by the Communists: in the Revolutionary Development program (1966-66), during the accelerated pacification campaigns (1968-700),[35] and then later in the community defense and local development plan (1970-72)[36]. The GVN never executed social mobilization and organization building with the skill of the Communists. But by 1971 Saigon's new approach had contributed to such a smothering of local insurgent activities that Hanoi, acknowledging the GVN breakthrough, was forced to plan a new military invasion.[37] The 1972 assault failed to break South Vietnam, and at a hideous cost to North Vietnam's army. But in 1973 and 1974 Hanoi kept up enough pressure so that, with the decline in U.S. aid, Saigon could not hold its hard-won position.

CONCLUSION AND PROGNOSIS

Vietnam demonstrated that the United States has distinct liabilities in countering revolutionary war movements and in orchestrating specially tailored limited-war strategies. Moreover, democracies cannot combat "wars of national liberation" unless they have the overriding support of their people *and can sustain the effort* for as long as it takes. Televising the battlefield is one sure way of eroding public support. The pluralistic, democratic nature of American society produces wide variations in our beliefs about political authority. We have no overarching doctrine of government. In contrast, Communist dictatorships and radical revolutionary movements have distinct advantages. Being authoritarian, they suppress dissent and control information. Their monocausal doctrines of politics lend themselves to the ruthless exploitation of changing situations.

In Vietnam our pluralistic traditions seriously diluted our search for strategy. The American government, even in war, must work in the open. Our foreign policy must constantly reconcile separate interests and factions. When we attempted to advise, and eventually direct, a counterinsurgency and then a major land war in Asia, we found that our pluralism (reflected in our fragmented bureaucracy) shaped our strategy. By spreading custody of the war's direction across competitive, largely uncoordinated agencies, we institutionalized our confusion. In neither Saigon nor Washington did we subject our agencies to effective control: there never was an American "proconsul" in the Vietnam War. The Army's recommendations were not what USAID wanted or what the CIA prescribed. State and USIS saw it still differently.

Saigon's limitations were equally fatal to the design of strategy. Inheriting the wreckage of France's colonial war, the governments of South Vietnam perpetuated a system of class, tradition, and wealth. Dominated by an oligarchical elite sitting atop a peasant base and held together by a garrison state, the power structure sought to restrict or prevent political participation by the masses. For the price of supporting Thieu, the urban-rural oligarchy was able to prevent serious reform of the system. Nor did it even have to try reforms as long as the Americans paid the bills and did a large amount of the fighting. By trying to do so much ourselves, we tended to fritter away the leverage we needed to bring the Saigon regimes around.

What can we say about future U.S. agency performance in revolutionary war situations? First, as long as congressional committees and the media pore over the CIA's every move, and the inevitable security leaks continue, the CIA will have real difficulty working against subversion in the Third World. And this could prove unfortunate, because American operations in Vietnam (and, particularly, in Laos) showed that the CIA was hard-nosed in its assessments, realistic and comparatively cost-effective in its operations. The Vietnam experience does not foster much confidence at this point that the Army can tailor its capabilities very well to unconventional warfare environments. The Army never wanted a counterinsurgency/stability operations mission in the first place—witness what happened to the Special Forces in the early 1960s. The Army's central mission remains the defense of Western Europe; second, to fight in Korea. In both cases the Army is prepared, understandably, to go all-out in a conventional, high-technology contest. The other major armed services—the Air Force and the Navy—have no capability or interest in counterinsurgency or nation building. The Marines showed realism in their Vietnam operations, but they must take their cues from the Navy when it comes to resources, budgets, and commitments. The Agency for International Development shows mixed results when it operates in unconventional environments. Yet the size of AID monies and programs continues to decline. More important, Communist insurgent activities are seldom countered with economic development schemes. The Department of State's and USIA's preferences for democratic approaches to revolutionary Third World predicaments are not realistic.

Thus we have found that conventional bureaucratic-military responses to revolutionary warfare do not work. They do not take into account the relevance of culture, social forces, and, above all, politics. They perceive socioeconomic problems and political problems through technological and administrative filters. They graft favored programs and resources onto foreign problems. They re-create reality in their own image, justifying progress by documenting effort. Conventional liberal-democratic responses to revolutionary warfare do not work either. They underestimate the role of force and violence. They do not take into account the salience of power, the necessity of creating, centralizing, and institutionalizing power before it can be shared. They apply Western values to non-Western problems. Since the collapse of Indochina, we have seen precious few efforts in the American government to develop a new nation-building and counterinsurgency doctrine, or specially tailored, realistic programs and strategies. No adapted machinery uniquely geared to cut across agency lines is in existence.

It is difficult to determine to what extent these weaknesses are understood in Washington. Most of the architects of our Vietnam policies, and our nation-building and counterinsurgency/stability operations programs of the 1960s and early 1970s, have left government. Mentally the Army is finished with counterinsurgency, although it lingers on as a potential responsibility. Army field manuals do throw some light on the problem. An examination of Army doctrine publications from the mid-1960s through the last several years shows a clear, if quiet, shift in confidence about the desirability and feasibility of U.S. military assistance and intervention in the developing world. Early manuals spoke of "areas and territories ravaged by insurgency," and were full of largely unqualified assumptions about our ability to help counterinsurgency. The counterinsurgency mission, we were told, commanded "equal priority with [Army] readiness for limited and general war missions." Now we find that the terms "counterinsurgency" and "stability operations" have given way to "internal defense and development." More attention is paid diagnosing the specific characteristics and problems of developing countries. More sophistication about various kinds of insurgencies and insurrection strategies is apparent, and there is an increased sensitivity to adviser relationships. "The primary purpose of U.S. Army assistance in [internal defense and development activities] ," states the current Army Manual, "is to increase the capabilities and efficiency of host country armed forces. . . . Overall U.S. assistance . . . will be commensurate with the magnitude and form of the threat to our allies while simultaneously being wholly consistent with the level of U.S. interest."[38] And further: "Advice may be the least desired assistance offered by [U.S. advisers] and only tolerated to obtain material and training assistance. Even when accepted, host country . . . leaders may not immediately act upon advice given by their U.S. advisors . . . often, what may appear logical to the adviser may not appear logical or practical for political, cultural, or economic reasons to those he advises."[36]

Rather than armed challenges to be overcome on battlefields, insurgencies should be viewed as *symptoms* of conditions and problems within societies (and often their governments) which need to be solved. As a consequence, criteria for U.S. military assistance and intervention in developing countries experiencing insurgency should focus around questions such as the following:

1. Does U.S. assistance push local government activities (civil, police, military) out in front?

2. Do our programs enhance or disrupt the ties between the government, the armed forces, and the people?

3. Does our involvement minimize disruption to indigenous patterns of life?

4. Do our programs create dependencies and expectations that cannot be fulfilled once our aid stops?

5. Do our programs overload the host country's mechanisms and/or capacities?

6. Does our intervention give the government's adversary a tailor-made propaganda cause? (alternatively do our programs enhance or subtract from the development of an environment sympathetic to the government's cause?)

7. Does our assistance increase the level of corruption in the society?

8. Do our programs train the wrong forces (perhaps those elements we are most familiar with)?

9. Is our assistance backed up with credible sanctions if misused by the host government?

10. Are U.S. advice and assistance tailored to the special requirements of the country and environment we are working in, or are they simply manifestations of "business as usual"?

Engaging in counterinsurgency is like trying to hug someone with a sunburn: everywhere you touch him, it hurts. To the degree that American security planners understand the extreme sensitivities in assisting other countries with their internal defense and development problems, our programs can help rather than hurt those we aid.

NOTES

1. See, for example, Secretary of State Henry A. Kissinger, "The Permanent Challenge of Peace: U.S. Policy toward the Soviet Union," February 3, 1976, San Francisco. The secretary expanded on these oral remarks in a speech at Dallas on March 22, where he said, "The United States cannot acquiesce indefinitely in the presence of Cuban expeditionary forces in distant lands for the purpose of pressure and to determine the political evolution by force of arms." He added, "An unopposed superpower may draw dangerous conclusions when the next opportunity for intervention beckons" (*New York Times,* March 23, 1976). 2. In response to Kissinger, Professor George Kennan, of Princeton, argued that not all regions were of equal importance to each superpower, that excessive intervention could equate to entrapment, and that the capabilities of the host regimes on the ground were critical (*Washington Post,* February 16, 1976, p. A15).

2. Samuel Huntington, cited in Bernard Brodie, *War and Politics* (New York: Macmillan, 1973), pp. 113-14.

3. R. W. Komer, "Bureaucracy Does Its Thing: Institutional Constraints on U.S.-GVN Performance in Vietnam," RAND Corporation Memorandum R-967-ARPA (August 1972).

4. This section draws principally upon the author's "How They Lost: Doctrines, Strategies and Outcomes of the Vietnam War," *Asian Survey* 15 (December 1975).

5. This is Jeffrey Race's thesis. See esp. chap. 4 of his *War Comes to Long An: Revolutionary Conflict in a Vietnamese Province* (Berkeley: University of California Press, 1972).

6. See Douglas Pike, *Viet Cong* (Cambridge, Mass.: M.I.T. Press, 1966); see also Stephen T. Hosmer, *Viet Cong Repression and Its Implications for the Future* (Lexington, Mass.: Heath, Lexington Books, 1970).

7. See Huntington's developmental analysis in Samuel Huntington, *Political Order in Changing Societies* (New Haven: Yale University Press, 1966), pp. 335, 343. The most intricate analysis of Diem's and Nhu's personzlied roles is in John C. Donnell, "Politics in South Vietnam: Doctrines of Authority in Conflict" (Ph.D. diss., University of California, Berkeley, 1964).

8. Douglas Pike, *War, Peace and the Viet Cong* (Cambridge, Mass.: M.I.T. Press, 1969), p. 128.

9. Robert Thompson estimates the North Vietnamese lost 130,000 combat forces, killed or disabled in the fighting, during this time. Thompson, *Peace Is Not at Hand* (New York: David McKay, 1974), pp. 121, 196.

10. Pike, *War, Peace and the Viet Cong,* pp. 108-67; Ian Ward, "Why Giap Did It: Report From Saigon," in *North Vietnam's Blitzkreig—An Interim Assessment,* ed. Brian Crozier (London: Institute for the Study of Conflict, October 1972), pp. 1-11; F. P. Serong, *Vietnam's Menacing Cease Fire* (London: Institute for the Study of Conflict, November 1974); Douglas Pike and James Haley, "Democratic Republic of Vietnam," and Carlyle A. Thayer, "Republic of Vietnam," in *Yearbook on International Communist Affairs,* ed. Richard F. Starr (Stanford, Ca.: Hoover Institution Press, 1975), pp. 429-39 and 440-54.

11. The most detailed and accurate analyses of opposing military activities in South Vietnam after the January 28, 1973, "cease-fire" are in Major General Charles J. Timmes, "Military Operations After the Cease-Fire Agreement, Part I and Part II," *Military Review* (August 1976, September 1976).

12. In early 1966, about 20,000 cadres were operating throughout the RVN. The number grew to 39,000 one year later, and topped out at about 48,000 cadres in 1969. They were never supposed to be "revolutionaries"; thus the GVN called them "Rural Construction" (Xay-Dung Dong-Tham), avoiding, in public, the American term "Revolutionary" (Cach Mang).

13. Rural Development Division, Community Development Directorate, "The Vietnamese Village" (Saigon: Hq. MACCORDS, May 2, 1970), p. 4.

14. Pike, *Viet Cong*, pp. 9-10.

15. Quote from Lucien Pye, describing classical Asian mandarin concepts, in his "The Roots of Insurgency and the Commencement of Rebellions," in *Internal War: Problems and Approaches*, ed. Harry Eckstein (New York: Free Press, 1964), p. 161.

16. The concept of "political community" in South Vietnam used here derives from Allan E. Goodman's excellent treatment of the problem in his *Politics in War: The Bases of Political Community in South Vietnam* (Cambridge, Mass.: Harvard University Press, 1973).

17. Theodore J. Low, "Making Democracy Safe for the World: National Politics and Foreign Policy," in *Domestic Sources of Foreign Policy*, ed. James N. Rosenau (New York: Free Press, 1967), p. 296.

18. *New York Times* (May 26, 1961): 12.

19. U.S. Department of State, *Political Development in South Vietnam*, Vietnam Information Notes, no. 5, Pubn. 8231 (January 1968), pp. 1-8. The problem of divergent views between State and Defense, and for that matter among all U.S. agencies in Vietnam, goes back to the early 1950s. Whereas State Department spokesmen almost always argued that U.S. policy should take the form of pressures on the GVN to reform and to liberalize its handling of dissent, of the press, and of the population so as to command popular support, Defense Department officials consistently regarded the GVN's difficulties as almost always proceeding from military, not political or administrative, inadequacies.

20. Three of Rowtow's essays are relevant. The first is Max Millikan and W.W. Rostow, *A Proposal: Key to an Effective Foreign Policy* (New York: Harper, 1957). The second is W.W. Rostow, *The States of Economic Growth: A Non-Communist Manifesto* (Cambridge: At the University Press, 1960). The third is Rostow's widely circulated speech, "Guerrilla Warfare in the Underdeveloped Areas," originally given at the U.S. Army Special Warfare School, Fort Bragg, North Carolina, on June 28, 1961.

21. Rostow, "Guerrilla Warfare."

22. Arthur G. Trudeau, Welcoming Address, in *U.S. Army's Limited War Mission and Social Seience Research Symposium*, ed. William A. Lybranc (Washington, D.C.: SORO/ American University, June 1962), pp. 11-12.

23. General William C. Westmoreland, "Progress Report on the War in Vietnam," *Department of State Bulletin* 57 (December 11, 1967): 785.

24. Colonel (later Marshal) Louis Lyautey, as quoted in Mark M. Boatner III, "The Unheeded History of Counterinsurgency," *Army* 16 (September 1966): 31. See also Joseph-Simon Gallieni, *Gallieni Au Tonkin 1892-1896* (Paris: Editions Berger-Levrault, 1941), pp. 219-20, in particular Annexe no. 1, "Principes de Pacification et d'Organisation."

25. The most careful analysis of the evolution of U.S. ground strategy in South Vietnam, and the debates within the Johnson administration in the spring and summer of 1965 on the relative merits of static defense, enclave, and search and destroy approaches, are in the official version of the "Pentagon Papers." See Department of Defense, *United States-Vietnam Relations, 1945-1967*, Vol 4, chap. 5 (Washington, D.C.: Government Printing Office, 1971), pp. 1-10, 33-135. General Westmoreland's description and defense of his strategy are in Westmoreland, *A Soldier Reports* (Garden City, N.Y.: Doubleday, 1976), pp. 174-96. Also relevant are U. S. Grant Sharp and W. C. Westmoreland, *Report on the War in Vietnam* (Washington, D.C.: Government Printing Office, 1969), p. 117; John H. Hay, Jr., *Tactical and Material Innovations*, Vietnam Studies (Washington, D.C.: Department of the Army, 1974), pp. 169-78; and Julien J. Ewell and Ira A. Hunt, Jr., *Sharpening the Combat Edge: The Use of Analysis to Reinforce Military Judgement*, Vietnam Studies (Washington, D.C.: Department of the Army, 1974), pp. 225-32.

26. Critics of the Westmoreland/De Puy strategy include Townsend Hoopes, *The Limits of Intervention* (New York: David McKay, 1969), pp. 62-66. See also Sir Robert Thompson, *No Exit From Vietnam* (New York: David McKay, 1969), pp. 129-31, 134-39. Westmoreland's rebuttal is in *A Soldier Reports*, pp. 148-49. Norman Hannah offers a different kind of criticism of Westmoreland, namely, that he was not aggressive enough, allowing his hands

to be tied in regard to invading Laos and possibly North Vietnam; see Hannah, "Vietnam: Now We Know," *National Review* (June 11, 1976): 612-16.

27. Ewell and Hunt, *Sharpening the Combat Edge*, pp. 75-95, 196-200.

28. Komer, "Bureaucracy Does Its Thing," p. 53.

29. The U.S. Military Assistance Command in Vietnam (MACV) and the ARVN JGS were aware of the damage U.S./GVN conventional firepower could inflict on the society. As General Westmoreland wrote: "Their tremendous firepower made it vastly more desirable that they fight in remote, unpopulated ares *if the enemy would give battle there"* (italics added); the problem was that Hanoi would not follow the script (U. S. Grant Sharp and W. C. Westmoreland, *Report on the War,* p. 132). Yet General Westmoreland also indicates that "Although South Vietnamese leaders asked at first that I restrict [the] American [combat] presence to remote areas, I declined, unwilling to see my [forces'] flexibility fettered and also conscious that American performance would set an example and a challenge to the face-conscious Orientals" (Westmoreland, *A Soldier Reports,* p. 196). By early 1966 the intensification of the war had produced estimates of the numbers of refugees ranging from 700,000 to 1,000,000. Evidence subsequently emerged that in 1965 and 1966, and at later times, the MACV under General Westmoreland either directly or tacitly authorized some *deliberate* refugee generation. See the February 1970 testimony of William Hitchcock and William Colby (U.S., Congress, Senate, Committee on Foreign Relations, *Vietnam: Policy and Prospects, 1970; Civil Operations and Rural Development Support Program: Hearings,* 91st Cong., 2d sess., 1970, pp. 221, 236).

30. Robert A. Packenham, "Approaches to the Study of Political Development," *World Politics* 17, 1 (October 1964): 113. See also Charles A. Joiner, "The Ubiquity of the Administrative Role in Counterinsurgency," *Asian Survey* 7 (July 1967: 550-44; and Charles A. Joiner, *The Politics of Massacre: Political Processes in South Vietnam* (Philadelphia: Temple University Press, 1974), esp. chap. 4.

31. Richard L. Clutterbuck, *The Long, Long War: Counterinsurgency in Malaya and Vietnam* (New York: Praeger, 1966), p. 81.

32. Thompson's comments were made in the Special Warefare Panel at the U.S. Army Operations Research Symposium, May 25-27, 1964, Rock Island, Illinois, reprinted in Hq. U.S. Army Weapons Command, *Proceedings of the U.S. Army Operations Research Symposium,* pp. 175-76.

33. One of the most articulate proponents of the administrative approach, and an acute scholar of Vietnamese history, particularly the Diem regime, is Dennis J. Duncanson; see his *Government and Revolution in Vietnam* (New York and London: Oxford University Press, 1968).

34. "It is an inescapable fact," stated the American ambassador to South Vietnam, General Maxwell Taylor, in his November 1964 briefing, "that there is no national tendency toward team play or mutual loyalty to be found among many of the leaders and political groups within South Vietnam." Excerpts from the briefing by Taylor, "The Current Situation in South Vietnam—November 1964," were printed in the *New York Times* (June 14, 1976).

35. The first accelerated pacification campaign of November 1968-January 1969 was generated from GVN and U.S. shock at the Communist Tet attacks. The Rural and Popular Forces were expanded to 400,000 men. Self-reliant local governments were given priority, and a new attack on the Communist infrastructure began. While full of defects, the accelerated pacification campaign proved that the government could operate a relatively controlled and organized civil-military pacification campaign. The takeoff for a government breakthrough in the countrysioe had occurred.

36. The 1969 and 1970 pacification and development plans were followed by the 1971 community defense and local development plan, which retained Thieu's emphasis on decentralizing the government and giving the villages an increased stake in their own security and development. The 1970 plan emphasized welfare assistance for the urban slums and

refugee camps and for fighting inflation. By 1971 land reform and the election process had taken over the central stage. In March 1972 the GVN commenced its 1972-75 four-year community defense and local development plan, but it was quickly postponed by Hanoi's April invasion. Overall setbacks were 15% to 20% of program goals, but very serious losses for the government occurred in Binh Dinh, Quang Tin, Quang Nam, Quang Tri, and Thua Thien provinces.

37. "By 1971 most of the population in the countryside was at peace and the amount of security achieved no longer a subject for official debate . . . the economic and political patterns of life had resumed" (Allen E. Goodman, "South Vietnam and the New Security," *Asian Survey* 12 [February 1972]: 121-22).

38. Department of Army, FM 100-20, *Internal Defense and Development: U.S. Army Doctrine* (Washington, D.C.: Department of the Army, November 1974), chap. 8, p. 11.

39. Army, *Internal Defense and Development*, chap. 7, p. 6. Compare the particulars in this document with earlier manuals—for example, Army, FM 31-21, *Special Forces Operations* (June 1965); Army, FM 31-23, *Stability Operations: U.S. Army Doctrine* (December 1967); and Army, RM 31-23, *Stability Operations: U.S. Army Doctrine* (October 1972).

THE UNITED STATES INTELLIGENCE COMMUNITY
AND MILITARY INTERVENTION

Paul W. Blackstock

Intelligence and covert operations constitute an integral part of the spectrum of intervention since, like other foreign policy determinations, the decision to intervene—either openly or secretly, using political or military means—rests, in theory, on the best information available to policy makers throughout the government. The collection, evaluation, and dissemination of such information is a primary function of intelligence. Estimates of the status, capabilities, and probable reactions of the state (and associated powers) which is the target of intervention should play an important role in the decision-making process. The production and dissemination of such strategic estimates is another major function of intelligence. Thus, how well or poorly the intelligence community functions, and the relationship between intelligence producers and the policy makers who consume their product, are important factors affecting military intervention. In this regard, the ambivalent character of the relationship between intelligence analysts and policy makers tends to restrict the rationally coordinated use of military intervention as an instrument of policy. Clandestine collection capabilities tend to be diverted to covert operations. The latter, in turn, frequently escalate into, or are followed by, some form of military intervention. Thus the incidence of military intervention tends to be reduced when restrictions limiting the use of covert operations are adopted.

During the Nixon and Ford administrations three key factors determined the parameters limiting the use of covert operations: (1) the national consensus, which shifted from support of the cold war to the favoring of détente; (2) the idiosyncratic factor linking intervention to the personalities of leaders in the White House, the National Security Council, and the office of secretary of state; and (3) institutional pressures from Congress, including Commissions of Inquiry into CIA Activities. B arring a sudden increase in tension levels within the general context of United States foreign policy, these factors could be expected to continue to affect the use of covert action and, by extension, military intervention throughout the later 1970s.

U.S. DOCTRINE CONCERNING INTELLIGENCE
AND POLICY MAKING

This study examines the relationship of the U.S. intelligence community and military intervention, beginning with a review of United States doctrine concerning intelligence, policy making, and covert operations; followed by a survey of academic criticism and congressional investigation of intelligence activities affecting foreign policy and intervention; organizational change and persistent dilemmas involved in the linkage between intelligence and covert operations; parameters affecting covert operations; and conclusions. Having stated our intent and scope, let us examine the ambivalent and necessarily idiosyncratic relationship between intelligence analysts and policy makers.

There are two main schools of thought on the relationship of intelligence to policy making. The traditional view holds that intelligence should be strictly separated from policy making and operations in order to retain its objectivity. The argument is that if the policy maker is supplied with complete and accurate information with respect to a problem calling for a decision, the options or responses will suggest themselves. At the very least, carefully evaluated information from an objective, unbiased source will increase the decision maker's chances of making a "correct" decision. The role of the analyst, like that of the intellectual, is to seek the truth, i.e., to find and present the facts, however critical of policy their implications may be. In order to do so, the analyst must stand aside and not be committed to any set of policy preferences which could affect his ability to perceive and present facts objectively. The late Allen Dulles stated that the Central Intelligence Agency was founded on the principle of "centralizing the main responsibility for the preparation and coordination of our intelligence analyses in an agency of government which has no responsibility for policy." He claimed that "Policymakers tend quite naturally to become wedded to the policies which they have been responsible for making. Prejudice is the most serious occupational hazard we have in intelligence work."[1]

A second view holds that intelligence is in fact, and should be, "policy-oriented." The consumer, i.e., the policy maker and operator, must supply guidance, not only in setting collection requirements but also for research and analysis, in order that the product may be pertinent or "relevant" to consumer needs and problems. However, as Sherman Kent warns, the closer the links between policy makers and analysts, the greater the danger that "intelligence will find itself right in the middle of policy, and that upon occasions it will be the unabashed apologist for a given policy rather than its impartial and objective analyst."[2]

Beginning in 1971-72, the author circulated a questionnaire on "Intelligence and Covert Operations: Changing Doctrine and Practice" among a representative group of thirty intelligence officers—two-thirds of whom had served at the directorate level in various agencies for an average of twenty-four years of government service. The results indicated considerable ambivalence on the relation of policy making to intelligence. While there was wide acceptance of the traditional view that intelligence should be separated from policy making in order to retain its objectivity, nevertheless two-thirds of the respondents believed that the policy maker must supply guidance to the analyst or producer in order that the product of the latter may be "policy-oriented" or relevant.[3]

The former head of the British Joint Intelligence Bureau (Defense), Major General Sir Kenneth Strong, makes a number of observations, based on forty years of experience, that effectively bridge this paradox:

> The relationship between Intelligence officers and policy-makers is of course difficult and complex. The generally accepted view that it is the duty of the Intelligence officer to "give just the facts, please" has little relevance in a modern governmental structure. In the first place, the facts are often such that the policy-makers are unable to interpret them without expert advice. Secondly, and obviously, the choice of facts is critical, and the Intelligence officer's decision as to which facts are relevant and which should be presented to the policy-maker is often the major initial step in the decision process. . . .
>
> On the other hand, there is a frequent temptation for policy-makers to use Intelligence data selectively to suit their own preconceived judgments or political requirements.[4]

Strong notes that intelligence is frequently blamed for operational or policy errors and suggests that the remedy lies in greater participation of intelligence officers in policy planning and operations:

> My experience is that operational and policy errors are often wrongly attributed to inaccurate or insufficient Intelligence. The tactical success of the Germans in the so-called Battle of the Bulge in the Ardennes in the closing stages of World War II was vociferously attributed to the failure of Intelligence staffs to provide warning of German intentions. An inquiry by General Bedell Smith immediately after the war absolved Intelligence of any failure on this occasion; such blame as could be attached to anyone was said to rest with the operational staffs. I think that this discussion of the attribution of blame for failures is a fruitless, though continuing, argument. The remedy lies in bringing Intelligence and operational staff more closely in contact, and I am convinced that Intelligence officers should participate directly in any important planning, policy or operational decision-making, both in war and peace. . . . In a sense, the objectives of Intelligence work are to have accurate forecasts of events or stages of development on the desks of decision-makers sufficiently early for them to

take action, or, failing this, to have accurate and imaginative estimates of situations on the decision-makers' desks at the same time as the news to which they refer is appearing on the press agency teletype. Obviously, sensible anticipation demands the cooperation of the policy-makers and planners, who must play their part by informing Intelligence staffs of the kinds of matters on which decisions are likely to be made, and the kinds of policies that are being developed.[5]

Divided policy-making and operational responsibilities, combined with career-conditioned and institutionalized rivalry, have created considerable tension between civilian and military elements within the American and other intelligence establishments.[6] A similar tension exists between policy makers and intelligence experts, each accusing the other of "intellectual arrogance." After noting such tension, General Strong suggests that the solution to this problem lies in better understanding and closer cooperation between the two elements in the decision-making process:

> No intelligence officer or agency can be right every time, just as no doctor can be infallible in his diagnoses and no lawyer can be certain of the adequacy of his advice on a complex problem. Not even the existence of a first-class Intelligence organization with access to all sources, staffed and trained by the most competent personnel, will guarantee that the right options will be chosen and the right policies pursued. It must, however, be added that there is often an element of intellectual arrogance in the posture of some policy-makers. ... I have often found myself viewing with appalling mistrust many of the generalizations on foreign affairs and foreign countries aired by those responsible for the development of policy.
>
> In practice, of course, a finely balanced cooperative system is vital if Intelligence and policy-making are to be sensibly related. In the first place, the Intelligence input must aim at being of such a consistently high quality as to acquire for itself a reputation for indispensability. Secondly, the policy-maker must ensure that the Intelligence staffs receive as much help as is possible in establishing their priorities, so that the bulk of their work will be relevant.[7]

In spite of increasing awareness throughout the government of the need for closer and better relations between decision makers and intelligence officers, the record in this regard is not encouraging. Ray S. Cline, former director of intelligence and research in the Department of State, from 1969 to 1973, has written a trenchant analysis of the role of intelligence in material decision making. Using the U.S. military alert of October 24, 1973, as a case study, Cline writes that "shortcomings in the handling of intelligence" were the result of (1) "failure to pass on evidence contained in Soviet statements on the situation" (in American-Soviet diplomatic exchanges); (2) "isolation of intelligence officers from thinking and key questions in the minds of policy officers"; and (3) "policy officers acting as their own intelligence analysts when they have neither technical knowledge nor time to weigh all the evidence objectively." Drawing on his experience as deputy director for intelligence in the CIA during the Cuban Missile Crisis of 1962, Cline draws the following doctrinal precepts:

1. Sharing of intelligence data and diplomatic correspondence at suitable levels is essential to careful decision-making.

2. Sharing of ideas and estimates among senior intelligence analysts and policy-planners is conducive to sound policy.

3. Basing key decisions on careful intelligence analyses is prudent and facilitates the public explanation that breeds confidence.[8]

In addition to institutionalized factors affecting the relationship between policy making and intelligence, the idiosyncratic element introduced by the personalities of policy makers and their advisers is important. American presidents and secretaries of state vary widely in their understanding of intelligence and their use or disregard of the intelligence product. As Ransom observes, "Many national policies are made with a seemingly willful disregard for intelligence. Domestic considerations are often given more attention than careful intelligence estimates. The best estimate, moreover, can never be a substitute for responsible political judgement. What it [intelligence] can do is attempt to insure that policy blunders are not made because known information has been wrongly evaluated or improperly disseminated."[9]

At times, under conditions of extreme secrecy on the part of the chief executive and the secretary of state, decisions involving military intervention have been made in spite of opposition by responsible experts in the Department of State, the intelligence community, or both. The Ford administration's support of an ill-fated Kurdish revolt in Iraq, in 1975, is a clear case in point. During the same period a task force composed of highly placed U.S. experts on Africa strongly opposed military intervention in Angola. Instead, "they called for diplomatic efforts to encourage a political settlement among the three factions to avert bloodshed." Owing to the idiosyncratic factor, their report was presented to the National Security Council "as merely one policy option" rather than as a recommendation.[10] Since these two cases are typical examples of covert operations, let us turn next to a brief examination of U.S. doctrine concerning such operations.

U.S. DOCTRINE CONCERNING INTELLIGENCE AND COVERT OPERATIONS

Covert operations are a part of the broad spectrum of foreign policy instruments ranging from friendly persuasion through normal diplomatic channels to the direct use of military force in open warfare. Political actions which would prove embarrassing if publicly exposed, such as the subsidizing, bribing, and/or blackmailing of politicians and parties, are conducted below the covert threshold, along with such activities as political assassination and similar acts of terror, and the clandestine use of political agents, mercenaries, and guerrillas to carry on subversive revolutionary or counterrevolutionary movements. Although states traditionally deny such interference in principle, most of these activities constitute aggressive intervention by one state in the internal affairs of another, and are frequently called political warfare. Their purpose is to extend the influence of one state over another. Influence tends to merge with control, and its ultimate extension is direct military intervention and conquest, in which case clandestine intervention escalates beyond the covert threshold into the open use of force. Political operations, both open and covert, have been called "competitive interference" or "informal penetration" by their advocates, and heralded as a "revolution in statecraft" in scholarly works which attempt to provide a theoretical basis for the analysis of foreign intervention.[11] Since the Watergate affair, covert operations have come under increasingly sharp criticism, culminating in extended congressional investigations in the mid-1970s.

Like other foreign policy actions, political warfare operations (both open and covert) depend on intelligence agency support to provide the information and estimates on which in theory they are based. Historically, however, they have often been conducted by special divisions of the foreign office, such as the so-called Asiatic Department of the Tsarist Russian foreign office. This practice changed during World War II, when the British Special Operations Executive (SOE) and its American counterpart, the Office of Strategic Services (OSS), were set up to carry out the political warfare missions of their respective governments.

Britain's wartime leader, Prime Minister Winston Churchill, created the Special Operations Executive not only to collect intelligence but also "to set Europe ablaze." The SOE and the OSS supported resistance movements in Nazi-occupied Europe which conducted widespread sabotage using guerrilla tactics. These later became known as "strategic services."[12] Since all political warfare and sabotage operations are hostile by definition, they can only be conducted secretly, by clandestine agencies using traditional espionage and counterespionage techniques.

As noted above, both the British SOE and the American OSS were established with the dual missions of clandestine intelligence collection and covert operations. The linkage between these missions, which is taken for granted in wartime, has been tacitly overlooked or neglected in intelligence doctrine dealing with the peacetime spectrum of intelligence capabilities and operations. The archives of intelligence agencies often remain classified for decades. Nevertheless, available historical records indicate that covert political action programs tend to originate as a natural, almost inevitable, extension of clandestine information collection in times of heightened international tension or whenever major powers consciously or unconsciously seek to expand their spheres of influence, especially in their relations with weaker or client states. This "iron law of development" may be alternatively stated as follows: "Whenever a government agency is given a clandestine collection mission and capability, its agents will tend to become involved in political actions or programs because the kinds of contacts they must make in order to carry out their primary mission have inevitable political overtones." In this regard Harry Rositzke, a former OSS agent who later became one of the Central Intelligence Agency's foremost specialists in clandestine collection, writes that "the kind of clandestine intelligence contacts that are still required, simply to keep on top of complex and important situations, cannot on occasion avoid having political overtones. The justification is, as it has been, to combat what remains the very large political activity of the Soviets and their allies."[13]

An interesting case study of the linkage between clandestine collection and operations comes from documents dealing with American intelligence in Moscow during the Bolshevik seizure of power and the Allied intervention, a period extending from October 1917 through October 1918. At that time, an American citizen of Russian-Greek ethnic origin, Xenophon B. Kalamatiano, who had represented American business interests in Moscow for several years, was recruited to run a clandestine intelligence collection agency listed on the table of organization of the Consulate General simply as the "Second Section." The available records indicate that Kalamatiano was a highly perceptive political analyst intimately acquainted with the Russian scene. However, he soon became closely linked with such British secret agents as Bruce Lockhart, Captain (later Brigadier General) George A. Hill, and Britain's "master spy," Sidney Reilly. As a result, he was arrested by the Soviets and charged with participation in "attempts to stage a counter-revolution in Moscow" known as "the Lockhart conspiracy." He was at first condemned to death, and although the sentence was later commuted to life imprisonment, it took four years of persistent State Department effort to secure his release from prison. Documentation on the Kalamatiano case is incomplete, since four of what were presumably the most sensitive and damaging record files were destroyed in the State Department before the others were transferred to the National Archives.[14] However, according to Lockhart's son, Robin Bruce Lockhart (himself a former British Naval Intelligence aide), "Peters, Vice-President of the Cheka in 1918, is on record as saying that of the various Allied Secret Services operating in Russia, that of America was the most compromised in the 'Lockhart plot'."[15]

In the disturbed period following World War II, the National Security Act of 1947 gave the Central Intelligence Agency (CIA) an intentionally broad charter to perform, in addition to intelligence collection and distribution, "such additional services of common concern as the National Security Council (NSC) determines can be more efficiently accomplished centrally" plus "such other functions and duties" as the NSC "may from time to time direct."

Under this broad formula the CIA has in practice performed a wide range of covert operations for political warfare purposes. In a passage which unwittingly illustrates the clandestine collection-covert operation syndrome in action, Rositzke authoritatively summarizes events and describes the origin of the CIA's cold war mission as follows:

When, in 1948, spurred by the Communist takeover in Czechoslovakia and the Italian political crisis, the National Security Council gave the CIA the responsibility for "political, psychological, economic, and unconventional warfare operations," the straightforward espionage mission of the AIS was enormously broadened, if not distorted. Known within the Service as "the PP mission," and originally carried out by a separate operating component within the CIA (the Office of Policy Coordination), these action operations and the new personnel responsible for them were soon integrated into the espionage and counterespionage service. This merger had a significant and enduring effect on the conduct and public image of American secret operations.

The cold war rationale for the covert action mission was simple: help stop the Russians. With Soviet troops poised to overrun Western Europe and "international communism" threatening the "free world" in France and Italy, Greece, Iran, Vietnam and China, with the military establishment severely reduced and State's diplomatic initiative stalemated, *the White House gave its own new "secret arm" the offensive mission to fight Russians with their own weapons. . . .*

The danger posed by these activities in the 1950's was not an illusion, and "covert action" became a (i.e., Soviet clandestine "political actions") popular expedient for taking American initiatives in the cold war without obvious official involvement. Presidents from Truman to Nixon were not reluctant to use it.[16]

This operational perspective has persisted, as, for example, when in December 1975 clandestine U.S. support of non-Communist guerrilla forces and factions fighting in the newly independent African state of Angola escalated beyond the covert threshold. This program was defended as necessary in order to demonstrate that the United States still has the national will to behave like a great power. This argument seemed "to revive the postulate that the United States must oppose any Russian adventure outside the Soviet bloc or lose credibility as a great nation and ally.[17] For their part, Soviet sources defended Russian support of Communist-led forces as legitimate aid extended to "wars of national liberation."[18]

The scope of covert operations has been extensive. The Directorate of Operations (formerly called Plans) is the CIA's single largest division and is responsible for all clandestine collection and covert operations and for the agency's eighty-five overseas stations. Employing an estimated 6,000-7,000 people, the directorate has had a budget of about $350 million, nearly half the CIA total.

Since the beginning of the cold war almost half of the clandestine personnel have been diverted from the task of collecting and processing information, as envisaged by those who established the CIA in 1947, to political warfare and paramilitary or even covert military operations, as in Laos and Vietnam. Following withdrawal of the United States from hostilities in Southeast Asia, many of the CIA's local agents were assigned to such tasks as reporting on the international drug traffic in the area, a traffic linked politically to Meo tribesmen and other elements formerly supported by the CIA. During his brief tenure as director of central intelligence, Schlesinger indicated interest in the intelligence aspects of the international drug traffic and international terrorism, represented by such acts as airplane hijackings and kidnappings.

What have been the basic assumptions underlying American political and military intervention in the so-called Third World, the major target of our covert operations during the cold war decades? They reflect a grossly oversimplified, black and white view of international relations, exemplified by the so-called domino theory. One of the many ironies connected with American intervention in Angola is that the domino idea was revived during a period in which the policy makers in U.S. foreign affairs emphasized political realism and sophistication. Rigorously pursued, the domino theory would reduce American policy until it consisted "largely of reactions to Soviet maneuvers whether or not American interests [were] directly challenged."[19]

In developing areas of the world, nationalism and the drive for modernization have produced a series of recurrent political and social revolutions which have displaced traditional elites and various colonial and postcolonial ruling groups. As new ruling elites in the Third World consolidate their power and privileges, the nepotism and corruption associated with traditional societies will almost certainly create deep political, economic, and social grievances. These in turn will lead to new consequences. In spite of heroic, if belated, U.S. efforts to arrest the process, this is clearly what happened to the Diem regime in South Vietnam, and the pattern will repeat itself elsewhere. Naturally the Soviets or the Chinese Communists, or both, will seek to exploit such indigenous revolutionary movements, employing their separate strategies of subversion or political warfare. However, the traditional cold war assumption that Communists will automatically succeed in capturing and controlling such movements, unless vigorously opposed by U.S. covert operations and counterinsurgency programs, is in error. The cycle of revolution in the developing areas is as open-ended as the process of modernization itself, from which it is inseparable. Even if local Communists attain power, they will probably be nationalists who will resist control by Moscow and Peking. This trend has been demonstrated in Southeast Asia, where there has been an undercurrent of rivalry between the Vietnamese and Chinese Communists, and where the former have been an obstacle to expansion of Chinese influence in the region.

CRITICISM OF INTELLIGENCE COLLECTION ACTIVITIES

The first and basic function of intelligence, gathering information, came under criticism during both the Nixon and Ford administrations as the result of a revived interest in "human intelligence (HUMINT)," i.e., information from human sources collected either openly or by means of clandestine techniques. As practiced between states, clandestine collection or espionage "is the attempt by one government to obtain secretly or under false pretenses information about another to which access is normally denied."[20] It has often been disparaged as producing "uncertain information from questionable people," the comment of Admiral Wemyss, the British First Sea Lord, at the end of World War I. With the advent of advanced technological means of surveillance, such as the U-2 and SR-71 reconnaissance planes, traditional espionage sources have been reduced to the point where they provide only an estimated five percent of information collected. However, the very success of technical sensors has indicated critical gaps in the information they can supply. For example, overhead photography can show a missile on a launcher. Radar intelligence can track it when fired, and telemetry intelligence (TELINT) can provide data on performance of the warhead. But only a well-placed espionage agent (read defector in place) can tell you what is in the warhead of an operational missile and what targets it is programmed to attack.

Since 1948 the CIA has directed espionage and covert political operations, frequently using the same agents for both purposes. As a result, the collection function has inevitably been downgraded, since the "action" (not to mention the rewards) has been largely in the covert operations area.

For at least the last two decades, the CIA stations abroad have been interested primarily in political warfare operations and have sought to recruit agents or sources who can be used for such purposes, primarily dissidents or others willing to engage in the overthrow of existing governments or to provide information needed for more subtle forms of intervention. Then, after a given covert operation has been approved, the emphasis shifts to developing additional sources who can provide information which will ensure its success. The main thrust of the stations' efforts is directed toward what in military terms is called *tactical* intelligence, whereas classical espionage has been aimed mainly at collecting information of strategic importance.

The collection requirements for espionage can be satisfied only by a radically different approach and by the recruitment of entirely different sources than the disaffected political activists who gravitate toward covert operations. What is needed are well-placed people who have access to plans, strategic dialogue, staff papers, decision making, etc.—sources who can provide information on strategic intentions rather than details with respect to hardware and capabilities. The latter kind of information can be provided by technical sensors. In addition, espionage must become responsive to Washington-based requirements rather than merely reporting general news based on hearsay evidence. The emphasis on covert operations has produced an essential mismatch between what is collected and what is needed to fill the gaps in the information provided by technical sensors. Moreover, the sources recruited for political warfare purposes rarely if ever have access to such information.

Clearly, clandestine collection and recruiting practices will have to be radically altered if there is to be any substantial improvement in U.S. espionage capabilities. But such a reversal is unlikely, given the bureaucratic influence of vested interests in the clandestine services, with their stake in the preservation of the status quo. The need to separate the clandestine collection effort from covert political operations has been recognized by such nonestablishment scholars as Henry Howe Ransom, as well as by dedicated professionals serving on the USIB Human Sources Committee. However, unless the need for such separation can be impressed on policy-making and executive levels within both the intelligence community and the government at large, the weight of vested interests will almost certainly perpetuate the present organizational structure. Probably only the President, working through the NSC channel, has enough influence to ensure that this basic reform is carried out.

ACADEMIC CRITICISM OF COVERT OPERATIONS

Serious criticism of covert operations began with the publication, in 1964, of the author's *Strategy of Subversion* and David Wise's and Thomas B. Ross's *The Invisible Government*. Both works, but especially the latter, called for closer scrutiny and control over the entire intelligence community. However, it was not until roughly a decade later, after the Watergate affair, that investigative journalists, such as Seymour Hersh of the *New York Times*, touched off sensational congressional investigations into the CIA's domestic activities. Covert operations then became matters of both public and especially congressional concern. Meanwhile, the groundwork for that concern had been laid by personal memoirs such as Patrick McGarbey's *C.I.A.: The Myth and the Madness* (New York, 1972), and Victor Marchetti's and John D. Mark's *CIA and the Cult of Intelligence* (New York, 1975), the latter an important, responsible critique which received wide publicity as the first book in American history to have been censored (by the CIA) prior to publication. Most damaging, from the CIA point of view, were Philip Agee's *CIA Diary*, published abroad (England, 1975), and *The Abuses of the Intelligence Agencies*, edited by Jerry J. Berman and Morton H. Halperin (Washington: Center for National Security Studies, 1975). Adding fuel to the fire coming from the private sector, Vice-President Nelson Rockefeller's commission on illicit CIA activities published its "Report to the President" in June 1975, in which the agency was found guilty of every serious allegation made against it privately. By way of contrast, the so-called Murphy Commission in its report devoted only a little more than one of its fifteen pages on intelligence to what is called "covert action," defined somewhat disingenuously as "activity abroad intended not to gather information but to influence events, an activity midway between diplomacy and war."[21]

The author's survey on intelligence and covert operations, mentioned earlier,

showed considerable ambivalence toward covert operations even among professional clandestine operators. Most of the thirty respondents regarded covert
operations as an essential arm of diplomacy, but at the same time subscribed to
the criterion that they should be used only as a last resort before the direct use
of military force in a prewar situation. There was also general agreement with
the proposition that "clandestine operational agencies are capable of preempting a policy-making role through operations which create situations of fact
to which national policy must later be readjusted, thus creating serious problems
of management and control"—not to mention the acute national embarrassment
which results when, as frequently happens, such operations are "blown" and
become public knowledge. A heavy majority of the respondents also agreed that
"covert operations have been oversold and overused as instruments of policy to
such an extent that on balance they have become counterproductive." For the
most part, professional analysts with long careers in collection, production,
estimates, and dissemination took the view that these purely intelligence
functions should be separated organizationally from politically oriented covert
operations. On the other hand, clandestine operators with mainly civilian
backgrounds favored the status quo, with covert operations housed under the
CIA. This is to be expected, given the strong institutional loyalties which
develop in all clandestine organizations. Almost all of the respondents, however,
agreed that effective control at the policy-making level has been inadequate in
the past, and that wherever covert operations may be housed they will present
problems in the future. With few exceptions, congressional monitoring and
control was regarded as inadequate and ineffective.

The Central Intelligence Agency declined to participate in the survey on
intelligence and covert operations. Nevertheless, public statements by former
CIA Director William Colby on the general utility of covert operations are
important in this regard. Although most of his professional experience had been
in clandestine operations, including the Phoenix program in Vietnam, Colby
publicly indicated a certain disenchantment with them in testimony before the
Armed Services Committee on July 2, 1973, when he stated that it was "very
unlikely" that the agency would again mount such wide-scale, covert military
operations as its support of the Meo tribesmen in Laos. Roughly a year later, in a
speech at a conference on the CIA and covert action sponsored by the Center for
National Security Studies in Washington, D.C., on September 13, 1974, Colby
amplified his position as follows: "It is advocated by some that the U.S.
abandon covert action. In light of current American policy, as I have indicated,
it would not have a major impact on our current activities or the current security
of the U.S. However, I can envisage situations in which the U.S. might well need
to conduct covert activity in the face of some new threat that developed in the
world."

My conclusions on the strategy of subversion, which were based on a study of
the historical evidence of covert activities available in the early 1950s and 1960s,
have since been reinforced by the record of subsequent operations in Southeast

Asia, Africa, and elsewhere. The most important of these conclusions may be summarized as follows:

1. The effectiveness of covert operations as a means of influence, control, or conquest has been overrated and their employment overemphasized—during periods of intense international tension and ideological crusades such as the cold war or "the lost crusade" in Vietnam.

2. The potential usefulness of covert operations tends in practice to be lost in a power struggle between the competing bureaucracies most directly involved, namely: *(a)* a Foreign Office or other top-level foreign policy agency; *(b)* a military establishment which provides logistic support, i.e., the arms or men or both required for armed insurrections, revolutionary movements, or "wars of national liberation"; and *(c)* a quasi-independent secret intelligence or security police organization which provides the intelligence support, or actively engages in covert operation, or combines both functions. Such divided policy-making and operational responsibilities (which are inevitable even under totalitarian regimes) tend to institutionalize bureaucratic rivalries and to create serious problems of management and control, as dramatically illustrated during the Bay of Pigs invasion of Cuba in 1961.

3. Divided policy-making and operational responsibilities also militate against the production of reliable intelligence estimates, on which covert operations are based, at three distinct levels: *(a)* strategic intelligence estimates which are likely to be badly distorted during times of mounting international tension or in a militant ideological or crusading atmosphere, as evidence by repeated "intelligence failures" in Vietnam; *(b)* built-in distortion factors present in even the most rationally organized intelligence systems, such as the feedback effect when information is collected and evaluated by operational personnel who stand to gain in personal reputation from the successful completion of projected covert undertakings; and *(c)* counterintelligence measures taken by the adversary to penetrate, expose, neutralize, or abort projected operations.

4. Covert operational agencies repeatedly disavow any policy-making function and are often excluded from a policy role by executive decree, national legislative regulation, or both. Nevertheless, such agencies are capable of preempting a policy-making role by operations which may predetermine or shape historical events, creating situations of fact to which foreign policy must then be readjusted, frequently under adverse or crisis conditions.

5. Under a blanket of "operational security" clandestine agencies can effectively sabotage foreign policy by bureaucratic deception and delay, or by operating in crisis situations on assumptions diametrically opposed to executive decisions. In such crisis situations the chief executive is a captive of his own staff "for the duration," like the commander in chief of allied armies in the field after a crucial battle is joined. For example, President Kennedy was clearly unable to obtain from the CIA compliance with a direct order to purge known Batista elements from the invasion force which landed at the Bay of Pigs. More recently, in spite of an order from President Nixton to destroy them, subordinate CIA

officials continued to stockpile certain toxic substances. Such incidents have dramatized what is now openly recognized as the difficult problem of securing effective command and control *within* clandestine agencies, as well as control from above by the chief executive of the state.

6. Once a covert agency has acquired the international reputation of controlling an effective "fifth column" abroad, this image can be exploited by other powers for their own political warfare or propaganda purposes, and the country becomes vulnerable to all sorts of irresponsible charges which complicate conduct of its relations with the rest of the world.

7. No matter how effectively managed or controlled, some covert operations are certain to be compromised and exposed, making the responsible government vulnerable to the charge of lying, i.e., of saying one thing in public (and often in its confidential assurances to other powers) while its agents abroad act in a directly contrary way. This has often resulted in serious embarrassment to the Foreign Office or State Department concerned, and to its representatives abroad.

8. The Great Powers have extended "friendly technical assistance" to emerging and client states, helping them build combined intelligence, security police, and covert operational agencies which have done much to increase political turbulence in the Third World with their provocations, plots, counterplots, and assassinations. Some of these provocations have precipitated international crises. The record of indigenous covert operational agencies in Sub-Saharan Africa has not been effective.[22]

9. Covert operations with limited objectives have a momentum of their own, once a program has started, that carries them to a point where they may bring about disastrous political consequences which were unforeseeable at the time of their initiation. Two examples from recent American and Soviet experience illustrate this principle. The first example was the much publicized U-2 incident in which, even on the eve of a planned U.S.-Soviet summit conference, surveillance flights over the USSR were continued, with the unexpected result that Khrushchev was able to exploit them for propaganda purposes and to abort the conference itself. The second example was the Soviet KGB deception or disinformation campaign which contributed to President Nixon's decision to visit the People's Republic of China and to seek U.S.-Chinese rapprochement. According to Arthur Cox, in August and September of 1969 the KGB mounted a major deception campaign which was orchestrated in several world capitals over a period of six months. In connection with armed Soviet-Chinese border incidents along the Ussuri River, KGB agents in Washington and London made explicit threats that the USSR was contemplating a preemptive strike and that "the use of nuclear weapons is not being exlcuded." For several months there was a flurry of inspired news items about aggressive Soviet intentions. "The KGB operation succeeded in pressuring the Chinese to resume the talks, but it also so alarmed the Chinese leaders that they put out feelers for secret negotiations with the United States . . . which led to President Nixon's visit to China and the ensuing breakthrough toward more friendly U.S.-Chinese relations. . . . Surely no

development has provided a greater setback to Soviet foreign policy, and to the extent to which the KGB contributed to this must be considered part of an incredible blunder."[23]

10. Whenever an adversary relationship exists between two powers the covert action agencies of each justifies its existence and operations on the grounds that the adversary is also conducting them. This tends to produce a stimulus-reprisal pattern, especially when reciprocating intervention occurs, a "mirror-image" situation is created in which each power condemns the other for intervention. This kind of pattern clearly developed in the case of reciprocal U.S.-Soviet intervention in Angola in late 1975 and early 1976. However, in regard to the much broader spectrum of U.S.-Soviet relations in general, Arthur Cox writes that "both CIA and KGB have been rationalizing the continuing existence of certain operations on grounds that the other is conducting such operations. ... Both organizations are flawed, both are dated, and both are still conducting political and psychological operations which tend to run counter to the objectives of their governments' foreign policies. Yet, the continuing existence of these organizations is used as a sort of litmus paper, by both sides, to test the true motivation and relative hostility of the other."[24]

CONGRESSIONAL AND COMMISSION INVESTIGATIONS

Ever since the clandestine Gulf of Tonkin incidents opened the door to large-scale military intervention in Vietnam, Congress has been painfully aware that covert operations can lead the nation unwittingly to war. The decision to wage war, many senators contend, should properly rest with Congress. As a result of the war in Vietnam and the Watergate affair, the CIA has come under heavier and more determined congressional scrutiny than at any time in its history. No less than five committees, four in the Senate and one in the House, were stirred by the Watergate disclosures to inquire into various aspects of the CIA's operations, and Chairman John C. Stennis of the Armed Services Subcommittee on intelligence stated that hearings would eventually be held on revising the agency's charter, the National Security Act of 1947.

Ironically, although Congress was aware of the need for closer surveillance over the CIA well before the Vietnam conflict, it failed to act decisively in this regard time and again. Since the National Security Act of 1947 and the 1949 Central Intelligence Act, nearly two hundred bills calling for closer surveillance of intelligence agencies have been introduced. Most of them attempted to establish a congressional committee to oversee the activities of the CIA. Only two of them ever reached the floor of Congress, where both were decisively defeated by more than two-thirds' majorities. In this regard, "it is significant that the Senate, on October 2, 1974, voted 68 to 17 not to prohibit further covert operations [the so-called Abourezk Amendment] and the House voted down a similar amendment."[25]

In spite of all the investigations and publicity, whether the Congress will in practice pass legislation which will provide for effective supervision over covert operations remains to be seen. The record for the period 1974-75 is mixed. According to Leslie Gelb, the 1974 amendment to the Foreign Assistance Act, which passed in the wake of disclosures of CIA involvement in the coup against the Allende regime in Chile, improved supervision only marginally:

> The law made the President personally responsible for covert operations, but did not define such operations. It was riddled with loopholes. For example, it said the operations had to be reported to Congress, "in a timely fashion"; in practice this has meant after the fact, when little can be done about it. The main contribution of the law was to enlarge Congressional knowledge of covert actions. Until that time, only the House and Senate Armed Services and Appropriations Committees were privy. These four committees had formed themselves into subcommittees with ties of friendship to the agency; even some of their members described their "oversight" as perfunctory. To this cozy situation the amendment added the Senate Foreign Relations Committee and the House International Relations Committee.... The fact is that many liberals stay away from all the intelligence subcommittees because they do not want to be tagged in the future with having tacitly approved an operation, even if they agreed with it, or because they want to be free to criticize if anything goes wrong.[26]

The June 1975 Rockefeller "Report to the President by the Commission on CIA Activities Within the United States" was a relatively fair, although somewhat apologetic, disclosure of CIA excesses and improprieties connected with domestic political surveillance during the 1950s and 1960s. The report's most conspicuous omission was the question of CIA complicity in plots to assassinate foreign leaders.

Under Frank Church, the Senate Select Committee on Intelligence focused its inquiry on assassinations, and in November 1975 published an interim report on the subject. Although press and television coverage was intense, it was also short-lived and failed to build public support for further investigation into the CIA's covert operations abroad. Then a fortuitous event suddenly changed the climate of public opinion in which both the Church committee and the House committee under Otis Pike were working. This was the assassination, on December 24, 1975, by unknown terrorists, of Richard Skeffington Welch, the CIA station chief in Athens, Greece. A small, anti-CIA magazine had identified Welch as a CIA official, although his agency affiliation had long been known to the kind of political terrorists who opposed CIA association with conservative regimes frequently controlled by military juntas. The emotional power of the tragedy was exploited as a means of creating hostility toward the congressional committees, and President Ford publicly hinted that inquiries into CIA methods was unpatriotic. As a result, in January 1976 the House of Representatives voted against publication of the final report of the Pike committee by a count of 246 to 124.

However, the Pike report was soon leaked to former CBS correspondent Daniel Schorr, and through him and other intermediaries to the New York *Village Voice*, where it was first published under banner headlines in February 1976. The substance of the Pike report was at once overshadowed by a public controversy over how it was leaked. The House Ethics Committee began a long investigation into the affair, which ended inconclusively with a mild rebuke to Schorr several months later, in October 1976. The *Voice* then published the Pike papers in a second, rearranged edition which included some new material. But again, in the preelection atmosphere of late 1976 the media virtually ignored the substance of the report.

Earlier in the year the Church committee had published a report on CIA covert actions taken to "destabilize" the Allende regime in Chile. Less damaging than the Pike papers, the Church report also failed to make much news or to stimulate debate on CIA covert action programs, such as the financial support of anti-Communist parties in the Italian elections which had taken place from the early 1970s onwards.

Thus by the fall of 1976 a combination of events had eroded the political base for controlling CIA covert operations as national attention turned to the presidential election campaign. Both candidates virtually ignored the complex problems involved in the management and control of covert operations in favor of campaign oratory about morality and leadership. However, several sources on the Church committee indicated that the issue might be taken up again "under the authority of the new Congressional oversight committee, and perhaps with the assistance of a new Democratic Administration."[27]

ORGANIZATIONAL CHANGE AND PERSISTENT DILEMMAS OF INTELLIGENCE

The war in Vietnam strained civil-military relations throughout the government and within the intelligence community, where problems of divided policy-making and operational responsibilities have always been abrasive, especially in regard to the management and control of covert operations. Moreover, rather than serving as a basis for policy making, CIA estimates and warnings were frequently ignored by the Joint Chiefs of Staff and the White House staff. It was against this background that, after his reelection, President Nixon decided to overhaul the two top-level agencies most concerned with decision making in the national security and foreign policy areas, i.e., the National Security Council and the intelligence community.

The reorganization of the intelligence community, which began under the

Nixon administration in November 1971, continued during the Ford administration and was carried out under the supervision of four successive directors of central intelligence, Richard Helms, James Schlesinger (who provided most of the impetus), William Colby, and George Bush. In its "Report to the President" dated June 1975, the Murphy Commission gave a carefully "screened" description of the structure and functions of the intelligence community as of that period. Appendix U: "Intelligence Functions Analyses" (volume 7 of the Murphy Comission report) includes an important article by Robert M. Macy, "Issues on Intelligence Resource Management," which evaluates a number of the organizational changes effected, many of which have resulted in improved management, and especially in tighter budgetary control.

Nevertheless, in spite of continuing reorganization of the intelligence community, stimulated by repeated congressional and other official investigations, certain persistent dilemmas remain. They cluster mainly around the problems of congressional restraint on executive power in general, and oversight of covert operations in particular. Any action taken in regard to the latter problem related directly to emerging limitations on military intervention, since, as indicated elsewhere in this study, covert operations tend to escalate into military intervention when less extreme forms of coercion fail to achieve their objectives. How far will Congress ultimately go in placing effective restrictions on covert operations? The answer to this question, according to Leslie Gelb, depends on whether the House and Senate are ready, at long last, to assume responsibility in the field of foreign intelligence. The issue is whether Congress is disposed to treat the matter of the CIA as a transitory problem—rolling a few heads, altering institutional facades and warning against violations of the law—or whether it sees the agency's activities as part of the Vietnam-Watergate experience, requiring some fundamental checks on the covert exercise of power.[28]

In sum, unless the historic confrontation, triggered by Watergate, between the executive branch of the government and Congress is resolved clearly in favor of Congress, no fundamental change in the role and functions of the CIA is likely. This applies to the presidential use of covert political and military operations as an instrument of foreign policy no matter how much "dirty tricks" may be publicly deplored when used to influence the electoral process at home. In this regard Nixon's secret bombing of Laos and Cambodia set a precedent which future presidents may be tempted to follow in similar circumstances.

Ever since Machiavelli, Western statesmen and politicians have been fascinated with the idea of combining the wiles of the fox with the strength of the lion. In the crusading atmosphere of the cold war and in Vietnam, it was hoped that covert operations might provide such a winning combination. That hope was based on ignorance, which has always been a poor counselor. Nevertheless, as long as the clandestine services of the CIA remain intact and available "as the President's loyal tool," the temptation to use them may prove as irresistible in the future as it has in the past. Certainly during 1975, a year when Congressional investigations and press exposures reached a climax, the lure of covert political action proved irresistible to both Secretary of State Kissinger and President Ford. During this period the administration poured millions of dollars through CIA clandestine channels into the hands of non-Communist parties in Portugal and, in a second such operation, funneled money and arms through President Mobuto of Zaire to support liberation movements in Angola, thus precipitating a confrontation on this issue with Congress that continued on into 1976.

Sometime in November 1975, an official who has had considerable experience at the directorate level of both the CIA and the Defense Intelligence Agency, but who prides himself on his objectivity, since he has no personal institutional axe to grind and no publicly stated positions to defend, made a number of observations with respect to the intelligence community, the substance of which are summarized below.

1. There have been real abuses and malpractices with the CIA which need to be corrected. Ironically, many of these lapses have been brought out by Colby himself, whose unprecedented candor in this regard has aroused much bitter opposition from old hands in the clandestine services who argue that he should have "stonewalled" any attempt to disclose them.

2. In a sense, congressional and other investigations have had a positive effect in that they have dramatized the need for a much tighter executive command, control, and accountability within the CIA itself. As a result, in addition to other internal reforms, the role and functions of the inspector general have been upgraded and secure channels established through which abuses may be reported at any level without fear of reprisal.

3. HUMINT, i.e., information collected either openly from knowledgeable persons or clandestinely from covert sources, is indispensable. Colby's position in this regard is unexceptionable: "In a world which can destroy itself through misunderstanding or miscalculation, it is important that our leaders have a clear perception of the motives, intentions, and strategies of other powers so that they can be deterred, negotiated about, or countered in the interest of peace or, if necessary, the ultimate security of our country. These kinds of insights cannot be obtained by means of technical sensors or analysis alone. They can only be obtained from closed societies by clandestine means of collection, i.e., espionage." However, the most valuable human intelligence usually comes from open sources. For example, the most important inputs in the national intelligence estimating process have come from reports of sophisticated and highly knowledgeable Foreign Service officers whose area expertise can never be replaced by technical sources. Ironically, because of the brush with which the whole intelligence business has been tarred, most Foreign Service officers would bristle at the idea of being thought of as sources. Moreover, because of the cloud over the agency, many overt sources outside the government have dried up to some extent.

4. Morale in the clandestine services is very low, since many aides who have

devoted the better part of their lives to what they regard as a necessary service believe that their roles and functions have not only been publicly tarred but seriously downgraded by management within the agency. As far as clandestine collection is concerned, many valuable sources that have been active have requested permission to lay low until the storm of investigations blows over. These tensions are harmful, but the damage is not irreparable.

5. Military capabilities, since they rest mainly on intelligence collected from open and technical sources, have not been appreciably affected by past and current investigations. The DIA and other service agencies will probably bear the brunt of future investigations, but in these groups the vulnerable spots are the result of inefficiency rather than of sins of commission.

6. In regard to congressional investigations of intelligence, the potential of their doing great harm if they continue endlessly cannot be overlooked. One of the worst effects is that top-level officials such as Colby have had to spend 60% to 80% of their time and energy on them, and have thus been diverted from their regular tasks. Under these conditions there is always the potential danger that an incipient crisis threatening national security—a small cloud on the horizon—will be either overlooked or its threat minimized. One of the most sensitive spots that needs better understanding and protection comes under the label of "sources and methods." There are two categories here. First, HUMINT sources, both open and covert, must be protected; otherwise, the open ones will soon dry up, and the clandestine ones may be compromised or even eliminated. Second, there are certain technical capabilities and sources which are truly secret, i.e., no other country really knows that we have them, and it is important that they *not* know. A familiar example is code-breaking, but there are also new advances in collection and processing which must be protected.

CONCLUSIONS

Sweeping recommendations as to how the intelligence community should be reorganized and its relations with policy makers and with Congress improved, especially in regard to the complex problems involved in the use and control of covert operations, are beyond the scope of this study. A well-balanced summary of the principal reforms advocated as a result of congressional and other investigations of the mid-1970s may be found in Taylor C. Belcher's article, "Clandestine Operations," in Appendix U of the Murphy Commission report previously noted.

President Ford's executive order of February 1976 indicated that any sweeping changes in the organization and functions of intelligence are unlikely unless Congress asserts far more control over the executive branch than it has in the past. This contingency also appears unlikely. Although Ford's executive order banned the use of assassination, he has publicly stated that he would not preclude the option of using less radical covert actions whenever he and his advisers judge them to be important to national security. The U.S. intervention in Angola is illustrative in this regard. The order also established an Operations Advisory Group, composed of top administration officials, to review and vote on all proposed covert operations.

During the Nixon and Ford administrations, three key factors have set the parameters limiting the conduct of covert operations. The first and most important has been the national consensus. For three decades American intervention abroad, both overt and covert, was rooted in a widely shared conviction that such intervention was necessary for waging the cold war. This consensus changed as exaggerated threat perceptions weakened under the impact of détente and the turbulent historical events of the 1960s and 1970s, events which radically changed the image of the CIA and its cold war mission. In this regard Belcher writes that

> The public was not antagonistic toward clandestine operations in the 1950's, when there was an easily perceptible threat. In the sixties, the situation changed rapidly as the Communist monolith began to show cracks. The enemy was not so apparent or so frightening. Added to this was the debate sparked by our deep and tragic involvement in Indo-China, where the secrecy surrounding the CIA's actions led to accusations of abuse of Presidential powers. Add to this the impact of Watergate and the newspaper accounts for CIA activities both at home and abroad, and one can readily understand why the CIA's image is so poor. The spate of critical exposes has inevitably led to considerable public discussion about the advantages and disadvantages of maintaining a covert action capability.[29]

The second factor is idiosyncratic, i.e., dependent on the kinds of personalities who gravitate to the centers of power and decision making in the American democratic system. With few exceptions, since World War II the highest executive, White House staff, and national security advisory positions have been held by activist, manipulative, and "hard-hitting" or aggressive personality types. This was especially true during the Nixon administration. Beginning in World War II, the OSS personnel recruiting and screening procedures were designed to assure a high percentage of such personality types, and that tradition has weighed heavily in the CIA clandestine services ever since. As a result there has been a pronounced element of machismo in these services, reflected in the more spectacular successes and failures of the agency. Other things being equal, the idiosyncratic factor might be expected to continue as a force making for increased use of intervention below the covert threshold. However, as noted above, the times had changed by the mid-1970s. The institutionalization of détente (even during the 1976 election year) and the emergence of a new national consensus favoring "consultation instead of confrontation" (a slogan popularized during the Nixon years) tended to reduce high-risk foreign policy initiatives on the part of the chief executive, especially when such actions were likely to run into congressional opposition. The U.S. intervention in Angola in 1976 was the principal exception to the long-range trend.

The third factor limiting the incidence of covert operations may be called, for want of a better term, "institutional pressures" from a variety of interrelated governmental and media sources. The former include presidential review agencies set up to approve or disapprove proposed covert action projects, as well as strengthened and reorganized congressional oversight committees. The latter include the omnipresent threat of exposure by the press and other media, which after Watergate played an increasingly important role in limiting the resort to covert action either at home or abroad. Similarly, the threat of renewed congressional and other official inquiries belongs in this category.

To conclude, barring some sudden and pronounced increase in threat perception and tension levels within the general context of United States foreign relations, these three factors could be expected to continue to restrict resort to covert action and, by extension, military intervention throughout the later 1970s.

NOTES

1. Allen Dulles in the essay condensation of *The Craft of Intelligence,* which appeared in *Harper's Magazine* (April 1963): 132.

2. Sherman Kent, *Strategic Intelligence for American World Policy* (Hamden: Connecticut: Archon Books, 1965), p. 201.

3. Paul W. Blackstock, "Intelligence and Covert Operations: Changing Doctrine and Practice," Department of Government and International Studies, University of South Carolina, 1973, p. 32.

4. Kenneth Strong, *Men of Intelligence: A Study of the Roles and Decisions of Chiefs of Intelligence from World War I to the Present Day* (New York: St. Martin's Press, 1971), p. 140.

5. Ibid., p. 132.

6. Paul W. Blackstock, *The Strategy of Subversion: Manipulating the Politics of Other Nations* (Chicago: Quadrangle Books, 1964), chapters 4 and 5, pp. 95-142.

7. Strong, *Men of Intelligence,* p. 156.

8. Ray S. Cline, "Policy Without Intelligence," *Foreign Policy* 17 (Winter 1975): 130-31.

9. Harry Howe Ransom, *The Intelligence Establishment* (Cambridge, Mass.: Harvard University Press, 1970), p. 21.

10. "The Pike Papers: House Select Committee on Intelligence CIA Report," p. 27, published by *The Village Voice* (October 1976).

11. See, especially, Richard Cottam, *Competitive Interference and Twentieth Century Diplomacy* (Pittsburgh: Univ. of Pittsburgh, 1967) and Andrew M. Scott, *The Revolution in Statecraft, Informal Penetration* (New York: Random House, 1965).

12. On SOE operations, see Michael Ford, *SOE in France* (London: Her Majesty's Stationery Office, 1966), based on official archives. Historians and political scientists have been denied access to comparable U.S. archives, and the only serious study in the field, based on secondary sources and extensive interviews, is Richard Harris Smith, *OSS: The*

Secret History of America's First Central Intelligence Agency (Berkeley: University of California Press, 1972).

13. Harry Rositzke, "America's Secret Operations: A Perspective," *Foreign Affairs* 53 (January 1975): 346.

14. Letter dated December 29, 1969, to the author from Mark G. Eckhoff, Director of the Legislative, Judicial, and Diplomatic Records Division, General Services Administration, National Archives and Records Service, Washington, D.C.

15. Robin Bruce Lockhart, *Ace of Spies* (London: Hodder & Stoughton), p. 159, n. 1.

16. Rositzke, "America's Secret Operations," pp. 341-42.

17. Graham Hovery, "Fog and Worse on Angola," *The New York Times* (December 30, 1975): 25. See also the official report of Kissinger's press conference on Angola and détente December 23, 1976 (Washington, D.C.: Department of State, PR 627/81).

18. Christopher S. Wren, "Africa: An Inviting Arena for Moscow," *The New York Times* (December 28, 1975): section 4, p. 1, in which a "well-placed Soviet insider" in Moscow is quoted as saying: "We've been supporting our friends in Angola for more than a decade. Why should we stop now just to satisfy Mr. Kissinger?"

19. Graham Hovey, "Fog and Worse in Angola."

20. See the author's article, "Espionage," in *The Encyclopedia Americana,* international edition (New York: Americana Corp., 1973), vol. 10, p. 584-87.

21. "Commission on the Organization of the Government for the Conduct of Foreign Policy," Report to the President (Washington, D.C.: Government Printing Office, 1975), p. 100; hereafter cited as The Murphy Commission.

22. Blackstock, *The Strategy of Subversion,* pp. 304-320.

23. Albert Cox, *The Myths of National Security* (Boston, 1975), pp. 110-11.

24. Ibid., p. 202.

25. Taylor G. Belcher, "Clandestine Operations," in Appendicies, volume 7, p. 68, cited in the report by The Murphy Commission.

26. Leslie H. Gelb, "Should We Play Dirty Tricks in the World?" *The New York Times Magazine* (December 21, 1975): section 6, p. 10.

27. Taylor Branch, "The Trial of the CIA," *The New York Times Magazine* (September 12, 1976).

28. Leslie H. Gelb, "Should We Play Dirty Tricks?" p. 20.

29. Taylor G. Belcher, "Clandestine Operations," p. 70.

PART V. MANPOWER AND PROFESSIONAL DILEMMAS

MANPOWER, MILITARY INTERVENTION, AND THE ALL-VOLUNTEER FORCE

Thomas A. Fabyanic

Although the term "military intervention" is open to a number of definitions, its interpretation here is restricted to the long-established meaning of armed interference by one nation in the internal affairs of another. Usually, the ostensible objective of such intervention is the "defense of some concept of ideal political order as conceived by the intervener," for which he is prepared to use limited military force.[1]

Throughout much of its history, the U.S. has intervened militarily in countries as close as Mexico and as distant as China and Russia. This trend has continued into the last half of the twentieth century, with military interventions in the Dominican Republic and Indochina. However, future intervention capabilities need to be assessed in terms of the effect of the recent U.S. decision to rely upon an all-volunteer force (AVF), for that force possesses vastly different characteristics and potential than the one which intervened in the Dominican Republic and Indochina.

Any decision to intervene militarily reflects, to a large measure, certain quantitative and qualitative dimensions of the military structure of the intervener; in this respect, the evolving size and composition of the AVF are noticeably different from the preceding conscript force. Another contrasting characteristic of the AVF is the degree to which it relies on reserve forces. There

AUTHOR'S NOTE: I am presenting these ideas as an individual. They have not been endorsed by any agency of the Department of Defense or the United States. These concepts are speculative and are intended only to serve as a basis for academic discussion. The author is indebted to the following individuals for their scholarly critique of the original draft: Professor William T. R. Fox, Institute of War and Peace Studies, Columbia University; Dr. Paul H. B. Godwin, Air University; Professor Morris Janowitz, University of Chicago; and Professor Jack Ladinsky, University of Wisconsin at Madison.

are numerous situations wherein military intervention by the U.S. would hinge on using selective reserve forces, since these are critical to the existing force structure. A final characteristic of the AVF that affects its intervention potential is the changed perception by the American public, government officials, and military leaders of its capability.

These qualities, which distinguish the AVF from the conscript force, have emerged during the four-year history of the voluntary system. The extent to which each differs from the corresponding characteristics of the conscript force is quantifiable and thus forms a measurable dimension of the AVF. The way each is conceptualized in relation to the intervention potential of the AVF is yet another analytical tool for evaluation. When conceptions and dimensions are applied in the developmental approach, the intervention potential of the AVF becomes of major significance, particularly to those concerned with military strategy.

CONCEPTIONS AND DIMENSIONS: FORCE SIZE

During the election campaign of 1968, both presidential candidates promised, if elected, to end military conscription and establish an AVF in the United States. Shortly after his election, Richard M. Nixon appointed an advisory commission on the AVF under the chairmanship of Thomas S. Gates, who had been secretary of defense. The President's Commission (hereafter referred to as the Gates Commission) considered the feasibility of obtaining various voluntary levels that ranged from 2.0 million to 3.0 million military personnel. It concluded that active-duty force levels within this range were possible if certain improvements were made in pay, conditions of service life, and recruiting capability.

Although the Gates Commission did not suggest a specific military manpower force level, a careful reading of the report indicates that a tentative objective was level between 2.25 and 2.5 million. Indeed, subsequently Secretary of Defense Melvin R. Laird requested, in February 1972, a force level at just under 2.4 million for FY 73.[2] This level was not obtained, however, and a series of requests for reductions began. The shortfall at the end of FY 73 was approximately 14,000, whereupon the secretary of defense lowered the manpower request to 2.23 million for FY 74. Despite the reduction in the total objective, a further shortfall of 72,000 occurred, for a combined shortage of over 200,000 for FY 73 and FY 74. Only a modest reduction in total force objectives was set for FY 75 levels; since then, recruitment has been sufficient to stabilize the force at approximately 2.1 million.[3] Table 1 demonstrates this downward trend in active-duty manpower levels under the AVF.

Table 1: DOD Active Duty Force

FY	Stated Objective	FY End Strength	Shortfall
1973	2,396,517	2,252,810	143,707
1974	2,233,000	2,161,000	72,000
1975	2,152,000	2,129,000	23,000
1976	2,087,000	2,080,997	6,003
1977	2,126,651	--	--

As can be seen from table 1, the decrease from the FY 73 objective to FY 76 end strength was 12.3%. Moreover, the FY 74 request of 2.23 million was described as a "base line force—the minimum force that the President and Secretary of Defense consider necessary to carry out national security objectives."[4] Yet a 6.5% reduction of that minimum force occurred between FY 74 and FY 76.

Within DOD, this downward quantitative trend has had the most effect on the U.S. Army. In FY 73 the Army established a force objective of 841,000, but ended the year with slightly less than 801,000. In the following year the requirement was lowered to 804,000, but Army strength fell to 783,000—its lowest since 1950. Since then the strength has stabilized at about 785,000.

Thus, for almost one and a half years after transition to the AVF, the Army consistently failed to attain its stated enlisted accession goals, despite increased pay, a more relaxed environment, and a doubling of its recruiting force. Increasingly it turned to particular groups, such as blacks and females, in an attempt to avert drastic recruiting shortfalls.

Emphasis on black recruitment rapidly expanded the black enlistment rate to 30%, increased their total representation in the Army to 22%, and brought their representation in some combat units to nearly 35%. Since blacks represented only 11.0% of the general population in the 17-44 age group, steps were taken by the secretary of the Army which eventually lowered the black enlistment rate to about 22% of all accessions.[5]

Emphasis on female accessions was increased by almost 60% between 1973 and 1974 and is scheduled to increase another 75% by 1978. The net effect of this effort will be to increase female representation among all the services from 1.6% to 6.2%. Nevertheless, within the Army more significant increases are possible, since it has concluded that between 20% and 35% of its positions could be filled by females. At present, 93% of the Army's enlisted military occupation skills are open to qualified female applicants. Only combat-related and otherwise hazardous positions are restricted to males; female officers are eligible to command all except combat or combat-support units.

The foregoing is significant because it demonstrates the Army's willingness to explore all possible accession sources to meet its manpower requirements.

Second, it is important because the effort failed to attain stated accession objectives, despite the heavy reliance on blacks and females. Failure to recruit and the corresponding decrease in the force structure continued until mid-1974, when the national economic downturn and resulting high unemployment appeared to resolve the recruiting problem temporarily. As shown in table 2, a striking correlation exists between unemployment and accession rates. This raises the question, of course, of the effect that a return to a more normal unemployment rate will have on the ability of the services to recruit adequate manpower to support a force level of approximately 2.0 million.

Perhaps one indication of possible force levels can be obtained by comparing the United States with Great Britain. Both nations share a cultural heritage, are industrially advanced, and possess voluntary forces which compete with the civilian sector for manpower resources by offering comparable wages for military service.

Since 1957 the British have maintained a voluntary force, but steady reductions in levels amounting to approximately 30% have occurred despite pay increases and recruiting innovations.[6] At present, male enlisted personnel in the British forces represent approximately 2.9% of total men in Great Britain between the ages of 18 and 45. Planned reductions now under way will drop the figure to approximately 2.6% by 1979.

By contrast, the U.S. has been attempting to maintain an enlisted force level of approximately 1.8 million, which represents about 4.6% of its male population between the ages of 18 and 45. Should the U.S. eventually discover

Table 2: Unemployment and Enlistment Relationships, 1973-74

Time Period	Unemployment Rate: Males and Females Aged 16 and Over	Percent Achieved of Army Enlisted Accessions
1973 Jan-Dec	4.9	87.8
1974 Jan	5.2	89.8
Feb	5.2	88.7
Mar	5.1	94.4
Apr	5.0	91.0
May	5.2	103.3
Jun	5.2	122.0
Jul	5.3	96.7
Aug	5.4	106.9
Sep	5.8	103.3
Oct	6.0	105.3
Nov	6.6	100.3
Dec	7.2	100.4

Source: U.S. Department of Labor, Bureau of Statistics; OASD, M&RA.

NOTE: A word of caution is in order, since the figures have not been refined to associate localized unemployment with recruiting results from the same area.

that the British effort represents a pattern inherent in Western industrialized societies, then it will find itself with an enlisted force structure of about 1.0 million. If the officer corps are included, the total force will amount to 1.2 million, about half the current size.

Lest one think that the U.S. and Great Britain are not sufficiently similar to support such a force size postulation, it should be remembered that by most standards the two countries are more alike than they are dissimilar. Moreover, the factors that affect the recruitment of a volunteer force primarily reflect perceptions of an institution and of the role of that institution in society. The two societies share a fear of large standing armies, a legacy from Oliver Cromwell.

But in addition to the problem of force level, the AVF has been confronted with the issue of quality, a factor that is less quantifiable from the standpoint of what is required and what is obtained. Although the degree of quality necessary in the armed forces may be an open question, it appears that the AVF is recruiting lower-quality personnel than its predecessor, the conscript force.

CONCEPTIONS AND DIMENSIONS: QUALITY

The armed forces measure quality by moral, physical, and mental standards. Since the advent of the AVF, however, there has been a tendency to expand the general meaning of quality to include other factors, such as social, economic, and racial representativeness in the armed forces. Indeed, the issue of representativeness has been argued for years by scholars such as Samuel P. Huntington, Morris Janowitz, and others, but it did not become a major item of professional or academic interest while conscription remained in effect. The peacetime draft, in all probability, did provide a reasonably balanced cross section of American youth for military service. Additionally, the criteria used under conscription enabled the services to maintain a reasonably high level of quality as measured by aptitude and education achievement. But with termination of the draft, public discussion began about quality in an AVF. For example, during the first meeting of a newly organized Senate Subcommittee on Manpower and Personnel, its chairman, Senator Sam Nunn of Georgia, stated that the issue of quality in the AVF

> does not simply to go the question of IQ, or the educational level of the new soldiers. Quality includes the whole spectrum of questions on the representative[ness], the motivation, and the patriotism, as well as the skill of our armed force personnel.[7]

Most of the issues raised by Nunn are complex; proper evaluation would require extensive testing and substantial analysis. But the degree of aptitude and educational achievement found in the AVF is quantifiable and easily compared with that in earlier periods of the draft. Until recently, the most commonly used standard test was the Armed Forces Qualification Test (AFQT), which basically is an aptitude test that measures arithmetical reasoning, word and tool knowledge, and pattern analysis. On the basis of test results, individuals are placed in categories I through V, as indicated in table 3.

Categories I and II are considered to be above average; III, average; and IV and V, below average. Category V personnel are legally exempt from military service.

During the first two years of the AVF, the measured aptitude of Army enlistees changed significantly. There were large declines in the above-average and growth in the average category, as shown in table 4.

However, the Army has improved accession quality as measured by AFQT by decreasing category IV personnel from 16.1% to 10% for FY 75, with a further decrease to 7% for FY 76. Yet it is not at all clear that small percentages of category IV personnel are wholly desirable, for it is the view of DOD that

> The learning capacity of new entries is adequate in meeting job requirements when the proportion of Mental Group IV personnel does not exceed about 22 percent. Conversely, when the overall proportions of Mental Group IV personnel falls below 15 percent, there is a tendency toward many people being under-challenged by their job assignment.[8]

Table 3: AFQT Category Determination

Mental Category	Percentile Score
I	93-100
II	65-92
III (a)	50-64
III (b)	31-49
IV	10-30
V	less than 10

Note: The services have moved away from AFQT; new aptitude test scores are converted to AFQT groupings for purposes of comparison.

Table 4: AFQT Comparisons: Conscript Force and AVF (in percentages)

	1965	1974	Percentage Change
I	8.1	2.0	75.3 decrease
II	33.5	23.0	31.3 decrease
III	41.7	58.9	41.2 decrease
IV	16.7	16.1	N/A
Total	100.0	100.0	

Source: OASD, M&RA.

Another qualitative measurement factor used by the services is high school education. As one may expect, the decrease in AFQT standings paralleled a decline in high school graduates among AVF accessions. During FY 64, for example, 67% of Army accessions were high school graduates; by FY 74 the figure had dropped to 56%. The number of high school graduates increased to 66% in FY 75, but it fell to 64% for FY 76.

As of 1976, therefore, qualitative measurements of the AVF did not appear to equal those of the conscript force, despite the effects of extremely high unemployment, which theoretically enables the services to select the best-qualified applicants. This suggests, of course, that improved economic conditions may adversely affect both the quantitative and qualitative dimensions of the AVF and require some of the services to lower standards, as they did during the early days of the AVF.

The Army, for example, lowered its quality objectives when it failed to attain its recruiting goals during the first six months of the AVF. The Army had set a 70% high school graduate accession objective during this period but found that such a goal led to shortages of about 2,000 recruits per month. Reluctantly, the Army eased the requirements and admitted the necessity of trade-offs between quality and quantity.[9]

With lower standards in effect, the percentage of high school graduates entering the Army fell throughout the last half of 1973. The average for the period was 54%; it dropped to 43% and 41% in November and December, respectively. In the following month, Congress established limitations that required a minimum of 55% high school graduates among accessions.

The attempt by Congress to raise the high school graduate percentage to a minimum of 55% was well intentioned, but it did create recruiting shortfalls. In testimony before the Senate Armed Services Committee during March 1974, the Marine Corps stated that the high school qualitative restrictions would limit Marine recruiting to the extent that a shortfall of 5.7% to 8.6% would occur in the enlisted force by June 1974.[10] In the previous year the Marine Corps had anticipated problems with qualitative requirements and acted to make the best of the situation. The Marine Corps felt that a high school diploma was primarily a measurement of motivation, the lack of which could be overcome by Marine Corps training. No lower limit for high school graduates was established; in FY 75, only 59% of Marine Corps accessions were high school graduates.

The Marine Corps' belief that its training could compensate for the lack of high school education proved incorrect. The Marine Corps acknowledged a quality problem in late 1975, when it admitted that possession of a high school diploma was "the most reliable preenlistment predictor that an individual will perform successfully from recruit training through expiration of active service." Moreover, it concluded that passing a General Education Development (GED) test was not an adequate substitute for having a high school diploma. In assessing its qualitative problems, the Marine Corps stated that "it was erroneously assumed that the advent of an All Volunteer Force would not substantially alter recruiting prospects since the great majority of past accessions had been volunteers."[11]

Convinced of the utility of high school education, the Marine Corps set and achieved an accession goal of 67% for FY 76 and has established a 75% goal for FY 77. Since it is doubtful that the Army can afford to attempt less, the demands for high school graduates by the services may go beyond practical limits in the near future. In addition, one must ask whether the high school diploma is an adequate primary measuring device. Clearly, its possession is the best means of identifying those most likely to complete an initial tour of duty with fewest problems in matters such as desertion, unauthorized absence, and drug abuse; but that does not mean that the diploma properly indicates needed quality. Given the increased sophistication of current and projected battlefield weapons technology, such as lasers, imaging infrared, and data-link systems, it is axiomatic that the qualitative demands of the services will increase.

This demand for quality accessions is increasing at precisely the same time that technology is making similar demands in the civilian sector. The services must compete for these resources, but the functions of supply and demand will impose quantitative limits. For example, despite 1976 national unemployment in excess of 7%, the United States Navy argues that competition in civilian industry for men trained in complex technical fields makes it difficult to retain them in the Navy. As a result, fleet-manning shortages between 20% and 30% exist in primary ratings, such as fire control technicians and electronic warfare technicians, that are critical to fleet readiness. The Navy reported similar shortages at the end of 1973, when unemployment stood at 4.9%. This further suggests that the relationship between unemployment and force quality may be far less than that between unemployment and quantity.

This particular problem in the Navy, and similar problems with highly skilled personnel in the other services, appears to be a problem of retention—another area in which the Gates Commission may have overstated the case for the AVF. Before FY 66, between 75% and 78% of armed forces' recruits served a single tour of duty. But despite high unemployment and improved conditions in the military, the current figure is nearly 80%, showing a regression of first-term reenlistment rates. Indeed, the figure may be higher for those whose skills are in demand by a civilian market that is becoming more technologically intensive.

Thus, the AVF is a force almost half a million smaller than originally sought and decreasing in size, while the quality of its ground forces seems lower than original expectations. To these two formidable problems one must add another, the cost of the AVF.

CONCEPTS AND DIMENSIONS: THE COST FACTOR

Some have estimated that the volunteer force costs about $3.5 billion a year, but I know that at hearing after hearing we come up with one small item after another which really is part of the volunteer force, ... [yet] not considered in this overall computation of costs. Therefore, I am not sure we have a very good fixation on ... the total cost.

The above statement, made by Sam Nunn when he chaired the Senate Subcommittee on Manpower and Personnel in August 1974, highlights the problem of defining the cost of the AVF. There exists little problem, however, in determining the total cost of manpower and its relationship to total military spending. Table 5 presents the trend of manpower cost and its percentage of the DOD budget.

Table 5 clearly shows the marked increase in personnel costs; but less obvious is the degree to which the AVF has contributed to that increase. The official assessment of AVF costs has varied. In early 1974 the secretary of defense provided a cost range from approximately $750 million to $3.7 billion, but chose the lower figure as the most realistic estimate of AVF cost.[12] A few months later an assistant secretary of defense placed the cost at about $300 million, a negligible sum indeed, which was computed using the methodology shown in table 6.[13]

Table 5: Manpower Costs[a] (in billions of dollars)

	FY 64	FY 74	President's FY 77 Budget Request
Defense Outlays	$50.8	$78.4	$100.1
Payroll Outlays			
Total military	13.5	24.4	27.4
Total civilians	7.7	14.2	17.1
Retired military	1.2	5.1	8.4
Total payroll	22.4	43.8	52.9
Personnel Support			
Outlays[b]	1.8	3.9	4.6
Percentage of Defense Outlays			
Payroll	44%	56%	53%
Personnel	4	5	5
Total	48	61	58
End Strengths of Regular Employees (in thousands)			
Active military	2,685	2,161	2,101
Civilians	1,176	1,109	1,036
Total	3,861	3,270	3,137

Source: **Manpower Requirements Report for FY 1977,** (Washington: Government Printing Office, 1976), pp. IX-4.

[a]Data exclude civil functions.

[b]Personnel support includes all nonpayroll costs of individual training, medical support (including CHAMPUS), overseas dependents' education, and recruiting and examining, plus half of base operations.

Table 6: AVF Cost Estimates, FY 1975 (in millions of dollars)

All-Volunteer Force Package	Budget Cost	Cost Avoidance
Administrative program (ROTC/ADV travel, other)	$ 496	
Enacted legislation (pay raise, ROTC, scholarship, bonus)	2,468	
Bonuses (proposed)	78	
Total	$3,042	
Base Costs		
Basic pay/allowances	$2,299	
Adjusted Total	$ 743	
Additional training costs avoided with reduced turnover		$400
Additional Selective Service costs avoided with discontinuation of draft		40
Estimated range of net AVF costs with reduction for cost avoidance		$300

Source: U.S. Senate, Committee on Armed Services, Hearings ("Fiscal Year 1975, Authorization for Military Procurement, Research and Development, and Active Duty, Selected Reserve and Civilian Personnel Strength"), 93rd Congress, 2nd session, Part IV ("Manpower"), Washington, D.C.: Government Printing Office, 1974, p.1619.

As the computations in table 6 show, the preponderant cost factor is basic pay and allowances, which amount to almost $3 billion. The reason given by DOD for not costing them against the AVF is that legislative enactments directed these pay increases before the initiation of the AVF. Essentially the increases were designed to make military pay and civilian pay comparable. The first step in the process was to match the pay of federal civil servants with pay levels of civilians in the private sector of the economy. Military pay, in turn, was then increased to match that of civilians within DOD. The second step was a compensatory increase, approved by Congress in 1971, primarily to provide a catch-up pay raise for junior officers and enlisted personnel. For the lower-ranking enlisted personnel, the increase was absolutely essential, since many at that time were paid at the so-called poverty level.[14]

These two increases substantially raised military pay and thus accounted for much of the increase in personnel costs between FY 64 and FY 74 shown in table 5. The increase for the average individual in the military is best understood by comparing the growth in Regular Military Compensation (RMC), which consists of basic pay, subsistence, quarters allowance, and the tax advantage gained by military personnel, since the last two items are nontaxable income. In absolute terms, the RMC increased from $4,380 in FY 64 to $9,380 in FY 75. After discounting for a consumer price index of 59%, the net RMC increase for FY 75 amounts to 55%.

The key question of AVF costs hinges, therefore, on whether the military pay increases legislated before the establishment of the AVF should be charged against it. DOD thinks not. Its view is that pay and allowances granted before the AVF was established were required as a matter of equity and thus were necessary and desirable.[15]

Notwithstanding this offered justification, the DOD view tends to draw a neat line between the end of conscription on December 31, 1972, and the effective start of the AVF on January 1, 1973. The line *cannot* be drawn, since efforts to establish the AVF predated 1973 by several years. For example, an extensive DOD study on a voluntary force was conducted as early as 1966 and concluded that an AVF was possible at substantially increased financial costs.[16] Furthermore, President Nixon promised, when he was campaigning in 1968, to end conscription and later directed the Gates Commission to develop a comprehensive plan for doing so. In 1970 the commission recommended adoption of an AVF and steps to be taken promptly toward that end. Moreover, according to the commission, the first step was "to remove the . . . [existing] inequity in the pay of men serving their first term in the Armed Forces."[17]

Thus there is no clear break between the AVF and its predecessor. Instead, there was a gradual movement toward establishing an AVF for most of the decade before it was adopted. And, although some pay improvements were both necessary and desirable, it is obvious that, without the significant pay increases granted prior to the AVF, there would be no AVF today. Indeed, Secretary of Defense Melvin R. Laird highlighted this in 1971, two years before the AVF, by stating that "the most serious obstacle of [sic] achieving zero draft is pay."[18] The pay increases subsequently granted must, therefore, be placed on the debit side of the AVF ledger. Once this has been done, the question then becomes one of degree—about which reasonable men can differ.

The highest DOD cost estimate for the AVF is $3.7 billion, a figure that includes pay comparability, recruiting and advertising, enlistment bonuses, education entitlements, and expenses to improve the living and working conditions of service personnel.[19] But even this estimate may be too conservative, for it can be shown that the cost of the AVF is much higher.

Table 7 compares personnel costs for FY 64 and FY 75 and shows a gross increase of $13.1 billion. After adjusting for inflation and deducting certain savings attributed to the AVF (see Table 8), one sees that the net cost of the AVF is $5.3 billion, or 43.2% more than the maximum cost estimated thus far.

Table 7: Selected Military Personnel Costs (in billions of dollars)

	FY 64	FY 75
DOD budget total (outlay)	$50.8	$85.8
Personnel costs		
Military basic pay	8.5	19.0
Military special pay and allowances	4.5	6.7
Family housing	0.5	0.9
Total pay and allowances	$13.5	$26.6

Source: **Annual Defense Department Report, FY 1975**, Washington, D.C.: Government Printing Office, 1974.

Table 8: AVF Cost Estimate (in billions of dollars)

FY 64 military personnel costs	$13.5 (From Table 7)
Consumer Price Index inflation factor: 54.8%	7.4
FY 64 military personnel costs (adjusted for inflation)	20.9
FY 75 military personnel costs	26.6 (From Table 7)
Real increase, FY 64-FY 75	5.7 (27% increase)
Less turnover and Selective Service savings	.4
AVF cost estimate	5.3

Source: U.S. Senate, Armed Services Committee, FY 75, pp. 1500-1501; 1619-20.

The primary contributing factor to AVF costs is the attainment of pay comparability. Under a voluntary military system, the armed forces continually must compete, in terms of pay and benefits, with the private sector for manpower and funds—both of which are finite resources. The competition, however, quickly establishes an inverse ratio between manpower levels and personnel costs. At present U.S. force levels are 18.6% below FY 64 strengths; while personnel costs necessary to maintain the reduced force are up, in real terms, by 27%, shown in Table 8.

Aside from this incongruous trend of decreasing manpower levels and increasing costs, the remuneration policies adopted to support the AVF have created a fixed relationship, between costs and force size, that effectively eliminates force-planning flexibility. Moreover, an inflationary economy exerts upward pressure on costs even when a stable force structure exists. This leads to some difficult choices for those who must provide for an adequate military posture. The aim is to slow the growth of manpower costs, primarily by limiting pay increases and by adjusting other items of compensation, such as housing, comissary stores, and retirement. Notwithstanding the practicality of these initiatives, the most optimistic projections show a savings of only $4.7 billion in the FY 77 budget.[20] This would reduce manpower costs from 58% to 53%, which would compare with 48% for FY 64. Moreover, planned alterations of compensation should be undertaken with full recognition of long-term consequences, since they surely will have some effect on recruitment and reenlistment trends. Perhaps more signfiicantly, alterations of compensation or benefits may offer incentives to those who view the military as one of the last mass groups of employees who have yet to be unionized.

Indeed, pay comparability in the AVF has placed the military in a quandary. Currently, 85% of active-duty military manpower costs are strength-related, which means that they are directly related to the size of the force.[21] Thus any meaningful reductions in manpower costs can be accomplished only by reductions in force size or major reductions in compensation. At present the emphasis appears to be on the latter.

The most significant aspect of the existing manpower cost and force level relationship, however, is the restriction it places on force level expansion. A draft DOD analysis indicates, for example, that if the U.S. returned to the enlisted force level of the Vietnam peak, the amount necessary to maintain the AVF instead of a conscript force would be $29.0 billion. In order for the AVF to sustain military operations at that level, it would be necessary to increase FY 75 defense spending of approximately $84 billion by an additional $73.5 billion.[22]

The Senate Armed Services Subcommittee on Military Manpower Issues addressed this issue by asking then Secretary of Defense James R. Schlesinger what would happen if it were necessary for the United States to increase manpower in the AVF to the level of the Vietnam period. "I do not believe we could obtain a sufficient force at acceptable budget levels," said Schlesinger, "and we would have to return to the draft."[23]

Perhaps the full effect of manpower constraints under an AVF is summed up best by Senator Sam Nunn:

> It is very disturbing to me . . . that if we . . . [revert] to any wartime footing, we will immediately have to go back to the draft. . . . It [further] disturbs me that we have a whole group of young people who would be shocked if all of a sudden we got into a war and the [concept of] the Volunteer Force evaporate[d].[24]

Few can doubt the assessments by Nunn and Schlesinger that force levels of the Vietnam period are unrealistic under the AVF concept. What also must be remembered, however, is that the principle of pay comparability precludes attainment of high force levels. In other words, it matters not if the forces are raised by the AVF, the draft, or mobilization of the reserves, because it does not appear that the nation can afford the payroll of large force levels. And to those who might suggest that military pay should be reduced under such circumstances, the Chief of Staff of the U.S. Army has replied: "It is inconceivable to me that we would pay men who were called upon to fight for this country less in wartime than they were receiving in peacetime."[25]

Thus it appears that the United States has put itself in a most undesirable position by creating an AVF, since such a force is feasible only when it competes in the manpower marketplace. The net result has been the creation of a terribly expensive force with practical limits on its expansion capability should the need for such expansion occur. But there is yet a worse dimension to the AVF. If it provides too small a force, or if it lacks credibility, then the force will be incapable of projecting real or perceived power to intervene militarily. Then it will be only a matter of time before a major military challenge is offered and the real cost of the AVF becomes manifest.

CONCEPTIONS AND DIMENSIONS: REPRESENTATIVENESS

In addition to the dimensions of quantity, quality, and cost, a drift toward racial and regional imbalance is emerging in the AVF. This trend may result, in a few years, in an AVF which finds itself in conflict with public attitudes as reflected in legislative assertiveness in matters of foreign policy and military intervention. For despite congressional restrictions, an unrepresentative force which is relatively small, highly capable, and eager to demonstrate its capabilities may be a powerful temptation to some future political leaders. Thus, in contrast to the previously discussed dimensions of the AVF, its lack of representativeness may suggest more rather than less intervention.

It is assumed that a representative force must reflect, in microcosm, the salient features of the society which it serves. And in a society such as the United States, where ethnic pluralism is strained by racial divisiveness, the racial composition of its armed forces is of major importance because it may bring the legitimacy of the force into question. Scholars concerned with this have described the racial changes occurring in the AVF and also have offered logical alternatives to ensure the formulation of a representative and thus politically legitimate force. Moreover, they have recognized that an unrepresentative and non-legitimate force may indeed call into question the legitimacy of the government which directs it.[26]

A generally less recognized but nonetheless equally significant aspect of representativeness is the regionalism which might characterize the armed forces; and in this respect the emerging trends of the AVF should sound a note of caution.

The draft, despite its many inequities, did provide a reasonably balanced geographical cross section of American youth; in so doing, it satisfied part of the representativeness equation, while simultaneously providing a continuous cadre of military veterans to the more antimilitary areas of the country. In contrast, the AVF appears to be drawing increasing numbers from the South and Southwest. For example, during FY 74 and FY 75, Army accessions from Southern states averaged 35% of total accessions, while those states represented only 27.6% of the population at large. More significantly, the Army oversubscribed blacks in the Deep South during FY 74 by ratios of 2:1, in terms of accession percentages and percentages of black males of military age within those states.[27] In all probability, this regional overemphasis was tempered somewhat, starting in FY 75, when widespread unemployment improved general recruiting conditions.

A more important regional trend in the AVF is the increased number of officers who come from Southern and Western states. For example, table 9 shows that, while total Air Force ROTC production declined approximately 20% between FY 70 and FY 75, ROTC officer production dropped 35% in the Ohio Valley region and 46% in the Northeast. In contrast, as overall ROTC graduates fell by 20%, the Southeast maintained its production in absolute terms and the South Central and Western regions actually increased their production of officers.

In addition to the increased overrepresentation from the South and West, the percentage of officers being provided by the USAF Academy is increasing, both

Table 9: USAF ROTC Production Trends

Geographic Areas	FY 70	FY 72	FY 72	FY 73	FY 74	FY 75	% Change
Northeast	769	668	537	404	378	413	-46.2
Ohio Valley	721	672	603	556	500	467	-35.2
North Central	715	773	665	518	478	482	-32.5
Middle Atlantic	551	516	484	485	420	443	-19.6
Southeast	538	552	541	516	452	534	- .7
South Central	583	617	667	690	644	603	+ 3.4
West	647	615	648	716	617	672	+ 3.8
Totals	4,524	4,413	4,145	3,885	3,489	3,614	-20.1

Source: Historical Data, Enrollment and Production Section, Air University, ROTC, Maxwell AFB, Ala.

absolutely and as a percentage of accessions. While ROTC production between FY 72 and FY 76 (forecast figure for FY 76) continued at a relatively steady rate of about 35% of Air Force officer accessions, USAF Academy graduates more than doubled as a percentage of total officer accessions, going from 6.8% to 15.6%.[28]

It should be clear that, if the foregoing trends are indicative of broader movements within the AVF, then the entire issue of force representativeness and legitimacy is of major significance. These trends suggest a narrowing of the sociopolitical base for both the officer corps and the enlisted force within the AVF. The net result can be a separate and distinct military force with extremely parochial views about itself and its mission.

The U.S. is now experiencing a period of legislative assertiveness, which, among other things, seeks to circumscribe military intervention as an instrument of foreign policy. Ample evidence of this congressional attitude can be found in the War Powers Act and the denial of military appropriations for Vietnam and Angola. Indeed, this assertiveness and its consequences appear to reflect the mood of the public and, moreover, seem to find additional support from at least the TV component of the national news media.[29]

Concurrently, however, it seems that the emerging AVF may be attracting those individuals who, by tradition and environment, wish to move in the opposite direction. Such individuals would tend to reinforce the elite corps of career officers whose "can do" attitude and professionalism demand that they provide the capability for maximum military responsiveness at all times, irrespective of attitudes in Congress or the public pertaining to its use or non-use. This narrow-based professionalism could lead to the development of both the necessary force structure and the strategy of employment for military intervention, despite the constraints of force size and the influence of the civilian leadership. Given the apparent trends in the dimensions of representativeness and legitimacy, they may tend to increase rather than to limit the possibility for military intervention.

TOTAL FORCE

Since the Korean War, the primary way to expand the force structure was through mobilization by conscription. Only selective activation of reserve units occurred during crises such as those which developed over Berlin, Cuba, and Tet, and in those cases the intent of the mobilizations was perhaps more political than military. Reserve forces, which stood at well over 2.0 million, were not mobilized for the war in Indochina, despite its duration and intensity, where mobilization seemed an obvious course of action. Instead, the United States preferred to conscript, and did so at an annual average of about 267,000.

The AVF, of course, has ended the possibility of maintaining large reserve forces whose wartime mission would be accomplished by conscripts. More important, the reduction of active force levels which has accompanied the AVF has forced the Army, for example, to rely upon reserve force augmentation in order to achieve its desired force structure. Between 1970 and 1973, as the United States moved toward the AVF, the Army reduced its divisions from seventeen and one-third to thirteen and cut its personnel strength by half a million. By 1975, the secretary of defense admitted that those reductions of active-duty ground forces had been too severe, and plans were made to correct them by innovations with reserve forces.[30]

After it had been agreed that a force structure of sixteen Army divisions represented a prudent risk force, the Army adopted a plan to create three additional divisions while adding only about 5,000 personnel to its active force of 785,000. Part of the plan called for reducing the combat-support ratio by converting tactical support units to combat units and assigning the tactical support mission to reserve forces. It was assumed, of course, that the reserve tactical support units would be maintained in a high state of readiness and deployed early in any conflict.

The second dimension of the Army plan called for even greater reliance on reserve forces. Within each of the new divisions, a full brigade, or one-third of its strength, would be provided by a reserve component brigade. As the plan developed, a fourth division was restructured to accommodate a reserve brigade.

Therefore, the sixteen-division Army force exists only if the combined elements of active and reserve forces are manned, equipped, and trained for combat. But despite official intent and action to maintain the readiness of these affiliated components, one must continually assess the degree and level of training that realistically can be accomplished by nonactive-duty Army forces. The task of accomplishing meaningful training, which requires joint maneuvers and total integration with the parent division, is a major undertaking, because of the limited time available to reservists; increasing their training availability time is extremely difficult, since most are fully employed in civilian life. Moreover, the equipment of the reserve components must match that of the active force, if total force training is to be effective. Given limited equipment availability, however, the establishment of priorities between the reserve components and active forces may be resolved only to the detriment of both.

A more important question, however, is whether the reserves will be utilized. Fundamentally, this is a question of political will and, as manifested in the Indochina experience, a step not easily taken by politicians. The necessity of activating the reserves under certain circumstances may be clear, but perhaps less obvious will be the political courage to do so. In recognition of this problem, a DOD request to Congress in late 1974 asked for legislation that would permit activation of up to 50,000 reservists for a ninety-day period without the declaration of a national emergency. The measure was signed into law on May 14, 1976.

Although in terms of numbers this projected call-up authority appears to be fairly limited, passage of the measure is of major significance. First, it grants to the President what appears to be unprecedented authority over nonactive-duty forces. Most surprising, this authority comes from Congress at a time when its record is replete with the exercise of congressional authority, which, after passage of the measure, would be protected in this matter primarily by the ninety-day limitation and the restrictions of the War Powers Act.

More important, however, the measure suggests a greater awareness of the emergent dependency of active-duty forces on the reserve elements. But a far deeper meaning of the measure may be the realization that the force structure, as constituted under the inherent limitations of the AVF, is inadequate for contingency operations. By inference, therefore, it suggests that the intervention capability of the AVF, without augmentation from reserve forces, is far less than that of the conscript force.

IMPLICATIONS FOR MILITARY STRATEGY

Conventional military wisdom holds that military strategy and force structure are the results of sequential events that begin with the formulation of national policy objectives. The policy, in turn, leads to a conceptualization of military, political, economic, and diplomatic strategies which are then forged into instruments capable of achieving the articulated policy objectives. From a realistic standpoint, however, such a formalized and structured methodology could never function, owing to the existence of numerous components in the national security system which continually exert modifying pressures on national policy objectives and the means to fulfill them.

In a democratic society attempting to cope with the vicissitudes of a postindustrial period, it is unlikely that all the elements of national power can be simultaneously orchestrated into a coherent strategy. For example, our security interests dictate that we must establish, along what may be called horizontal lines, a geographical area of security which may be at odds with economic interests structured along vertical lines. The result is an apparent dichotomy, for the U.S. would expend huge sums of money on defense to deter a potential adversary, while simultaneously engaging in trade relationships with the same potential adversary that are not too far removed from "most-favored-nation status." This complicates the determination of what constitutes a "vital interest" and thus adds uncertainty to the formulation of foreign policy and, consequently, attendant military strategy. Moreover, it is becoming increasingly obvious that there are limits to the effectiveness of military power, and that realization, in turn, constrains foreign policy objectives. Thus the relationship between our foreign policy and military strategy is not support of the former by the latter, but a relationship that is inherently reciprocal.[31]

Usually, there is basic compatibility between foreign policy objectives and the military capability necessary to secure those objectives, by intervention if necessary. At times, however, capabilities and objectives may be out of phase. This now may be occurring in the United States, where a traditionally manpower-intensive force finds itself confronted with substantial military commitments, while manpower is denied as the transition is made to a capital-intensive force of unparalleled technological sophistication.

There is little reason to assume that the United States can alter the equation by increasing military manpower levels, which further suggests that military commitments and contingency plans requiring intervention forces may well be revised downward. However, a selective increase in capability of existing forces, augmented by reserves, may offset the decreased manpower levels evident in the AVF. But if the force level reductions that have taken place thus far reflect a trend inherent in politically advanced and technologically oriented societies that rely upon voluntary forces, then profound alterations of our entire military system are inevitable.

It appears that the inability to recruit adequate numbers of ground-combat personnel in the early days of the AVF resulted in successive reductions in force size, which gradually led to structural changes such as alteration of the combat-support ratio and extensive reliance on reserves. Despite the decreased manpower, however, the cost of military manpower continued to rise and, with inflationary pressures, contributed to lowered military readiness of the AVF. Also, essentially the reserve components have remained unready operationally, owing to equipment shortages.[32] It must be recognized that, while some of these problems may be transitory, the availability of adequate numbers of qualified manpower is crucial.

Notwithstanding current force capability trends, however, innovations are under way to overcome what appears to be decreased military intervention capability. The Army, for example, has created an elite force of "quick strike" ranger units which can be rapidly deployed from the United States to any accessible area of the world where a U.S. presence may be desired. The doctrine whereby they would be used, however, is uncertain at this point. A new initiative by the USAF is the airlift-enhancement program, which calls for increased strategic airlift deployment capability and includes plans for a large aerial tanker to reduce reliance on foreign bases during force deployments.

The combination of "quick strike" ranger units and increased airlift capability, together with acceptance of the hypothesis that froce capability affects its use or non-use, may conflict with emerging nonintervention attitudes by U.S. society and proscriptions against the use of military force by Congress. Whether military officers will develop such a doctrine of employment is uncertain, but they are faced with a new set of challenges that require a changed doctrine for military intervention. Such a doctrine would call for rapid deployment of highly specialized forces; swift and decisive employment to achieve clearly stated and obtainable objectives; and immediate withdrawal to comply with legal proscriptions and to prevent formulation of domestic opposition.

It is not assumed that a particular type of military capability and a supporting doctrine would lead to involvement by virtue of their existence (although the opposite can be argued).[33] It must be realized, however, that we live in an era of significant political, social, and economic change, in which the requirement for conventional military intervention capability may remain extensive. Moreover, we must also realize that some of our current interests and presumed commitments may be beyond the capability of the emerging force, despite innovations.[34]

A most significant factor to be considered by military planners is the influence the AVF will have on the Clausewitzian concept of appeasement and escalation as tools of mutual reciprocation in military intervention.[35] Crises in which military intervention is an option usually erupt suddenly and allow little time for rigorous analysis. Action and issues are often clouded by inadequate intelligence, rapidly changing military conditions, complex political considerations, and many other variables. This explains, in part, the propensity of military leaders to plan for a worst-case scenario.

By grossly oversimplifying the Clausewitzian construct of reciprocity of appeasement and escalation, and by postulating that measurably smaller intervention capability exists within the AVF vis-à-vis its predecessor, one can conceptualize a wide range of results from possible interventions supported by the AVF. Before the AVF, the United States, with its perceived ability to escalate military intervention to extremes, tended to ignore basic asymmetries between fundamentals such as offense and defense. Aided by what can be characterized as a hubris of technology, the U.S. tended to construct military force equations (between itself and potential adversaries) in which it controlled the key variables.

With the AVF, the U.S. now must reassess its role in similarly constructed equations, since it may no longer possess the capability to escalate to extremes, technological innovations notwithstanding. The United States must now accept the use of deescalation as a tool of reciprocity when an intervention option occurs, for precious little escalatory potential exists.

Recognition of this changed role of the United States in future military intervention equations can lead to the development of a simplistic model which would highlight intervention priorities based on emerging military potential.

This model should be visualized as a group of concentric circles, with the U.S. in the innermost circle. The first concentric circle out from the center is occupied by Western European allies and Japan. The relationship between the center and first circle is characterized by horizontal economic ties, occasionally strained by sociopolitical values that diverge from the U.S. structure, but reinforced by external threats that cannot be confronted unilaterally by Japan or Western Europe. Because of forward basing by the United States in the first circle, ample military capability exists to consider military intervention by the United States should it be deemed appropriate. Obviously, the U.S. capability for successful intervention would decrease in proportion to the strength of the country in which the intervention was contemplated.

In the second concentric circle we find Cuba, Mexico, and Canada. Cuba is an opposition but is offset by Canada, which is in mutual alignment with U.S. military capability. Mexico is neutral but can effectively oppose by gaining political and moral support from nations in the outer concentric circles. The capability for intervention by the U.S. in this circle is high because the locations are adjacent, which would permit application of preponderant mass by the U.S. This is not to say that such intervention would be successful, but rather that U.S. capability to intervene is of a high order.

The third concentric circle contains the countries of Central America, Latin America, and the Middle East. It is bounded by the last concentric circle, which contains Korea, the Persian Gulf area, Africa, and nations which are of less significance to the U.S., such as major powers against whom intervention is impossible (USSR, PRC, etc.), and countries over which the latter exercise hegemony. The capability of intervention in these last two circles is quite low, for the operative factors are time, distance, space, and the key variable of available manpower.

In the not too distant past, the United States may have possessed the capability to intervene, for example, in an area such as the Persian Gulf. A large standing army, availability of reserve manpower, and a functioning conscript authority could have provided the perception of adequate forces to properly manipulate the intervention equation. The AVF, however, may have modified, or at least tempered, such beliefs.

CONCLUSION

The United States has entered a new era, in which military intervention cannot be undertaken with the same assurance that has characterized the past, for it is unlikely that manpower levels provided by the AVF will permit the U.S. to manipulate intervention equations to its advantage. In this sense, the reduced force levels of the AVF will have a restraining effect on intervention decisions. But perhaps more significantly, the inability of the AVF to expand rapidly (as could its conscript predecessor) may seriously limit the escalation potential of the United States and force it to use deescalation as a tool of reciprocity when the possibility of intervention occurs. This would represent a new dimension of the conceptualization process used by those who formulate military strategy.

The United States must recognize this reality and not attempt to rely on mechanistic means, such as rapid reaction forces and enhanced strategic airlift, to obviate the manpower limits inherent in the AVF. Indeed, the very creation of an AVF by a nation which holds superpower status may suggest the need for reassessment of many traditional concepts, of which military intervention is but one.

NOTES

1. Urs Schwarz, "Great Power Intervention in the Modern World," *Problems of Modern Strategy* (New York: Praeger, 1970), pp. 176-77.

2. *National Security Strategy of Realistic Deterrence, Annual Defense Department Report, FY 1973,* (Washington, D.C.: Government Printing Office, 1972), p. 155. (Hereafter all such reports will be referred to as *Annual Defense Department Report* with appropriate years.)

3. It is necessary to recognize that Congress may not approve requested force levels for various reasons, such as its estimate of the recruiting capabilities of the services. For example, the FY 73 request of 2.4 billion was reduced by congressional authorization to 2.33, but the services ended the year with 2.25. Nevertheless, in testimony before the Senate Armed Services committee, the Army requested Congress not to base its authorization on congressional "estimates of the Army's capability to recruit toward an end strength" (U.S. Congress, Senate, Committee on Armed Services, *Fiscal Year 1975 Authorization for Military Procurement, Research and Development, and Active Duty, Selected Reserve and Civilian Personnel Strengths: Hearing,* 93d Cong, 2d sess., p. 4 ("Manpower"), March 21, 22, and 26, 1974, p. 1627 [hereafter referred to as SASC, FY 1975]).

4. U.S., Congress, Senate, Committee on Armed Services, *Fiscal Year 1974 Authorization for Military Procurement, Research and Development, and Active Duty, Selected Reserve and Civilian Personnel Strengths: Hearings,* 93d Cong., 1st sess., p. 8 ("Manpower"), June 11, 12, 13, 27; July 13, 14, 27; August 3, 1973, pp. 5201, 5222.

5. *New York Times* (February 21, 1974); *Washington Star–News* (October 29, 1974).

6. Thomas A. Fabyanic, "Manpower Trends in the British All-Volunteer Force," *Armed Forces and Society* 2 (Summer 1976): 553-72.

7. U.S., Congress, Senate, Subcommittee of the Committee on Armed Services, *Military Manpower Issues of the Past and Future: Hearings,* 93d Cong., 2d sess., August, 1974, p. 3 (hereafter referred to as Nunn Committee).

8. *Annual Defense Department Report, FY 1974,* p. 100.

9. *New York Times* (July 29, 1973).

10. SASC, FY 1975, pp. 1481, 1595.

11. Report on Marine Corps Manpower Quality and Force Structure submitted by Gen. Louis H. Wilson, USMC, Commandant of the Marine Corps, to Senate Armed Services Committe on December 31, 1975, p. 2 of Executive Summary.

12. *Annual Defense Department Report, FY 1975*, p. 179.

13. SASC, FY 1975, p. 1620.

14. Ibid., p. 1500; *Manpower Requirements Report for FY 1975* (Washington, D.C.: Department of Defense, February 1974) pp. xi-20.

15. *Annual Defense Department Report, FY 1975*, p. 179; SASC, FY 1975, p. 1619.

16. U.S., Congress, House, Committee on Armed Services, *Review of the Administration of the Selective Service System: Hearings,* June, 1966, pp. 9999-10174.

17. Letter of Transmittal, President's Commission on An All-Volunteer Force, February 20, 1970 ([Gates Commission Report] Washington, D.C.: Government Printing Office, 1970).

18. *Annual Defense Department Report, FY 1972*, p. 134.

19. *Annual Defense Department Report, FY 1975*, pp. 179-80.

20. *Annual Defense Department Report, FY 1977*, pp. 219-25.

21. *Manpower Requirements Report for FY 1975*, pp. xi-3.

22. Andrew Uscher and Daniel Huck, "Is the AVF a Peacetime Concept?" (unpublished draft of Cost Analysis for Alternative Force Sizes, October, 1974).

23. Nunn Committee, p. 26.

24. Ibid., p. 56.

25. Ibid., p. 1527.

26. Morris Janowitz and Charles Moskos, Jr., "Racial Composition in the All-Volunteer Force: Policy Alternatives," *Armed Forces and Society* 1 (Fall 1974): 109-23. For an alternative view, see Alvin J. Schexnider and John Sibley Butler, "Race and the All-Volunteer System," *Armed Forces and Society* 2 (Spring 1976): 421-32.

27. Defense Manpower Statistics for FY 1974, Office of the Assistant Secretary of Defense, Manpower and Reserve Affairs.

28. Air University, USAF ROTC, Maxwell AFB, Alabama.

29. See, e.g., James A. Johnson, "The New Generation of Isolationists," *Foreign Affairs* 49 (October 1970): 136-46; Bruce Russett, "The Americans' Retreat from World Power," *Political Science Quarterly* 90 (Spring 1975): 1-21; Ernest W. LeFever, *TV and National Defense: An Analysis of CBS News, 1972-73* (Boston, Virginia: Institute for American Strategy Press, 1974).

30. *Annual Defense Department Report, FY 1976 and 1977*, pp. iii-15.

31. Bernard Brodie, "Vital Interests: By Whom and How Determined," *National Security and American Society,* ed. Frank N. Trager and Philip S. Kronenberg (Lawrence, Kansas: University Press of Kansas, 1973), pp. 63-78.

32. *Annual Defense Department Report, FY 1977*, pp. 200-205.

33. Graham T. Allison, "The Military and American Society," *The Annals* (March 1973): 17-37.

34. See, e.g., James R. Schlesinger, *Annual Defense Department Report, FY 1976 & 1977,* pp. iii-32. Secretary Schlesinger argues that in the absence of increased airlift it would make more sense to reduce some of our more distant and informal commitments.

35. See Raymond Aron, "Clausewitz's Conceptual Systems," *Armed Forces and Society* 1 (Fall 1974): 49-59, for a related discussion on Clausewitz's method of analysis.

PROFESSIONAL PROBLEMS AND ADAPTATIONS

Sam C. Sarkesian

Since the end of World War II, while conventional military forces have remained essential ingredients of strategic deterrence, their utility for intervention has declined. At the same time, there have been a general persistence in political confrontations and an expansion of diplomatic maneuverability. Within the context of general interstate tension, this has created a vastly different environment for the resolution of conflicts. Domestically, the legacy of Vietnam remains a critical conditioning factor in U.S. military posture, while the issues raised by the volunteer military system compound the problems of adjustment to the changed environment. As a result, the U.S. military profession is faced with a series of difficult problems which have a direct bearing on the character of professionalism and on the ability of the military to engage successfully in foreign operations.

The purpose of this paper is to examine professional problems stemming from the new dimensions of military purpose—those specifically related to military intervention. In examining these issues, we will explore the relationships among international constraints, domestic values, and military purpose. Consideration will also be given to institutional and professional dimensions associated with the advent of the volunteer military. In this context, important questions are also raised regarding concepts of war, institutional orientation, and professional ethics.

There are six premises basic to this study. (1) The assumption is that military intervention means the commitment of U.S. military forces to a foreign

AUTHOR'S NOTE: The author wishes to thank Charles C. Moskos, Jr., for his valuable assistance. Selections from his paper "Trends in Military Social Organization," prepared for delivery at the conference on "The Consequences of Military Intervention," the University of Chicago, June 17-19, 1976, were included in this paper.

operation. (2) The least probable limited war is a direct confrontation between the U.S. and USSR or the U.S. and China. If one does occur, it is likely to involve the deployment of tactical nuclear weapons. (3) Deployment of tactical nuclear weapons is likely to escalate the confrontation and may be viewed by the "enemy" as a strategic factor that crosses the threshold into general war. (4) Professional issues are primarily, but not exclusively, focused on professionalism within the ground forces. Given the nature of sea and air warfare, professional problems are more likely to be strongly associated with ground-force commitment. (5) Limited wars are most likely to occur in nondeveloped regions, i.e., the Third World.[1] (6) Strategies of limited war remain elusive. The experience of Vietnam did not necessarily establish a policy of "no more Vietnams." Indeed, the acceptance of such a policy would hamper the development of a flexible and prudent approach to the prospects of limited war.[2]

Although limited wars are conditioned by their own special characteristics, they cannot realistically be separated from considerations of overall military capability and nuclear deterrence. Limited war and nuclear deterrence are part of an integrated military continuum. The ability to deter means the ability to maintain an effective limited-war readiness in all arms, and to maintain such readiness in the absence of actual hostilities. Thus the U.S. military is faced with problems of combat readiness in a series of contingencies ranging from general nuclear war to indirect confrontation. Equally important, the strengths and weaknesses in any major contingency have an effect on other capabilities.

There are, nevertheless, special features of limited war that distinguish it from other categories of warfare. The fundamental characteristic is restraint. "What distinguishes limited war from total war? The answer is that limited war involves an important kind and degree of restraint—deliberate restraint. . . . The restraint must also be massive . . . the restraint necessary to keep wars limited is primarily a restraint on means, not ends."[3]

The "ends" do have an important conditioning function, however. If complete annihilation of the enemy is a goal, for example, it is unlikely that other restraints will have any real meaning.[4] Thus political goals must be realistic in terms of the ultimate outcome of limited war—that is, military strategy must be effectively linked to political purpose. More important, political purpose must be identified and articulated so as to ensure legitimate military purpose. This matter will be addressed in more detail later.

Wars can also be limited by restraint on the use of force, to include the type of weapons deployed. The presumption is that weapons of a strategic nature—those that have the propensity of escalating the conflict—and weapons indiscriminate in their targets either will not be used or that their use will be very carefully restrained.

In such circumstances, the nation with a major strategic capability may well find that it is severely limited in its ability to bring to bear its military power. Brodie, for example, observes:

Among the military lessons we have learned is that restraint in the application of force–in order to keep that application compatible with its purpose–may make the force applied ineffective for its purpose. Thus to grant sanctuary and to withhold tactical nuclear weapons may be utterly correct policy, but such restraints have to be recognized as being costly, possibly very costly, in military effectiveness. For the future, this is bound to mean, and should mean, not fewer limitations upon the use of force, but rather fewer occasions for applying force under circumstances requiring such restraints.[5]

The nature of force applied and the type of weapons deployed are also contingent on the character of the limited war. Until the last decade, limited war has generally been associated with a Korean type of conflict. Essentially, this rested on the premise that the war would be reminiscent of a World War II type of setting, with its identifiable front lines, conventionally organized enemy, and use of generally conventional military tactics within specified geographical boundaries. Since the late 1950s, however, the changed nature of the international system has significantly influenced the character of limited war. It is more likely that limited wars will now include a mix of conventional and unconventional ingredients.[6] For example, it is improbable that an intervening power will be able to gain a foothold and maintain itself in another nation without first defeating a conventional force, and–more important–successfully defeating a hostile population conducting a "people's war." Indeed, one can reasonably argue that the defeat of the enemy's conventional forces may be the less difficult part of the operation.

Limited wars are also characterized by the use of surrogate forces or wars by proxy.[7] Beginning in Greece (1947), the United States adopted a policy of using advisory teams to assist and in many respects supervise the indigenous forces in combating opponents. As we learned in South Vietnam, however, the use of surrogate forces can lead directly to the use of combat personnel to support and eventually supplant indigenous forces.

Finally, military intervention (employing ground forces) must utlimately face the problem of disengagement. South Vietnam provides an example of the chaos and trauma associated with disengagement during an impending defeat. South Korea, on the other hand, illustrates the quicksand quality of intervention–even after twenty years, U.S. troops are still deemed necessary to prevent recurrence of war. Indeed, disengagement could trigger political as well as military events that could well erode the very purpose of the initial intervention.

These characteristics raise four salient features about and for U.S. policy. First, there is an inherent asymmetry. That is, under a number of circumstances it is conceivable that the limited-war involvement of the U.S. may be met by total war by the "enemy." Second, limited war is very political in character. In light of the nationalistic sentiments, the delicate balance of terror between superpowers, the general antagonism toward any action that hints of imperialism, and the general North-South tensions in the world, U.S. military intervention may create political pressures and responses beyond the boundaries of conventional military capability. Third, military intervention may have limited use and be politically counterproductive. Moreover, to succeed, the application of force may require subtle and low-visibility operations rather than conventional military intervention. Fourth, in any case, the rules of the game of limited war must be clearly articulated and generally accepted by the protagonists. In light of the first three features, it appears highly unlikely that rules regarding limited war that are directly connected with political and nationalistic issues will be accepted if they limit a power's ability to achieve political goals. This may well destroy the very purpose of the intervention in the first place. It is within these general policy considerations that professional military problems are addressed.

CHANGING MILITARY ORGANIZATION

Military purpose and professional problems are also manifested in the context of changing conceptions of military organization. There is a need, therefore, to examine the proposition that the American military is moving from a predominantly institutional format resting on professionalism to one resembling that of an occupation. This proposition also assumes that the concept of a "calling" inherent in professionalism is considerably reduced when economic and status considerations become paramount. While it is not necessary to predict such a shift, it is necessary to be aware of its possibility and its implications.

Terms like "occupation," "profession," or "institutional format" are imprecise in both popular and scholarly discussions. Nevertheless, each contains connotations which distinguish them from one another. For our purposes, these distinctions can be described as follows.

An *occupation* is legitimated in terms of the *marketplace*, i.e., prevailing monetary rewards for equivalent skills. In a modern industrial society, employees usually enjoy some voice in the determination of appropriate salary and work conditions. Such rights are counterbalanced by responsibilities to meet contractual obligations. The occupational model implies that the priority inheres in self-interest rather than in the task itself or in the employing organization. A common form of advancement of group interest is the trade union.

A *profession* is legitimated in terms of specialized expertise, i.e., a purpose that transcends individual self-interest in favor of a presumed higher good. A *calling* in an *institutional format* usually enjoys high esteem in the larger community because it is associated with self-sacrifice and complete dedication to one's role. A calling does not command monetary reward comparable with what one might expect in the general economy. But this is often compensated for by an array of social benefits that simultaneously signal the institution's intent to take care of its own and set the institution apart from the general society.

Members of an institution do not organize into self-interest groups. If redress for grievance is sought, it is through "one-on-one" recourse to superiors or a trust in the paternalism of the organization.

Of course, such models are as much caricatures as they are descriptions of reality. In the armed forces, moreover, the situation is complicated in that the military has elements of all three models. But the overarching and clearly dominant trend in contemporary military social organization is the decline of the institutional format and the corresponding ascendancy of the occupational model.

Whether the occupational model will become the organizational model for the professionals, i.e., the officer corps, is problematical. In the current professional environment, there is resistance to the idea of professionalism defined in terms of economics. Indeed, there is evidence to suggest that many in the profession seek a professional purity based on time-honored concepts of duty, honor, country.

Although there were precedents before the emergence of the all-volunteer force in early 1973, the end of the draft was the major influence moving the military away from an institutional format. In contrast to the all-volunteer force, the selective service system was based on the premise of citizenship obligation—with concomitant low salaries for draftees—and the ideal of a broadly representative enlisted force (though this ideal was not always realized). In fact, the occupational model was clearly the foundation of the philosophic rationale of the 1970 *Report of the President's Commission on an All-Volunteer Armed Force* (Gates Commission Report).[8] Instead of a military system anchored in the normative values of a calling—captured in words like duty, honor, country—the Gates Commission explicitly argued that primary reliance for recruiting an armed force be based on monetary incentives determined by marketplace standards. Perhaps the ultimate in monetary inducements has been reached in the "bonus" used to recruit young men into the combat arms since the end of the draft.

While the termination of the selective service system is the most dramatic change in the contemporary military system, other indicators of the trend away from the institutional format toward the occupational model can be noted: (1) the significant salary increase given the armed forces since 1971 in an effort to make military salaries competitive with civilian rates; (2) proposals to make civilian-military pay "comparable," e.g., doing away with the allotment system in which service remuneration is partly determined by the service member's marital and family status; (3) proposals to eliminate or reduce a host of military benefits, e.g., subsidies to commissaries and exchanges, the G.I. Bill, health care for dependents, the pension system; (4) the separation of work and residence locales accompanying the growing proportion of enlisted men residing off the military base; (5) the increasing reluctance of many military wives at officer and noncom levels to participate in customary social functions; and (6) the growing discussion about the legality and relevance of trade unions for active-duty military personnel. These trends highlight the tendency toward the occupational model in the emergent military organization.

INSTITUTIONAL CHARACTER AND CONSTRAINTS

While the changing organizational mode may have a long-range effect on military purpose and professionalism, the military institution as it is now structured creates immediate professional problems. The nature of the volunteer force, problems of combat readiness, and demands of institutional loyalty impose operational definitions on the environment that limit the professional's ability to develop flexible and realistic responses to limited war.

The volunteer military places manpower and budgetary constraints on the ability of the U.S. military to undertake external operations.[9] Put simply, volunteer forces have limited manpower.[10] Conducting sustained operations in any given limited-war situation requires a reservoir of replacements and the ability to expand force levels. This may mean involvement of the National Guard, reserves, or both, as well as the possible reinstitution of the selective service system. In view of the attitudes of the American people and the nature and character of limited war, it is unlikely that such policies will gain the support of Congress or the public. On the other hand, the nature of volunteer forces may isolate the military from society to an extent where, even if they were committed to external operations, they would receive little support from the American people.

Budgetary restraints prohibit significant expansion of the military establishment during peace to meet sustained limited-war contingencies. While the defense budget may increase to meet perceived Soviet advances in nuclear missiles and military capability, it is unlikely that much financial support will be provided for additional manpower and limited-war capabilities that are not directed at the Soviet Union or major war contingencies.

Many professionals lack faith in the ability of the volunteer forces; they see, as a result, a general weakening of the American military purpose.[11] Indeed, there seems to be a latent fear that the American forces will find it difficult to conduct limited wars, in terms not only of quantity but also of quality of forces. Moreover, professional concern about such matters is reflected in institutional preoccupation with raising the general quality of the military for the purposes of pretraining for combat. Thus general education, remedial training, recruiting incentives, and administrative techniques may become institutional programs and goals at the expense of serious combat training.

Aside from constraints imposed by the volunteer system, there are constraints associated with combat readiness. This is a term used to signify the degree to which the military forces are capable of conducting successful military operations. Combat elements of the military must remain in a state of perpetual readiness. This is perhaps one of the most perplexing training problems facing the military. It is clear that maintaining a high level of combat readiness during times of relative peace is a difficult matter, even more difficult when the identity of the enemy is not clear. Moreover, maintaining combat readiness over long periods presumes a general consensus that there is indeed a threat. Because of the current environment and the inclination of the American people to oppose foreign adventures, it is not clear how the institution will be able to maintain a consistent combat readiness.

Force structure is generally based on the conventional concepts associated with general war. The concept of "forces in being" that is the basis for U.S. force structures presumes a capacity to conduct wars with current manpower levels. Moreover, this approach rests on the premise that the most likely future wars will be fought and ended quickly, with little or no time for mobilization. Thus, the forces-in-being idea gives only secondary consideration to cadre or mobilization posture and to force structures for conducting limited-war operations.

With the decline of mass armies, the ability of the United States to immediately respond militarily rests on the quantity and quality of the volunteer force. The four to six month preparatory period necessary to upgrade reserve forces for combat operations makes it unrealistic to assume that such forces can be considered a quick reaction force—"forces in being."

In light of these considerations, the U.S. military appears to be developing a narrow operational perspective—the use of nuclear weapons in support of ground operations. That is, there is a strong propensity for the main military effort to be directed toward European-style combat, resting on the assumption that tactical nuclear weapons will be available to support ground operations. Yet the new dimensions of military purpose demand a multidimensional military posture in a variety of combat environments.

Finally, the institution, in any case, demands loyalty. Since the military institution and the profession rest on time-honored concepts, duty, honor, country, and the demand for institutional loyalty and obedience, there is little room for resistance to institutional demands and to orders from above. The demand for prompt and unquestioning response is so ingrained in the professional ethos that it is inconceivable that many officers would question either institutional policies or orders from superiors. This critical inquiry from within the profession is reduced to almost meaningless rhetoric, while institutional orientation precludes flexibility and adaptability.

The problems with respect to institutional considerations seem clear—institutional demands and requirements do not foster a military purpose responsive to the new environment, nor do they respond to the broader demands of professionalism. Equally important, there does not appear to be a political perspective that is realistically tied to the capabilities of the military institution. Given the close relationship between deterrence capacity and a range of contingencies from general nuclear war to indirect confrontation, the U.S. military appears to be inadequately prepared to engage successfully in limited-war operations.

PROFESSIONAL AND INSTITUTIONAL ADAPTABILITY

In the post-Vietnam period, the most difficult task of adaptability has faced the ground forces and related units under pressure to maintain an effective force for military intervention. Two interesting trends can be discerned: one is an effort to create elite ground forces; the second, paradoxically, has been to contract military functions out to civilian personnel and civilian agencies. Both are manifestations of the trend toward the occupational model.

Proponents of elite units have typically been accorded a mixed reception in American military circles.[12] Because elite units could be regarded as an institution within an institution, specialized fighting units often found themselves at the margin of or even at odds with the regular command structure. But if the armed forces continue to move toward an occupational model, the status of elite units in military social organization will be fundamentally different from that of past experience. In reaction to the occupational model, that is, certain numbers of servicemen—largely through self-selection—will gravitate toward units where the traditional qualities of the military are maintained and valued.

Preliminary evidence indicative of the new circumstances of elite units is found in a study of four combat battalions (conducted in spring 1975).[13] These battalions, all stationed in the southeastern United States, represented all combat units. There were, in ascending order of "eliteness," an infantry battalion, a tank (armored) battalion, an airborne infantry battalion, and a ranger battalion. A representative sample—between 85 and 90 lower-ranking soldiers (pay grades E-3 and E-4) from each battalion—were surveyed for social background characteristics and attitudinal items measuring military commitment.

There was wide variation in the racial compositions of the battalions. Blacks were 53.3% of the infantry, 51.7% of the armored, 22.0% of the airborne, and 9.3% of the rangers; the white ratios were the inverse of the black figures. For the same pay grades, the Army-wide figure was 23.7% black in 1975. Certainly the southeastern regional basis of the recruitment pool contributed to the disproportionate number of blacks in the armored and infantry battalions. But this only puts into sharper contrast the fact of the nearly all-white composition of the ranger battalion.

Parallel comparisons can be made for educational levels. The proportion of soldiers who had at least some college was 10.9% in the infantry, 11.8% in the armored, 17.2% in the airborne, and 30.2% in the rangers. It is important to note, however, that even when race was held constant, the educational differences between the units persisted, although they were somewhat less pronounced. Contrary to much conventional wisdom, the most elite combat units in the all-volunteer Army are largely made up of middle-class white youth. At the same time, the nonelite units that constitute the large bulk of the ground combat arms are overproportionately representative of lower-class, less educated, and minority groups—though not nearly to the extent of the armored and infantry battalions described here.

The soldiers were asked about their willingness to serve in hypothetical combat situations. Miniature scenarios were presented for six hypothetical situations: (1) an invasion of the U.S. by a foreign enemy; (2) a fight against revolutionaries in America; (3) defense of a U.S. ally in Western Europe—say, Germany; (4) defense of a U.S. ally in the Far East—say, Korea; (5) defense of a U.S. friend in the Middle East—say, Israel; and (6) an overseas civil war in which the government asks for American help. Of course, it is extremely risky to extrapolate, from attitudes toward hypothetical situations, predictions of actual behavior in a real combat circumstance. Nevertheless, these items do offer themselves as primitive indicators of level of military commitment.

Table 1 gives the percentages of soldiers who stated they would either volunteer or willingly follow orders to serve in each of the hypothetical combat situations. Two patterns of response appear in these data. First, willingness to serve is highest—as one would anticipate—in defense of the United States from a foreign invasion. Not so expected, however, is the finding that combat willingness varies hardly at all whatever U.S. ally may be invaded. Second, and most important for our purposes, the more elite units, especially the rangers, consistently indicated a greater willingness to go into combat, while the nonelite units—especially the infantry battalion—just as consistently indicated the greatest reluctance to do so.

Additional data dealt directly with the salience of the institutional versus the occupational model of military social organization. For contrast, we focus our

Table 1: Percentage of Troops Who Would Volunteer or Willingly Follow Orders to Go Into Combat in Hypothetical Situations, by Type of Unit

Combat Situation	Rangers	Airborne	Armored	Infantry
U.S. invaded by foreign enemy	97.8%	93.4%	88.5%	81.4%
Fight revolutionaries in America	96.4	77.6	71.1	59.2
Defend Western European ally—Germany	92.9	77.8	75.8	59.4
Defend Far Eastern ally—Korea	92.9	75.5	75.6	60.4
Defend Middle Eastern friend—Israel	90.5	76.4	73.6	58.3
Overseas civil war in which government asks for American help	84.5	72.2	64.3	52.8
(modal number of cases)	(86)	(90)	(87)	(90)

Source: Charles W. Brown and Charles C. Moskos, Jr., "The Volunteer Soldier—Will He Fight?" **Military Review** (June 1976).

attention on the two polar units—the ranger battalion and the infantry battalion. A series of items probed for the reasons that the soldier had joined the service. Among the infantrymen, 61.1%, compared with 28.2% of the rangers, stated they had difficulty in finding a decent civilian job; 50.6% of the infantrymen, compared with 37.7% of the rangers, said the combat enlistment bonus was an important factor; and 59.4% of the infantrymen, compared with 58.1% of the rangers, agreed with the statement that the "Army should try to maintain traditions which make it different from civilian life."

The evidence thus indicates that soldiers who were most compatible with the institutional format of the military were also the soldiers most likely to indicate their willingness to serve in combat. Conversely, for those soldiers most in accord with the occupational model, the level of military commitment was markedly lower. Yet, because of the ascendant occupational model, a small number of young men—disproportionately white and middle class—are being self-selected into the most traditional of combat groups—the elite units of the all-volunteer Army. In terms of military social organization, we are witnessing a differentiation—both in social composition and in military commitment—*within* the ground combat arms and not just *between* the combat arms and the technical support branches.[14]

Another consequence of the ascendant occupational model departs entirely from formal military social organization. This is the use of civilians to perform tasks which by any conventional measure would be seen as military in content.[15] The private armies of the Central Intelligence Agency have long been an object of concern within the regular military command. But what is anomalous in the emerging order is that, rather than assigning its own military personnel, the U.S. government increasingly gives contracts directly to civilian firms—with salary levels much higher than comparable military rates—to perform difficult military jobs. In other words, the very structure of the military system no longer encompasses all military functions.

It is hard to overstate the extent to which the operational side of the military system is now reliant on civilian technicians. The large warships of the U.S. Navy are combat-ineffective without the technical skills of the contract civilians who permanently serve aboard those ships. Major Army ordnance centers, including those in the combat theater, require the skills of contract civilians to perform necessary repairs and assembly. Missile-warning systems in Greenland are in effect civilian-manned military installations run by firms responsible to the U.S. Air Force. In Southeast Asia and Saudi Arabia, private companies such as Air America and Vinnel Corporation are given U.S. government contracts to recruit civilians who carry out military activities. Bell Helicopter and Grumman have established a quasi-military base in Isfahan, Iran, staffed by former American military personnel who train Iranian pilots. The American monitoring force in the Sinai is contracted out to private industry; the government retains only policy control.

External political considerations certainly impinge on the decisions to use civilian contracts for military tasks. But if task efficiency is the issue, there is also a more nagging implication. Military personnel cannot or will not perform arduous long-term duty with the efficacy of contract civilians. The trend toward employing contract civilians to do military tasks could well be the culmination of the industrialization of the military purpose.

While these questions primarily focus on the enlisted structure, they do have an influence on professionalism. If the occupational model and contract civilian roles are to become the accepted norm, beliefs conducive to organizational and societal respect—the whole notion of military legitimacy—become untenable. If military legitimacy erodes, the very basis of military professionalism erodes. Indeed, the uniqueness of military purpose that has been the basis of professional expertise and authority in society will become very suspect. Moreover, the ability of the military to respond to a range of policy alternatives and contingencies will be significantly diminished.

MILITARY PURPOSE AND SOCIETY

The contradictions between military purpose and values of society create one of the most complex problems, one involving matters of values, attitudes, and linkages between the military and the political system. Additionally, questions regarding legitimacy, civil-military relations, institutional norms, and individual behavior patterns are inherent parts of the issue. Thus military professionalism and military purpose cannot realistically be studied outside the context of the values and attitudes of society. Military legitimacy is bestowed by society. Consequently, the ability of the military to conduct limited wars is not solely a function of combat effectiveness; it is a combination of this factor and legitimacy—specifically, the legitimacy of purpose.

Professional ethics and institutional purpose are the cornerstones of military legitimacy. These are linked in explicit and at times subtle ways. If there is a high degree of interpenetration between the military and society (as there is likely to be in modern democratic societies), the military is sensitive and responsive to the values and perceptions of society. Military purpose must be congruent with social values and at the same time correspond to professional military perspectives. In sum, society bestows legitimacy on the military through its acceptance of the military's purpose and the perception that social norms are closely linked to professional ethics and behavior.

Military legitimacy alone does not necessarily lead to successful application of military power; however, military posture is an essential factor. (As used here, "legitimacy" does not refer to the legitimacy of the profession in the wider context of the political system, but to professional esteem, prestige, and credibility—a legitimacy of purpose and professional ethics.) There must be a supportive balance between military legitimacy and military posture. It is difficult to be precise about the degree of each required in any given period or combat situation. The post-Vietnam era demands one particular intermix, while the Korean War demanded another. One may reasonably argue that the Vietnam involvement never achieved an effective intermix. Military power, to be effective, not only must have a military institution capable of engaging in combat; it must also have the material and political support of, as well as psychological linkage with, society. In simple terms, the military can only be as effective as society will allow; conversely, if society supports the military's involvement in conflict, the military must have the proper posture to effectively apply military power. This is the basic premise behind the concept of "management of violence in the service of the state." The state identifies the enemy; society provides the political-psychological wherewithal to carry out necessary policies; and the military implements the will of the state. These elements are interrelated and must reinforce each other if military policy is to be successful.

Military legitimacy rests primarily on image, values, prestige, and purpose; military posture rests on organization, training, technology, and leadership. In other words, military legitimacy is primarily a psychological, or subjective, dimension; military posture, on the other hand, is primarily organizational, with emphasis on quantitative standards, i.e., objective.

To ensure an effective degree of military power, therefore, there must be symmetry between military legitimacy (subjective) and military posture (objective). There is always the danger of asymmetry—where subjective factors, for example, may become increasingly dominant, while objective factors become less able to achieve minimum influence on application of military power. This situation can lead to the politicization of the military and a high degree of civilianization, eroding the professional basis of the military institution. Similarly, objective factors may become dominant, subduing the influence of subjective factors to such a degree that the military perspective dominates the political institutions—a garrison state condition.

In a democratic society, asymmetry is most likely to develop as a result of contradictions between subjective and objective factors. Thus, the perceptions of society regarding military purpose and behavior may not be in accord with professional military perceptions—indeed, may be absolutely opposed to them. The military in a democratic society cannot remain in this kind of asymmetric relationship with society without its institutional purpose and cohesion being destroyed. Given the relationships between society and the military in a democratic system, political and social forces will generate pressures for the restoration of symmetry—even at the expense of the military institution. This is particularly relevant in the conduct of limited wars.

Equally important, policies followed by the government in committing ground and other military forces to limited-war situations create tension among professional purpose, ethics, and society. Professional propensities to use military force to its maximum to achieve quick and decisive victory are mitigated by society's tendency to demand proper behavior in the conduct of war and clearly articulated military purposes within a context of acceptable political goals. Moreover, while many military men see "military intervention as potentially necessary," the attitudes of society questions the need for such action.   In such circumstances, the military establishment and the profession become particularly susceptible to divisiveness and lack of credibility created by the contradictory demands of society and of military purpose.

Democratic society, moreover, assumes that there is a high moral quality in its value system. In this regard, one of the more important elements affecting society's perceptions of the military (and thus military legitimacy) is the correlation between individual behavior and the norms of society. On a more mundane level, the individual actions of a soldier on the battlefield must meet some minimum societal norms while conforming to certain professional expectations. Thus the professional's military effectiveness rests in no small measure on the correspondence of professional behavior with the moral quality of the social values in his society.

Military purpose and moral quality, according to one scholar, are crucial in determining the legitimacy of military purpose.

> How then, are we to assess the vast powers that the military has come to hold over millions of American citizens? Simply, the military's powers are legitimate to the extent—and *only* to the extent—that they are in the first instance, consonant with contemporary standards of justice and humanity, and then only when the foreign policy which the military carries out is both (1) directly related to the defense of the nation or its closest democratic allies, and (2) by elected officials whose decisions are guided by the will of the people as expressed through the political process.[17]

Most civilians would accept this premise; but a soldier-scholar writes, "One would be hard pressed to find a mature professional soldier who would accept Barnes' premise."[18] The problem seems fairly clear: while the professional views his mission through operational lenses, the civilian views it through political lenses. More specifically, the purposes of the political system are the boundaries within which military purpose operates. Political purposes must therefore be congruent with the general will of society if military purpose is to succeed. Yet there is some contradiction between these concepts and professional perceptions.

The problem is equally complex in contingencies involving the use of tactical nuclear weapons. The threshold between tactical nuclear war and general war is thin, even if such a distinction were to be accepted. To accept the deployment of tactical nuclear weapons, society must perceive the crisis as clearly threatening the national security. Equally important, decision makers will be placed in the quandary of trying to distinguish between actions that require a tactical nuclear response and those in the general-war category. The reluctance to use nuclear weapons in less than general wars remains embedded in the institutional decision-making process. However, rational arguments regarding the substitution of nuclear weapons for military manpower remain. Indeed, how this can be accomplished while maintaining restraint and within limited political goals remains a mystery—indeed, a dilemma. As Knorr observes, "The uncertainty about whether escalation can be avoided looms very large. And this uncertainty itself is therefore apt to deter these [nuclear] powers from lightly initiating even the most limited application of military force against each other."[19]

The issues and relationships between military purpose and society are best summed up by a noted military historian:

> To use—and restrain—its immense social, economic and political influence wisely and effectively, the Army obviously must hold itself in close rapport with the people. To secure military success in so complex and difficult a way as the one in Vietnam, it must also depend upon its rapport with the people. Unless the people decide that the war in Vietnam is in truth their way, the Army must finally fall.[20]

ETHICAL PROBLEMS

The problems arising from relationships and requirements among professionalism, society, and the military institution are, in the broader sense, questions of professional ethics. The fundamental ethical question confronting the military profession is how to accommodate itself to its growing volunteer character, while reinforcing its links to society, and maintain its uniqueness as a profession able to respond to the new environment.

Answers to these questions will not be found in more elaborate technology, increased military discipline, isolation, or aloofness from society, but in understanding the role that the military plays in society and appreciating the "politics" of democratic systems. This requires a commitment to the idea that the military professional is part of the American political system and civilian value structure. The military must understand the political "rules of the game" not only of their own institution but also those prevailing in the broader political system.

Seen this way, professional ethics takes on a wider meaning and is particularly sensitive to individual attitudes and behavior. More specifically, ethical questions become linked with the purpose and utility of military force; the degree of political influence of the military within the political system or nature of civil-military relations; the extent to which individual military officers can become involved in the "politics" of the political system; and the conflict between individual conscience and institutional demands.

Questions, for example, about the utility and purpose of military force require basic rethinking of professional purposes. Should military forces serve society in other ways than preparation for and waging of war? There are a number of advocates of using the military force peacefully, involving it in civic action, educational programs, and social welfare roles. Indeed, some would argue that waging war is not sufficient to sustain professional purpose. A system of ethics, they would claim, cannot be based solely on a concept of "management of violence."

Concern over civil-military relations focuses on such problems as the influence of military men over political decisions. As important is the question of national priorities. Should military men be concerned in their military calculus with domestic priorities? Or should there be a purely military perspective based on the assumption that other branches of government provide executive and legislative monitoring? To what degree should the military reinforce civilian value systems?

In this context, questions are raised about the professional as opposed to the political nature of military service. While some argue that professionalism is enhanced by a nonpolitical military, others argue that only through political knowledge can professionals properly fulfill their responsibilities. Indeed, some scholars advocate political soldiers who are at home in a political environment—particularly that associated with limited war.

> We must understand that nowadays the armed forces of a nation are instruments of external politics and must be trained for such activities. In this sense, I say yes to political activity by our military commanders; they must be highly trained in external politics, otherwise they will carry their political naïveté into highly sophisticated political arenas, seeing communists under every bush, and, worse still, supporting political losers purely because they seem affluent and respectable on the surface. Military commanders must be trained in armed diplomacy, a training that must start in their early years. Most important, they must be trained in political and social science which is as important as technological education in the armed services.[21]

Legitimate dissent is an essential part of the political dimension of professionalism required for the conduct of modern limited war, among other things. In addition, legitimate dissent allows a close linkage between the junior and subordinate levels of the military establishment and the senior levels—something lacking in the conduct of the Vietnam War. Indeed, this lack had much to do with the difference between the realities of the war in the field and those perceived in Saigon. In limited wars, when the military instrument is directly involved in a Vietnam type of environment, responsiveness and appreciation of the senior officers toward the attitudes of small-unit commanders is a necessity. The political and social intertwining is most apparent at the lower-unit operational levels and must be translated into operational considerations at all levels. In the long run, legitimate dissent will provide a new dimension to the professional ethos that will make it more responsive to the necessities of policies requiring military intervention. It will provide the impetus to clearly articulate the military position; it will allow a variety of views to be assessed, broadening the generally monolithic view of the professional's perspective on military purpose.[22]

Within the profession there is also concern about the relationship between individual behavior and institutional norms. One of the most illuminating views comes from a study of military professionalism conducted at the U.S. Army War College. This states, in part,

> It is impossible to forecast future institutional climates with any degree of reliability. Nevertheless, it is not unreasonable to state as consequence of the present climate: it is conducive to self-deception because it fosters the production of inaccurate information; it impacts on the long term ability of the Army to fight and win because it frustrates young, idealistic, energetic officers who leave the service and are replaced by those who will tolerate if not condone ethical imperfection; it is corrosive of the Army's image because it falls short of the traditional idealistic code of the soldier—a code which is the key to the soldier's acceptance by a modern free society; it lowers the credibility of our top military leaders because it often shields them from essential bad news; it stifles initiative, innovation, and humility because it demands perfection at every turn; it downgrades technical competence by rewarding instead trivial, measureable, quota-filling accomplishments; and it eventually squeezes much of the inner satisfaction and personal enjoyment out of being an officer.[23]

This conclusion by a group of military professionals considering their own profession has serious ramifications for the meaning of professional ethics. If such conditions are generally prevalent, what alternatives are available to rectify the problems? To what degree will the profession respond to—or allow—internal dissent? Can professionals refuse to carry out illegal orders? Are there institutionalized processes which foster reasoned dissent without evoking institutional retaliation against the dissenting officer?

As important, this conclusion points to an erosion of performance quality, as well as ethical imperfection. It also suggests the existence of a particular kind of professional, working at the highest levels of military hierarchy, symbolizing the profession to the community, and dictating the nature of the military value system and civil-military relations. What ethical standards are likely to prevail if those who consider career success the dominant norm become the professional elite? Professional problems associated with limited war therefore raise a number of broader issues about military purpose, civil-military relations, and the boundaries of professionalism in general. Yet existing interpretations of professional ethics are likely to obscure the fundamental meaning and study of issues raised here, while perpetuating what McWilliams labels "bureaucratic tendencies," which include "conformity, careerism, and cultivation of right attitudes."[24]

Thus the traditional perspectives on the use of military force, institutional loyalty, and mission orientation reinforced by situational ethics rationalize narrow professional perspectives as the key to institutional and individual success.

CONCLUSIONS

It would, of course, be traditional to respond to the questions addressed here by stating that the military requires better training, leadership, motivation, management, and tactics. Yet the answer may lie not in "better" everything but in recognizing the limits of intervention. It seems unlikely that the U.S. will be able to intervene in limited situations with hopes for a "neat surgical" operation. On the contrary, it is more likely that military intervention will increase the politicization of the conflict and stimulate a nationalistic reaction, while exposing the United States to internal tensions and conflict. Increasingly, this will erode "professionalism" while decreasing the legitimacy of the military institution at home.

The difficulty is clear. Military intervention raises serious problems of military purpose. Not only are there major linkages between society and military purpose, but also among professionalism, society, and military purpose. Without relatively clear goals and unambiguous roles and purpose for the military in modern limited war, military professionalism will be unlikely to be able to maintain the ethical and purposeful posture so necessary for retaining its legitimacy and its linkage with society. Equally important, the political-psychological dimensions of modern limited war may quickly involve the intervening power in the political-social systems of an alien culture. The professional ethos and traditional perspective do not provide professional dimensions for sustained operations in such an environment. Thus a problem is created not only involving the pursuit of policy in modern limited war but also involving that policy's actual conduct.

When viewed from the policy level, it is clear that there are political-psychological limits to the application of military power. These limits, translated into strategic terms, militate against a policy of committing troops into the ambiguous, multidimensional environment associated with modern limited war. If military policy is to be successful, there must be symmetry between military legitimacy and military purpose.

Thus the military profession has three options. First, it can retreat into a rigid and narrow professionalism in which military men are unconditional servants of the state. This stance suggests a robotlike response to political leadership, once the military follows it unquestioningly.

Second, the profession can assume a civil service role in which civilian politics, unionization, salary concerns, and fringe benefits become the major motivation for individual officers. To civilianize the military this far would very likely erode its professional uniqueness and render it easily vulnerable to political manipulation. In the long run, it would create dangers not only for the profession but for the whole political system.

Third, the profession can develop a new rationale in which the military is seen as more than the unconditional servant or simple paid employee of the state. This would require that the military acquire understanding and expertise, a sense of realistic and enlightened self-interest, and professional perspectives transcending the boundaries traditionally associated with duty, honor, and country. The profession must accept a political dimension—not partisan politics; it must be capable of dealing with environments that are not purely military, and recognize the professional military man's right to engage in politics within a domestic system, as long as he adheres to the rules of the game. In this third option, the profession would see itself as a political interest group trying to reach the civilian leadership and the public to explain its case and develop a consensus for its objectives. To implement this option requires a military leadership and profession which have a specific but limited political posture.

We are not suggesting that military professionals should make political decisions about the goals of the political system, in peace or in war. But surely they must be equipped to look beyond immediate exigencies and develop the intellectual tools and insights to appreciate the interdependence between war and politics. Such a perspective is not acquired in professional military schools—at least not in the present curriculum. To present the "military" point of view in a judicious and well-articulated manner, military professionals must understand the total concern of the political system. They must go beyond the simple loyalty of "managers of violence in the service of the state." Moreover, war itself raises questions of morality which require more than a "military" solution.

While the Janowitz thesis of a constabulary force is fundamental to this consideration, the option here is broader in scope. Not only should military men be prepared to perform duties in non-war situations, but they need develop a political awareness, gain realistic insights into the operation of the American political system, and establish legitimate procedures for advocacy of military interests. This presumes for example, that the education of a military officer needs to go considerably beyond the "military" skills presently predominate in senior military schools. It also presumes that "political" knowledge in the broad sense is an inherent part of the professional perspective.

This option of retreating to narrow professionalism is a more comfortable position, and has been the mythical basis for civilian-military relationships for some time. But it relegates the professional military men to an unthinking role hardly adequate to the complexities of modern military life and present and future world politics. The second would transform the military into a civil service in which self-interest rather than national purpose motivates action. The third option is clearly the most challenging and useful; yet it, too, has its dangers. Not only must the profession accept a political dimension to its ethical values, but it must always remember that it remains a servant of the state and is not an autonomous decision-making body. To take on this critical political dimension is only a short step from assuming a self-righteous stance as the ultimate arbiter of society's political disputes. The third option provides a wider range of activity, mainly consultative, for the professional officer. Indeed, it requires an active, responsible self-interest and a nonpartisan involvement in the policy-making process and in politics in general. The American political system is based partially on the assumption that groups and interests must have access to policy makers; articulation and aggregation of interests on a wide scale, unemcumbered by government restrictions, are basic premises of democratic society. Even the military ought to be given the opportunity to argue its case within the accepted rules of the game.

From the individual point of view, the third option requires the profession to recognize the limits of military institutional demands and individual subservience, including combat situations. The institutionalization of healthy skepticism, reasonable inquiry, and legitimate dissent would do much to reinforce the worth of the "individual" while providing momentum for innovation, imagination, and self-examination. Obviously, this option requires substantive changes in professional ethics and a broader view of military professionalism.

NOTES

1. Robert E. Osgood, "The Reappraisal of Limited War," in *American Defense and Detente; Readings in National Security Policy,* ed. Eugene J. Rosi (New York: Dodd, Mead, 1973), pp. 468-69. The author concludes, "These doubts seem likely to lead to a marked differentiation of interests in the application of containment—a downgrading of interests in the Third World and a greater distinction between these interests, and those pertaining to the security of the advanced democratic countries . . . What they seem to preclude, at least for a while, is any renewed effort to strengthen military deterrence and resistance in the Third World by actively developing and projecting United States' capacity to fight local wars."

2. Ibid., p. 470. The author notes, "What we are almost certain not to witness is the perfection of limited-war conceptions and practice in accordance with some predictable, rational calculus and reliable, universal rules of the game. The conditions and modalities of international conflict are too varied, dynamic, and subjective for limited war to be that determinate." See also Herbert K. Tillema, *Appeal to Force: American Military Intervention in the Era of Containment* (New York: Thomas Y. Crowell, 1973). According to Tillema, the United States has been involved in four overt military interventions since World War II: Korea, 1950; Lebanon, 1958; Vietnam, 1961; and the Dominican Republic, 1965. These are considered overt military interventions because of the commitment of ground troops. Thus in the thirty years since the end of World War II, the United States has been involved in four limited-war situations requiring U.S. ground troops. Although in two instances, the Dominican Republic and Lebanon, casualties were few and numbers of troops small, the total casualties of the four interventions is over 80,000 killed and thousands more wounded and disabled. Tillema discusses these interventions and what he perceives as the basis for U.S. policy. Equally interesting is his discussion of why the U.S. did not intervene more frequently, given the nature of the international environment over the past thirty years.

3. Bernard Brodie, *War and Politics* (New York: Macmillan, 1973), pp. 127-28.

4. Osgood, "Reappraisal of Limited War," p. 471. According to the author, "A limited war is generally conceived to be a war fought for ends far short of the complete subordination of one state's will to another's and by means involving far less than the total military resources of the belligerents, leaving the civilian life and the armed forces of the belligerents largely intact and leading to a bargaining termination . . . the term local war is not often reserved for the great number of local conventional wars in which neither of the superpowers is directly or indirectly involved. The difficulty of defining limited war arises partly because the relevant limits are matters of degree and partly because they are a matter of perspective, since a war that is limited on one side might be virtually total from the standpoint of the other, on whose territory the war is fought. Furthermore, a limited war may be carefully restricted in some respects (e.g., geographically) and much less in others (e.g., in weapons, targets, or political objectives)."

5. Brodie, *War and Politics,* p.358.

6. The Chinese Communist victory in 1949 provided a modern demonstration for the remainder of the world of the effectiveness of a "people's war." Regardless of the number

of failures, the disagreement over tactics, and the sacrifices required, "people's war" became a symbol and a model, not only for use against colonial powers but also against established regimes and their supporters.

7. Klaus Knorr, *On the Uses of Military Power in the Nuclear Age* (Princeton, N.J.: Princeton University Press, 1966), p. 108.

8. *President's Commission on an All-Volunteer Force, Report* (Washington, D.C.: Government Printing Office, 1970).

9. Zeb B. Bradford and Frederic J. Brown, *The United States Army in Transition* (Beverly Hills: Sage, 1973), pp. 38-42.

10. For example, at the height of the Vietnam War, there were approximately 500,000 U.S. military men in Vietnam. To prosecute the war and still maintain some semblance of a worldwide military posture, there were over 1.3 million men drafted into the Army over the period 1965-69. Additionally, there were close to 1 million enlistments and reenlistments. Thus, for the Army alone, over 2 million men were either inducted or enlisted over a five-year period. For the same period of time, over 5 million personnel were either drafted or enlisted in all of the services.

11. Frank Margiotta, "A Military Elite in Transition: Air Force Leaders in the 1980's," *Armed Forces and Society* 2, 2 (Winter 1976): 155-184.

12. See Roger A. Beaumont, *Military Elites* (Indianapolis: Bobbs-Merrill, 1974) pp. 171-84; and Sam C. Sarkesian. *The Professional Army Officer in a Changing Society* (Chicago: Nelson-Hall, 1975), pp. 93-102.

13. Charles W. Brown and Charles C. Moskos, Jr., "The Volunteer Soldier–Will He Fight?" *Military Review* (June 1976).

14. Charles C. Moskos, Jr., "The Emergent Military: Civil, Traditional, or Plural?" *Pacific Sociological Review* 16, 2 (April, 1973): 255-79; David R. Segal, et al., "Consequence Isomorphism and Interdependence at the Civil-Military Interface," *Journal of Political and Military Sociology* 2 (Fall 1974): 161-71; Bradford and Brown, *U.S. Army in Transition,* pp. 189-202; William L. Hauser, *America's Army in Crisis* (Baltimore: Johns Hopkins University Press, 1973), pp. 207-18; and Sarkesian, *The Professional Army Officer,* pp. 93-102.

15. The original argument that the military was being segmented into a civilianized technical component and a traditional combat element is found in Moskos, "The Emergent Military." Extensions of the "plural military" thesis are found in Bradford and Brown, *U.S. Army in Transition;* Hauser, *America's Army in Crisis;* and Segal "Consequence Isomorphism."

16. Jerald G. Bachman and John D. Blair, *Soldiers, Sailors and Civilians: The "Military Mind" and the All-Volunteer Force* (Ann Arbor, Michigan: Survey Research Center, 1975), p. 62.

17. Peter Barnes, *Pawns: The Plight of the Citizen-Soldier* (New York: Alfred A. Knopf, 1972), p. 8.

18. Hauser, *America's Army in Crisis,* p. 88.

19. Knorr, *On the Uses of Military Power,* pp. 99-100.

20. Russell F. Weigley, *History of the United States Army* (New York: Macmillan, 1967), p. 556.

21. Michael Elliot-Bateman, "The Form of People's War," in *The Fourth Dimension of Warfare,* ed. Michael Elliot-Bateman (New York: Praeger, 1970), 1:147.

22. On the need for dissent, see William P. Mack (USN-Ret.), "The Need for Dissent," *New York Times Magazine* (January 12, 1976).

23. U.S. Army War College, *Study on Professionalism* (Carlisle Barracks, Pa.: USAWC, June 30, 1970), pp. 28-29.

24. Wilson C. McWilliams, *Military Honor after Mylai* (New York: Council on Religion and International Affairs, 1972), p. 28.

PART VI. DOMESTIC CONSTRAINTS

CHANGES IN AMERICAN PUBLIC ATTITUDES TOWARD INTERNATIONAL INVOLVEMENT

John E. Mueller

This chapter represents an effort to assess historical changes in popular American attitudes toward the cold war, and particularly toward various of its ancillary concerns: international tensions, the fear of war, isolationism, the willingness to confront and combat international communism, support for military intervention, and support for defense spending.

Data will be drawn from a wide assortment of public opinion polls conducted since World War II in which relevant questions have been posed.[1] Of particular interest are the results obtained in a nationwide poll commissioned by the Chicago Council on Foreign Relations and carried out in December 1974 by Louis Harris and Associates.[2] In this poll a wide variety of pertinent questions were asked, and it will be the particular burden of this discussion to put some of the results obtained into a broader historical perspective. Specifically: do the results of this poll suggest that the American public has substantially changed in its attitudes toward aspects of the cold war and international involvement, or are the results generally in line with those obtained by polls in earlier and in later years?

After a technical digression in the first part of the discussion, the second part assesses two opinion phenomena of the 1970s: the decline of international tensions (as measured by a decreased fear of major war) and the acceptance of defeat in Indochina. With this as background, the third part investigates how these experiences have affected American attitudes toward three policy areas: military intervention, isolationism, and defense spending.

THE PROBLEM OF QUESTION WORDING

It is necessary to begin on a rather tedious methodological note, one developing ideas and a point of view that will recur repeatedly in this analysis. This is a concern, almost a preoccupation, with the precise wording of the poll question under consideration.

The public opinion polling process can be seen as a fairly primitive stimulus-response situation. In a rather odd social context the respondent is peppered with a series of questions by an interviewer who is a perfect stranger. The questions range over all sorts of issues, many of which the respondent has spent almost no time thinking about. And, if the respondent has thought about the issue before, it is often the case that no determined opinion has been reached.

Nevertheless, there the interviewer is, ready to record for all posterity the respondent's reaction to a battery of questions, many of which are of necessity rather simplistic or banal. For the respondent the situation often is confounding and embarrassing, as well as flattering—few people, after all, are accustomed to having their every word taken down as some sort of holy writ (or at least as valued ephemera).

Accordingly, most respondents do their best to oblige and are willing, with all the instant profundity they can muster, to react on the spot to the series of questions.

That is what the public opinion polls measure.

The data so gathered can be a valuable aid in understanding popular attitudes, but they must be handled with great care. In particular, it is necessary to pay close attention to the precise nature of the question-stimulus to which the respondent fashions a hasty reply, because on many issues seemingly minor changes in the wording of the question can profoundly alter the shape of the response.[3] Respondents often seem to react as much to the tone or context of the question, or to key words in it, as they do to its objective content.

In the present situation, for example, if poll questions on U.S. military intervention have the word "Communist" in them, they simply are not the same questions as ones without that key word, no matter how similar they may be on other grounds. Similarly, "help defend" is not the same as "send American troops," nor is "did we make a mistake in Vietnam" the same as "was the Vietnam War worth fighting."

A splendid example of this is furnished in the Chicago Council poll. On two different pages of the questionnaire the respondents were asked if they wanted defense spending expanded, cut back, or kept at its present level (table 1). The questions were very similar. As the Council's report observes, however, the context of one question (A in table 1) was such that tradeoffs with other government expenditures were *implied*.[4] The result was that this formulation of the question found the public 10 percentage points more willing to cut defense expenditures.

It should be stressed that neither version of the question is in any sense "loaded" or "biased." Both are perfectly sensible formulations to get at the issue in question. But the results certainly suggest that to conclude 32% (or 42%) of the American public "thinks" that defense spending should be cut is purest nonsense. Public opinion polls are entirely incapable, with any degree of

Table 1: Question Wording–Defense Spending

A. (Hand respondent card A.) "Here is a list of present federal government programs. For each, I'd like you to tell me whether you feel it should be expanded, cut back, or kept about the same." (Read list and record below for each item.) 1. Aid to education. 2. Defense spending. . . .

B. "Do you think that we should expand our spending on national defense, keep it about the same as it is now, or cut back our defense spending?"

	A	B
Cut back	42%	32%
Keep same	38	47
Expand	14	13
Not sure	6	8

Source: John E. Rielly, **American Public Opinion and U.S. Foreign Policy** (Chicago: Council on Foreign Relations, 1975), p. 16.

precision, of answering questions like "What percentage of the American public thinks defense spending should be cut?"

The kinds of public opinion analyses that have the most merit involve *comparisons*. We can compare subgroups on a single poll to see how they react to the same question; we can compare responses to the same question asked at different points in time to assess trends; and we can compare different questions or different formulations of a question, to see what kinds of words or contexts alter the response patterns.[5] Such analyses are not necessarily sure to be successful, but at least they are not fundamentally flawed at the outset.

It is this perspective that will be applied in the observations that follow.

TWO OPINION PHENOMENA: THE DECLINE OF INTERNATIONAL TENSIONS AND THE ACCEPTANCE OF DEFEAT IN INDOCHINA

At least two aspects of the public's perceptions of international affairs in the mid- 1970s, in a period of continued détente with the Soviet Union and relaxed hostilities with mainland China, differ from those of the active phases of the cold war.

First, there was a marked decline in perceptions of international tensions, as indicated by a substantial reduction in the fear of war; and, associated with this, there was a reduced sense of urgency in international affairs in general. Second, the public, after the extended agonies of the war in Indochina, accepted defeat there with remarkable equanimity.

Decline of International Tensions

A valuable poll indicator of public perceptions of international tension can be found in response to questions about the imminence of a major war. It is clear that concerns that another world war may be around the corner became much less in the 1970s than they often were in the past—particularly compared to the chilliest periods of the cold war, which began to thaw about 1963. This says nothing about the *reality* of the situation, of course; it may be that World War III loomed closer in the mid-1970s than in, say, 1948 or 1951 or 1962. But it seems that public (and probably official) expectations about such a calamity declined. People became, in short, more relaxed, more sanguine about a major conflagration. Realistic or not, this perspective probably informs other attitudes, including those about defense spending and perhaps about some forms of military intervention.

In national opinion surveys conducted since World War II, the American public was asked some two hundred times about its expectations of a major war. The question, in various permutations, was of the form, "Do you expect the United States to fight in another world war within the next _____ years?"[6]

The question was often posed in surveys in the 1940s and 1950s, and the polls generally discovered considerable peaks of popular concern about the dangers of a nuclear war with the Soviet Union—a concern largely neglected by purveyors of fifties' nostalgia. The question has appeared only infrequently in polls conducted after 1963, however. This is probably an indication of relaxed tensions, since poll questionnaires tend to be filled with items of current topical interest, and something that is no longer being discussed simply doesn't get queried. The newspapers, which are the chief customers of the polling organizations for these kinds of questions, want topicality, not history.

To a degree, the change in the concern about an imminent world war can be seen in the few data points available for the period after 1962. In April 1963, a bare six months after the tumultuous Cuban Missile Crisis, expectations about a world war in five years had reached a very low level historically, while fewer people expected a world war within one year than in any earlier poll. (However, tensions as measured by these two questions had risen by the time they were last asked—in mid-1965 and early 1966, as the United States was moving directly into the Vietnam War. Although the public was probably thinking more of a major war with China than with the Soviet Union, the data suggest that war expectation questions might well have generated interesting newspaper copy. By that time, however, the polling agencies had lost the habit.)

The decline of tensions over a war with the Soviet Union can be seen more specifically in two other comparisons.

Twice Gallup has asked the American public to look twenty years into the future and to decide which of a list of things "will have happened by then"—one item being "Atomic war between Russia and America." The question was first posed in December 1959, at one of the mellowest points in the cold war period.

Khrushchev had recently visited the United States and the "Spirit of Camp David" was abroad in the land. The question about war in five years had been asked two months earlier, and had reached its lowest recorded level. In that atmosphere Gallup found 17% selecting atomic war with Russia as being one of the things that "will have happened" in twenty years. When the question was again posed ten years later, in October 1969, the expectation level had dropped from this already rather low score to an almost unmeasurably small 8%.[7]

A second comparison is afforded by responses to the question, "Do you expect the United States to fight in another world war within the next ten years?" This question was posed repeatedly in the late 1940s and early 1950s. It generally garnered affirmative responses from well over 50% of the population, reaching a high of 83% at the worst stages of the Korean War. After a long interval the question was once again posed in spring 1976, when it slumped essentially to its lowest recorded level: 43%.[8]

It would be helpful to have some really extensive data to demonstrate this relaxation of tensions, but the limited amount available (as well as common sense) argue that in this important area there has been a decidedly nontrivial change in international perceptions. The American public still had plenty of things to worry about in the mid-1970s, but concern about an imminent nuclear war was much less prevalent than it was in the 1950s and early 1960s.[9]

Associated with this decline in tensions was a somewhat more general feeling of reduced urgency in international affairs. Up until the mid-1970s international concerns were important in the American public's sensibilities. There was the concern over war, over the contest with international communism, over American prestige abroad, over the exigencies of international leadership.

There were fluctuations in these attitudes, of course, and much of the concern persisted. But in the wake of Vietnam, and with détente a feeling of relaxed urgency seemed to predominate. Indicative of this, perhaps, was the election campaign of 1976, the first since World War II in which there was no feeling of international urgency, much less crisis. The campaign of 1948 had been conducted during various crises in Europe, including the Berlin blockade; in 1952, there was the Korean War; in 1956, there were simultaneous crises in Suez and Hungary; in 1960, the debate was over who could best handle Khrushchev over issues like Berlin, Cuba, Laos, and the Congo; in 1964, 1968, and 1972, Vietnam policy in various ways was a central concern. In contrast, the 1976 campaign was dominated by domestic—particularly economic—considerations.

It is easy to overemphasize the public's interest in foreign policy issues. Study after study in the last thirty years has found a remarkable lack of awareness and interest in these issues. In the tumultuous 1960s, for example, polls found that a quarter of the public professed not to know "if there is any Communist government in China now." And the percentage of people found to be alert to an international issue tends to depend on whether it was in last night's headlines or not.[10]

But the post-Vietnam relaxation and essential unconcern does seem special (although, of course, it may prove to be only temporary). Nothing seems urgent in the cold war-Vietnam sense. Commentators have almost found their favorite word, "crisis," inapplicable to foreign affairs. A Roper poll conducted in June 1976 gave respondents a list of twenty-two issues and asked them to select the two or three that seemed most important to them. The international issue that did best ("The budget for national defense") came in tenth.[11] Similar findings are reported for 1976 by Watts and Free: of thirty-one problem areas ranked by respondents, the most popular intentional item ("Keeping our military and defense forces strong") came in eleventh.[12]

Acceptance of Defeat in Indochina

If the comparative thawing of the cold war, and a consequent reduction in tensions, in war expectancy, and in a sense of international urgency, constituted one of the major international events of the 1960s and 1970s, another was surely the war in Vietnam. The war, it is often observed, was a "trauma" for the American public—it came close to "tearing the country apart."

An evaluation of the war is partially tapped in one set of questions on the Chicago Council survey—which was conducted *after* direct American military involvement had ended with the "Peace with Honor" settlement of January 1973 but *before* the final Communist victories there in spring 1975. Respondents were handed a list of international events and asked to designate which were "proud moments" in American history and which were "dark moments." The results, tabulated in table 2, show Vietnam *(before* the final collapse, remember) viewed as a comparatively dark moment (though it would have been helpful to have had more potential dark moments for comparison—such as the Bay of Pigs, the "fall" of China or Cuba, the U-2 crisis, etc.). It would be interesting to have this question repeated later, to see whether the defeat made the Vietnam "moment" seem even darker.[13]

One of the more impressive events of recent years was how casually the American public accepted the Communist victories in Vietnam in the extraordinary debacle of spring 1975. During the course of the war, many observers warned that a Communist victory in Vietnam might have a dire impact on American politics. A rise of a new McCarthyism (in simplistic analogy with the "fall" of China) was often predicted. Indeed, an argument sometimes given for continuing the war was that a loss there would cause unbearable strains and recriminations in American politics.

Of course, nothing of the sort happened. In part, this was probably because of the rather gradual way the United States left the war. U.S. troops were doing little ground fighting by 1972, and American bombing ended with the "Peace with Honor" settlement of January 1973. By the time of the 1975 defeat, the war had been decoupled from American sensibilities to a substantial degree and the public watched the collapse with considerable detachment.

Table 2: "Dark" and "Proud" Moments in Recent U.S. History, 1974

"Here's a list of international events that the United States has been involved in in recent history. For each, please tell me whether you think it was a proud moment in American history, a dark moment, or neither a proud moment nor a dark moment."

	Proud Moment	Dark Moment	Neither	Not Sure
1. U.S. role in the founding of the United Nations	82%	4%	9%	5%
2. U.S. role in the Korean War	22	41	27	10
3. Nixon's trip to Communist China	60	9	24	7
4. U.S. role in the Vietnam War	8	72	15	5
5. The Berlin airlift	53	7	15	26
6. CIA involvement in Chile	7	41	19	34
7. Kennedy's handling of the Cuban Missile Crisis	53	18	14	15
8. U.S. involvement in the Dominican Republic	10	20	27	43
9. U.S. role in World War II	69	12	11	8
10. The founding of the Peace Corps	81	2	10	7
11. The Marshall Plan of aid to Europe	56	6	15	23
12. U.S. sending emergency aid to Bangladesh	76	3	11	11
13. American support of Israel during the October 1973 war	43	11	29	17

Source: Chicago Council of Foreign Relations Codebooks.

In fact, the public may have written off Vietnam as a bad debt quite a bit earlier. Table 3 details data on a central poll question posed during the war: Was Vietnam a "mistake"; As can be seen, support for the war had already reached low levels as early as 1968, with residual support presumably coming from only the most tenacious of hawks.

With this perspective on the war, and with American troops no longer engaged in Vietnam, Americans seem to have been quite willing to forget the whole thing. The Chicago Council survey in 1974 found the public giving about as much attention to "what's happening in Vietnam these days" as it was to "the war in Cyprus."[14] So boring had Vietnam become for Gallup that, after the "Peace with Honor" settlement, he never even bothered to ask the American public again whether it felt the war was a mistake—in fact, he largely gave up on the issue as early as 1971.

What is particularly incredible is that the collapse in Indochina was actually used by the man who presided over it, President Gerald Ford, as a point in his favor in his reelection campaign of 1976. When he came into office (1974), he argued, the country was still involved in the war; but now (1976) it was not. His opponent never seemed interested in pressing the point, nor did the President's opponents from the Right within his own party.

Table 3: Support and Opposition in the Vietnamese War, 1964-73

A. "In view of the developments since we entered the fighting in Vietnam, do you think the U.S. made a mistake sending troops to fight in Vietnam?" (AIPO)

B. "Do you think we did the right thing in getting into the fighting in Vietnam or should we have stayed out?" In 1964 and 1966 this was asked only of those who said they had been paying attention to what was going on in Vietnam (80% of the sample in 1964, 93% in 1966). (SRC)

For each question the numbers represent, in order, the percentages in support of the war (Pro), in opposition (Con), and with no opinion (DK).

	A			B		
	Pro	Con	DK	Pro	Con	DK
November 1964				47%	30%	23%
August 1965	61%	24%	15%			
March 1966	59	25	16			
May 1966	49	36	15			
Bomb oil dumps						
September 1966	48	35	17			
November 1966	51	31	18	47	31	22
Early February 1967	52	32	16			
May 1967	50	37	13			
July 1967	48	41	11			
October 1967	44	46	10			
Bunker, Westmoreland visit						
December 1967	46	45	9			
Tet offensive						
Early February 1968	42	46	12			
March 1968	41	49	10			
April 1968	40	48	12			
GOP Convention						
August 1968	35	53	12			
Democratic Convention						
Early October 1968	37	54	9	30	52	18
Nixon elected						
February 1969	39	52	9			
September 1969	32	58	10			
January 1970	33	57	10			
March 1970	32	58	10			
April 1970	34	51	15			
Cambodia invaded						
May 1970	36	56	8			
November 1970				30	49	20
January 1971	31	59	10			
May 1971	28	62	11			
November 1972				29	57	14
January 1973	29	60	11			
Settlement						

Sources: John E. Mueller, **War, Presidents and Public Opinion** (New York: Wiley, 1973), pp. 54-55; Gallup Opinion Index (GOI) 92; and SRC Codebooks.

SUPPORT FOR MILITARY INTERVENTION, ISOLATIONISM, AND DEFENSE SPENDING

It seems, then, that rather imperfect poll data are suggesting two things about American popular attitudes toward international events in the mid-1970s: (1) a relaxed sense of concern about an imminent world war accompanied by a reduced feeling of urgency about international affairs in general; and (2) an almost bemused acceptance of defeat in Indochina.

How have international events affected attitudes toward military intervention, isolationism, and defense spending?

Attitudes Toward Military Intervention

The unhappy experience with Vietnam, however calmly accepted, is unlikely to inspire any desire for a repetition. But in considering attitudes toward military intervention abroad, it seems useful to divide the issue area into two subareas: (1) support for intervention to aid a friendly power that has been attacked by the Communists; and (2) support for intervention for a less tangible purpose—to prevent the spread of communism. The model for the first kind of intervention might be a war something like the one that was fought in Korea. Models for the second kind would be intervention in Greece in 1947, Lebanon in 1958, the Dominican Republic in 1965, and, carried to its logical extreme, Vietnam in 1961 and 1965.

Military intervention to aid an attacked friendly power. Over the course of the last thirty years various polls have been conducted which included questions about U.S. military intervention to aid friendly countries that have become the (hypothetical) victims of a foreign invasion.

The wording of these questions varies considerably and, insofar as can be determined, the response is affected in major ways if (a) the hypothetical attackers are specifically identified as "Communist" or "Soviet," and (b) the questions ask about sending U.S. troops, as opposed simply to "helping defend" or "coming to the aid or defense of" an attacked power. The data in table 4 have been used in one paper to suggest a "substantial drop" by 1974 in support for military intervention.[15] But, as can be seen, the 1974 question (from the Chicago Council survey) differs from the earlier two in important ways: it is more specific in asking about sending *U.S. troops* and it does not specifically ask about turning back a *Communist* or *Soviet* attack. Because of these differences, we would expect the last question to show less support for military intervention. And it does.

It might well be argued that the difference of a mere ten or twelve percentage points between the surveys suggests that support for military intervention did *not* drop, since that much variance is probably attributable to changes in

Table 4: Question Wording–Military Intervention

September 1970: "There has been a lot of discussion about what circumstances might justify the United States going to war in the future. Do you feel if each of the following happened it would be worth going to war again or not? . . . Western Europe were invaded by the Communist."

Go in	51%
Stay out	32
No opinion	17

June 1972 (Agree or disagree): "The United States should come to the defense of its major European allies with military force if any of them are attacked by Soviet Russia."

Go in	52%
Stay out	32
No opinion	16

December 1974: "There has been a lot of discussion about what circumstances might justify U.S. military involvement, including the use of U.S. troops. Do you feel if . . . Western Europe were invaded, you would favor or oppose U.S. military involvement?"

Go in	39%
Stay out	41
No opinion	20

Source: **Harris Survey Yearbook of Public Opinion** (New York: Harris, 1971), pp. 86-87; William Watts and Lloyd A. Free, **State of the Nation** (New York: Universe Books, 1973), p. 281; Rielly, **American Public Opinion**, p.18.

question wording.[16] In fact, it seems to be the case, on the basis of a variety of poll results, that *public support for military intervention to defend against an invasion of a friendly power was much the same in the mid-1970s as it was in earlier years in the cold war, going back at least to 1950.*

There are four sets of data to support this assertion: *(a)* a comparison of one question asked in the Chicago survey of 1974 with a question asked in 1951; *(b)* a comparison of questions asked during the Korean War with ones asked during the first half of the Vietnam War; *(c)* some Gallup results that allow a fairly systematic comparison of attitudes from 1971 with those of 1975; and *(d)* a question that traces opinion on the issue between 1972 and 1976.

a. Table 5 shows a comparison between 1951 and 1974. Both ask about supplying troops to help defend Yugoslavia against an attack by Soviet or Communist armies. Both find about the same (small) percentage in favor. Other countries were asked about by NORC in the early 1950s and by the Chicago Council poll in 1974 but, alas, Yugoslavia is the only country they *both* asked about.

b. Table 6 supplies data from polls in which Americans were asked about the advisability of getting involved in other Koreas and other Vietnams. The Korean

Table 5: Military Intervention to Help Yugoslavia, 1951 and 1974

August 1951: "If Communist armies were to attack Yugoslavia, do you think the United States should stay out of it, or should we help defend them?" (If "help defend"): "Should we send American troops to help them or just send military supplies?"

15%	Send troops

December 1974: "There has been a lot of discussion about what circumstances might justify U.S. military involvement, including the use of U.S. troops. Do you feel if . . . the Soviet Union attacked Yugoslavia after Tito's death, you would favor or oppose U.S. military involvement?"

11%	Help Yugoslavia (send troops)
65	Stay out
24	Not sure

Sources: For August 1951, NORC Codebooks; for December 1974, Rielly, American Public Opinion, p. 18.

War polls have an extra response category, "It depends." If these people are crudely allocated into the other three categories (or even if they aren't), the comparable 1967 Vietnam results (questions B and C) turn out to be rather similar to those found for the equivalent period in the Korean War, 1952 or 1953.

Questions D and E are included in table 6 to show what happens when the question tosses the "U.S. troops" issue into the question and leaves out the "Communist" issue: compared to questions B and C, "support" for military intervention drops considerably.

c. There are data available (table 7) to allow a comparison of a poll from 1971 with one conducted in mid-April 1975, at the time of the collapse of the U.S.-supported governments in Indochina—events which could hardly be expected to increase support for the interventionist cause. Opposition to U.S. military interventions is generally higher in the later poll, but not greatly so, *particularly* considering the circumstances under which it was conducted. Furthermore, the percentage in favor of intervening with *troops* is hardly changed at all.

Of the ten to twelve countries for which 1971-75 comparisons are possible, there are five that show an increase of at least 8 percentage points in the "stay out" category between the 1971 and 1975 polls. Two of these, India and Turkey, received a lot of rather bad press during the interim, while the drop in attachment to Nationalist China is probably attributable to the substantial relaxation of tensions between the United States and mainland China that occurred between 1971 and 1975. Since the 1975 poll was conducted during the collapse of the U.S. position in Indochina, it is hardly surprising to find an 8-point rise in the "stay out" sentiment with respect to Thailand—indeed, that change almost seems rather small under the circumstances.

Table 6: Getting Involved in Other Koreas, Vietnams

A. "If Communist armies attack any other countries in the world, do you think the United States should stay out of it, or should we help defend the countries, like we did in Korea?"

		Stay Out	Help Defend	It Depends	No Opinion
1950	September	14%	66%	15%	5%
	December	28	48	15	9
1951	August	28	53	13	6
	December	30	52	13	5
1952	June	33	45	15	6
	October	31	45	18	6
1953	August	36	45	13	6
	November	26	52	17	5
1955	October	28	52	14	6
1956	November	24	52	20	4

B. December 1967: "In the future, do you feel the United States has an obligation to defend other Vietnams if they are threatened by Communism?"

	39%	44%		17%

C. December 1967 (Roughly): "Should the U.S. go to the defense of Thailand if that country were threatened by Communism?"

	36%	42%		22%

D. October 1967: "If a situation like Vietnam were to develop in another part of the world, do you think the U.S. should or should not send troops?"

	57%	29%		14%

E. January 1969 (same): 62   25   13

Sources: NORC Codebooks; Mueller, **Wars, Presidents and Public Opinion**, pp. 111-12.

The other major increase in the "stay out" category is more difficult to assess: West Germany. The 11-point increase is quite striking and cannot be explained by any apparent changes of policy or circumstances. It is hard to put the change down to a generally increased isolationism, however, because the percentage favoring the use of U.S. troops changed hardly at all and because a comparable increase in the "stay out" category is not found in questions about somewhat similar countries such as England and Japan.

Included in table 7 are some data from a Harris poll conducted in 1969. In general, there is a considerable drop in support for military intervention between the Harris 1969 poll and the two Gallup polls of the 1970s.

I am inclined to discount this apparent change, however. First, it seems odd that precipitous decreases would be found in support for military intervention

Table 7: Military Intervention to Help Various Countries, 1969, 1971, 1975

April 1969: "If . . . were invaded by outside Communist forces" would you favor American action with "U.S. armed forces," "military and economic aid," or "stay out"? (Harris)

April 1971, April 1975: "In the event a nation is attacked by Communist-backed forces, there are several things the U.S. can do about it—send American troops OR send military supplies but not send American troops OR refuse to get involved. What action would you want to see us take if . . . is attacked?" (Gallup)

		Armed forces Troops	Aid/ Supplies	Stay Out	No Opinion
West Germany	1969	38	21	28	13
	1971	28	41	22	9
	1975	27	32	33	8
Israel	1969	9	35	39	17
	1971	11	44	33	12
	1975	12	42	37	9
Japan	1969	27	15	21	37
	1971	17	34	38	11
	1975	16	35	40	9
England	1971	37	33	19	11
	1975	37	30	24	9
India	1969	22	15	40	23
	1971	7	40	39	14
	1975	7	34	47	12
Mexico	1969	52	24	13	11
	1971	45	26	19	10
	1975	42	25	23	10
Thailand	1969	25	15	37	23
	1971	11	36	38	15
	1975	10	32	46	12
Brazil	1969	34	18	28	20
	1971	16	36	33	15
	1975	15	33	39	13
Nationalist China (Taiwan)	1969	26	15	36	23
	1971	11	30	45	14
	1975	8	27	54	11
Canada	1969	57	22	11	10
	1971	–	–	–	–
	1975	57	19	14	10
Saudi Arabia	1975	7	27	54	12
Philippines	1969	30	17	19	34
	1971	–	–	–	–
	1975	29	34	26	11
Turkey	1971	10	36	37	17
	1975	9	29	49	13

Sources: Time, May 2, 1969; Bruce Russett and Miroslav Nincic, "American Opinion on the Use of Military Force Abroad," Yale University, n.d.; GOI 121, July 1975.

between 1969 and 1971, with nothing comparable being found between 1971 and 1975. It is also troublesome that the "no opinion" percentage in the Harris poll is generally so much higher—suggesting less interviewer persistence (not necessarily a bad thing)—which makes comparison more difficult.

But, most important, the 1969 question is worded differently: it asks about support for the use of U.S. *armed forces,* not U.S. *troops.* For some, "armed forces" probably suggested air raids and artillery bombardment, a more palatable alternative than "troops," which suggests the foot soldier. That's enough, probably, to explain the difference.

d. Finally, table 8 details some data from the 1972-76 period that were generated by a question about coming to the defense of major European allies attacked by Soviet Russia. There is something of a decline of support for intervention in the 1972-75 period, perhaps paralleling the drop found in the Gallup findings for 1971-75 for West Germany noted above. By 1976, however, this small decline in support for intervention had been more than reversed.[17]

Military intervention to prevent the spread of communism. All the questions noted above are about American willingness to aid in the event of an armed attack against another country. Mostly, it seems, the public, by 1976, was as willing to help as it ever had been. However, there is another kind of military intervention—getting involved militarily simply to stop the spread of communism, rather than to defend against an outright invasion. As already noted, this would envision a situation less like Korea in 1950 and more like the Dominican Republic in 1965 or Lebanon in 1958.

The data on this score are presented in table 9, and they suggest a rather considerable drop in enthusiasm between 1968 and 1976 for these kinds of ventures.

Thus, although the word "communism" still inspires a negative response in the American public, and opposition to Communist *invasions* of friendly lands may be as high as ever, there is probably a more relaxed feeling about the rather generalized and airy "threat" of communism than there once was. One poll found, in 1964, a composite score of 86 (out of a possible 100) of "worry" about "the threat of communism at home and abroad." This figure had dropped to 79 in 1968, and to 69 in 1972 and 1974, then rose somewhat to 74 in 1976.[18]

Table 8: Military Intervention to Aid European Allies, 1972-76

"The United States should come to the defense of its major European allies with military force if any of them are attacked by Soviet Russia."

	1972	1974	1975	1976
Agree	52%	48%	48%	56%
Disagree	32	34	34	27
Don't know	16	18	18	17

Source: William Watts and Lloyd A. Free, "Nationalism, Not Isolationism," **Foreign Policy** (Fall 1976): 17.

Table 9: Military Intervention to Prevent the Spread of Communism, 1968-76

"The U.S. should take all necessary steps, including the use of armed force, to prevent the spread of communism to any other parts of the free world."

	1968	1972	1976
Agree	57%	46%	44%
Disagree	29	43	43
Don't know	14	11	13

Source: Watts and Free, State of the Nation, p. 217; Watts and Free, "Nationalism, Not Isolationism," p. 23.

In the summer of 1951, in the midst of the Korean War, NORC asked: "If you had to choose, which would you say is more important—to keep Communism from spreading, or staying out of another war?" Faced with this unpleasant set of alternatives, 63% favored stopping communism, while 29% wanted to stay out of war.[19] It would be interesting to have this question repeated now, but, even though precise comparison is not possible, the question has enough similarities with the question in table 9 to be instructive. In 1951, 63% were willing to go to war to stop the spread. A difference seems to be present.

It would also be interesting to have earlier polls to compare with one result in the Chicago Council poll of 1974. The respondents were presented with a list of eighteen "possible foreign policy goals that the United States might have." Each was to be rated on its importance. "Containing communism" was first on the list in the questionnaire. Fully 13% of the public (and 16% of the leaders sampled) found this to be "not important at all" as a goal, and 27% (and 49% of the leaders) found it to be only "somewhat important."[20]

With respect to opinion about military intervention abroad, then, the data seem to be suggesting one constancy and one change from the days of the cold war. Americans seem to be about as willing as ever to aid friendly countries, particularly major allies, if they suffer foreign invasion; but Americans also seem to be less willing to agree to military intervention aimed merely at stopping the spread of communism. To simplify, it seems that public support in the mid-1970s for another war like Korea might be as high as it ever was, but that support for another Vietnam would be lower. The public's apparent ability to contain its enthusiasm for Secretary of State Henry Kissinger's 1975 gambol in Angola is entirely consistent with these findings.

Trends in Isolationism

Table 10 supplies poll data gathered over the last twenty-one years on several isolationist questions—ones which ask respondents whether they would prefer the United States to be an active participant in world affairs or to have it be aloof and independent.

Table 10: Questions on Isolationism, 1945-76

A. "Do you think it will be best for the future of this country if we take an active part in world affairs, or if we stay out of world affairs?" (NORC, AIPO)

B. "Do you feel that since the war this country has gone too far in concerning itself with problems in other parts of the world, or not?" (NORC, SRC)

C. "Would it be better for the United States to keep independent in world affairs—or would it be better for the United States to work closely with other nations?" (AIPO)

D. "The United States should mind its own business internationally and let other countries get along as best they can on their own. Do you agree or disagree?" (GOI)

For each question the numbers represent, in order, the percentages with an isolationist response, an interventionist response, and no opinion.

	A			B			C			D		
	Stay Out	Active Part	No Opinion	Too Far	Not	No Opinion	Keep Independent	Work Closely	No Opinion	Mind Business	No	No Opinion
October 1945	19	70	11									
1947	25	68	7									
April 1949				41	50	9						
September 1949	25	67	8									
October 1949				48	41	11						
January 1950	24	57	9									
June 1950				36	54	10						
November 1950	25	64	11									
December 1950	25	66	9	36	48	13						
October 1952	23	68	9	55[a]	32	12						
February 1953	22	73	5									
August 1953							15	78	7			
September 1953	21	71	8									
April 1954	25	69	6									
October 1954				41[a]	46	12						
March 1955	21	72	7									
November 1956	25	71	4									
April 1963							10	2	8			
October 1964	16	79	5									
June 1965							16	79	5	18	70	12
1967												
February 1968										27	66	7
February 1969							22	72	6			
1972										35	56	9
March 1973	32	65	4									
January 1974										41	47	12
December 1974	24	66	10									
Spring 1975	35	60	4							36	52	12
Spring 1976	32	63	5							41	49	10

Sources: Mueller, Wars, Presidents and Public Opinion, p. 110; Rielly, American Public Opinion, p. 12; Current Opinion, April 1975; NORC Codebooks; Watts and Free, "Nationalism, Not Isolationism," p. 17.

[a] "Some people think that since the end of the last world war this country has gone too far in concerning itself with problems in other parts of the world. How do you feel about this?" (SRC) Qualified isolationist and internationalist responses are included in the figures given; they total 9% and 7% for the 1952 survey, respectively, and 6% and 6% for the 1954 survey.

Isolationism so measured grew during the Vietnam War, as it did, at least in the responses to question B, during the Korean War. Some of this perceived growth during the 1960s may be artifact, however. Isolationism, as measured by the A, C, and (presumably) D questions, was at a historic low in the 1963–65 period as the Vietnam War was beginning–an effect, perhaps, of American success during the Cuban Missile Crisis and of the improving relations with the Soviet Union. To a degree, then, Vietnam may have caused isolationism to increase to more historical levels.

Nevertheless, the figures for the mid-1970s in the A and D columns are generally quite high. The question is, will they remain so? The evidence is mixed.

Tracing the A question, one sees an unprecedently high isolationism reading in spring 1973, in the aftermath of the "Peace with Honor" settlement in Vietnam. In the Chicago Council survey of December 1974, however, isolationist sentiment had again slumped to its general historical average–normalcy, perhaps. But the spring 1975 reading, in the midst of the Indochina collapse, is again quite high, a particularly remarkable change because this rather bland question has proved to be, generally, rather imperturbable, as poll questions go. By spring 1976, isolationism had perhaps begun to decline again.

On the other hand, the behavior of the generally more volatile question D is essentially in the opposite direction: isolationism down in 1975, up in 1976.

It seems safe to conclude, then, that isolationism in the wake of the Vietnam War was higher than ever before, but it would be unwise to speculate about whether this phenomenon will prove to be lasting.[21]

Support for Defense Spending

Historical poll data demonstrate rather clearly that popular support for cutbacks in defense expenditures became far higher in the 1970s and late 1960s than it was during the cold war period. Russett has presented data on this,[22] and table 11 gives samples from his data from the 1950s and updates his findings for the period since 1969 (see also table 1).

In the 1950s, support for reductions in defense expenditures was comparatively low. For example, question B in table 11, asked in 1957, found only 9% supporting reduction, even though the question contained the reminder that "the biggest part of government spending goes for defense."

The C and D questions allow a comparison between spring 1960 and the late 1960s (unfortunately, no good data for the time in between seem to exist). A rather dramatic change is evident.

Then the D and E series indicate that the change was not a fleeting one–it persisted into the mid-1970s. The data from 1976 indicate a little mellowing, but certainly not back to the level of the 1950s.

Finally, the F and G questions, which are of substantially different form than the others and can only be compared to each other, also suggest a degree of

Table 11: Attitudes on Defense Spending, 1951-76

A. "During the coming year, do you think we should cut down the amount we are spending on our rearmament program, keep it about the same, or spend even more on our armed forces?" (NORC 302) (NORC 334)

| April | 1951 | Cut down | 8% | Keep same | 39% | Spend more | 44% | DK | 9% |
| December | 1952 | | 11 | | 52 | | 31% | | 6 |

October 1955 Same, except "arms program" instead of "rearmament program" (NORC 378)

| | | Cut down | 8% | Keep same | 60% | Spend more | 26% | DK | 6% |

B. "The biggest part of government spending goes for defense. Do you think this sum should be increased, decreased, or kept about the same as it was last year?" (AIPO 579)

February 1957 Decreased 9%

C. "There is much discussion as to the amount this country should spend for national defense. How do you feel about this—do you think we are spending too little, too much, or about the right amount?"

| Spring | 1960 | Too much | 18% | About right | 45% | Too little | 21% | DK | 16% |

D. Same, except "the government in Washington should spend for national defense and military purposes" instead of "the country should spend for national defense."

July	1969	Too much	52%	About right	31%	Too little	8%	DK	9%
November	1969		46						
March	1971		49		31		11		9
February	1973		42		40		8		10
September	1973		46		30		13		11
September	1974		44		32		12		12
February	1976		36		32		22		10

E. "We are faced with many problems in the country, none of which can be solved easily or inexpensively. I'm going to name some of these problems, and for each one I would like you to tell me whether you think we're spending too much money on it, too little money, or about the right amount . . . (9) the military, armaments and defense."

April	1973	Too much	38%	About right	45%	Too little	11%	DK	6%
April	1974		31		45		17		7
April	1975		31		46		17		7
Spring	1976		27		42		24		7

F. "Choose between "The Federal government should reduce spending for military and defense purposes" and "The Federal government should not reduce spending for military and defense purposes."

| October | 1974 | Reduce spending | 55% | | Not reduce spending | 45% |

G. "Government spending for military defense should be reduced."

| February | 1976 | Agree | 37% | Disagree | 52% | No opinion | 11% |

Sources: Bruce Russett "Revolt of the Masses;" NORC Codebooks; GOI 112, October 1974; NDPSS Codebooks; GOI 113, November 1974; New York Times, February 13, 1976; GOI 129, April 1976.

mellowing in 1976—though, again, still not to the levels of the 1950s (similar questions from that time cited by Russett generate much lower support for reductions).[23]

While support for cutting back defense spending reached higher levels in the 1970s than in earlier years, Rielly's analysis of the 1974 Chicago data suggests that this support was by no means firm and unyielding.[24] He finds that around half of those in favor of defense reductions could be dissuaded if they were convinced that reduced spending either would increase unemployment or would cause the United States to fall behind the Soviet Union in military strength. Accordingly, any politician inclined to see reduced defense spending as a popular issue must bear in mind the fact that it would become far less popular if the opposition were able successfully to raise the specter of potential Communist superiority or of unemployment. The conduct of the candidates in the 1976 election—when Jimmy Carter soft-pedaled his previous support for cutbacks in defense expenditures—suggests the soundness of Rielly's observation.

CONCLUSIONS

On the basis of the available data, it has been argued that there are two important elements in American perspectives toward international affairs in the mid-1970s. First, in the persistent atmosphere of détente with the Soviet Union and, to a degree, with mainland China, the American public came to be far less fearful of a major war and found less urgency in international affairs in general than was the case in the 1940s, 1950s, and 1960s. Second, the public weathered the war in Vietnam and the final collapse there with remarkable equanimity.

With these elements as background, trends in American popular perspectives toward three specific areas of international behavior were assessed: attitudes toward military involvement, attitudes toward isolationism, and attitudes toward defense spending.

American attitudes toward *military involvement* seem unchanged in one area, changed in another. Despite the experience of Vietnam, the public did not appear to be distinctly less willing than it once was to come to the aid of a friendly power that is subjected to invasion by a Communist power. In particular, it would seem that popular support for commitments to defend places like Western Europe or Japan against Communist attack was about as high as ever. On the other hand, the Vietnam experience and the reduced sense of urgency apparently reduced support for the idea of going to war, or using armed force, simply to prevent the "spread" of communism to other areas.

In general it seems, therefore, that the public remained willing to stand behind firm defense commitments to major allies if they are attacked, but became less willing than it once was to support intervention designed to stop communism when the threat is less than a direct military attack.

American attitudes toward *isolationism* changed to a degree. Isolationism grew somewhat during the Vietnam War, as it had during the Korean War. It is not clear how lasting this increased isolationism might be, however. Some polls suggest a mellowing of isolationism by 1976; others found it persisting.

American attitudes toward *defense spending* were considerably different in the 1970s than they had been in the 1950s and early 1960s: support for a cutback in defense spending was far higher, though this support was by no means firm and unyielding. Some of this is to be expected in the wake of Vietnam, a disillusioning experience with military force if there ever was one. In addition, the decline of international tensions is also relevant. If military expenditures are in part a preparation for war, and if war—at least thermonuclear war—seems less likely to occur, it makes sense to some (though it might seem folly to others) to relax this preparedness somewhat and to use the money for other purposes. Arguments in favor of military spending are much more likely to convince someone who fears a major war within the next two years than they are to convince someone who sees no such imminent calamity. And, as the data presented above suggest, while many people at various points in the cold war saw a major war as imminent, fewer seemed so concerned by the mid-1970s.

NOTES

1. A number of abbreviations are used to cite these data sources: AIPO (American Institute of Public Opinion—the Gallup poll); *GOI (Gallup Opinion Index)* The number following citation refers to issue; NORC (National Opinion Research Center); NDPSS (National Data Program for the Social Sciences—General Social Survey); and SRC (Survey Research Center).

2. See John E. Rielly, *American Public Opinion and U.S. Foreign Policy* (Chicago: Chicago Council on Foreign Relations, 1975).

3. Another concern is sampling variability, particularly if data going back to the 1940s are used. See John E. Mueller, *War, Presidents and Public Opinion* (New York: Wiley, 1973), chap. 1; and Norval D. Glenn, "Problems of Comparability in Trend Studies with Opinion Poll Data," *Public Opinion Quarterly* 34 (Spring 1970): 82-94.

4. Rielly, *American Public Opinion*, p. 16.

5. We can also compare them with our expectations of how the poll should come out—for what that is worth. The precise figures on a poll do have concrete meaning sometimes—if they are measuring a simple, specific behavioral act (like voting) rather than attitudes or opinion. See Mueller, *War, Presidents and Public Opinion.*

6. For more detail, see John E. Mueller, "Public Expectations of War," (Paper delivered at the American Political Science Association Convention, September 1975).

7. Data from Roper Public Opinion Research Center, Williamstown, Mass.

8. NDPSS Codebooks. A somewhat related set of questions appeared in polls conducted during the 1960s and 1970s. The question was, "Under present circumstances, how worried or concerned are you about the danger of a major world war breaking out in the near future?" A composite score on this question of 90 (out of a maximum possible of 100) was registered in 1964. This slid to 83 in 1968, to 66 in 1972, to 65 in 1974, and then rose somewhat to 74 in 1976. William Watts and Lloyd A. Free, "Nationalism, Not

Isolationism," *Foreign Policy* (Fall 1976): 11; idem, *State of the Nation* (New York: Universe Books, 1973), pp. 39, 280.

9. See also Rielly, *American Public Opinion,* p. 10. While tensions over a *major* war relaxed, the Vietnam experience suggested to the public that other kinds of war were still possible. One question, "Do you expect the United States to fight in another war [not a *world* or *major* or *nuclear* war] within the next 10 years?" found 56% answering affirmatively in spring 1973 in the wake of the Vietnam "Peace with Honor" settlement. In spring 1975, in the context of the Indochina collapse, this figure rose to 70%, then declined to 57% in spring 1976 (NDPSS Codebooks).

10. Mueller, *War, Presidents and Public Opinion,* pp. 2, 113-14n.

11. *Current Opinion* (September 1976).

12. Watts and Free, "Nationalism, Not Isolationism," pp. 9-10.

13. The Korean War is also seen as an especially "dark moment," and it may be that the agonies of Vietnam have helped to reduce the retrospective popularity of the earlier war. For some evidence on this point, see Mueller, *War, Presidents and Public Opinion,* pp. 171-72. The popularity of the Cuban Missile Crisis on this list seems rather low—particularly since President Kennedy's name is specifically associated with it.

14. Rielly, *American Public Opinion,* p..9.

15. Bruce Russett and Miroslav Nincic, "American Opinion on the Use of Military Force Abroad," Yale University, n.d.

16. One question on the Chicago Council survey generated a fantastically *low* percentage in favor of not intervening: "Now let me hand you this card with four statements on it. Please read these four statements and tell me which *one* comes closest to describing your own view of what the United States should do *if friendly countries are attacked.*" The response was as follows:

23%   The United States should send *military*   aid, economic aid, and, if necessary, send *American troops and manpower.*

37   We might send some *military aid* as well as *economic aid,* but we should not involve any American troops or manpower.

22   We might send some *economic aid,* but we should not send military aid and should not involve any American troops or manpower.

9   The United States should *not* send any military aid or economic aid, and should *not* send any American troops or manpower.

9   Not sure

This question generates only 9% in favor of doing nothing, the lowest percentage favoring complete nonintervention on any poll I have seen dealing with this general issue. The reason for this, of course, is not that total isolationism fell into severe disfavor in December 1974, but rather that the third alternative, proposing a very modest kind of aid, is unique in the questions used on this topic and proves to be very seductive to many of those who would otherwise opt for the fourth alternative (and perhaps to others as well). Accordingly, the question cannot be used for making historical comparisons. (Chicago Council Codebooks.)

17. Watts and Free ("Nationalism, Not Isolationism," p. 17) find a parallel dip and rise for Japan: "The United States should come to the defense of Japan with military force if it is attacked by Soviet Russia or Communist China."

	1972	1974	1975	1976
Agree	43%	37%	42%	45%
Disagree	40	42	39	37
Don't know	17	21	19	18

Other related data: the percentage who professed to worry a "great deal" or a "fair amount" about "maintaining close relations with our allies and keeping our military alliances strong" stood at 68% in a 1964 poll and *rose* to 75% in 1968, remained the same in

1972 (Watts and Free, *State of the Nation* [1973], p. 39), and rose further to 78% in 1974 (William Watts and Lloyd A. Free, *State of the Nation, 1974* [Washington, D.C.: Potomac Associates, 1974], p. 320).

18. Watts and Free, *State of the Nation* (1973), p. 39; idem, "Nationalism, Not Isolationism," p. 11. Interestingly, while the public may be less belligerently anti-Communist than it once was, it does not appear to be less hostile to communism as a form of government. One poll question asked, "Thinking about the different kinds of governments in the world today, which of these statements comes closest to how you feel about communism as a form of government: It's the worst form of all; It's bad, but no worse than some others; It's all right for some countries; It's a good form of government." Posed three times between 1973 and 1976, the question found some shift *toward* the perspective that "Communism is the worst form of all" (NDPSS Codebooks).

19. NORC Codebooks.

20. Rielly, *American Public Opinion*, p. 13; and Chicago Council Codebooks.

21. Watts and Free have compiled a composite internationalist/isolationist index; its behavior between 1964 and 1976 is plotted in Watts and Free, "Nationalism, Not Isolationism," p. 21. To create this index they have homogenized the results of several questions (five in 1964 and 1968, seven in the later years), a procedure that is dangerous at best. One of the questions included is agreement or disagreement with this statement: "The United States should cooperate fully with the United Nations." Agreement with the statement, not surprisingly, dropped enormously (from 72% to 46%) over the period. While this reflects clear disillusionment with the United Nations, it is not clear how this specific attitude relates to the more general phenomenon of isolationism. One could give up on the United Nations without giving up on internationalism.

22. Bruce M. Russett, "The Revolt of the Masses: Public Opinion on Military Expenditures," in *New Civil-Military Relations*, ed. John P. Lovell and Philip S. Kronenberg (New Brunswick, N.J.: Transaction, 1974), pp. 57-88.

23. Not only was there far more support in the mid-1970s for cutbacks in military spending, but, unlike the situation in the 1950s, the setiment for such reduction came disproportionately from the attentive public. The Chicago Council survey found its sample of national leaders in 1974 to be substantially more in favor of defense reductions than the general public (Rielly, *American Public Opinion*, pp. 16-17). And the Gallup breakdowns by education for question D in table 10 for the 1969-74 period show the college-educated to be 10 or more percentage points more likely to support cutbacks in defense than the grade-school educated *GOI* 50, 71, 101, and 112). By contrast, NORC breakdowns for question A (in table 11) in the 1950s either show the college-educated to be 15 percentage points more in favor of spending *increases* (April 1951) or else they find little difference by education (December 1952 and October 1955) (NORC Codebooks). There may have been some mellowing on this score also. The Gallup responses to the D question in 1976 show the college-educated to be only 5 percentage points more in favor of defense cuts *(GOI* 129). Part of this may be a kind of "follower" effect among the better-educated (see Mueller, *War, Presidents and Public Opinion*, chaps. 4 and 5). See also Russett, "The Revolt of the Masses"; and Bruce Russett, "The Americans' Retreat from World Power," *Political Science Quarterly* 90 (Spring 1975): 1-22. Incidentally, it should not be assumed, in assessing these questions, that the public has any confident *quantitative* feel for the level of defense spending. In July 1969 and again in February 1976 Gallup asked, "Offhand, do you happen to recall about how much of every *dollar* is now spent for military and defense purposes?" Fully 70% refused to guess, and most of those who did were pretty far off *(GOI* 50, p. 10; *GOI* 129, p. 21). See also Mueller, *War, Presidents and Public Opinion*, pp. 62-63.

24. Rielly, *American Public Opinion*, pp. 16-17.

NATIONAL DECISION MAKING AND

MILITARY INTERVENTION

Paul R. Schratz

The collapse of U.S. policy in Vietnam raises fundamental questions on the future role of military force in support of American foreign policy and the processes by which national decisions involving the resort to force are made. In an era of increasing complexity in the interrelation of politics, economics, and security, direct use of military power appears to be of declining utility even though world leaders see armaments to be of increasing necessity. The military profession, as a consequence, finds itself shaken by two revolutions—externally in strategy and policy, internally in technology and organization. Fundamental questions arise on the structure of national decision making and the strategic and tactical doctrines upon which such actions are based.

Of primary interest to our inquiry is a careful examination of the governmental structure for the conduct of foreign policy that was completed by the Commission on the Organization of the Government for the Conduct of Foreign Policy, the so-called Murphy Commission, on June 30, 1975.[1] Particularly important is an appended contract research program on national security policy and the conduct of future war. Many questions arise. What are proper restraints on military intervention? How does the structure give appropriate weight to perspectives and political, military, economic, and social interest in policy making? Congressional influence as a conditioning and limiting factor in the exercise of military power is too often neglected. What are proper criteria by which the national security organization should be both shaped and judged? How does American tradition influence policy making both affirmatively and negatively? What general tasks are performed by the "Permanent Government," and how can the existing balance of interests and perspectives, vested and weighted in the 1940s to meet the problems of a cold war era, be shaped to achieve American purposes in the world of the 1980s? The commission devoted primary scrutiny to executive-congressional relationships and, within the executive branch, to the interrelationships of State, Defense, and other departments and agencies in the national security apparatus. Too little study was devoted to internal considerations relative to the Defense role in national security policy, however, and a preliminary examination is necessary in this respect.

I

The American approach to war, and particularly the role of the military in shaping and pursuing foreign policy goals, is unique in many respects. American policy makers and the structure of the American policy machinery rarely stimulate consideration of war as an instrument of policy as Clausewitz saw it. War is not visualized as an integral and unavoidable part of political evolution but as a lamentable aberration, a detour in the historical process, a moral evil. Clausewitz claimed that war is merely another kind of writing and language for statesmen, and that the thread of policy must run through the intervening period of hostilities to the peace beyond.

The writings of Mahan on the influence of sea power on history shaped the imperial policies of Britain, Japan, and Germany at the turn of the twentieth century. In the U.S. they stimulated new thinking toward a closer relation of military power to the needs of national security. Political and military leaders proposed a Council of National Defense on several occasions, prior to World War I, to shape U.S. planning toward two principles: (1) war is an extension of politics; and (2) wars, if fought, would be short, offensive, and waged with resources stockpiled at the outbreak. The experience of war, 1914-18, drastically changed thinking on both premises. The stalemated war on the Western front, rather than an extension of politics, was something completely separate from other aspects of the nation's life, and economic mobilization became the single most important ingredient of military victory in modern wars.

Over the years these postwar convictions increasingly shaped attitudes toward national security planning. Interest in political-military planning fell to a dangerously low level. Thoughts about war were far more drastic than they might otherwise have been. Emerging doctrines on the role of air power, applied later to intercontinental missiles, showed a purely punitive function wholly removed from political purpose. The emphasis on national economic mobilization was greatly expanded and war once again became wholly separate from politics.[2]

The isolation of war from politics stimulated pursuit of idealistic goals as the precondition for peace—"unconditional surrender," "there is no substitute for victory." Even when the diplomat and the warrior seemed to speak in the same tongue, as in Korea and Vietnam, the dialect was not the same. Lacking a close interrelationship between war and policy, the U.S. developed a remarkable capacity to defeat the enemy in the field, yet could neither prevent war from occurring nor achieve a satisfactory peace in the aftermath. War seen as a necessary evil becomes a crusade. American wars fought as crusades were eminently successful in the field; the question remains as to how well the political objectives were served by resort to the force of arms.

The cleavage in American thought in the relation of politics and power, of diplomacy and war, has unfortunate consequences. Limiting themselves to the military aspects of policy as properly their concern, the military leaders' participation in the policy process contributes to strategic and doctrinal deficiencies that prevent conceptualizing force in other terms. War becomes a contest of logistics rather than of politics.

On the civilian side, important political consequences inextricably embedded in events are traditionally isolated from policy as "purely military matters." The self-imposed isolation of political and military elements generates overreliance on military considerations and too easily subordinates national goals to military policy. Political leaders have rarely understood fully the role—and limitations—of military power in seeking the ends of policy. Military leaders, through misguided deference to the principle of civilian control of the military, are overreluctant to participate fully in the policy process. The result, therefore, is an enigma of policy devoid of military participation yet dominated by military considerations. In Vietnam, civilian deference to military advice, dominated by "purely military considerations," contributed to overmilitarization of an essentially political problem, to pursuit of a guerrilla war with conventional field tactics, and to measurement of success in the field in engineering rather than in political terms.

The American experience in war isolated the exercise of power vertically from its admixture with policy and horizontally from a cooperative and unified land, sea, and air effort. Behind a façade of voluntary cooperation, the Army, Navy and Air Force went separate ways in separate worlds. Despite spasmodic attempts at coordination, there was no liaison with the State Department to either complicate or enrich planning; prior to World War II, no agency short of the President himself existed to coordinate the Army, Navy, and State Departments, or the output in national policy, strategy, operations, and weaponry. Common or joint activities of the military services in peace and war were governed by the principle of "mutual cooperation." The services were not really expected to coordinate with the State Department. Wartime commanders were expected to reach friendly agreement on how best to coordinate forces in battle; the goals both presumably sought were accepted as given. Cooperation was a wholly individual action, and the lack of it, even when deliberate and at a critical moment, was rarely called to account until the failure of cooperation, both political and military, contributed to a national disaster at Pearl Harbor.[3]

Despite the weaknesses, coordination among the military services went far beyond that achieved in adapting military means to the aims of foreign policy. The institutions necessary for a sustaining and evolving civil-military relationship prior to World War II simply failed to develop. Army and Navy officers frequently had a voice in foreign policy decisions, and were often used by State as an alternate source of information on conditions abroad, but there was always tension: the military officer did not want to exercise a "political" role, to share in the actual policy making process. He preferred to be furnished with firm guidelines and directives on policy needs. The officers of the Army and Navy were insufficiently educated in political affairs, were isolated from the mainstream of civilian thought, as well as from policy making, and were often compelled to rely on their own insufficient sources of information.[4] In consequence, they were victims of a world outlook which caused them to interpret international events almost exclusively in terms of strife and conflict, competition and war—interpretations, therefore, bordering on fantasy.

No U.S. war plan before 1939 recognized that we might be called upon to fight alongside allies. The unified and combined commands of World War II and Korea were neither fully unified nor directly responsive to their designated commanders. Forces were normally assigned for tactical operations only; for other functions the parent services were in a controlling position. The role of diplomacy was rarely considered, and still more rarely thought to be relevant.

Yet the "military mind" existed almost as frequently in civilian as in military circles: if the military leaders were not able to effectively plan the closely integrated use of force in politics, the diplomatic service was even less able to do so. In the rare cases where particular diplomats may have had a clear perception of the skilled use of force, the weakness of State Department organization, and its extreme reluctance toward coordinated planning with the military in any form, frustrated execution. Through World War II there was, in short, no effective reconciliation of force with diplomacy in the U.S. policy process. Further, policy makers had no conception that courses of action which they generally viewed as altruistic often succeeded in building, in the long term, only resentment.

II

With the establishment, in 1947, of a formal "national security" organization, the primacy of the State Department as the key organ for the practice of diplomacy was superseded. The National Security Act sought primarily a new and unified organizational structure for security policy at the national level. The primary goal was unification of the armed services; political, military, and, to a degree, economic coordination were secondary. Even though the integration of national political, military, and economic resources under a common structure modified considerably the traditional role of the department, State still was not consulted in the early congressional hearings with Army and Navy military and civilian leaders; with unification, processes of international diplomacy, long a sacred preserve of the diplomat, passed into the realm of an interagency council. A great many issues heretofore negotiated in direct bilateral discussions now came properly within the function of the National Security Council.

The 1947 national security organization, at best a transition affair, underwent a decade of legislative change before emerging, under Eisenhower's impetus in 1958, as a reasonably sophisticated *formal* structure for national security planning and decision making. Separate sea, land, and air warfare were gone, and defense planning was placed on a national basis, with military control to be exercised through functional unified commands utilizing elements of any or all of the services. The services retained ground, sea, and air roles to "provide, train, and equip" forces for the unified combatant commands. In Eisenhower's words,

> Complete unity in our strategic planning and operational direction is vital. It is therefore mandatory that the initiative for this planning and direction rest not with the separate services but directly with the Secretary of Defense and his operational advisers, the JCS. . . .
>
> No military task is of greater importance than the development of strategic plans. . . . Genuine unity is indispensable at this starting point. No amount of subsequent coordination can eliminate duplication or doctrinal conflicts which are intruded into the first shaping of military programs.[5]

Nevertheless, the responsibility for "the first shaping" of strategic planning and doctrinal development by the Joint Chiefs of Staff—repeated three times in the Eisenhower message—was delegated by them to the services, where large and prestigious staffs dominate the planning process.

Pertinent Army, Navy, and Air Force manuals continue to underplay joint roles and to propagandize service values.[6] National objectives are referred to only casually and in broad, general, philosophical terms. Air Force doctrines are offensive and punitive, while Army and Navy doctrines are defensive and retaliatory; for the Air Force visualizes a short war of extreme violence, and the Army and Navy see longer wars of attrition.

Such doctrinal guidelines are grossly inadequate for joint, multiservice, or national needs; they are inadequate for service needs as well. The strategy they define emerges without political content, and joint doctrine for multiservice operations thirty years and two wars later remains in a primitive state of development. The important and unresolved question is, how can one train commanders for the needs of future way if they do not in their career experience, study or develop or exercise joint doctrine essential to leading such forces in future war?

In the military strategic planning void, it was the political leadership which took the initiative in major postwar strategic revisions of 1950, 1953, 1961, and 1967. The irrelevance of doctrines such as massive retaliation, however, indicates a void in political-military thinking and in the proper role of force in diplomatic, economic, and other policies which it presumably serves. The relation of power and values, war and diplomacy, has not been bridged. The McNamara revolution affected primarily the *managerial* function of Defense. It was hardly in the interest of the defense secretary to further unify the military services in their *operational* role. Systems analysis made the services more competitive in weapons procurement but, since they lacked either a doctrinal base or true joint goals, it further intensified parochial differences. Managerial efficiency plus doctrinal deficiency in Vietnam combined to prove to the world that the ability to manage a war is not the same as the ability to fight one. In sum, the Defense reorganization in 1958 contributed significantly to a sound *formal* structure for the department, but the *informal* organization for national security planning substituted horizontal bargaining and interservice rivalry for traditional vertical military-civilian bargaining.

The Secretary of Defense rarely considers the Joint Chiefs of Staff as his planning body, and it functions only marginally as an advisory body in national decision making. In its foreign policy role, therefore, the Defense-JCS structure can hardly be classed as adequate, the defects being conceptual and administrative as well as organizational.

The continued rejection, implicit or explicit, of the premise that war is an instrument of policy stimulates overreaction and overmilitarization. The diplomat, hopelessly outclassed through his own contingency planning weaknesses, defers to the military leadership. The JCS, which defers on political issues to the State Department and the White House, produces military advice largely devoid of political content.[7] In a world where no problem is strictly military or strictly political, the policy void has limitations on both sides. Every recent president has found it necessary to ask the JCS to base its advice not only on narrow military considerations but on broad-gauged political and economic factors as well. Military problems cannot be looked at as self-contained technical issues to be treated without regard to their political context (as in the classic example of Herman Kahn's *On Thermonuclear War)*, nor can they be transformed into something approaching an exact science endowed with strictly defined concepts, rigorous analysis, and quantitatively distinguishable models. A national security structure formally involving the Pentagon in policy making in theory, therefore, has in practice operated to reduce the political content and to rationalize foreign policies in military terms. The military concentration on the means of applying force in ways subtle and unsubtle distorts policy making in any other terms. Political problems considered in military terms emphasize military options; superior Pentagon staffing soon makes them military problems.[8]

The national strategic planning deficiencies can be classed as a lack of positive, general, near-term goals, a lack of unity of purpose in joint aims, and a lack of a body of basic doctrine in current unified operations. These deficiencies keep the military chiefs prisoners of the separate services which they head. Admirals and generals who think in service terms in peacetime can hardly be expected to plan in unified terms in war; strategic planning as a service function rather than as a unified function grossly limits their conceptual grasp. The doctrinal void both limits the quality of advice to the civilian leadership in national planning and frequently places a straitjacket on operational performance in the field. The emerging unity among the services developing from closer interrelation of functions requires further organizational change before operational necessity and the growing harmony of function can hope to overcome traditional service methods of doing business. The need for increasing participation of Defense in the policy process should be recognized and encouraged, not for the purpose of aiding the domination of policy issues where responsibility lies elsewhere, but to diminish the tendency to rationalize foreign policies in military terms.

The paradox of alienation from, and domination of, policy by Defense interests, in short, constitutes the milieu in which the Murphy Commission sought to devise a more effective organization of national security elements in the conduct of foreign policy.

III

The commission, looking externally at the national security function, found that a primary problem for the President was the need for alternate sources of advice on military issues—including honest dissent from the established view. Morton Halperin points out that the military has a virtual monopoly on providing information about readiness and capabilities of U.S. or even allied forces and the effectiveness of American combat operations. The prestige and influence of the military leaders, particularly in their relations with Congress (and the right to inform congressional committees directly of their differences with administration policy) highlights the difficulty. On a diplomatic move, the President can turn to career foreign service officers, businessmen, intelligence specialists, and others for legitimate advice; such alternative sources are rare in the military. In addition, the personal style of the President and his advisers exerts a paramount role in decision making. The structure should allow an opportunity for a serious look at Defense matters from other than a Defense viewpoint at preselected critical or turning points. The importance of such a review has been well stated by a qualified student of national security organization:

> When individuals in the U.S. Government consider a proposed policy change, they see quite different things. A proposal to withdraw American troops from Europe, for example, is to the Army a threat to its value, a threat to its command organization, its budget and size; to OMB a way to save money; to Treasury a balance-of-payments gain; to State a threat to good relations with NATO; to the president's Congressional Advisor an opportunity to remove a major irritant in the President's relations with the Congress. The differences come from the differing currencies in which they define the issue as well as the stake—whether they see a threat or an opportunity.[9]

Each participant sees the issue within the extremes of threat and opportunity. Within each agency, vested interests present divergent views which cloud agency positions. The heart of the American system of policy making is a resolution of competing interests. The military establishment must take political, military, and other factors increasingly into account, and its executive group must blend the wisdom of civilian and military personnel. In order for a military establishment to function—and recognizing that military force has no intrinsic worth aside from its utility in achieving political ends—it must have purpose, policy, objective, and scope. These are determined by the political authority, with due regard for the role of other agencies in national security planning, primarily through a much clearer mandate and responsibility for subordinate actions, including a wide choice of alternative and dissenting views prior to choice.

Perhaps the real value of the Murphy Commission findings emerges more in the contract research program, in the conception of the problem of organizing for foreign affairs, than in the substantive recommendations. The central issue in organizing for foreign affairs appeared to be the vesting and weighting of perspectives and interests—not in organization per se, but rather in *which* perspectives are introduced and *what* weights are given in regular processes of decision and action.

In the commission study of defense and arms control, the three general tasks seen as performed by a government organization are as follows:

Structuring the Permanent Government. The national security organization represented initially the perspectives and interests set up in response to problems of the cold war of the late 1940s. Is the present balance of perspectives and interests appropriate for achieving American purposes as shaped and weighted by an admittedly bloated national security establishment of the 1970s and 1980s, 99% of whom are members of the Permanent Government, an executive establishment that does not change with presidents or administrations?

Managing the Departments and Agencies. Given the structure and processes of the Permanent Government, is the balance between departments and their political managers appropriate for the problems of the late 1970s and 1980s, and are the skills of the department managers, given the instruments they control, adequate for the job?

Central Decision and Coordination. Often ill-defined and poorly recognized, the problem of central decision and coordination has dominated discussion of national security organization for a decade and a half. Judgments must be made as to (1) whether the principal formal mechanism for central coordination, the NSC, is sufficiently broad in perspective for present and future problems; (2) whether the sharp line between domestic and foreign policy issues in both formal and informal coordinating mechanisms is appropriate for current problems; and (3) whether the search should continue for a single, dominant mechanism to perform the task of central decision and coordination.

In the structure of the Permanent Government with respect to military intervention, for example, a remarkable change has occurred. Before World War

II, the number of U.S. military and government employees concerned with foreign affairs was minuscule; today it is enormous, organized by function and agency to deal with the multiple facets of international affairs wherein each department has a partial, deliberately parochial definition of "the problem" of foreign policy. Such factors conspire to produce and nourish vested interests regardless of the administration in power. For example, Secretary of Defense McNamara made his fateful choice of the F-lll as the biservice, limited-war fighter plane of the 1960s from a choice of specific operational requirements defined by the Air Force Tactical Air Command alone, and which reflected TAC interests rather than those of the secretary of defense and the President. The fighter that emerged did not have capabilities suited for the Kennedy administration's limited-war strategy but instead was designed for a nuclear mission McNamara meant to deemphasize.

During the period of the cold war, after World War II, we saw that security defined in military terms became the overriding purpose abroad, both in concept and in organizational form. The concept has now changed, but the organizational form remains. In contrast with earlier eras of American history, U.S. foreign policy became substantially "militarized." The predominant feature of the post-World War II quarter-century was the global expansion of American military influence. At the height of this expansion, circa 1968, the U.S. had defense treaties with forty-two nations, 3.5 million men under arms in "peacetime," with 1.1 million stationed abroad, manning 2,200 military bases in thirty-three countries. The Defense bill for the first twenty-five years surpassed a trillion dollars; the foreign aid bill exceeded $150 billion.[10]

The military instrument sought neither control nor domination, but merely a counter to perceived Communist threats to Free World security and independence. Since the principal instrument of involvement was military force, the military and Defense professionals played a primary role both abroad and in Washington. As suggested earlier, the National Security Act of 1947 gave form and structure to the fact that U.S. involvement in foreign affairs would no longer be a responsibility for representation and negotiation by the State Department but would involve many departments, primarily Defense and the military departments as partners in providing for U.S. national security. The "Declaration of Policy" introducing the 1947 act states as much. From that time, principal declarations of U.S. foreign policy objectives and directives became Basic *National Security* Policy, *National Security* Action Memoranda, and *National Security* Decision Memoranda.

Militarization of foreign policy resulted not from independent action by military leaders, nor from organizational structure, but primarily from the conceptions and judgments of presidents and largely civilian advisers about the importance of the military threat. This was powerfully reinforced by the ease of mobilizing support in Congress and in the country for foreign policy objectives justified in military terms, and the ease of White House entry into tough bureaucratic issues of diplomacy or security when symbols of "national security" are involved.

The size, strength, and character of the Department of Defense and the network of troops and advisers abroad substantially affect (1) the recognition of foreign policy problems as "threats" requiring action; (2) the flow of information about problems recognized and unrecognized; (3) the alternative actions and their relative attractiveness; (4) the pressures in decision making; and (5) the character of actions taken. The expansion of the military establishment *followed* expansion of American foreign policy objectives, not vice versa. Once established, the structure continues to influence American foreign policy objectives. The impact we have abroad is not simply a function of people and money, but these indicators are suggestive. The ratio between Defense Department and State Department resources in budget is 150 to 1; in personnel, 30 to 1, in employees abroad, 100 to 1. Pressures toward military intervention in future crises must be examined under these circumstances.

The Murphy Commission case studies document the heavy weight of security considerations defined in military terms rather than in economic, domestic, or foreign policy terms. For example, Defense Department budgets are not formally reviewed by the State Department or other external viewers, although the Office of Management and Budget requests such reviews on other department budgets.[11] Weapons are acquired by a military defining process which in many critical choices are poorly matched to national strategic objectives (F-lll, ABM, FDL); weapons for national purposes which do not reinforce the need of a service develop slowly or not at all (smart bombs, hard-site ABM);[12] and weapons tend to oversophistication and "goldplating," threatening to price the country out of the war-fighting business (MBT-70, Trident). Future requirements for projecting American presence and power require a skillful balance between service conceptions of weapons needs and broader foreign policy objectives. Military strategy and doctrine are frequently deficient, often leaving serious gaps between presidential or secretary of state conceptions and military practice. Glaring divergencies between policy goals and the military conduct of the war appeared in Vietnam.

In structuring the bureaucracy the Permanent Government, in national security affairs as elsewhere, has many incentives to expand and few to contract. Bypass mechanisms are easier to create than to cancel; each administration leaves additional residue for its successors. The Permanent Government has reached elephantine proportions, and the effect on the practice of foreign policy is pernicious. Sheer, unmanageable size is the root problem in Washington and overseas today, in two distinct ways: numbers of people and multiplicity of chains of command. Of the two, the latter is by far the more serious.

The second general task performed by a governmental structure, managing the departments and agencies to achieve national objectives, is particularly important in light of the greatly increased complexity of possible future military interventions. Can one expect the military services to develop weapons the nation needs, such as a missile, when the military leader responsible for the choice may have devoted a career to a manned aircraft or an aircraft carrier?

Despite presidential or secretary of defense initiatives in weapons programs, most of the action most of the time is taken by departments and agencies constituting the Permanent Government (or not taken at all). Departments and agencies are created to pay special attention to particular aspects of a problem. Over time—and not much is required—these organizations develop their own conceptions of how they should fulfill the mission. Organizational structure creates departmental parochialism that is reinforced by the environment; the manner in which departments interpret designated missions reflects the needs of the organization as well as of the mission.

A central role of the President and his administration, therefore, is to appraise needs, judge priorities and the national interest, and ensure that departmental action effectively serves a broader conception of national needs. This is achieved by reorganization where necessary, by use of independent and implementation analysis, by careful attention to personnel recruitment, placement, and training (none of the commission case studies, for example, found a secretary of state making a real effort to manage the activities of the department), and by better understanding of the processes secretaries are charged with managing.

The remaining task performed by a governmental structure is central decision and coordination. As a general rule, foreign relations cannot be separated sharply into "security," "foreign policy," and "economics." They are intermingled, and each is part of a broader problem of domestic politics. Virtually no issue of importance in foreign relations falls exclusively within the domain and control of a single department or agency. An agency is influenced by the perspective and task which are more narrowly its own, by the concerns of its particular impact in national decisions. In the NSC and elsewhere, participants represent agency views; it is extremely difficult to "negotiate" an agency position for the broader goal without loss of prestige and influence within the agency and supporting staff. To a large degree the needs of a President and those of "his" officialdom are incompatible. The critical variable affecting which mechanisms are used is the President himself: his personal preferences and style and the degree to which confidence flows downward.

Efforts to legislate structure for high-level centralized management and decision, therefore, cannot succeed. The NSC exists only to serve the President; he alone can decide on how he wishes to use it. For centralized management and decision on issues in which the President is personally involved, any executive structure that he does not find useful will go unused.

IV

Subject to the above, the national policy and decision processes with respect to military intervention in future crises appear to need several changes, primarily to lessen the militarization of policy options inherent in the present system. The

Murphy Commission contract research program—not seen by the commissioners themselves, unfortunately—suggests a number of corrective measures, including the following:

• Creation of a strong representative of broader security and foreign policy perspectives to identify problems, provide information, devise alternatives, make and implement routine decisions. Preferably this representative would be created within the Department of State at undersecretary level, with an appropriate staff of perhaps one hundred professionals; alternately, it would be a separate unit of a greatly enlarged NSC staff.

• Joint SecState/SecDefense preparation, presentation, and defense of a Foreign and Defense Policy statement to supersede the current Defense Posture Statement. Assuming adequate competence in State, this statement would be presented jointly to the Armed Services and Foreign Relations committees.

• Development of a strong Foreign Service capability for "foreign assessment" in addition to routine political reporting.

• Creation of a Military Operations Analysis Office in OSD focused on military operations and capable of systems analysis and implementation analysis. (Rejected by the SecDef)

• Transfer of military staff responsibility for military operations under unified command to a single military officer with a separate staff for military operations.

• Addition of the secretary of the treasury and the President's scientific and economic advisers to NSC membership and redefinition of assignments of presidential assistants to break down the sharp distinction between "foreign policy" and "domestic" issues. (Not supported by President Ford.)

Throughout the study and research program, the conclusion emerges repeatedly that the national security structure, augmented by a strong and capable Defense staffing organization, is able to, and usually does, overwhelm the presumably dominant State role in policy. Unless the Department of State can be strengthened root and branch, throughout its structure in Washington and abroad, there is little hope that militarization of policy will cease to flourish.

The commission research program identified a number of satellite functions, or subtasks, related to foreign policy which also merit attention. These are (1) implementation; (2) articulating foreign policy goals and guidelines; (3) attending to the longer run; (4) assessing foreign governments; and (5) making ad hoc adjustments for personalities and operating styles. Not included in the commission study, but equally necessary, is (6) follow-up and evaluation of performance.

Implementation is at least half the problem in most important decisions and actions. Presidents and administrations dominate important decisions; bureaucracies dominate implementation. Choice among options rests primarily with the President and his associates. When a decision has been made, the predominant influence over the character of the action shifts to the implementor, generally the Permanent Government. Perceptions, objectives, and constraints differ one from the other. The broader the directive, the wider the latitude for interpretation and for slanting implementation toward the organizational needs and interests of the implementor. The understanding, by policy and program decision makers in both the executive and the legislature, of institutional factors affecting implementation has been poor. The important issue is to narrow the gap between decision and implementation.

Articulating foreign policy goals and guidelines is a difficult and elusive problem. Effective procedures for central decision and coordination on the basis of a reasoned conception of foreign policy objectives will not guarantee an effective American foreign policy. Postwar goals and guidelines have broken down. No longer does the attentive public or other participants in American policy making know what American policy is for and about. Basic assumptions and simplifications about international politics, how to define security, what constitutes threats to the U.S.—earlier axioms have given way to widespread uncertainty on these issues. The chief recent inadequacy in articulating foreign policy goals is nothing more than inattention. Overriding concerns for secrecy, a penchant for puffery, and intolerance for argument or debate cloud both participation and understanding.

Failure in *attending to the longer run* usually follows overconcentration on the immediate at the expense of the important, and a government tendency to react to problems rather than to initiate solutions. Policy choices should be made on the best projections of longer-run consequences, a difficult alternative frequently because of uncertainty about the future and the possible sacrifice of immediate needs. The circumstances of decision making in the U.S. government—short terms in office, domestic constituencies—tend to shorten the time horizon. Improved long-run perspectives require higher-quality forecasting, better long-term judgment in the regular processes of governmental decision, a heightened awareness of the importance of long-term consequences, better longer-run planning staffs and advisory panels, better understanding of the dynamics of change, and longer-term (five-year) funding authorizations.

The task of *assessing foreign governments* is a critical component of foreign policy choice: understanding why foreign governments take certain actions, predicting actions they are likely to take, predicting the effect of proposed U.S. initiatives (and redesigning U.S. actions to achieve the desired impact). The U.S. government has not been well served in foreign assessment. Presidents and other policy makers have not understood why foreign governments took certain actions, have acted on poor choices about actions of allies and opponents, and have formulated U.S. actions which have been counterproductive. Assessing foreign governments is a major function of State (where it is called "political reporting and analysis") and the intelligence community, and one of increasing future importance. However, State's performance has been poor overall, poor in comparison to CIA assessment, and poor in terms of reasonable expectations. Its defects—which are characterized by description rather than analysis, too narrowly defined politics, avoidance of inference or prediction, and argumentative, generalized, or irrelevant briefs cloaked in obscure English—illustrate the weaknesses in the foreign service capabilities, goals, training, incentives and awards, as well as ignorance of Washington concerns and arrogance of ambassadors. In Washington, the department lacks the capability to either improve or fully understand field action, and does not raise sharp questions with embassies or require better assessment.

The task of *making ad hoc adjustments for personalities and operating styles* is a problem of organizational structures, procedures, tradition, directives—and presidential intentions. The State Department vacuum in analysis, decision making, and implementation has gradually been filled by an expanded NSC staff. In some ways this has led to distortion through competing preferences about policy, and to competition for power and influence. The chief executives should, and should be expected to, make explicit ad hoc adjustments in operating procedures—deliberately frustrating organization charts and the logic of organizational design—to fit the capabilities of key individuals to his personal needs.

Inherent in both the style and the structure of decision making is the task of *follow-up and evaluation of performance.* Chief executives and agency heads should, routinely and ad hoc, perform independent study and evaluation of (1) decisions, actions, and operations, both failures and successes, in relation to both short- and long-term goals; (2) quality of implementation and analysis; (3) accountability by commanders at all levels; (4) performance of individuals; and (5) cost in both resources and manpower.

V

The congressional role in foreign policy and congressional-executive relations with respect to military power and national policy are important adjuncts of national decision making which have received too little attention from participants and scholars alike. Under the Constitution, the Congress and the executive share important responsibilities with regard to foreign policy—war power, treaty powers, and the appointive process. Congressional control of the purse strings is a powerful instrument of both foreign and domestic policy. Congress also has sole power to regulate foreign commerce, but in practice has delegated much of it to the executive. The executive-legislative process in theory is reciprocal and consultative, with powers of Congress keyed to the phrase "advise and consent."

To get the Constitution off on the right foot, President George Washington dutifully visited the Hill to seek such advice. He found it so abusive that he strode from the Senate chamber swearing "never to return to this place"—a tradition unbroken until President Ford's visit a few days after his inauguration in August 1974. (Although warmly received by his former colleagues, Ford is not known to have returned.) During the interval, the presidential potential in foreign affairs had grown to dramatic proportions, in part because of an essentially unpredictable attitude by Congress even in its moments of greatest influence.

The failure of President Wilson to consult Republican members of the Foreign Relations Committee in his deliberations on the Treaty of Versailles led to the destruction of the League of Nations. A generation later, Congress ratified the UN Charter with the provision that American troops would be committed to UN action only after a Special Military Agreement had been negotiated with the UN Security Council and approved by Congress. The agreement failed to be negotiated only because of the deepening cold war between the two most powerful members of the Security Council.[13]

Yet the Truman Doctrine, the Marshall Plan, and the UN Relief and Rehabilitation Agency (UNRRA) could hardly have been established without Senate Foreign Relations Committee leadership under Senator Vandenberg. The antiballistic missile (ABM) debate and the Vietnam War brought about new roles for the Congress in shaping and articulating public opinion on national security matters. The vast increase in international trade and investment problems in the 1970s contributed to important growth of the Congress in regulating commerce. The annual defense debate, and congressional decisions on the size of the armed forces, the ships, planes, missiles, and other weapons of war, exert major influences on foreign policy and the military support of diplomacy worldwide. Yet these congressional pressures are essentially negative—they tend to hobble the free play of diplomacy by placing limits on resources rather than extending the leverage of the resources themselves.

Perhaps no area of potential influence gives the legislators more difficulty than the power to initiate war, which was vested exclusively in Congress by the Constitution, but, prior to the recent War Powers Resolution, was virtually under the exclusive control of the executive.[14] The "dog of war" which Thomas Jefferson thought had been tightly leashed to the legislature somehow had shifted into the executive kennel. Modern armaments tend to emphasize the executive role. It is often asserted that the initiation of nuclear war could not possibly await congressional authorization; at the other extreme it is contended that limited wars and interventions are inappropriate for congressional action. There being no wars available other than "limited" and "unlimited," congressional power is essentially nullified, at least until the congress can find a medium-sized war in which it can participate. Therein lay the origin of the war powers legislation.

For several years congressional leaders sought to restore the balance in the war-making process through ad hoc efforts. Such relatively mild measures as a "Sense of the Senate" resolution calling on the President not to undertake commitments to war without congressional sanction, repeal of the Tonkin Gulf resolution, and resolutions barring use of American ground forces in Thailand, Laos, and Cambodia generally failed. President Nixon ignored such warnings by expansion of the war into Laos and by widespread use of American air power in Laos, Cambodia, and North Vietnam. Congress retaliated at last with additional restrictive legislative action culminating in the War Powers Resolution, passed over a presidential veto, which prevents the President from sending American troops into combat overseas for more than sixty days without the expressed consent of Congress.

Although the resolution was an expression of popular protest of an unpopular war, there may be unanticipated and far-reaching consequences. The President must resolve an overseas crisis in less than sixty days or risk congressional failure to grant an extension. Once American troops are committed, the inducement to use tactical nuclear weapons in order to reach an early decision may be too strong to overcome. Note that Defense Secretary Schlesinger on several occasions deliberately drew attention to the presence of U.S. nuclear weapons in South Korea, pointedly adding that American troops will not get drawn into another prolonged Vietnam type of war. President Ford has refused on several occasions to rule out first-strike use of American nuclear weapons. In reply to a press conference question, he stated that "we had a change of some degree about a year and a half ago, when I took office . . . to maximize our flexibility." Defense Secretary Rumsfeld in the FY-77 posture statement echoed that "we do not preclude . . . first use of nuclear weapons in the defense of our interests." Chairman of the Joint Chiefs General George Brown, discussing tactical nuclear weapons in the current military posture statement, added that "a theory of controlled and limited escalation is inherent in the possibility of this employment." The resolution was never intended to increase presidential reliance on nuclear weapons, and the linkage to the War Powers Resolution is not clear. The conclusion is strong, however, that by reducing the President's other options, the effect will be to increase the likelihood of nuclear war.

Other consequences may be equally adverse to congressional intent. As a practical matter it is difficult to recall a sizable intervention which was not popularly supported for at least sixty days. If this be true, then the effect is a delegation of short-term war-making power to the President. Senator Javits, cosponsor of the Senate version of the bill, stated that it would give "the President more authority to do what is necessary and proper in an emergency than he now possesses." Congress would appear to have little choice in most cases but to ratify executive initiatives.

The War Powers Resolution was clearly a protest against the closed, one-man policy process of the late Nixon administration. Other, less publicized, congressional actions seem better oriented to favorable long-term consequences, although they also show a high element of indecision and paradox. Recent increases in staff competency are long overdue. The ABM action and the movement toward a functional, mission-oriented congressional budget analysis both offer promise. Yet close observers of congressional-executive relations with respect to foreign policy see little beyond continued subservience of the legislature to the executive. The Murphy Commission report is timely, therefore, and offers valuable indicators on these trends.[15]

An interview survey of 105 congressmen chosen in a statistically random selection found widespread and strong dissatisfaction with the role they perceive the Congress is playing in foreign policy. Yet congressmen are generally satisfied with the executive role and differ widely on what the congressional role should be—its nature, extent, and limits. They express strong support for organizational changes, yet do not see such changes as significant. Most dissatisfaction focuses on inadequate information from, and consultation with, the executive; this lack hampers them from reaching their own conclusions on policy matters, and hence from fulfilling an adequate "review and oversight" role. Desiring to participate in shaping and modifying policies, and, when necessary, to check, reverse, or initiate policy in cooperation with the executive, they nevertheless do not see direct participation by legislators in the conduct of foreign policy as appropriate.

The significant procedural change toward a unified budget of functional, mission-oriented programs found strong support but an undercurrent of pessimism toward adoption. The measure, one of sixteen suggested reform proposals in the foreign policy field suggested by the Murphy Commission study, received 76.8% support (17.2% opposed); adoption, however—estimated in the Pentagon as inevitable for the FY 78 budget—was seen as likely by only 57.1% (42.9% seeing it as unlikely).

A tabulation of the sixteen reform proposals, a summary of congressional attitudes and an analysis of legislators' support are appended as tables 1, 2, and 3 (see pp. 364-366). From these data it can readily be concluded that the Congress continues to satisfy itself with the rhetoric of legislation, leaving the hard work of implementation, from policy making to evaluation, to the executive. Actions to restore the power of the Congress—taken, pending, or proposed—are largely tactical and cosmetic. A revitalized role of Congress in policy making appears to be less a problem of organizational change than of the will and energy of the members. If the Congress continues to lack either in sufficient degree, the executive role will continue to dominate except during those rare historic periods of executive weakness.[16]

Edward Laurence made a careful analysis of the role of Congress in the defense policy process and the reasons for executive dominance. He concludes that Congress is not organized to participate effectively in the defense policy process and can do so only in the absence of executive consensus. The executive dominance is enhanced by a monopoly of intelligence and technology so that Congress may process only options among those programs proposed by the executive.[17]

The Murphy Commission analysis confirms the legislative branch weakness.

Careful reading of the commission report with respect to congressional-executive relations fails to disclose any pattern of recommended initiatives of the Congress in foreign policy adequate for sophisticated analysis, except in a negative sense.[18] With a knowledgeable, well-informed, and articulate Vice-President pleading the executive role in the commission discussions, and generally less informed and less persuasive members of Congress defending the legislative role, it is understandable that the heart of the problem of separate or shared executive-congressional powers was never reached. The congressional members in some instances, in fact, appeared far too willing to interpret events with respect to the War Powers Resolution with a strong bias of self-interest.

The Statement of Purpose of the Joint War Resolution claims that it "will apply to the introduction of United States Armed Forces into hostilities, or into situations where imminent involvement in hostilities is clearly indicated by the circumstances."[19] The commission study asserts that reports "by the President to the Congress concerning military evacuations at Danang, Phnom Penh and Saigon, and the recovery of the merchant ship *Mayaguez* and its crew," tested the constitutionality of the consultation and reporting sections of the resolution. In fact, however, the military evacuations made no test whatever of constitutionality; they indicated far less the imminence than the termination of hostilities in Southeast Asia. The recovery of the merchant ship *Mayaguez,* even though casualties were suffered, involved no remote "imminent involvement" in hostilities as contemplated in the resolution. In both instances President Ford simply carried out his oft-repeated promise to keep Congress informed. He stated as much to congressional members at the *Mayaguez* briefings; contrary to the statement in the commission report, this information was repeated to the commission by the Vice-President.

VI

It is neither necessary nor desirable—or even possible, perhaps—to offer in crisp summary form an ideal structure for national security decision making. Some order can be sought from the wide variety of determinants discussed here without being overly prescriptive. Numerous models for national decision making are available to serve the ends of policy oriented toward possible need for military intervention in future years. Structural, conceptual, and empirical variants, both formal and informal, successful and unsuccessful, have been tested in the recent past. But what is ideal for one era may be inappropriate for another. Above all, what is ideal for the personal style of one president may be inappropriate for his successor, and if inappropriate it will be unused.

Within the Defense Department, the unity of the services desired by the President, the Congress, and the American people is embodied in the relevant legislation, and is probably preferred by most occupants of the Pentagon as well. It becomes increasingly necessary, therefore, to reexamine the conditions which stimulate parochialism in order to reduce the harmful effects of rivalry, to increase the sophistication of policy planning, and to emphasize the subsidiary role of the Defense Department in national security policy making. The most persistent criticism is the militarization of foreign policy. Lacking sound doctrinal guidelines for interservice operations, strategy remains captive to technology and policy is driven by weaponry. Technology and modern weaponry without sound guidelines will lead only to militarism.

The President and national policy makers have ample sources of political and economic counsel; they have few sources of military advice other than the Pentagon. Pentagon advice is reinforced by the influence and prestige exerted by the JCS in the Congress, on the public, and on the not wholly disinterested defense industry. The sheer size of the military bureaucracy generates vested interests in programs of its foreign clients, which in turn generate pressure for military aid and intervention. The proliferation of foreign policy-oriented staffs in the Defense Department (ISA, JCS, the intelligence agencies and service staffs) dominates the policy process with military-oriented views, dilutes State Department authority, and further weakens political-military control.

Policy making is also overbalanced by a national security structure performing many tasks of negotiation and diplomacy traditional to the State Department. The NSC, necessary in some form as a policy making body for major matters, also frequently tends to isolate the chief executive from the operational agencies by the addition of another layer to the process. Excessive centralization of control of U.S. foreign policy in the White House in turn contributes to a further weakening of the State Department role and locates the decision process under circumstances where dissenting views are least likely to be expressed. These problems are hardly new. They were noted in a far less complex security structure by the first Hoover Commission, which cautioned against presidential overinvolvement in foreign affairs without proper executive branch consultation.

Elements such as the above weaken the full play of diplomacy and contribute to undue military influence on decision making. What is of major concern to students of administration is that these difficulties distort what should be a permanent nonpartisan and inconspicuous institution occupying a key but subordinate role in the foreign policy process. As long as the policy process is dominated by the national security structure, however, the military role will be preeminent. With preeminence comes the danger of both use and abuse of the military instrument in crisis situations. It is vital that control be retained firmly in the civilian executive. The challenge is to make the structure fully responsive to national goals and not merely to the military perspective of those goals.

For all its flaws, the performance of the national security structure in recent years has gradually become more effective. The same can hardly be said—despite encouraging indications in the antiballistic missile crisis in 1970—of the role of the Congress in national security policy. The Murphy Commission, an initiative of Senator Fulbright and the Senate Foreign Relations Committee, sought to counter the Nixon concentration of power. Given the diverse constituencies of the Congress—uncentralized, undisciplined, and uncontrolled, yet influenced by disciplined and controlled power blocs; forward-looking, yet with both eyes firmly on the constituencies—it is extremely difficult to organize congressional support, easy to mobilize opposition, and impossible to predict either continuity or a specific direction. With the dominance of interest politics in Congress, its role may never be coequal with the executive in foreign policy. Lacking the capacity to exert legislative influence other than in a subordinate and generally negative role, Congress may find that its well-meant efforts, such as the War Powers Resolution, could be counterproductive in achieving the desired effect.

Perhaps it is premature to expect the Murphy Commission, at least initially, to make a significant contribution to the conduct of foreign policy. Many of the abuses of the Nixon administration were overtaken by events in the transition to the Ford administration. The continued lack of bipartisan support in Congress, however, will delay major initiatives in the organization for foreign policy until there is a new administration and new leadership in both the White House and the Congress.

Looking to the future with the framework of the immediate past in mind, one is inclined to support the claim of an aspiring presidential candidate that the soundest element of our governance is the American people themselves, and that popular sanction on national policy, for all the inherent pain and frustration, has been in the end the counsel of wisdom.

NOTES

1. *Report of the Commission on the Organization of the Government for the Conduct of Foreign Policy, 1973-1975* (Murphy Commission) (Washington, D.C.: Government Printing Office, 1975). •

2. William Young Smith, "The Search for a National Security Planning Machinery, 1900-1947," (Ph.D. diss., Harvard University, 1960).

3. See Laurence J. Legere, *Unification of the Armed Forces* (Washington, D.C.: Office of the Chief of Military History, Department of the Army, 1950), p. 2.

4. Richard D. Challener, *Admirals, Generals, and Foreign Policy, 1898-1914* (Princeton, N.J.: Princeton University Press, 1973), p. 405.

5. "Special Message to the Congress in Reorganization of the Defense Establishment, April 3, 1958," *Public Papers of the Presidents* (Washington, D.C.: Government Printing Office, 1958), pp. 278-79.

6. The 1971 U.S. Air Force basic doctrine uses the term "aerospace" 38 times, down from 108 in the 1959 edition; "U.S. Air Force" 24 times, the Joint Chiefs of Staff and Department of Defense only once. No reference is made to the Army, Navy, or Marine Corps.

7. It cannot be discovered that a secretary of state ever appeared before a military appropriations committee to discuss policy implications of a military budget. General George C. Marshall, a great military leader with unique qualifications in relating policy to war, declined, as secretary of state, to testify before Congress on the budget because it might be "misinterpreted as an effort by him to introduce a military factor into his work."

See Warner Schilling, *Strategy, Policy, and Defense Budgets* (New York: Institute of War and Peace Studies, Columbia University Press, 1962). See also Smith, "The Search for a National Security Planning Machinery."

8. A compilation was made by this author for the Murphy Commission of the literature on the defense structure with respect to national security decision making by official commissions, panels, study groups, unofficial (government-supported) analyses, unofficial works by former bureaucrats, and books by outside organizations and scholars. Of approximately ninety such studies, 125 specific defects were alleged with respect to the role of the Defense Department in the foreign policy process. More than 50% of the recommendations (67) are in regard to inadequate planning and strategic or doctrinal deficiencies; over 25% of the remainder allege military domination of policy. Only 10% of the recommendations refer to inadequate civilian guidance; another 10% refer to overorganization, too many layers, awkward staffing, or options set up at low level.

9. Morton H. Halperin, "The Decision to Deploy the ABM: Bureaucratic Policies in the Pentagon and White House in the Johnson Administration" (Paper presented at the American Political Science Association meeting, September 1970).

10. There were 380 major installations abroad in 1965; today there are 283, 232 of which are in three countries; 181 in Germany, 27 in Japan, and 24 in Korea.

11. Under a 1975 law requiring the executive branch to provide arms control impact statements with new weapons programs proposed to Congress, Pentagon compliance has been questionable. The analysis of the cruise-missile on arms control failed to mention that the weapon was one of the keys to the stalemated strategic arms limitation treaty (SALT II) negotiations with the Soviet Union. Such statements are claimed by Congress as confirmation of congressional suspicions that the executive branch—Defense in particular—has no inclination to treat it as an equal partner.

12. The widely publicized "smart bomb" was available in 1967 but was not tried in Vietnam until 1972, not even when such a weapon was needed for important and politically sensitive targets such as the Hanoi-Haiphong bridge complex. The earlier use of laser-guided weapons, allowing great reductions in size and number of missions, would have had profound implications on the scale of the bombing effort, the civilian casualty rates, the number of aircraft, pilots, and crews lost, and hence internally on aviation training programs, aircraft procurement, and the Air Force budget. Recommendations for greater use fell on deaf ears. No recommendation came from the field, at least when losses were low, because Defense criteria for bombing effectiveness were measured by number of missions and tonnage, not by accruacy. The Tactical Air Command, long committed to the assumption that nuclear weapons would be used, did not include a serious war-fighting capacity. Tactical bombing had become a lost art.

13. Jacob Javits and Don Kellermann, *Who Makes War: The President and the U.S. Congress* (New York: Morrow, 1973).

14. Public Law 93-148, November 1, 1973.

15. See the Murphy Commission report, vol. 5, app. M, "Congressional Survey" (Washington, D.C.: Government Printing Office, 1975). Twenty senators and eighty-five representatives participated in the survey.

16. Arthur M. Schlesinger, "The Runaway Presidency," *Atlantic Monthly* (November 1973): 51.

17. Edward J. Laurence, "The Changing Role of Congress in Defense Policy Making," *Journal of Conflict Resolution* 20 (June 1976): 213-53.

18. The Murphy Commission, a joint congressional and executive task force, was an initiative of the Senate Foreign Relations Committee.

18. Cited in the Murphy Commission report, p. 198.

Appendix 1: Legislators' Appraisals of Sixteen Foreign Policy Proposals

Subject of Question	Support				Likelihood			
	Support	Oppose	Neutral	n	Likely	Unlikely	Unsure	n
More GAO monitoring of overseas programs	84.1%	11.9%	4.0%	(101)	74.0%	22.9%	3.1%	(96)
Eecutive "unify" budget categories into single authorization for foreign affairs activities of all departments	76.8	17.2	6.0	(99)	57.1	42.9	–	(91)
Define executive branch consultation obligations with Congress ..	73.0	17.0	10.0	(100)	70.4	29.6	–	(88)
More joint committee hearings, action Senate & House foreign affairs committees	70.0	20.0	10.0	(100)	39.8	58.1	2.1	(93)
Submit Executive Agreements to Congress	62.5	22.2	15.3	(104)	44.3	54.6	1.1	(97)
Executive-legislative liaison committee to exchange information of mutual interest	57.4	27.8	14.8	(101)	44.0	53.6	2.4	(84)
Create Foreign Affairs Research Institute for original policy oriented research	56.4	34.7	8.9	(101)	53.8	45.1	1.1	(91)
Change CIA statutory mandate to report equally to Congress & executive	55.6	35.2	9.2	(54)	39.1	58.7	2.2	(46)
Increase congressional oversight of CIA by direct appropriation for funding	54.7	26.4	18.9	(53)	62.5	35.4	2.1	(48)
Tie executive funds in foreign affairs to full information and access to documents	53.0	36.0	11.0	(100)	37.6	62.4	–	(85)
Strengthen foreign policy committees	46.5	40.4	13.1	(99)	34.4	61.3	4.3	(93)
Question period for secretary of state on floors of Congress	45.6	47.6	6.8	(103)	19.2	80.8	–	(99)
Establish congressional General Counsel's Office to represent legislative interests	39.2	49.0	11.8	(102)	34.8	63.0	2.2	(92)
Form Committee on National Security from combined Armed Services and Foreign Relations/Foreign Affairs Committees	28.4	59.8	11.8	(102)	13.7	84.2	2.1	(95)
Foreign affairs liaison offices staffed by Congress in major executive agencies	27.4	60.8	11.8	(102)	13.2	81.3	5.5	(91)
Create "Department of Peace" cabinet with primary responsibility in formulation & conduct of foreign policy	23.5	70.4	6.1	(98)	12.1	87.9	–	(91)

Source: Report of the Commission on the Organization of the Government for the Conduct of Foreign Policy, 1975-1975 (Washington, D.C.: Government Printing Office, 1975).

Appendix 2:   Congressional Attitudes Toward Sixteen Proposals: A Summary

MAJORITY Support *and* Favorable Assessment* in BOTH HOUSES:

> Require Executive to "unify" budget categories
> Give GAO more authority to monitor overseas programs
> More precisely define executive consultation responsibilities

MAJORITY Support in HOUSE; MAJORITY Favorable Assessment, BOTH HOUSES:

> Increase congressional oversight of CIA

MAJORITY Support and NEAR MAJORITY Favorable Assessment, BOTH HOUSES:

> Require executive branch to submit all Executive Agreements
> Establish executive-legislative liaison committee

MAJORITY Support in BOTH HOUSES but LESS THAN MAJORITY Favorable Assessment:

> Encourage more joint hearings, legislative activity
> Tie executive spending to information, documents

MAJORITY Support and Favorable Assessment in HOUSE ONLY:

> Create congressional Foreign Affairs Research Institute

MAJORITY Support, HOUSE ONLY:

> Bring more foreign policy legislation under jurisdiction of Foreign Affairs, Foreign
>   Relations Committees
> Revise statutory mandate of CIA

NEAR MAJORITY Support and Favorable Assessment, SENATE ONLY:

> Establish congressional General Counsel's Office

NEAR MAJORITY Support, HOUSE ONLY:

> Provide for secretary of State questioning on floor

NO MAJORITY Support or Assessment in EITHER HOUSE:

> Create Foreign Affairs liaison offices staffed by Congress
> Create "Department of Peace" cabinet
> Combine Armed Services and Foreign Affairs/Foreign Relations Committees to form
>   Committee on National Security

---

*Favorable Assessment = "50-50 or better" chances.

Appendix 3: Legislators' Support of Proposals and Assessment of the Proposals' Likelihood

Proposal (Question)	Support[a]	Likelihood[b]		n
		Likely	Unlikely	
More GAO monitoring of overseas programs	Support	85.2%	15.8%	(85)
	Oppose	16.7	83.3	(12)
Executive "unify" budget categories	Support	62.5	37.5	(76)
	Oppose	26.7	73.3	(17)
Define executive branch consultation	Support	87.7	12.3	(73)
	Oppose	23.1	76.9	(17)
More joint committee hearings, action	Support	53.1	46.9	(70)
	Oppose	5.3	94.7	(20)
Submit Executive Agreements to congress	Support	56.4	43.5	(65)
	Oppose	10.0	90.0	(23)
Executive-legislative liaison committee	Support	65.3	34.7	(58)
	Oppose	4.8	95.2	(28)
Foreign Affairs Research Institute	Support	82.4	17.6	(57)
	Oppose	9.7	90.3	(35)
Change CIA statutory mandate	Support	59.2	40.7	(30)
	Oppose	6.7	93.3	(19)
Increase congressional oversight of CIA	Support	78.6	21.4	(29)
	Oppose	25.0	75.0	(13)
Tie executive funds to information, documents	Support	61.3	38.6	(53)
	Oppose	9.1	90.9	(36)
Strengthen foreign policy committees	Support	56.8	43.2	(65)
	Oppose	8.6	91.4	(40)
Question period for secretary of state	Support	32.6	67.4	(47)
	Oppose	8.6	91.3	(49)
Congressional General Counsel's Office	Support	78.3	21.6	(40)
	Oppose	–	100.0	(50)
Committee on National Security	Support	39.3	60.7	(29)
	Oppose	1.8	98.2	(61)
Foreign affairs liaison office	Support	43.5	56.5	(28)
	Oppose	–	100.0	(62)
"Department of Peace"	Support	30.4	69.6	(23)
	Oppose	4.9	95.1	(69)

[a] Excludes "Pro/Con" and "don't-know" responses.
[b] "Likely" includes "50-50 or better" responses.

PART VII. EPILOGUE: TOWARD CONCEPTUAL REFORMULATION

BEYOND DETERRENCE:

ALTERNATIVE CONCEPTUAL DIMENSIONS

Morris Janowitz

In assessing the changing role of force in international relations, it is necessary to consider whether the existing conceptual categories derived from scholarship in this area are appropriate and clarifying. In particular, the analytical relevance of the key term "deterrence" needs to be called into question. Deterrence is the key concept for linking military strategy and operations to the manifold policies and practices of the United States in its international relations. In reassessing the precision and implications of the term "deterrence," there is no implicit or explicit judgment of its value—theoretical and operational—in the period 1945 to 1975. Social scientists must strive to make use of timeless categories, but at the same time, and especially in the context of international relations, they must take into consideration the changing historical context. Thus, a reassessment involves not only analytical questions, but the central issue of the changed historical context as well.

STABILIZING AND DESTABILIZING MILITARY SYSTEMS

The central assumption of this analysis is that the classical categories for analyzing military organization and strategy must be reconceptualized in the era of nuclear weapons and decline of colonial rule.[1] The idea of "stabilizing"

AUTHOR'S NOTE: This chapter is an explication and reformulation of a conceptual framework presented in "Toward a Redifinition of Military Strategy," **World Politics** 26 (July 1974): 473-508.

and "destabilizing" military systems is offered as an alternative to the classical language–balance of power, offensive-defensive, and strategic-tactical military structures.

It is no simple matter to define and give concrete content to the terms "stabilizing" and "destabilizing" when speaking of military structures, but their essential elements can be identified. These concepts supply a basis for reassessing international relations during the years since 1945, and for examining alternative approaches to the search for military détente They also help to give meaning to the oft-repeated observation that, from the point of view of Western nations with multiparty political systems, the role of violence in international relations has undergone fundamental changes.[2]

First, the concepts of stabilization and destabilization are based on the recognition that total war, as prepared for and practiced by the nations of Europe and the United States and Japan during World Wars I and II, is no longer viewed as an instrument for achieving national goals.[3] To the extent that rationality operates, the outbreak of "major" war between industrialized nations is no longer defined as inevitable. A military force based on conventional mobilization for total war gives way to a force in being, which is designed to achieve deterrence.

Second, the overseas colonial empires of advanced industrial nations have, in the main, come to an end through voluntary withdrawal, or political agitation, or, in a limited number of cases, as the result of military engagements.[4] Colonial rule has given way to varieties of assistance in the building of military and paramilitary institutions in the so-called developing nations, and to support for armed conflict either between or within these nations.[5]

As a result, the legitimacy and utility of every specific military preparation and operation have been judged in terms of new criteria which, in a kind of shorthand, have come to be called deterrence. Deterrence is equated with a reduction of the chances for and avoidance of the outbreak of major war between the advanced industrial powers, and with the inhibition of peripheral and limited war. But the term has limitations–and not only because it has been overused and misused. It deals mainly with military affairs and military goals and does not adequately encompass the range of processes and objectives required for an international order that seeks to avoid war.[6] In short, deterrence as a concept has been mainly negative–and therefore of limited import for analyzing the organizational goals of military institutions. However, to speak of stabilized military systems and the search for stabilization is, first, to indicate the multiple goals of military institutions: avoiding general war and reducing or inhibiting limited war. But second, an emphasis on stabilized military systems encompasses the goals of a controlled level of military expenditures and expanding arms control, as well as a reduction in mass personal insecurity generated by the arms race. Given the dangers of accidental nuclear war, miscalculations leading to escalation of international tensions, and the sheer organizational complexity of managing nuclear military systems, new forms of communication and negotiation are required between "adversaries" if one is to speak of stabilized military systems.[7] In these terms, the management of military institutions involves the creation of an international arena which would improve economic intercourse and enhance the opportunity for political solutions to global tensions and imbalances. There is no assumption that the internal sociopolitical structures of "adversaries" need to change or converge for steps to be taken in the political and military spheres. Stabilization hardly implies maintenance of the status quo; to the contrary it refers to an orderly process of social and political change based on persuasions and groups processes, rather than on the application of coercion.

Since, for industrialized nations, military intervention operates under marked limitations—which tend to increase—the notion of stabilizing versus destabilizing military systems is designed to explore these limitations and to assess the full range of impact that the military function has in the international arena. It is designed to avoid utopian thinking during a period of redefinition of national interests, since it assumes that stabilized military systems are required if positive goals in international relations are to be established.

The conception of stabilizing versus destabilizing military systems rests on an interdisciplinary or general social science perspective. Military technology supplies the point of departure for the conception, which starts conventionally with economic elements and uses political elements as coordinating mechanisms. In recent years, there have also been efforts to incorporate psychological elements.[8] With the declining legitimacy of military force—because of the utter destructiveness of military technology and because of the internal sociopolitical tensions of an advanced industrial society—the social dimensions of international relations come into prominence. The notion of legitimacy and the crisis of legitimacy in military force constitute one formulation of the sociological dimension of international relations. It is dangerous to develop a sociological model of international relations, since it can quickly reduce itself to issues of manpower and morale or questions of ethics divorced from political reality. But, basically, the changing function of the military is in part a reflection of the realistic issues of norms and legitimacy.[9] The analysis of international relations can therefore be enriched by the appropriate infusion of the sociological analysis of institutions, social structures, and institution building.

Two interrelated assumptions about the nature of advanced industrial societies and the impact of the industrial order offer a point of departure. They are relevant for linking the transformation of the internal social structure of an advanced industrial nation with trends in the international arena.

First, there is a profound diffusion or dispersion of power and authority within the advanced, industrialized nation-states and in the linkages between these states and the rest of the world community. A striking paradox of course exists: elements of diffusion and dispersion are compatible with elements of persistent and increased concentration of power and authority. We cannot assume that we are dealing with a closed system; however, the contemporary process of transformation of authority is difficult to comprehend.

Sociologists have spoken of functional interdependence to describe the process by which the division of labor in institutions becomes more complex and specialized. Manheim has offered the notion of "fundamental democratization" to point to the normative and political implications of this development in the social order.[10] There is some merit in this formulation, although there is also a possibility of confusion, since he does not use "democracy" in the parliamentary sense. He is oriented to the residual power that emerges as formerly excluded groups increasingly enter the mainstream of society. In the United States, the trend toward "fundamental democratization" first became noticeable during the mobilization efforts of World War I, but its full implication developed and became more manifest during the second Indochina war.

Since 1945, the most striking development in the internal social structure of Western parliamentary democracies has been the residual power that accrues to formerly excluded or low-status groups—minorities, unskilled workers, youth, old people, and women. The complexity of the division of labor and the functional interdependence plus new normative trends are key elements. Often the power of these groups is more negative than positive, but that is the implication of residual power. The new trends do not negate the persistence of extensive disparity and inequality in resources and privileges. This observation merely seeks to place the residual power in the context of the social structure of an advanced industrial society, where its results is an increase in political tension and an undermining of political legitimacy. The difficulties of making effective political decisions become central. There is persistent tension between elite groups and pervasive veto groups. Political systems can operate on the basis of a gap between aspiration and actual practice, but the strains from the pressure of fundamental democratization are profound on the domestic scene. They result in chronic social conflict or national political stagnation, rather than in new revolutionary circumstances.[11]

At the international level, the same diffusion of power and authority can be noted. It reflects changes in internal domestic matters and in the structure of international relations.[12] The phrase, "the shift from a bipolar to a multipolar world community," fails to capture adequately the complexity and content of this transformation. The diffusion of power involves the linkages among major nation-states; and simultaneously, within each region, a related process occurs among the smaller nation-states. The dispersion of residual power is striking, despite the enormous concentration of resources among the advanced industrial nations. As in the case of patterns of internal domestic authority, the increase in functional interdependence is operative; normative and ideological values have enlarged impact. Some writers believe that this fundamental democratization among nations, especially in the context of nuclear weapons systems, should result in invigorated competition with attendant international stability, in an analogue to the competitive process of the marketplace. However, the actual process of dispersion of power and authority produces no inherent increase in stability. As in the case of the impact of fundamental democratization on domestic social structure, the effects on international relations are persistent tension and great difficulty in achieving accommodation and effective political decisions.

The second assumption about advanced industrialism is that, both internally and internationally, the interplay of force and persuasion undergoes a transformation. An admixture of these elements has traditionally been the central element in diplomacy. The calculus of force and persuasion has been modified so that there is good reason to speak of an increase and intensification in their fusion or articulation, including the threat of force. In the period of mass armies and traditional warfare among industrialized nations up through World War I, there seems to have been a phasing or periodicity in the use of persuasion and coercion.[13] There was more of a separation between normal international relations and the application of force. The breakdown of the balance of power led to the use of force, and "victory" was pursued by the means at hand. Although there were intermittent periods of high tension, war followed peace and peace followed hostilities.

Under the technology and politics of deterrence and involvement in peripheral warfare, the threat of force and its actual use are more continually invoked, with concurrent efforts at persuasion. The process is one of gradually escalating and deescalating force, of simultaneously "fighting" and "negotiating," of pursuing divergent means in different specific sectors of the international arena. In part, this process reflects the effort to avoid the use of great amounts of force; in part, it reflects the consequences of greater functional interdependence, in which the opposing powers must take into consideration the enlarged arenas of common interest. There is, at each step, a potent inhibition against using more powerful weapons. The symbolic aspects of force become more and more central. The fusion of force and persuasion partially reflects changes in the normative structure of international relations.

In Western political democracies, the same transformation in the balance of force and persuasion manifests itself internally—for example, in the efforts to control race relations, student protests, and labor relations, and even in the handling of bank robbers. The police are prepared to use personnel who specialize in negotiations with bank robbers holding hostages rather than to apply the force at their disposal. The application of force is not a periodic, all-or-nothing event; rather, it is a continuous aspect of the social process, which must be moderated in terms of self-interest and the possibility of unanticipated consequences.

The consequences of both *(a)* increased functional interdependence and "fundamental democratization" of residual power and *(b)* the fusion of and moderation in the use of force and persuasion is a new level of complexity and fragility in international relations. It is not enough to assert that, because of nuclear weapons, there has been no major or total war directly between advanced industrial nations for more than a quarter of a century although levels of tension and the scope of armed conflict have been persistent and unacceptably high, and there has been persistence of warfare through third parties. It is necessary to offer hypotheses about the increased limits of military intervention since the end of World War II.

Inequality is an outstanding aspect of the international order, and the same can be said of the internal social structure of any society, advanced or not. Over the last quarter century, inequality among nations has probably declined less than inequality within nations, especially within advanced industrialized states. Of course within advanced industrialized states, those persons who are not members of the middle majority—i.e., the sick, the aged, elements of the unskilled, and welfare recipients—may well find themselves with enduring disabilities that exclude them from the material benefits of affluence.

In some fundamental sense, the role of military force is designed to support the inequalities among nations, or at least does so in fact (as domestic police power contributes to internal social stratification). This assertion does not deny that military force contributes to the maintenance of a world "order"—no matter how unstable—in which economic, educational, and administrative processes can and do operate to reduce existing degrees of inequality.

However, the hypothesis appears relevant that, at the international level, the capacity of advanced industrialized nations to maintain their economic advantages by reliance on military force has markedly declined. The cost of a military establishment is so huge that there is an important advantage to be gained by reducing or even limiting military expenditures than by using the threat of force to achieve economic advantage.[14] Critics of a variety of political persuasions now generally concede that *military expenditures are not needed* to maintain the economic vitality of a "capitalist" society in the West, and that they are a tremendous burden to the Soviet Union during its continuing press for industrial growth.[15] Nuclear weapons rule out the possibility of drastically restructuring the "zones of influence," as was done after World War II. Moreover, on the contemporary international scene, the less developed nations will not as readily succumb to a show of the flag or a military presence. Of course, this does not rule out specific intervention to deny important resources to an opponent. To use the language of economics, the marginal utility of the military function has declined.

In addition, there are grave limitations to the psychological returns of a military force with nuclear weapons. "National security" and "defense of the motherland" are in part a matter of psychic security and of honor, prestige, and the positive attraction of membership in a collectivity. The phrase "world politics and personal insecurity," offered by Harold D. Lasswell, is a focal but neglected aspect of the transformation of international relations. The sheer accumulation of weapons—especially nuclear weapons—does not necessarily reduce anxiety.

The mass of the citizenry continues to support policies which are represented as essential for nuclear deterrence, although there may be extensive political debate about alternative strategies and levels of budgetary allocation. Popular support for national security is in part an expression of personal anxiety. However, the threat of mass destruction produces privatization as well as moral revulsion. There has been a long-term decline in enthusiasm for national war making. Popular support at the outbreak of World War I gave way to realistic participation during World War II, and the prospect of a third world war produces psychological numbness.[16] Since 1945, sharp outbursts of neutralism have reflected these feelings. During a period of military détente such feelings will become more prominent, and, although likely to be limited to a minority of the population, "psychological" neutralism can have extensive political consequences.

The mass media—especially television, in its day-to-day reporting of violence from Indochina to Northern Ireland—serve to increase the negative psychological consequences of military intervention. Military institutions have a diminished ability to contribute to psychological security: the reality and the imagery of violence produce higher levels of personal insecurity, leading to apathy and withdrawal.[17] In short, the perspective toward international relations that is appropriate for the application of the concept of stabilizing versus destabilizing must be multidimensional.

The formulation of stabilizing versus destabilizing is more useful for assessing the contemporary function of the military in international relations than the classic concepts of strategic versus tactical, or offensive versus defensive. The classic terms can be used to describe the technological dimensions of the military, but the notion of stabilizing and destabilizing is designed to reflect the politico-military processes at work in international relations. As shown above, the terms "stabilizing" and "destabilizing" compel us to consider the socio-political context of military systems in the search for a viable international system: the avoidance of nuclear war and the containment of peripheral military confrontations.

APPROACHES TO MILITARY DÉTENTE

The central issue is to assess the stabilizing versus destabilizing consequences of alternative approaches to military détente recognizing the asymmetrical compression of conscripted manpower for the NATO forces in contrast to the Warsaw Pact states. A review of the years 1945 to 1968—from the first use of nuclear weapons to the active negotiations between the United States and the Soviet Union on strategic arms limitations—is a precondition for assessing the trends that emerged after 1968, when the second phase in post-World War II international relations began.

To speak of stabilized systems of nuclear weapons implies the expectation that future weapons development will be economically manageable and will not present the political specter of a perpetual, overpowering, and uncontrollable "doomsday" arms race, although some continuous change would be built in. In other words, nuclear weapons can be managed without consuming excessively large amounts of resources and producing such high levels of personal insecurity as to transform advanced industrial society into a type of garrison state in which the search for more and "better" nuclear systems becomes an omnipotent goal.

The hypothesis can be offered that between 1945 and 1968, although there was no explicit system of arms control, the development of nuclear weapons remained within tolerable limits of stabilization. However, the deployment of conventional forces in Southeast Asia had a destabilizing effect on that area and, in turn, on worldwide relations.

It was a period when deterrence operated to avoid the outbreak of nuclear war without any fundamental politico-military realignments that could be viewed by any of the three central powers as basically threatening to the structure of the world community. However, the period 1945-68 was only partly stabilizing at the level of nuclear weapons. Insufficient steps were taken to develop explicit systems of arms control, and there was inadequate anticipation of a future in which more complex nuclear weapons would be deployed and in which economic and political factors would require a more active search for military détente. The destabilization caused by military intervention in the second Indochina war not only reduced and delayed the United States' ability to take the initiative in negotiating with the Soviet Union on strategic arms limitation and a restructuring of conventional forces in Western Europe, but also contributed to increased destabilization throughout the world community, especially in the Middle East.

In the years immediately after WWII, it was clear that, while the United States had "numerical" superiority in nuclear weapons, the possibility of an outbreak of nuclear war was very remote, although effective steps had to be taken to prevent accidental warfare or miscalculation. The bulk of the strategic literature of that period, predicting or accounting for developments, can be readily dismissed. It would have been too much to expect the United States' political elite to begin realistic negotiations with the Soviet Union in 1950 on the basis of nuclear parity, which was to develop only at the end of the 1960s as a prerequisite of the SALT talks. However, there was no possibility of preventing the Soviet Union from achieving such parity if the United States was to remain a humane and democratic society.

In essence, the political leaders of the Soviet Union and the United States recognized the utter destructive capacity and unpredictability of nuclear weapons in any military confrontation between NATO and Warsaw Pact nations. The achievement of nuclear deterrence and relative stability between 1945 and 1968 is a reflection not merely of weapons systems, but also of political arrangements and normative patterns at the international level. The social structure and political posture of the United States initially ruled out a preventive attack on the Soviet Union. The NATO military system had at its disposal an adequate number of ground forces to achieve its deterrent role in the nuclear context. The ground-force structure of NATO, especially the very sizable American contingent, indicated a relatively stable political context, uninfluenced by the fears of a nuclear holocaust that could have produced excessive neutralism. Also, there was no move toward an independent European deterrent under Franco-German hegemony, which would have been highly destabilizing from the point of view of Soviet-American relations. Moreover, the military presence of the United States ensured the continued division of Germany, which was essential for the postwar reconstruction of both Western and Eastern Europe and for the long-term stability of the West.

During the Eisenhower administration, while the Soviet Union was engaged in the first steps toward nuclear parity, there was in the United States an extensive effort to develop a civilian defense system. This effort collapsed, initially because of public indifference and later because of congressional reluctance to allocate the required funds. After a very brief period of limited hysteria, the penetration of a doomsday outlook into their day-to-day life proved to be unacceptable to the citizens of the United States, who thereby served to contain the level of international tension. A massive civilian defense program would have been destabilizing at that time because it would have weakened the credibility of the United States' strategic intentions of avoiding nuclear war. It would also have weakened the social fabric of the United States by further distorting the values of everyday life.

The effectiveness of nuclear deterrence in the NATO-Warsaw Pact balance was enhanced by the limited but symbolically significant efforts at international arms control. These steps produced no more than marginal technical adjustments, but they underlined the intention to keep military developments within credible and acceptable limits. (The accords started with the denuclearization of Antarctica, partial test bans, prohibition of nuclear weapons in outer space and in the sea bed, and construction of the "hot line.")

In contrast to the relatively stabilized military balance—conventional and nuclear—in Western Europe, which lasted until the middle of the 1960s, the progressive deployment and utilization of military force in the Far East had a very different impact, which was essentially destabilizing. In essence, the basic source of the destabilization was the failure to develop political arrangements with Communist China; such efforts were blocked from 1947 on by domestic American political agitation. All available evidence indicates that, at the close of World War II and subsequently, Communist China would have been amenable to political initiatives comparable to those which were launched after 1968, and which would have taken into consideration the relations of China both with the Soviet Union and with other nation-states of the Far East and Southeast Asia. Instead, American foreign policy sought to mechanically apply the format of Western Europe without appropriate adaptation to the realities of the social structure of the Far East.

For a brief time, the possibility of the use of "tactical" nuclear weapons to support the declining fortunes of the French in Indochina, particularly in the context of "white" military forces against Asiatic formations, proved highly destabilizing. This prospect created the specter of disaster for the world community. It was effectively avoided, but at the cost of extensive destabilizing consequences.

Deployment of conventional forces, especially ground forces, failed to take into account the process of decolonization and emergent nationalism in the Far East and in Southeast Asia. After the defeat of Japan, the reimposition of colonial systems was not militarily feasible and was sure to be politically destabilizing. Initially, United States policy was oriented toward the goal of decolonization and the emergence of independent nation-states with their own indigenous military forces. The conventional United States military presence had to conform to these politico-military requirements. In the British and Dutch colonies, the objective was basically achieved, but lack of political decisiveness in Indochina presented the crucial and fatal exception. (The political error was rooted not only in first tacit and then open support of French military intervention, but also in allocating a role in China in the initial occupation of Indochina.)

In retrospect, although there is no point in rewriting history, if the Nixon policies toward Nationalist China on Formosa—which were implemented after 1968—had been initiated in 1956-47, alternative political and military arrangements for Korea, and particularly Indochina, might have been possible. However, prolongation of the second Indochina war was a major destabilizing process in the international arena after 1945. One of the causes was the limited effectiveness of U.S. military intervention, especially in its conventional strategic air attacks, and the absence of adequate international political legitimacy of the effort. Later, limitations in the North Vietnamese military effort emerged. The failure of their tank offensive in spring 1972 (which was blunted by tactical airpower) and the increased accuracy of United States bombing of the North in the fall of 1972 created the military conditions for the acceptance of a "cease-fire." It was clear, however, from the early 1960s on, that a contraction of American military involvement in the second Indochina war depended on a direct initiative by the United States to satisfy the political objectives of Communist China.

The vast amount of documentation on the outbreak of the second Indochina war has obscured the central issue: the demise of the determined United States military opposition to deploying ground forces on the mainland of Asia, which had become especially strong after Korea. The leaders of this opposition were called members of the "never-again club." Before 1960, key U.S. military leaders had been opposed to large-scale ground involvement in Southeast Asia. Likewise, the limits of intervention had been recognized in the military plans that were developed, calling for 1 million to 1.2 million men as the requirement for a ground force in Vietnam.[18]

It is arbitrary to take 1968 as the starting date of the second era in post-World War II politico-military development, and no doubt it will be subject to later reformulation. In that year, however, the internal political scene in the United States changed, because of the election of President Richard M. Nixon, to permit deescalation of the war in Vietnam, and to make possible new political initiatives with the Soviet Union and, later, with Communist China. President Nixon's election also permitted the political decision to start unilateral disarmament in the United States by ending the draft. In effect, 1968 was a political benchmark for response to developments which had been in progress since the early 1960s—for example, the growing "numerical nuclear parity" of the Soviet Union, the increased complexity of nuclear weapons, the limitations on American intervention in the second Indochina war, the increased recognition of the limitations of military assistance programs to the developing nations, the emerging tension between the Soviet Union and China, and the internal problems of advanced industrial countries, including the Soviet Union.

The initiatives toward détente sought a new stabilization, but contained actual and potential elements of destabilization. Starting in 1968, the legitimate utility of military force required new arrangements to stabilize the nuclear deterrent under conditions of nominal nuclear parity. It is of course assumed that political elites in the United States would not accept "marked" Russian nuclear superiority. A stabilized nuclear deterrent cannot be defined only in technological terms, namely, as an inhibited commitment of economic resources. Politically, it would be necessary to prevent both reactive neutralism and aggressive nationalism in Western Europe. On one hand, reactive neutralism would lead to significant pressure to opt out of nuclear defense arrangements because of distrust of American intentions as being either too "forward" or too "unreliable," and might be assisted by high levels of privatization. On the other hand, aggressive nationalism might be attended by pressure for a more forward European defense posture. The political requirement of stabilized nuclear deterrent would also involve the avoidance of an independent Western European deterrent, especially under Franco-German domination, which would be gravely destabilizing to United States-Soviet relations.

The conflicts—technical, administrative, and political—encountered in the Strategic Arms Limitation Talks underline the enormous difficulties of institution building for military stabilization after 1968. However, the main objectives of strategic arms limitations began to emerge. The stabilizing elements of strategic arms arrangements include negotiations as permanent mechanisms; improved unilateral and bilateral photoelectronic surveillance; further limitations on weapons testing; on-site nuclear explosion inspection; limitations on new launching complexes, including antiballistic missile systems and submarines; negotiations concerning new types of missiles, such as the cruise-missiles; and improved "hot-line" procedures, including the stationing of joint military commissions in neutral territories. Moreover, the emerging patterns of strategic arms limitations face the incredibly complex task of political accommodation with

Communist China.[19] This last is especially crucial, since the United States would produce gravely destabilizing potentials if it were to seek to enhance its world position by a balance-of-power strategy of "playing off" the Soviet Union against Communist China.[20] These rivalries are likely to maintain themselves of their own accord, with destabilizing consequences. Negotiations with Communist China on strategic arms limitations might well begin earlier rather than later.

However, the core problem is not technical. It remains political, and is related in particular to the changed military function. The major political thrust of the period after 1968 has been to link strategic arms limitation negotiation to the issues of conventional forces in Western Europe. The stability of deterrence depends on the relevant contribution of conventional forces to the mechanics of deterrence, to internal political balance in the NATO structure, and to the political stability of each constituent nation. Paradoxically, despite the vast expenditure of the United States military, the central stabilizing element rests on the supply of an adequate number of conventional ground forces in Western Europe. The unilateral introduction of the all-volunteer force complicated this task; but with a viable professional reorientation, an adequate force with legitimate military utility can be maintained even without conscription.[21]

GOALS OF U.S. MILITARY FORCES

There is little point at this juncture in spelling out alternative scenarios or patterns of strategic force deployment. Instead, the issue rests on recognizing the goals of U.S. military forces under a foreign policy which is searching to design a new world order. It makes no difference whether one believes that the world arena should be seen as a single interacting field of forces or whether one believes that regional differentiation is operative. It is a tautology to claim that the absence of peace is the result of a failure to develop an international order; but it is a useful tautology, since it implies that the use of military forces in creating world order must be considered. Such a world order would not be fixed, static, and without tension; it would have its conflicts, instabilities, and ambiguities. But the measure of a trend toward meaningful world order would be signified by a decline in risk-taking for marginal advantage and a substantial reduction in direct confrontations that are seeded with dangerous elements of escalation; and even more important would be a decline in the imagery and reality of an unorganized world community locked into a doomsday search by the superpowers for a military weapons system to produce "superiority."

There can be no doubt that the United States would have to be the prime agent of initiative in this search for stabilizing military systems. The goal will not be reached by simply reacting to Soviet policies. It is also the case that the NATO-Warsaw Pact relations supply the central arena for such initiatives. The "drift toward the Left" in Western European governments hardly implies automatic destabilization, although it does complicate day-to-day management of the balance of politico-military forces.

It is best not to think in terms of strategic military objectives, but rather to identify a process of strategic adaptation. In the search for a stabilized foreign policy, the United States would seek to influence the Soviets to accept the premise that it desires a world order in which it would not station conventional ground forces outside Western Europe (correspondingly, the same would hold true for the Soviet Union, in that its external ground force deployment would be limited to Eastern Europe). The size of these forces would be subject to negotiations under mutual-balanced-reduction in the light of military and political requirements for nuclear deterrence and the worldwide search for military détente. The United States would maintain a meaningful but delimited multiple-purpose contingency force on active duty, supported by a contracted but effective ready reserve. This force would have a reinforcement potential for NATO and, at the same time, serve as a deterrent to Russian ground-force deployments outside the Warsaw Pact.

These conditions would alter the role of naval forces. A stabilized military balance would involve the deployment of naval forces by both sides as an element of the NATO-Warsaw Pact mutual deterrence on both the North Atlantic and the East Mediterranean flanks. It can be expected that a naval presence ranging widely over the globe, for diffuse objectives of national prestige and presumed political advantage, will continue, with only marginal politico-military consequences. Greater expansion of naval power—as, for example, in the Indian Ocean—presents potentials for delimited elements of destabilization, but local nationalist setiment serves as a partial counterweight. There is also the ever present issue of avoiding naval accidents, which is already being pursued by direct negotiation and treaty between the Soviet Union and the United States.[22]

Strategic analysts will of course point to the profoundly destabilizing impact of the direct and indirect U.S./USSR politico-military confrontations outside of the European theater, each of which presents a special case. Korea serves as an example. The resolution or stabilization of this confrontation rests on the exploration of whether a U.S. commitment can be achieved by withdrawal of its ground forces, leaving only air and naval units in that theater. More generally, elements of destabilization operate in the competition which the United States and the Soviet Union have generated in the developing nations. However, since 1968, a more realistic perspective has been emerging as military assistance programs are seen to have very limited military utility. The general trend does not negate some profoundly unstabilizing focal points. The military assistance programs in connection with the unending Arab-Israeli conflict are central. However, the pattern of response since the outbreak of hostilities in 1973 in the Middle East indicates that the strategic process there is not merely the result of the overriding calculus of the superpowers. Instead, the scope for initiatives that client states have serves as the basis for a containment of the destabilizing components. Of continuing centrality is the resolution of the politico-military tensions created by the persistence of white political supremacy in the southern portions of Africa. This struggle is particularly destabilizing because of the moral issues it raises.

But the generalized and diffuse confrontation between the U.S. and the USSR in the so-called Third World has been transformed and muted in good part by the political definition which has come to be held by the superpowers and the importance of nationalist sentiment in these nations. The ability of major powers to alter the political structure of developing nations by political manipulation, subversion, support of guerrilla groups, and other types of covert operations has no doubt been exaggerated, although there have been particularly striking cases of this kind of activity. These attempts may well continue, even though massive efforts in Latin America, for example, have failed. Moreover, in the Western political democracies, there is growing recognition that measures of defense against internal subversion depend on viable political leadership as much as on military or paramilitary institutions. The appeals to nationalistic sentiment and the reliance on indigenous political resources have demonstrated their effectiveness, so that a belief in the inevitable success of Communist-dominated coups and revolts has come to an end. This is not to overlook the destabilizing elements of direct colonial rule where it still persists. However, under conditions of nuclear deterrence, there is real danger that military officers will seek to maintain a traditional definition of the military function by such means as a strong emphasis on various forms of "counterinsurgency." The specter of Western officers and intelligence operatives "going native" and leading indigenous forces dies hard, especially when the Soviet Union and China continue to give military assistance to the developing nations. But, for a stabilized world balance, the less direct the intervention the better, since such a policy allows nationalism to operate as a counterpressure.

In partial summary, it can be said that narrower limits of the military function have emerged for advanced industrialized nations, especially those with parliamentary institutions. But to speak of narrow limits hardly alters the centrality of force—especially force that is legitimate and oriented toward stabilizing international relations.

INSTITUTION BUILDING FOR MILITARY STABILIZATION

The fusion of new concepts with the day-to-day realities of military organization has presented, and continues to present, deep problems in institution building. The behavior and perspectives of the military are influenced as much by the immediate realities of manning particular weapons systems as they are by the formulation of doctrine. These realities maintain traditional combat philosophies. It is true that, in the parliamentary nations of the West, the terminology of deterrence has been incorporated into the language of the professional officer. There is much discussion of the phrase "peacekeeping through a military presence." The phraseology of the deterrent force in the format of a constabulary or various alternatives is extensively debated in military circles. The formulation presented in *The Professional Soldier* continues to require clarification and explication. "The military establishment becomes a constabulary force when it is continuously prepared to act, committed to the minimum use of force and seeks viable international relations rather than victory, because it has incorporated a protective military posture."[23] However, verbal pronouncements are not reliable indicators of institutional change.

It is difficult to assess the actual and potential capacity of a military organization to transform itself and to meet its changed function. To move beyond the strategy of deterrence and consider issues of stabilization versus destabilization will be even more difficult. In the Soviet Union, the existence of a capacity to fight a conventional war in Europe, the possibility of intervention in the countries of Eastern Europe, and the confrontation on the Sino-Soviet border help to maintain traditional perspectives. However, the specter of nuclear weapons and their relation to conventional military operations has produced an equivalent but highly muted debate in Soviet professional circles about the nature of the military profession under nuclear arms.[24]

Comparison with the medical profession may be appropriate. In order to develop preventive medicine, a separate structure and, in effect, a separate profession—the specialist in public health, with different training, career, and perspective—had to be brought into being. Clearly, it is not feasible to think in such terms in the case of the military. The transformation in professional capacities must take place within existing operational units. For the military profession, the overriding consideration is whether a force effectively committed to a deterrent philosophy, to peacekeeping, and to the concept of military presence can maintain its essential combat readiness.

To the detached outside observer, this problem hardly appears insoluble, but to the professional officer it is a central preoccupation. Does deterrence carry with it the seeds of its own destruction? Will such a strategy, especially under a parliamentary system, undermine the credibility of the military? Can a military force maintain combat readiness without any combat experience or its equivalent? Does not an inherent advantage accrue to nations under single-party political systems which accord the military a different social position and a broader range of functions—functions that presumably make it more viable? The focus is on the U.S. military establishment, since the movement toward stabilizing military systems rests on its initiatives and adequacy.

Institution building in the military—creating and maintaining a stabilized force for deterrence—must be seen as an aspect of the long-term decline of the mass armed forces based on conscription. The expansion of the military organization to fight a total war had the paradoxical consequence of "civilianizing" the military. The line between the military and the larger society weakened because of military dependence on civilian industry and science, and because of the impact of the mobilization of large numbers of civilians for wartime service. "Total war" made both soldier and civilian objects of attack, and served further to attenuate the distinction between the two sectors of society. Notions such as Lasswell's "garrison state," Mills's "power elite," and Eisenhower's "industrial-military complex" served to highlight the political problems associated with the expansion of the military and the blurring of the distinction between the military and civilian sectors.[25]

The emergence of an all-volunteer military slows the trend toward civilianization. While there is no return to highly self-contained military establishment, the "new military" displays a strong preoccupation with maintaining its organizational boundaries and corporate identity. Top military leaders, in particular, struggle to maintain the distinctive features, qualities, and mystiques of military life as they see them. Although they are dependent on technical expertise, they press to select for the highest command posts those who have had combat experience; as the opportunities for combat decline, the emphasis is on at least operational experience. The military continues to recruit top leaders from those who have attended the prestigious military academies. It seeks to build housing on military bases and to maintain the separate structure of the community and its own style of life. The issues of civilian control are changed under the volunteer force structure, and focus more and more on maintaining the social integration of the military into the larger society.

In any military organization, there is a gap between the "big ideas" of military function and the immediate tasks which military personnel must continually perform. Military leaders hope that day-to-day routine will create, or at least contribute to, a sense of military readiness and essential social solidarity. In essence, the more a unit during its normal routine is a military force in being, the more able it is to maintain the sense of military distinctiveness. There are, of course, limits to this—for example, when the tasks become excessively tedious or irksome.

Thus, the Air Force is the service best able to recruit personnel and maintain morale under voluntary manpower systems, because the routines of flying aircraft create military units in being. Even missile crews and radar units, because of the deadly character of the weapons they handle, feel a sense of urgency which helps them to overcome boredom. Naval units have traditionally represented a force in being and maintained a group solidarity derived from the vitality of seamanship. However, the tedium and pressure of the new naval life—for example, of the submarine at sea for months and months—have transformed some of these conditions and increased the problems of recruitment and self-conception.

The crisis of the military style of life is sharpest in the ground forces. Here the gap between preparation and training and presumed combat is the greatest. Training is only periodic and often lacks the sense of urgency, reality, or risk that routine operations in the Air Force and Navy entail. Airborne and parachute units are closest to units in being, because of the risk and danger in training. As a result, parachute training, ranger training, and wilderness activities are emphasized, not only because of their functional importance but to maintain the professional ideology of combat readiness and military distinctiveness.

Combat readiness is a genuine problem, for there is insufficient experience to satisfy operational military officers.[26] The pressure of this uncertainty carries the danger that the military will develop an inflexible posture likely to stand in the way of pragmatic adjustment to emerging realities. One possible response is the acceptance of doctrines which distort the utility of military force in international relations and which are excessively ideological, absolutist, and assault-oriented. The essential issue is to restructure the organizational milieu of the military so that combat readiness is not an expression of personal aggressiveness or rigid ideological perspectives, but rather a meaningful element of organizational effectiveness.

Available data on education and socialization in the military supply no assurance that the process of transformation in the profession will be automatic or certain. In reality, the dominant impact of socialization is negative. Military socialization does not fundamentally alter the attitudes of recruits; it merely rejects those who do not conform to central norms and values. Moreover, the longer the time men spend in a military career, the more homogeneous their orientation becomes; and, all too often, the more pessimistic are their views on international relations.[27]

Tough training is necessary and may make for group loyalty, but it does not necessarily guarantee the professional perspectives required for a deterrent force. Moreover, as Marine Corps experience documents, there appears to be a modest supply of human beings, even in an advanced industrial society, who are prepared to expose themselves to the extreme rigors of training required by that service. But the responsibilities given to such men are limited to initial military assaults.

To adapt to the current realities of international relations, the military profession must have a conceptual clarity about its strategic purpose. The new element is that such understanding cannot be reserved to the top leadership. In appropriate degrees, all professional levels must be aware of the redefined aspects of the military function. In fact, professionalism is not to be delimited in terms of skill, but must include the dimension of awareness of the goals and purposes beyond deterrence. An educational system which assumes that an officer is trained for a tactical mission and subsequently educated for strategic goals as he advances through the military hierarchy has become irrelevant and outmoded.

Since men are not guided by strategic concepts alone, group cohesion and collective motives are essential. In the United States, particularly in the aftermath of the war in Vietnam, core elements in the military are deeply concerned with keeping alive their concept of the "fighter spirit." In Western Europe, the military forces acknowledge this problem but are less concerned, since they accept the validity of their training and operational format. One cannot separate self-conceptions from public reputations. In comparison with the military in Western Europe, and especially in Great Britain, the lower prestige and social standing of the United States military do appear to contribute to its concern with "tough" military virtues.

Standards of personal behavior are a central issue. If it is to be seen as legitimate and reliable, a force which handles nuclear weapons cannot engage in the deviant practices found in civilian life. The constant screening of "human factors" becomes part of military medicine, and the personal and social controls required to deal with the difficult and tedious tasks of the "new military" will have to be different and more constrained than those in the civilian society.

In a parliamentary democracy, it has been assumed that an officer corps which is not excessively self-recruited and which is reasonably representative of the larger society would have a political orientation compatible with the larger society and would have internalized the advantages of civil control.[28] There can be no explicit political criteria of recruitment into the officer corps. The professional soldier—officer or enlisted man—has the right to personal privacy and to civic involvements, provided he does not engage in partisan behavior. Moreover, it is assumed that he will remain integrated into the larger society. (In the Soviet Union, political reliability is required and enforced by police controls, and the military is isolated from the larger society in order to ensure continuing loyalty to the Party.)

However, in an all-volunteer force, especially in nations with a long tradition of citizen-soldiers, all of these assumptions are being tested.[29] The strategic conceptions of deterrence and of stabilized military systems which do not produce tangible "victories" create high levels of professional tension and frustration, especially in a period of strong antimilitary sentiment. Recruitment becomes more difficult and the recruits tend to be less representative of the larger society. The potential danger is not simply that the military will become ingrown and socially isolated, although there is clearly a trend in this direction. The real danger is that the military will become both ideologically rigid and more specialized in its contracts with civilian society, and that these contracts may move it toward a more explicitly conservative and rightist orientation.

The result of such a trend would not be the emergence of a potential cadre for counterrevolution. Rather, the military would emerge as one additional element of political controversy in a society already racked with extensive political conflict and dissension. Unless this alternative can be avoided, the military is likely to operate as a pressure group against the realistic military policies required in the search for a new pattern of stabilization in international relations.[30]

The formulations of social research are designed to clarify political and social alternatives; but they should be constructed so as to reduce the possibility of self-fulfilling prophecies. Thus it is necessary for this analysis of international relations and military institutions to return to its point of departure. The assumptions of "fundamental democratization" and the interpenetration of coercion and persuasion reflect the continuity between the internal social structure of an advanced industrial society and the transformed processes of international relations. The emergence of nuclear weapons and the decline of colonial rule have combined to decrease the relevance of traditional conceptions of military intervention that are concerned with the "defeat"· of national adversaries or the drastic restructuring of the balance of power. In a very crude way, the term "deterrence" represented a partial, incomplete, and ultimately unsatisfactory advance that sought to recognize realities and to reformulate international political analysis. The intellectual limitations of the notion of deterrence are varied; basically, the term denotes the military objectives without adequately encompassing the political, social, and moral ends. But alternatively, the idea of stabilization is designed to highlight the necessity of achieving political, economic, and social goals rather than maintaining the status quo.

In a period of search for military détente, the increased obsolescence of the notion of deterrence rests not merely on the changed character of the threat of national adversaries, although this is a relevant dimension. The concept of stabilizing versus destabilizing military systems is an attempt to explicate more specifically their political and moral objectives. It is an intellectual orientation concerned with the potentialities and limitations of military systems in creating new rules and new norms which are designed to reduce the threat of nuclear and limited war and at the same time to enhance the process of orderly change at the international level.

In each historical period, it is essential to avoid the extrapolation of trends that characterize much of international relations analysis. Therefore, the formulation of stabilizing versus destabilizing military systems should highlight the built-in limitations in any search for military détente. Moreover, it does not deemphasize the centrality of force in international relations. I am hopeful, however, that it does offer a sharper set of categories for estimating changes in the utility and the legitimacy of the military function.

NOTES

1. Bernard Brodie, *Strategy in the Missile Age* (Princeton: Princeton University Press, 1959); David W. Tarr, *American Strategy in the Nuclear Age* (New York: Macmillan, 1966).

2. Raymond Aron, *The Century of Total War* (New York: Doubleday, 1954); Albert Wohlstetter, "The Delicate Balance of Terror," *Foreign Affairs* 37 (January 1959): 211-34; Joseph Frankel, *International Politics; Conflict and Harmony* (London: Allen Lane, 1969).

3. Thomas C. Schelling, *Arms and Influence* (New Haven: Yale University Press, 1966). Despite the author's language and particular style, this volume contains valuable materials on the actual pattern of communication and interaction between the United States and the Soviet military force.

4. Rupert Emerson, *From Empire to Nation* (Cambridge, Mass.: Harvard University Press, 1960); Clifford Geertz, ed., *Old Societies and New States: The Quest for Modernity in*

Asia and Africa (New York: Free Press of Glencoe, 1963).

5. Morris Janowitz, *The Military in the Political Development of New Nations* (Chicago: University of Chicago Press, 1964); S.E. Finer, *The Man on Horseback* (London: Pall Mall Press 1962); Philippe C. Schmitter, *Military Rule in Latin America* (Beverly Hills: Sage Publications, 1973).

6. For an analysis of the changed political meaning of nationalism in international relations, see John Herz, *International Politics in the Atomic Age* (New York: Columbia University Press, 1959); F.H. Hinsley, *Power and the Pursuit of Peace* (Cambridge: Cambridge University Press, 1963).

7. The concept of "stabilizing" versus "destabilizing" military systems does not necessarily assume the idea of equilibrium in international relations, but it is compatible with the analysis of historical change.

8. The pioneer effort was Harold D. Lasswell, *World Politics and Personal Insecurity* (New York: Free Press, 1965); see also Alix Strachey, *The Unconscious Motives of War* (London: Allen and Unwin, 1957); Maurice L. Farber, "Psychoanalytic Hypotheses in the Study of War," *Journal of Social Issues* 11, 1 (1955). 29-35.

9. See, for example, Richard H. Tawney, *The Acquisitive Society* (New York: Harcourt, Brace and Row, 1920).

10. Karl Mannheim, *Man and Society in an Age of Reconstruction* (New York: Harcourt, Brace and Company, 1940), pp. 109-29.

11. Ralf Dahrendorf, *Class and Class Conflict in Industrial Society* (Stanford: Stanford University Press, 1959); Barrington Moore, *Reflections on the Causes of Human Misery and Upon Certain Proposals to Eliminate Them* (Boston: Beacon Press, 1972).

12. Francis H. Hinsley, *Sovereignty* (New York: Basic Books, 1966).

13. Hans Speier, *Social Order and the Risks of War* (Cambridge, Mass.: M.I.T. Press, 1969).

14. Stockholm International Peace Research Institute, *World Armaments and Disarmaments,* SIPRI Yearbook 1973; See also SIPRI Yearbooks for 1968-1969, 1969-1970 and 1972; United States Arms Control and Disarmament Agency, *World Military Expenditures 1971* (Washington, D.C.: U.S. Government Printing Office, 1972).

15. Stanley Lieberson, "An Empirical Study of Military-Industrial Linkages," in Sam C. Sarkesian, ed., *The Military Industrial Complex: A Reassessment,* Sage Research Series on War, Revolution and Peacekeeping, Volume II (Beverly Hills: Sage Publications, 1972), pp. 53-94.

16. Ernst Kris and Nathan Leites, "Trends in Twentieth Century Propaganda," *Psychoanalysis and the Social Sciences* 1 (1947): 393-409.

17. For an evaluation of the impact of violence on television on social personality, see U.S. Public Health Service, The Surgeon-General's Scientific Advisory Committee on Television and Social Behavior, *Television and Growing Up: The Impact of Televised Violence* (Washington D.C.: U.S. Government Printing Office, 1972).

18. It remains to be explained why the U.S. military did not follow its own professional judgment. The appropriate form of dissent would have been token resignation of the Chief of Staff, particularly the Chief of Staff of the ground forces, when he was assigned a task that he believed could obviously not be achieved with the resources placed at his disposal. The publication of *The Pentagon Papers* has probably postponed an analysis of this central issue, since the answer lies not in examination of specific documents but in the analysis of the workings of a military bureaucracy which in effect has become "overprofessionalized"— more prepared to follow orders than to exercise independent professional skill and judgement.

19. Morton Halperin, *China and Nuclear Proliferation* (Chicago: University of Chicago, Center for Policy Studies, 1966).

20. Raymond L. Garthoff, *Sino-Soviet Military Relations* (New York: Praeger, 1966).

21. Morris Janowitz, "Volunteer Armed Forces and Military Purpose," *Foreign Affairs* 50 (April 2972): 427-43; Erwin Hackel, "Military Manpower and Political Purpose," *Adelphi Papers* no. 72 (London: Institute for Strategic Studies, 1970).

22. Union of Soviet Socialist Republics, *Prevention of Incidents on the High Seas* (Agreement signed at Moscow, 1972).

23. Morris Janowitz, *The Professional Soldier* (New York: Free Press, 1971), 418.

24. John Erickson, "Soviet Military Power," *Strategic Review* 1 (Spring 1973).

25. Harold D. Lasswell, "The Garrison State," *American Journal of Sociology* 46 (January 1941); C. Wright Mills, *The Power Elite* (New York: Oxford University Press, 1956).

26. The concern to maintain combat readiness also pervades the Russian forces. Their leaders are deeply concerned that they have had no combat experience for a quarter of a century; in their own terms, the occupation of allied socialist nations is not considered war. Their response has been to conduct frequent large-scale maneuvers, with which they are obsessed. The threat of a Sino-Soviet confrontation supplies a realistic stimulant. Russian military leaders cannot engage in candid discussion of these issues, and very little is known of the scope and quality of their thinking of these points. They must accept the insistence of political leaders that ideological training is a device for maintaining combat readiness—although, of course, they are fundamentally aware of its limitations.

27. Bengt Abrahamssor, *Military Professionalization and Political Power* (Beverly Hills: Sage Publications, 1972); John P. Lovell, "The Professional Socialization of the West Point Cadet," in Morris Janowitz, ed., *The New Military: Changing Patterns of Organization* (New York: Russell Sage Foundation, 1964), pp. 119-59; David E. Lebby, "Professional Socialization of the Naval Officer: The Effect of the Plebe Year at the U.S. Naval Academy," unpublished Ph.D. dissertation (University of Pennsylvania, 1970).

28. Samuel P. Huntington, *The Soldier and the State* (Cambridge, Mass.: Belknap Press of Harvard University, 1957).

29. Morris Janowitz, "The U.S. Forces and the Zero Draft," *Adelphi Paper* no. 94 (London: Institute for Strategic Studies, 1973).

30. For one of the earliest sociological explications of the norms required for an international order, see Charles Horton Cooley, *Social Process* (New York: C. Scribner's Sons, 1918), p. 256.

ABOUT THE CONTRIBUTORS

Paul W. Blackstock is a Professor of Political Science at the University of South Carolina. He is known for his expertise concerning U.S. intelligence activities and is the author of numerous articles and books on the topic. His publications include *Strategy of Subversion* and *The Secret Roads to World War II*.

Davis B. Bobrow is Professor and Chair, Department of Government and Politics, University of Maryland. His areas of interest include policy science, defense policy, political development, and political communication. He was a Rhodes Scholar from 1956-1958 and received his graduate degrees from the Massachusetts Institute of Technology. He is the author of numerous articles on international political decision-making and national security affairs.

James F. Digby serves as Executive Director of the California Arms Control and Foreign Policy Seminar and as a Senior Staff member of the Rand Corporation. He formerly headed Rand's Operations Department and was an early contributor to Rand thought on the use of counterforce attacks and the design of forces for controlled response. His publications include a chapter in *The Other Arms Race* and "Precision-Guided Weapons," an IISS Adelphi Paper.

Thomas A. Fabyanic is a career officer with the U.S. Air Force. His flying experience included tactical airlift operations and combat missions during the Vietnam war. He received his graduate degree from St. Louis University and was an Assistant Professor of History at the U.S. Air Force Academy. He has also served as a Research Associate at the Institute of War and Peace Studies, Columbia University and is a faculty member at the Air War College, Maxwell Air Force Base.

Maury D. Feld is a sociologist who has written extensively on military institutions. He pursued graduate studies at the University of Montpellier, France and the University of Basel, Switzerland. He is the author of the book *The Structure of Violence: Armed Forces as Social Systems,* which combines a sociological and a historical perspective.

Lawrence E. Grinter serves as the Director, East Asia and Western Pacific Studies, The National War College, Washington, D.C. He received his graduate degrees in political science from the University of North Carolina. His areas of research and teaching interest include comparative politics, Asian politics, and civil-military relations. He is the author of many articles dealing with the political and military activities of Southeast Asia and U.S.-Pacific relations.

Roger Hamburg received his Ph.D. from the University of Wisconsin and is an Associate Professor of Political Science at Indiana University, South Bend. He teaches Soviet foreign policy, American foreign policy, and international politics. He is the author of articles dealing with Soviet and Chinese politics and Soviet activities in Latin America.

Morris Janowitz is Distinguished Service Professor of Sociology, University of Chicago and is the Chairman of the Inter-University Seminar on Armed Forces and Society. His major fields of interest include civil-military relations and urban sociology. He is the author of *The Professional Soldier* and *Social Control of the Welfare State.*

Joseph J. Kruzel is an Assistant Professor of Political Science at Duke University. He graduated from the U.S. Air Force Academy and pursued graduate work at Harvard University. His dissertation title was "Preconditions and Consequences of Arms Control Agreements." He served as a member of the U.S. delegation to the SALT talks from 1970-1972 and is the author of several articles on arms control.

Michael MccGwire is Professor of Maritime and Strategic Studies at Dalhousie University, Halifax, Nova Scotia. He also serves as the Director of the university's Center for Foreign Policy Studies. Mr. MccGwire is a retired Royal Navy Commander and is the author of many articles dealing with Soviet naval power and the military use of the seas.

John E. Mueller is a Professor of Political Science at the University of Rochester. His teaching and research concerns are in the fields of defense policy, international relations, and quantitative methods. He received his graduate degree from the University of California, Los Angeles, and his dissertation concerned balloting patterns in California. He is the author of articles dealing with public opinion for policy decisions, voting activities, quantitative measurement in international relations, and the volume *War, Presidents, and Public Opinion.*

John R. Pickett is a retired U.S. Air Force officer who has served as consultant to the Congressional Office at the Pentagon. Mr. Pickett has a Master's degree in systems analysis and specializes in airlift issues. He is pursuing a doctoral degree in the Department of Statistics, University of Georgia.

Sam C. Sarkesian is Professor and Chair, Department of Political Science, Loyola University of Chicago. He serves as the Associate Chairman of the Inter-University Seminar on Armed Forces and Society. Mr. Sarkesian retired from the U.S. Army as a Lieutenant Colonel in 1968 and is pursuing research interests in the areas of military professionalism and African studies. He is the author of *The Professional Army Officer in a Changing Society* and the editor of *Revolutionary Guerilla Warfare.*

Paul R. Schratz was a Mershon Scholar at Ohio State University where he received his Ph.D. in political science. He has been a faculty member of the National War College and the Naval War College, and a guest scholar at the Brookings Institution. Mr. Schratz also served on the President's Commission of the Organization for the Conduct of Foreign Policy.

Caesar D. Sereseres received his advanced degrees from the University of California, Riverside, is an Assistant Professor of Political Science at the University of California, Irvine, and a consultant to the Rand Corporation. His research interests include American foreign policy, institutional development in Latin American, and Mexican-American politics. Mr. Sereseres has written on Chicano and Spanish-speaking community problems, U.S. military aid to Latin American, and American foreign policy activities in Latin America.

Richard Smoke, the co-author of the 1974 Bancroft Prize-winning volume, *Deterrence in American Foreign Policy,* received his Ph.D. from the Massachusetts Institute of Technology in 1972. He has served as a Fellow of the Center for Advanced Study in the Behavioral Sciences and is a Research Fellow of The Wright Institute, Berkeley. His research interests include U.S. national security policies, arms control and disarmament issues, and the psychology of public policy decision-making. He is also the author of *Controlling Escalation.*

Lewis S. Sorley prepared this manuscript shortly before assuming a position with the Intelligence Community Staff in Washington. He has served as a policy analyst in the Office of the Secretary of Defense and in the Office of the Chief of Staff of the Army, and has been a member of the faculty at the Army War College and at West Point and is a doctoral candidate in American foreign policy at the Johns Hopkins University.

Ellen P. Stern received a Master's degree from the School of International Relations, University of Southern California, in 1974. She serves as the Associate Editor of *Armed Forces and Society: An Interdisciplinary Journal.*

INDEX

AABNCP, 115
Acheson, Dean, 37, 39-40
Administrative approach doctrine, 246-247
Advanced Airborne National Command Post, 115
Advanced Tanker Cargo Aircraft program, 148
AFSATCOM, 115
Air Force ROTC production trends, 294-295, with table
Air Force Satellite Communications, 115
Airlift, 137-149
    airlift enhancement program, 299
Alerts. See Military alerts
Algeria, 245
All-volunteer force
    combat willingness of troops, 311-312, with table
    cost factors, 288-293, with tables
    effects of lowered manpower levels, 298
    ethical problems, 316-318
    force size, 282-285; table on 283
    Gates Commission, 282, 307
    implications for strategy, 297-300
    lack of faith in, 308
    professionalism in, 295
    quality of, 285-288, with tables
    representativeness, 293-295
    social composition and commitment, 312
    unemployment and enlistment levels, table on 284
    See also Army, U.S.
American, See United States
Angola, 171, 173
    Cuban intervention in, 65, 205

Soviet intervention policy, 65-66
Arbatov, Georgi, 50-51
Arms limitation, 133-135
Arms transfers
    evaluating, 219-223
    to Middle East countries, 219-20
    to nonindustrial nations, 214
    volume of, tables on 235
Army, U.S., 287
    elite ground forces, 310-311
    professional adaptability, 310-313
    reliance on reserves, 296-297
    See also All-volunteer force
Aron, Raymond, 122
AVF, See All-volunteer force

Balance of power doctrine, 69
BMP combat vehicle, 192
Brezhnev, Leonid, 51, 52, 67-68

C^3, 101-118
    horizontal C^3, 109
    vertical C^3, 109
C-5 capability, 147-148
Centers of power, diffusion of, 25
Central Intelligence Agency, See CIA
Chicago Council poll, 324-325, 328-329
China, People's Republic of, 53-54
    See also Sino-Soviet antagonism
Church Committee, 272-273
CIA
    Congressional investigations, 250, 257-258, 271-273
    criticism of covert operations, 267-271
    Directorate of Operations, 264
    founding principles, 258
    National Security Act (1947), 263
    Watergate scandal, 274